Production and Operations Management

Production and Operations Management
A Self-Correcting Approach

SECOND EDITION

Ralph M. Stair, Jr.
Florida State University

Barry Render
George Mason University

ALLYN AND BACON, INC.
Boston • London • Sydney • Toronto

Library of Congress Cataloging in Publication Data

Stair, Ralph M.
    Production and operations management.

    Includes index.
    1. Industrial management.   2. Operations research.
3. Production management.   I. Render, Barry.   II. Title.
HD31.S66 1984   658.5   83-24359
ISBN 0-205-08137-1

Printed in the United States of America

10 9 8 7 6 5 4 3 2   88 87 86 85

To
Lila and Rhonda

Contents

Preface ▬▬▬▬▬▬▬▬▬

HOW TO USE *PRODUCTION AND OPERATIONS MANAGEMENT: A SELF-CORRECTING APPROACH*

To the Student

This book has been designed to assist you in learning the concepts and techniques of production and operations management. The production-operations management course is an integral part of the curriculum in many colleges of business and administration today. It is intended to provide you with an understanding of the kinds of problems found in managing a business, government, or nonprofit organization (be it production- or service-oriented). An additional purpose is to give you experience in tackling common production or operations problems by familiarizing you with the most important approaches to the design, operation, and control of productive systems.

Each of the nineteen units in this book contains a complete, straightforward explanation of the subject at hand, together with several carefully explained examples and self-correcting problems. The problems allow you to progress through the material at your own pace. A correct answer means that you have mastered the material and that you can proceed to new material. An incorrect answer alerts you to a misunderstood concept or a computational mistake. The self-correcting problems in this book will give you immediate feedback on your progress at any point. You will be able to move forward with confidence after each correct answer, and you will be able to pinpoint and correct any problems that you may encounter as a result of an incorrect answer.

Space has been provided in most cases for your calculations and answers. When appropriate, we have included graphs and tables to make it easier for you to layout and solve the problems. In case you should need additional room, however, we suggest that you keep a pad of paper handy.

Whatever the order in which your class progresses through the units of this book, it will surprise you that the material is not nearly as complex or difficult as you may have imagined it would be. The problems of production and operations management are no more difficult than any other subject. Just proceed example by example, and problem by problem. This approach is a tried-and-true method by which many students before you have learned the concepts of production and operations management efficiently and effectively.

To the Instructor

Production and Operations Management: A Self-Correcting Approach is suitable for undergraduate- and graduate-level courses in production management, operations management, management science, and quantitative analysis. Although this book may be employed as a supplement to assist the student in mastering the concepts and techniques of production and operations management, it has also been used quantitative analysis. Although this book may be employed as a supplement to assist the student in mastering the concepts and techniques of production and operations management, it has also been used successfully as a problems-oriented *text*. The book is so complete and clear in coverage of major production and operations management topics that, when supplemented with other materials and resources (such as outside readings or cases and your own experience), it will more than suffice as a primary learning aid—and will fulfill the production management requirement of the American Assembly of Collegiate Schools of Business (ASCSB). Financially, this option is very popular with students.

We have designed all of the material and problems to be straightforward and easy to learn, and we hope that our extensive student testing has rendered the book error free. You will find that the examples and self-correcting problems are comprehensive and realistic. In addition, the nineteen units allow great flexibility in course design and presentation.

In this second edition, you will find expanded treatment of forecasting (Unit 6), facility location (Unit 11), and MRP and capacity planning (Unit 8). We have also added new chapters on aggregate planning (Unit 12) and job shop scheduling (Unit 18). At the end of each unit, unsolved homework problems are included.

Acknowledgments

The authors gratefully acknowledge the reviews and comments of Professors Ogden H. Hall at the University of New Orleans, Robert Hall at Indiana University, Bruce A. Skalbeck at St. Cloud University, Kenneth Ramsing at University of Oregon, Erwin Saniga at University of Delaware, Phillip A. Vaccaro at Salem State College, William V. Gehrlein at University of Delaware, Benny D. Bowers at University of North Carolina, Charlotte, Leo Simpson at Eastern Washington University, Jugoslav S. Milutinovich at Temple University, Robert F. Berner at State University of New York, Buffalo, A. J. LaPorte at Salem State College, and John G. Wacker at Iowa State University. We also thank Toni Williams for her excellent typing support.

Production and Operations Management

Unit 1

Production and Operations Management in Perspective

Humans have been eating and sleeping and producing goods and services since the beginning of time. The formal study of how people can more efficiently and effectively produce goods and services, however, has been investigated only in the last century. Progress in this area is due in part to rapid advances in technology and to new processes. When you compare the dramatic progress of the last several years with that made in the previous hundred years, you realize how fast today's society is changing. Changes in technology and life-style have had a profound effect on the types and number of products and services available. In order to gain insights into the future, let us begin Unit 1 by investigating historical developments that relate to the production of goods and services. We will delve into the management of production and operations systems and then go on to explore in the remaining eighteen units topics that comprise our treatment of production and operations management.

A HISTORICAL PERSPECTIVE

In the last two centuries we've seen dramatic changes in our society. Although Greek and Chinese academicians long ago wrote about management, it was not until around 1910 that the first principles of scientific management were developed. Frederick W. Taylor is considered by many experts to be the father of the principles of scientific management. Taylor investigated management, time study, and work study concepts. At roughly the same time, Frank and Lillian Gilbreth studied the motions of workers. Their motion studies led to many conclusions about work and the human activities involved with work. A few years later, Henry Ford experimented with assembly lines, Henry L. Gantt developed a special type of scheduling chart, and F. W. Harris investigated one of the first inventory control models that minimized inventory cost. In the 1930s Shewart, Dodge, and Romig pioneered basic quality control concepts that are still in use today in many organizations. Since the 1930s, there has been an explosion in the number of new quantitative and qualitative techniques applied to the analysis of productive systems. These techniques include linear programming, PERT, and simulation, among others.

Changes in the goods and services demanded by society have also occurred. The consumption of durable goods has grown slowly but steadily, yet the demand for services has skyrocketed. In the 1930s and 1940s, most graduates of business administration programs found careers with manufacturing organizations. Today, however, business school graduates are finding jobs and starting careers in hotel, restaurant, and tourism administration; public utilities and transportation; city, state, and federal government; and athletic organizations. The growth of service industries has had and will continue to have a profound effect on business administration programs.

With changes in management style and societal needs for goods and services have come advances in data and information processing. Information that was impossible or too expensive to produce several years ago is now obtainable at low cost and with little effort. Thus, decision makers are able to use information not previously available to make better choices. Computerized data-processing advances have not only provided more goods and services for society but have also made them cheaper to produce.

These historical developments have had a great impact on the scope and meaning of production and operations management. Today's typical course in production and operations management is significantly different from the course you might have taken ten years ago. And a course in production and operations management ten years in the future will most assuredly be different from those being offered today.

WHAT IS PRODUCTION AND OPERATIONS MANAGEMENT?

"Production management," "operations management," and "production and operations management" are three common textbook titles. In each book you examine, however, you will find different definitions of the three terms. Before *we* discuss and define production and operations management, let us first investigate a production and operations system. In its simplest terms, such a system is one that transforms raw materials and inputs by a certain process or a variety of transformation activities into a desired product. Usually the product is a good or service. Figure 1.1 reveals the essence of a production and operations system.

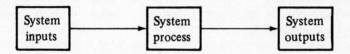

Figure 1.1. A Production and Operations System

In Figure 1.1 it is apparent that almost all organizations in the private and public sector fit into the category of production and operations systems. Thus, in addition to traditional manufacturing companies, we can consider organizations such as hospitals, nursing homes, hotels, and governmental agencies of all types to be production and operations systems. Furthermore, these organizations control production and operations to obtain the desired goods and services. They do so by monitoring the system and taking corrective action when necessary, as shown in Figure 1.2.

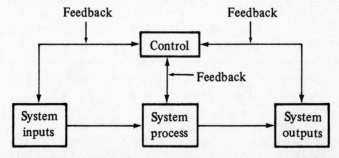

Figure 1.2. A Production and Operations System with Feedback

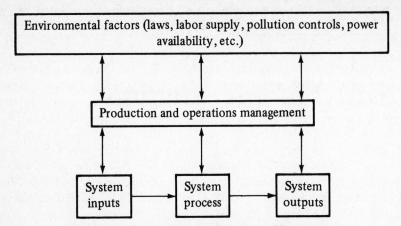

Figure 1.3. Production and Operations Management

Figure 1.3 graphically displays the scope of the field. Production and operations management deals with problems that directly relate to the design and operation of those resources used in producing goods and services. Managing such a system requires a variety of diverse and sometimes complex analyses. You will come across examples and problems involving production and operations analysis throughout this text.

The birth of any operations and production systems normally begins with project planning. Management often uses such concepts as PERT and PERT/Cost, which we'll cover in Unit 19, in addition to computer simulation, cost-volume analysis, and financial analysis (see Units 2, 3, and 15). Related techniques that deal with product selection include decision-making criteria and linear programming, the topics of Units 4, 9, and 10. Once some of the initial planning has been completed, facility location, transportation methods, layout design, and work measurement are normally analyzed next. You will find these concepts discussed in Units 11–14. After a production and operations system has been established, such problems as inventory control, quality control, and service systems must be explored, and we'll investigate these topics in Units 5, 7, 8, and 16. Finally, a fully functioning production and operations system requires regular maintenance, the subject of Unit 17. The concepts and techniques outlined above represent the essence of this book. They also represent today's most commonly used and discussed tools of production and operations management. These tools assist the manager in the design, operation, and control of operations and production systems.

Cost-Volume Analysis

Most organizations in the private sector exist for one reason: to make a profit. Moreover, most corporations have as their primary goal the maximization of profts. As a result, one of the oldest and most widely used financial techniques is the formal analysis of cost-volume relationships. And one frequently computed quantity is the *break-even point,* which is the number of units that an organization must sell to just break even, in other words, to have zero profit.

Although it is common to use break-even analysis for long-range projects, it is especially useful for short-run planning when costs can be divided into fixed costs and variable costs. Figure 2.1 shows how we can determine graphically the point at which revenues are equal to costs (the break-even point).

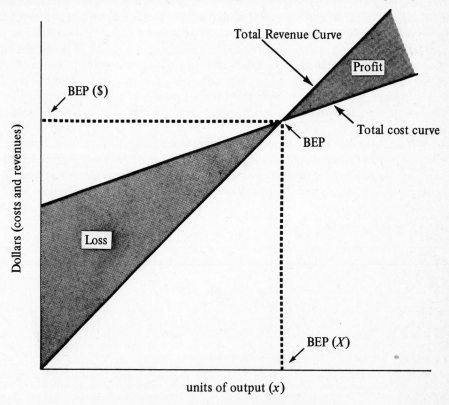

Figure 2.1. Cost-volume Analysis

Where in Figure 2.1 the following terms are used:

$$\text{BEP} = \text{break-even point}$$

$$\text{BEP}(x) = \text{break-even point in units}$$

$$\text{BEP}(\$) = \text{break-even point in dollars}$$

ALGEBRAIC SOLUTION

Although we can determine the break-even point graphically, it is much easier to compute it algebraically, by equating total revenues with total costs. Let

$$\text{TR} = \text{total revenue} = Px$$

$$P = \text{price per unit}$$

$$x = \text{the number of units}$$

$$\text{TC} = \text{total costs} = F + Vx$$

$$F = \text{fixed costs}$$

$$V = \text{variable costs per unit}$$

Setting total revenue equal to total costs, we get

$$\text{TR} = \text{TC}$$

$$Px = F + Vx$$

Solving for x, we get

$$\text{BEP}(x) = \frac{F}{P - V}$$

and

$$\text{BEP}(\$) = \text{BEP}(x) \times P$$

$$= \frac{F}{P - V} \times P$$

$$= \frac{F}{1 - V/P}$$

$$\text{profit} = \text{TR} - \text{TC}$$

$$= Px - F - Vx$$

$$= (P - V)x - F$$

Using these equations, we can directly solve for break-even point and general profitability.

EXAMPLE 2.1

Given the following data, determine the break-even point in units and dollars.

$$P = \$7/\text{unit}$$

$$V = \$2/\text{unit}$$

$$F = \$80,000$$

1. $\text{BEP}(x) = \dfrac{F}{P - V}$

   $= \dfrac{80,000}{7 - 2}$

   $= 16,000$ units

2. $\text{BEP}(\$) = \text{BEP}(x) \times P = 16,000 \times 7$

   $= \$112,000$

   or

   $\text{BEP}(\$) = \dfrac{F}{1 - V/P} = \dfrac{80,000}{1 - 2/7}$

   $= \$112,000$

PROBLEM 2.1

Given the following data, calculate BEP (x), BEP $(\$)$, and the profit at 100,000 units:

$$P = \$8/\text{unit}$$

$$V = \$4/\text{unit}$$

$$F = \$50,000$$

BEP (x) =

   =

BEP $(\$)$ =

   =

profit at 100,000 units =

   =

GO-NO-GO DECISIONS

Break-even analysis is useful in a variety of situations. The equations developed earlier in this unit are valuable tools for analyzing "go" or "no-go" decisions, as the following example demonstrates.

EXAMPLE 2.2

An electronics firm is currently manufacturing an item that has a variable cost of $.50 per unit and a selling price of $1.00 per unit. Fixed costs are $14,000. Current volume is 30,000 units. The firm can substantially improve the product quality by adding a new piece of equipment at an additional fixed cost of $6000. Variable cost would increase to $.60, but their volume should jump to 50,000 units due to a higher-quality product. Should the company buy the new equipment?

1. Profit before $= (P - V)x - F$
   new equipment

$$= (\$1 - \$.50)\,30{,}000 - \$14{,}000$$

$$= \$1000$$

2. Profit with $= (\$1 - \$.60)\,50{,}000 - (\$14{,}000 + \$6000)$
   new equipment

$$= \$20{,}000 - \$20{,}000$$

$$= \$0$$

Therefore, it is not advisable to buy the new equipment.

PROBLEM 2.2

The electronics firm in Example 2.2 is now considering the new equipment coupled with a price increase to $1.10 per unit. With the higher-quality product, the new volume is expected to be 45,000 units. Under these circumstances, should the company purchase the new equipment and increase the selling price?

SUMMARY

In this unit we have studied cost-volume relationships. Cost-volume analysis makes several assumptions: (1) all costs are either fixed or variable; (2) both costs and revenue factors are known with complete certainty; and (3) a dollar received today is the same as a dollar received in the future. If these assumptions are valid, cost-volume analysis is useful in a variety of situations. We can determine whether to make or buy a particular product, decide among several manufacturing processes for given volumes of production, and decide whether or not to sell a new product line and drop an old product with cost-volume analysis. In cases for which these assumptions are not valid, however, either this kind of analysis must be modified or other approaches must be employed. In Unit 3, we will investigate situations in which the time value of money is important. There we will explore concepts such as present value and internal rate of return. And Unit 4 will discuss decision making under risk and uncertainty.

ANSWERS

2.1 1. BEP $(x) = \dfrac{50,000}{8-4}$

   $= 12,500$ units

2. BEP $(\$) = 12,500 \times 8$

   $= \$100,000$

3. Profit $= (8-4) \times 100,000 - 50,000$

   $= \$350,000$

2.2 1. Profit with

   price increase $= (\$1.10 - \$.60)\, 45,000 - \$20,000$

   $= \$2500$

2. Profit before

   new equipment $= \$1000$

The results indicate that the company should purchase the new equipment and implement the price increase.

HOMEWORK PROBLEMS

2-1. Currently, EZ Developing, Inc. (EZD) is using a moderately expensive photographic processor to develop film from professional cameras. The equipment has a fixed cost of $30,000. Each roll of film developed costs EZD $6.30. The charge to customers for processing is $8.50.

The executives of EZD are now considering two alternative film developing processes. The System 200, manufactured by an American company, has an initial purchase price of $42,000. The cost per roll of film, however, is only $5.10. The alternative is to acquire the XT 400 device, manufactured by a Japanese company. The XT 400 has a fixed cost of $55,000. The developing cost per roll, however, is $4.95.

Regardless of the system chosen, EZD still plans to sell its services to customers at a rate of $8.50 per roll. Currently, there is a demand for 40,000 rolls of this particular type of film per year, and this is expected to continue into the future. EZD can either stay with the existing system, acquire the System 200, or acquire the XT 400. Which alternative would you recommend?

2-2. Mark Martinko is currently considering the possibility of developing manufacturing facilities to produce a new type of fishing pole. The fishing pole would have a price of $8.00. Mark estimates that the fixed cost could range anywhere from $10,000 to $11,000, the variable cost could range from $4.00 to $6.00, and the volume could range anywhere from 4,000 units to 6,000 units. Unfortunately, Mark has no idea what the fixed cost, variable cost, or volume will be. Therefore, he would like to try several different conditions to see what effect these conditions would have on the break-even point in units and the overall profitability.

For the first condition, Mark would like to use a fixed cost of $10,000, a variable cost of $4.00 per unit, and a volume of 4,000 units sold. The second condition should have a fixed cost of $10,000, a variable cost of $5.00, and a volume of 4,000. The third condition Mark would like to test has a fixed cost, again, of $10,000, but the variable cost has increased to $6.00, while the volume remains at 4,000 units. For the fourth, fifth, and sixth conditions, Mark would like to hold the fixed cost equal to $11,000 and the total units sold equal to 4,000 units. For the fourth condition, variable cost should start at $4.00. For the fifth condition, variable cost should be $5.00, and for the sixth condition, variable cost should be $6.00. For the seventh, eighth, and ninth conditions that Mark would like to test, he would like to hold fixed cost equal to $10,000, and increase the units sold to 6,000. For the seventh condition, variable cost should start at $4.00. For the eighth condition, variable cost should be $5.00, and for the ninth condition, variable cost should be $6.00. For the final three conditions that Mark would like to test, conditions 10, 11, and 12, he would like to hold fixed cost equal to $11,000 and the number of units sold equal to 6,000. For the tenth condition, variable cost should again start at $4.00 per unit. For the eleventh condition, variable cost should be equal to $5.00 per unit, and for the twelth condition, variable cost should be equal to $6.00 per unit.

Mark would like you to determine both the break-even point in units and the profit for these twelve conditions. You may wish to use a table with each row representing a different condition. Which condition will give Mark the best overall profitability?

Unit 3

Financial Analysis

Organizations usually have two sources of financial funding: internal and external. Retained earnings are the major source of internal funds, while external sources can usually be divided into debt capital and equity capital. One of the most difficult decisions facing the operations manager is the allocation of funds among competing investment alternatives. These investments include:

1. Acquisition of facilities and equipment
2. Production of new product lines
3. Repair and maintenance of existing equipment and facilities
4. Research and development
5. Raw materials and inventory
6. Increased labor force for existing and new production

Operations managers must decide how to allocate scarce resources among different investment alternatives. Different cash flows, project lengths, and so on, necessitate a method of comparing investment alternatives and choosing those investments that bring the organization closer to its goals and objectives. The types of analysis used to compare investment alternatives are many and varied, but the most common include *payback period, net present value,* and *internal rate of return.* This unit not only explores these techniques, but it looks at the consequences of depreciation and taxes as well.

PAYBACK PERIOD

Payback is one of the most commonly used and easiest-to-compute methods of financial analysis. It ranks investments according to the time it takes each investment to pay back in profits the initial investment. Thus, if an initial investment is $500.00 and the return is $100.00 per year, the payback period is five years.

EXAMPLE 3.1

General Manufacturing Services (GMS) is considering three investment alternatives. Each alternative requires an investment of $15,000, but the cash flows for the three investments differ significantly. Calculate the payback period for each investment.

(continued)

Year	Cash Flow for Investment A	Cash Flow for Investment B	Cash Flow for Investment C
1	$7000	$5000	$4000
2	6000	5000	4000
3	6000	5000	4000
4	2000	5000	4000
5	1000	5000	4000
6		5000	4000
7			4000
8			4000
9			4000
Life of investment	5 yr.	6 yr.	9 yr.
Payback period	2.33 yr.	3 yr	3.75 yr.

The payback period for investment A is 2.33 years because it takes that long for the returns to equal $15,000 ($7000 + $6000 + $6000/3 = $15,000). The payback period for investment B is 3 years, and the payback period for investment C is 3.75 years. For investment C, it takes 3.75 years at $4000 per year to pay back the initial investment [$4000 + $4000 + $4000 + .75 ($4000) = $15,000]. If the payback period is the criterion, the best strategy is investment A because it has the shortest payback period.

PROBLEM 3.1

Rank the following investments according to payback period. Each alternative requires an initial investment of $20,000.

Year	Cash Flows for Investment 1	Cash Flows for Investment 2	Cash Flows for Investment 3
1	$ 1,000	$7000	$10,000
2	1,000	6000	5,000
3	3,000	5000	3,000
4	15,000	4000	2,000
5	3,000	4000	1,000
6	1,000	4000	1,000

(continued)

7	–	4000	1,000
8	1,000	2000	–
9	–	–	1,000

When the cash flows are the same each year, we can calculate the payback period with the following formula:

$$\text{Payback} = \frac{\text{investment} - \text{salvage value (if any)}}{\text{profit/year}}$$

EXAMPLE 3.2

The cost of purchasing and installing a new price of equipment is $85,000. The salvage value is $15,000. If the investment returns a profit of $9500 per year, what is the payback period?

$$\text{Payback} = \frac{\$85,000 - \$15,000}{\$9500} = 7.37 \text{ yr.}$$

PROBLEM 3.2

What is the payback of an investment that costs $123,545 and has a salvage value of $44,560? The annual profit from the investment is $14,667.

Although the payback period method is easy to understand and compute, it has some severe limitations. First of all, it does not consider any returns after the payback period. Thus, in Example 3.1, investment 1, with a payback period of 2.33 years, would always be preferable to investment 2, with a payback period of 3 years, according to the payback period criterion. Even if investment 2 returned over $1 million between years 5 and 10, investment 1 would still be chosen over investment 2 because returns after the payback period are not included in the calculation. The payback period remains the same. Thus, the life of the investment is not a factor in the decision. Investment 2 could have a long life with high returns, but if investment 1 has a smaller payback period, the payback criterion favors its choice. The second limitation of the payback analysis is that it does not take into account the time value of money. One hundred dollars today is worth more than $100 received ten years from now. In fact, if $100 were invested in a savings account at an interest rate of 8 percent, it would be worth more than $200 in ten years. This is the time value of money concept. Look at Problem 3.1. Note that investment 1 and investment 3 have the same payback period. But the returns of investment 3 are higher in the first two years. Placing these early returns in a bank or reinvesting them would yield further profits. With respect to the time value of money, investment 3 is more attractive than investment 1, even though their payback periods are the same. The next section reveals how the operations manager can incorporate interest into investment decisions.

INTEREST CONSIDERATIONS

If you invest $100.00 in a bank at 5 percent for one year, your investment will be worth $100.00 + $100.00 (0.05) = $105.00. If you invest the $105.00 for a second year, it will be worth $105.00 + $105.00 (0.05) = $110.25 at the end of the second year. Of course, we could calculate the future value of $100.00 at 5 percent for as many years as we wanted by simply extending this analysis, but there is an easier way when we express this relationship mathematically.

For the first year:

$$\$105 = \$100 \, (1 + 0.05)$$

For the second year:

$$\$110.25 = \$105 \, (1 + 0.05) = \$100 \, (1 + 0.05)^2$$

In general,

$$F = P \, (1 + i)^N$$

where:

F = the future value (such as $110.25 or $105)

P = the present value (such as $100.00)

i = the interest rate (such as 0.05)

N = the number of years (such as 1 yr. or 2 yr.)

In most investment decisions, however, we are interested in calculating the present value of a future cash flow. Solving for *P* we get

$$P = \frac{F}{(1 + i)^N}$$

PROBLEM 3.3

An investment will produce $1000 two years from now. What is the amount worth today; that is, what is the present value, if the interest rate is 6 percent?

When the number of years isn't too large, the above equation is effective. When the number of years, *N*, is large, the formula is cumbersome. For twenty years, you would have to compute $(1 + i)^{20}$. Without a sophisticated calculator, this computation would be difficult indeed. Interest rate tables such as Table 3.1 alleviate this situation. First, let's rearrange the present value equation:

$$P = \frac{F}{(1 + i)^N} = F \times \text{(a factor)}$$

where the factor $= 1/[(1 + i)^N]$ and again *F* = future value. Thus, all we have to do is to find the factor and multiply it times *F* to calculate the present value *P*. The factors, of course, are a function of the interest rate *i* and the number of years *N*. Table 3.1 lists some of these factors. Now present value problems are much easier to compute.

EXAMPLE 3.3

An investment will produce $1000 two years from now. What is this amount worth today (namely, the present value) if the interest rate is 6 percent?

To solve this problem, we simply look in Table 3.1 for an interest rate for 6 percent and two years. The factor is 0.890, and thus the present value is $1000 (0.890) = $890.00.

Table 3.1
Present Value of $1

Year	1%	2%	3%	4%	5%	6%	7%	8%	9%	10%
1	0.990	0.980	0.971	0.962	0.952	0.943	0.935	0.926	0.917	0.909
2	0.980	0.961	0.943	0.925	0.907	0.890	0.873	0.857	0.842	0.826
3	0.971	0.942	0.915	0.889	0.864	0.840	0.816	0.794	0.772	0.751
4	0.961	0.924	0.888	0.855	0.823	0.792	0.763	0.735	0.708	0.683
5	0.951	0.906	0.863	0.822	0.784	0.747	0.713	0.681	0.650	0.621
6	0.942	0.888	0.837	0.790	0.746	0.705	0.666	0.630	0.596	0.564
7	0.933	0.871	0.813	0.760	0.711	0.665	0.623	0.583	0.547	0.513
8	0.923	0.853	0.789	0.731	0.677	0.627	0.582	0.540	0.502	0.467
9	0.914	0.837	0.766	0.703	0.645	0.592	0.544	0.500	0.460	0.424
10	0.905	0.820	0.744	0.676	0.614	0.558	0.508	0.463	0.422	0.386
11	0.896	0.804	0.722	0.650	0.585	0.527	0.475	0.429	0.388	0.350
12	0.887	0.788	0.701	0.625	0.557	0.497	0.444	0.397	0.356	0.319
13	0.879	0.773	0.681	0.601	0.530	0.469	0.415	0.368	0.326	0.290
14	0.870	0.758	0.661	0.577	0.505	0.442	0.388	0.340	0.299	0.263
15	0.861	0.743	0.642	0.555	0.481	0.417	0.362	0.315	0.275	0.239
16	0.853	0.728	0.623	0.534	0.458	0.394	0.339	0.292	0.252	0.218
17	0.844	0.714	0.605	0.513	0.436	0.371	0.317	0.270	0.231	0.198
18	0.836	0.700	0.587	0.494	0.416	0.350	0.296	0.250	0.212	0.180
19	0.828	0.686	0.570	0.475	0.396	0.331	0.277	0.232	0.194	0.164
20	0.820	0.673	0.554	0.456	0.377	0.312	0.258	0.215	0.178	0.149

Year	11%	12%	13%	14%	15%	16%	17%	18%	19%	20%
1	0.901	0.893	0.885	0.877	0.870	0.862	0.855	0.847	0.840	0.833
2	0.812	0.797	0.783	0.769	0.756	0.743	0.731	0.718	0.706	0.694
3	0.731	0.712	0.693	0.675	0.658	0.641	0.624	0.609	0.593	0.579
4	0.659	0.636	0.613	0.592	0.572	0.552	0.534	0.516	0.499	0.482
5	0.593	0.567	0.543	0.519	0.497	0.476	0.456	0.437	0.419	0.402
6	0.535	0.507	0.480	0.456	0.432	0.410	0.390	0.370	0.352	0.335
7	0.482	0.452	0.425	0.400	0.376	0.354	0.333	0.314	0.296	0.279
8	0.434	0.404	0.376	0.351	0.327	0.305	0.285	0.266	0.249	0.233
9	0.391	0.361	0.333	0.308	0.284	0.263	0.243	0.225	0.209	0.194
10	0.352	0.322	0.295	0.270	0.247	0.227	0.208	0.191	0.176	0.162
11	0.317	0.287	0.261	0.237	0.215	0.195	0.178	0.162	0.148	0.135
12	0.286	0.257	0.231	0.208	0.187	0.168	0.152	0.137	0.124	0.112
13	0.258	0.229	0.204	0.182	0.163	0.145	0.130	0.116	0.104	0.093
14	0.232	0.205	0.181	0.160	0.141	0.125	0.111	0.099	0.088	0.078
15	0.209	0.183	0.160	0.140	0.123	0.108	0.095	0.084	0.074	0.065
16	0.188	0.163	0.141	0.123	0.107	0.093	0.081	0.071	0.062	0.054
17	0.170	0.146	0.125	0.108	0.093	0.080	0.069	0.060	0.052	0.045
18	0.153	0.130	0.111	0.095	0.081	0.069	0.059	0.051	0.044	0.038
19	0.138	0.116	0.098	0.083	0.070	0.060	0.051	0.043	0.037	0.031
20	0.124	0.104	0.087	0.073	0.061	0.051	0.043	0.037	0.031	0.026

PROBLEM 3.4

What is the present value of $5600 when the interest rate is 8 percent and the return of $5600 will not be received for twelve years?

The above equations are used to determined the present value of one future cash amount, but there are situations in which an investment generates a series of uniform and equal cash amounts. This type of investment is called an *annuity*. For example, an investment might yield $300 per year for three years. Of course, you could use the above formula three times for years 1, 2, and 3, but there is a shorter method. Although there is a formula that we can use to solve for the present value of an annual series of uniform and equal cash flows (an annuity), it is easier to use a table that has been developed for this purpose. Like the normal present-value computations, this calculation involves a factor. The factors for an annual series are in Table 3.2. The basic relationship is

$$S = R \times (\text{a factor from Table 3.2})$$

where:

S = the present value of a series of uniform annual receipts

R = the receipts that are received every year for the life of the investment (the annuity)

The present value of a uniform annual series of amounts is an extension of the present value of a single amount, and thus Table 3.2 can be directly developed from Table 3.1. The factors for any given interest rate in Table 3.2 are nothing more than the cumulative sum of the values in Table 3.1. In Table 3.1 for example, 0.952, 0.907, and 0.864 are the factors for years 1, 2, and 3 when the interest rate is 5 percent. The cumulative sum of these factors is 2.723 = 0.952 + 0.907 + 0.864. Now look in Table 3.2 where the interest rate is 5 percent and the number of years is three. The factor for the present value of an annuity is 2.723 as you would expect. Although Table 3.2 is a cumulative sum of the values in Table 3.1, Table 3.2 can be very helpful in making financial decisions as you will see in the following examples and problems.

EXAMPLE 3.4

River Road Medical Clinic is thinking of investing in a sophisticated new piece of medical equipment. It will generate $7000 per year in receipts for five years. What is the present value of this cash flow?

(continued)

Use an interest rate of 6 percent.

$$S = R \times \text{(a factor from Table 3.2)} = \$7000\,(4.212) = \$29{,}484$$

The factor from Table 3.2 was obtained by finding that number when the interest rate is 6 percent and the number of years is five.

PROBLEM 3.5

River Road Medical Clinic is contemplating another investment that would require the same initial investment. The salvage value for both investments is $0.00. This other investment, however, will generate $8600 per year in receipts. The life of the investment is only four years. What is the present value of this investment? Use the same interest rate as in Example 3.4.

There is another way of looking at Example 3.4 and Problem 3.5. If you went to a bank and took a loan for $29,484 today, your payments would be $7000 per year for five years if the bank used an interest rate of 6 percent compounded yearly. Thus $29,484 is the *true* present value of the investment in Example 3.4. The same type of statement can be made for the investment in Problem 3.5. Thus, everything else being equal, the investment in Problem 3.5 is better than the investment in Example 3.4 because of the higher present value. We should pause here to make an important point; interest rate considerations are very important. Without the present value computations you may have made the wrong decision because the total cash receipts for the investment in Example 3.4 are greater than the cash receipts on Problem 3.5 ($7000 × 5 = $35,000 is greater than $8600 × 4 = $34,400).

NET PRESENT VALUE

Many experts consider the net present value method to be one of the best methods of ranking investment alternatives. The procedure is straightforward; you simply compute the present value of all cash flows for each investment alternative. When deciding among investment alternatives, you pick the investment that has the highest present value. Similarly, when making several investments, investments with a higher net present value are preferable to investments with a lower net present value.

Table 3.2
Present Value of an Annuity of $1

Year	1%	2%	3%	4%	5%	6%	7%	8%	9%	10%
1	0.990	0.980	0.971	0.962	0.952	0.943	0.935	0.926	0.917	0.909
2	1.970	1.941	1.914	1.887	1.859	1.833	1.808	1.783	1.759	1.735
3	2.941	2.883	2.829	2.776	2.723	2.673	2.624	2.577	2.531	2.486
4	3.902	3.807	3.717	3.631	3.546	3.465	3.387	3.312	3.239	3.169
5	4.853	4.713	4.580	4.453	4.330	4.212	4.100	3.993	3.889	3.79
6	5.795	5.601	5.417	5.243	5.076	4.917	4.766	4.623	4.485	4.354
7	6.728	6.472	6.230	6.003	5.787	5.582	5.389	5.206	5.032	4.867
8	7.651	7.325	7.019	6.734	6.464	6.209	5.971	5.746	5.534	5.334
9	8.565	8.162	7.785	7.437	7.109	6.801	6.515	6.246	5.994	5.758
10	9.470	8.982	8.529	8.113	7.723	7.359	7.023	6.709	6.416	6.144
11	10.366	9.786	9.251	8.763	8.308	7.886	7.498	7.138	6.804	6.494
12	11.253	10.574	9.952	9.388	8.865	8.383	7.942	7.535	7.160	6.813
13	12.132	11.347	10.633	9.989	9.395	8.852	8.357	7.903	7.486	7.103
14	13.002	12.105	11.294	10.566	9.900	9.294	8.745	8.243	7.785	7.366
15	13.863	12.848	11.936	11.121	10.381	9.711	9.107	8.558	8.060	7.605
16	14.716	13.576	12.559	11.655	10.839	10.105	9.446	8.850	8.312	7.823
17	15.560	14.290	13.164	12.168	11.275	10.476	9.763	9.120	8.543	8.021
18	16.396	14.990	13.751	12.662	11.691	10.826	10.059	9.370	8.755	8.201
19	17.224	15.676	14.321	13.137	12.087	11.157	10.336	9.602	8.949	8.365
20	18.044	16.349	14.875	13.593	12.464	11.469	10.594	9.817	9.127	8.514

Year	11%	12%	13%	14%	15%	16%	17%	18%	19%	20%
1	0.901	0.893	0.885	8.77	0.870	0.862	0.855	0.847	0.840	0.833
2	1.713	1.690	1.668	1.646	1.626	1.605	1.586	1.565	1.546	1.527
3	2.444	2.402	2.361	2.321	2.284	2.246	2.210	2.174	2.139	2.106
4	3.103	3.038	2.974	2.913	2.856	2.798	2.744	2.690	2.638	2.588
5	3.696	3.605	3.517	3.432	3.353	3.274	3.200	3.127	3.057	2.99
6	4.231	4.112	3.997	3.888	3.785	3.684	3.590	3.497	3.409	3.325
7	4.713	4.564	4.422	4.288	4.161	4.038	3.923	3.811	3.705	3.604
8	5.147	4.968	4.798	4.639	4.488	4.343	4.208	4.077	3.954	3.837
9	5.538	5.329	5.131	4.947	4.772	4.606	4.451	4.302	4.163	4.031
10	5.890	5.651	5.426	5.217	5.019	4.833	4.659	4.493	4.339	4.193
11	6.207	5.938	5.687	5.454	5.234	5.028	4.837	4.655	4.487	4.328
12	6.493	6.195	5.918	5.662	5.421	5.196	4.989	4.792	4.611	4.44
13	6.751	6.424	6.122	5.844	5.584	5.341	5.119	4.908	4.715	4.533
14	6.983	6.629	6.303	6.004	5.725	5.466	5.230	5.007	4.803	4.611
15	7.192	6.812	6.463	6.144	5.848	5.574	5.325	5.091	4.877	4.676
16	7.380	6.975	6.604	6.267	5.955	5.667	5.406	5.162	4.939	4.73
17	7.550	7.121	6.729	6.375	6.048	5.747	5.475	5.222	4.991	4.775
18	7.703	7.251	6.840	6.470	6.129	5.186	5.534	5.273	5.035	4.813
19	7.841	7.367	6.938	6.553	6.199	5.876	5.585	5.316	5.072	4.844
20	7.965	7.471	7.025	6.626	6.260	5.927	5.628	5.353	5.103	4.87

EXAMPLE 3.5

Quality Plastics, Inc., is considering two different investment alternatives. Investment A has an initial cost of $35,000 and investment B has an initial cost of $30,000. Both investments have a useful life of six years. The cash flows for these investments are given below. The cost of capital or the interest rate (i) is 8 percent.

Investment A Cash Flow	Investment B Cash Flow	Year	Present Value Factor at 8%
$10,000	$9000	1	0.926
$10,000	$9000	2	0.857
$11,000	$9000	3	0.794
$12,000	$9000	4	0.735
$11,000	$9000	5	0.681
$ 5,000	$9000	6	0.630

To find the present value of the cash flows for each investment, we multiply the present value factor times the cash flow for each investment for each year. The sum of these present value calculations minus the initial investment is the net present value of each investment. The computations appear in the following table:

Investment A Present Values	Investment B Present Values	Year
$9260 = (0.926)($10,000)	$8334 = (0.926)($9000)	1
$8570 = (0.857)($10,000)	$7713 = (0.857)($9000)	2
$8734 = (0.794)($11,000)	$7146 = (0.794)($9000)	3
$8820 = (0.735)($12,000)	$6615 = (0.735)($9000)	4
$7491 = (0.681)($11,000)	$6129 = (0.681)($9000)	5
$3150 = (0.630)($5,000)	$5670 = (0.630)($9000)	6

	Investment A	Investment B
Totals:	$46,025	$41,607
Minus Initial Investment:	−35,000	−30,000
Net Present Value:	$11,025	$11,607

The net present value criterion shows investment B to be more attractive than investment A because it has a higher present value. In this example, it was not necessary to make all of those present value computations for Investment B. Because the cash flows are uniform and equal, Table 3.2 gives the present value. Of course, we would expect to get the same answer.

(continued)

As you recall, Table 3.2 gives factors for the present value of an annuity. In this example, the payments are $9000; the cost of capital is 8 percent; and the number of years is six. Looking in Table 3.2 under 8 percent and six years, we find a factor of 4.623. Thus the present value of this annuity is (4.623)($9000) = $41,607. Look at the above table. Indeed, we get the same value, as expected.

PROBLEM 3.6

Barry Manufacturing has to make a decision between two investment alternatives. Investment A has an initial cost of $61,000, and investment B has an initial cost of $74,000. The useful life of investment A is six years, while the useful life of investment B is seven years. Given a cost of capital of 9 percent and the following cash flows for each alternative, determine the most desirable investment alternative according to the net present value criterion.

Investment A Cash Flow	Investment B Cash Flow	Year
$19,000	$19,000	1
$19,000	$20,000	2
$19,000	$21,000	3
$19,000	$22,000	4
$19,000	$21,000	5
$19,000	$20,000	6
	$11,000	7

INTERNAL RATE OF RETURN

The internal rate of return is another popular method used in deciding among competing investment alternatives. Instead of giving the present value of an investment, the internal rate of return gives the return in percent that an investment will bring to an organization. The same concepts, tables, and formulas that are used in the present value analysis are also used in the computation of the internal rate of return. Furthermore, these methods are equivalent. They will result in the same decision.

The internal rate of return is that interest rate i that will result in the present value of the future cash flows being equal to the initial investment. Stated in other terms, the internal rate of return is that interest rate i that will result in a zero net present value. When there is only one cash flow in the future, we can determine the internal rate of return directly by using logarithms or a scientific calculator.

EXAMPLE 3.6

Andy Lange, a real estate investor, considers only investments with an internal rate of return of 9 percent or greater. He is considering investing \$89,000 in a plot of land near Lake Jackson. Andy is confident that the property will be worth \$100,000 in two years. What is the internal rate of return for this investment?

To determine the internal rate of return, Andy must equate the initial investment of \$89,000 to the present value of the future cash flow. This can be done as follows:

$$\text{Initial investment} = \text{present value of the future cash flows}$$

$$I = \frac{F}{(1+i)^N}$$

where:

I = the initial investment, which is \$89,000 in this case

$$\frac{F}{(1+i)^N} = \text{the present value of the future cash flow.}$$

F = the future cash flow, in this case, \$100,000

N = the number of years, which is 2 for this example

i = the internal rate of return

In order to determine the internal rate of return, we solve for i in the above equation:

$$I(1+i)^N = F$$

$$(1+i)^N = \frac{F}{I}\left(\frac{C_I}{C_0}\right)$$

$$1+i = \sqrt[N]{F/I} \text{ or } \left(\frac{F}{I}\right)^{\frac{1}{N}}$$

$$i = \sqrt[N]{F/I} - 1 \text{ or } \left(\frac{F}{I}\right)^{\frac{1}{N}} - 1$$

(continued)

Now we can determine the internal rate of return by placing the appropriate values in the equation:

$$i = \sqrt[N]{\$100{,}000/\$89{,}000} - 1 \text{, or with } N = 2,$$

$$= \sqrt{1.12359} - 1$$

$$= 1.059999 - 1$$

$$= 0.059999$$

The internal rate of return is 0.059999, or about 6 percent, which is below Andy's investment policy. Thus, he should not invest in this plot of land. Because the investment was for two years (N), we had to take the square root of 1.12359. If N were greater than 2, we would need a scientific calculator to determine the internal rate of return.

The procedure used in Example 3.6 works if there is only one future cash flow. When there are several future cash flows, as is usually the case, it is more difficult to solve directly for the internal rate of return. Instead of receiving $100,000 at the end of the second year, let's assume that Andy will receive $50,000 at the end of the first year and $50,000 at the end of the second year. Here is the equation that Andy would have to grapple with in trying to directly solve for the internal rate of return:

$$\$89{,}000 = \frac{\$50{,}000}{(1+i)^1} + \frac{\$50{,}000}{(1+i)^2}$$

Solving for i in this equation is not a simple task, although it can be done. When there are ten years of cash flows, there will be ten terms with i raised to a different power in each. Instead of solving directly for i, you would generally use a trial-and-error approach. You would select an interest rate and make all of the present value computations. If the net present value were not zero, you would try another interest rate. You would repeat this procedure until the initial investment came close to equalizing the present value of the future cash flows.

Because there are some excellent programs that make the appropriate calculations to determine the internal rate of return for investments, we will not force you into hours of grueling and complex computations. It is simply the purpose of this section to reveal the concepts and procedures of this approach.

EXAMPLE 3.7

The initial cost of an investment is $36,000, and it will return $6000 per year for nine years. What is the internal rate of return?

In this problem, we must find the interest rate that will force the present value of $6000 per year

(continued)

for the next nine years to be equal to the initial investment which is $36,000. Since this is the present value of an annuity, we can use Table 3.2 to find the appropriate interest rate. We will start at 6 percent then go to 7 percent, and so on, until the present value of $6000 per year for the next nine years is about equal to $36,000. The following table shows this trial-and-error procedure:

Trial Number	Interest Rate	Present Value Factor (Table 3.2)	Present Value of Cash Flow	Comments
1	6%	6.802 × $6000	$40,812	*i* is too low
2	7%	6.515 × $6000	$39,090	*i* is too low
3	8%	6.247 × $6000	$37,482	*i* is too low
4	9%	5.985 × $6000	$35,910	*i* is too high but is very close

   Thus the internal rate of return is between 8 and 9 percent. The present value at 9 percent is so close to $36,000 that, for all practical purposes, the internal rate of return is 9 percent. To obtain a more exact answer, we can follow a trial-and-error procedure using the present value formula or we can interpolate the information in the above table. Interpolation is the process of determining the value of a function that is between two known values. In this case, we would want to determine the internal rate of return when it is between two values in the table.

   The procedure used in Example 3.7 is called *trial and error.* If the present value is tremendously different from the initial investment, we don't have to increment the interest rate by 1 percent. In Example 3.7, we could have tried 8 or 10 percent. The number of trials may be different, but the answer will be the same. In the next problem, you may have to try several different interest rates to find the internal rate of return.

PROBLEM 3.7

The initial cost of an investment is $65,000. The return is $16,000 per year for eight years. What is the internal rate of return?

(continued)

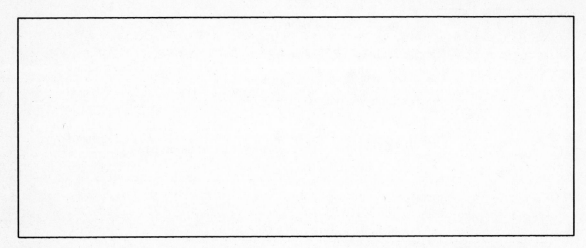

When the annual cash flows are not the same, then a large table (such as the one in Example 3.5 or in Problem 3.6) is necessary to compute the present value for each interest rate. The computations are more difficult, but the trial-and-error process is the same.

DEPRECIATION AND TAXES

Net present value and internal rate of return are excellent ways of evaluating investment alternatives. Both of these methods analyze cash flows. Unfortunately, one of the major cash flows of most organizations is to federal, state, and local governments in the form of taxes. Thus it is very important to consider the effect of taxes on investment alternatives. If you are in the 50 percent tax bracket and if you do not take an allowable deduction of $100,000, you will be paying $50,000 more in taxes. If you had taken this deduction, you would have an additional $50,000 to invest. With a progressive tax structure and increasing inflation, many organizations find that their buying power is the same, but their taxes are higher. Thus, in recent years, tax considerations have become more and more important.

Since many organizations have a large investment in equipment, depreciation is an important tax consideration. Depreciation can be deducted as a business expense. If the depreciation on a piece of equipment in the first few years of the investment is higher, the taxes will be lower, and the company will have more cash to invest in the first few years of the investment. As you might imagine, the IRS has strict laws regulating how a company can depreciate assets or equipment. It is necessary, therefore, to understand these methods of depreciation and their effects on cash flows. First, we will investigate the various methods of depreciating an asset.

Most assets decline in value each year the asset is used. Consequently, the IRS allows the use of several procedures to depreciate an asset. The methods to be discussed in this unit are:

1. Straight line
2. Sum-of-the-years-digits
3. Declining balance

The corresponding formulas are:

$$D_i \text{ (straight line)} = \frac{I - S}{N}$$

$$D_i \text{ (sum-of-the-years-digits)} = \frac{(I - S)(N - i + 1)}{\Sigma N}$$

$$D_i \text{ (declining balance)} = \frac{B}{N} \text{(book value of the asset)}$$

where:

$I =$ the initial investment in dollars

$S =$ the salvage value in dollars

$D_i =$ the depreciation in year i in dollars

$N =$ the life of the investment in years

$B =$ the declining balance factor (usually 2, 1.5, or 1.25)

$\Sigma N =$ the sum-of-the-year-digits. When N is 4, ΣN is $1 + 2 + 3 + 4 = 10$

These formulas may seem formidable until you see how they are used in an example. We will start by investigating the use of straight-line and sum-of-the-years-digits methods in the next example and problem. Then we will delve into declining balance.

EXAMPLE 3.8

An asset has an initial cost of $65,000 and a salvage value of $15,000. The life of the asset is four years. Compute the depreciation for each of the four years using the straight-line method and the sum-of-the-years-digits method.

First of all, you will note that both methods have the term $(I - S)$, which is the initial value minus the salvage value. For this example, $(I - S) = \$65,000 - \$15,000 = \$50,000$. For the sum of the years digits, you will have to compute ΣN, which is $1 + 2 + 3 + 4 = 10$ for this problem. Having completed these preliminary computations, we can employ the following table to calculate depreciation using straight line and sum of the years digits.

(continued)

Year	Straight Line	Sum of the Years Digits
1	$\dfrac{\$50,000}{4} = \$12,500$	$\$50,000 \left(\dfrac{4}{10}\right) = \$20,000$
2	$\dfrac{\$50,000}{4} = \$12,500$	$\$50,000 \left(\dfrac{3}{10}\right) = \$15,000$
3	$\dfrac{\$50,000}{4} = \$12,500$	$\$50,000 \left(\dfrac{2}{10}\right) = \$10,000$
4	$\dfrac{\$50,000}{4} = \$12,500$	$\$50,000 \left(\dfrac{1}{10}\right) = \$\ 5,000$
Totals:	$50,000	$50,000

Notice that the straight-line depreciation is the same for all years; it is simply the initial value minus the salvage value divided by the number of years. The sum-of-the-years-digits is not much more difficult to compute. For the first year, where $i = 1$, $N - i + 1$ is $4 - 1 + 1 = 4$. For the second year, $N - i + 1$ is 3, for the third year it is 2, and so forth. Each year this term decreases by one, and the first year it is equal to the life of the investment (four years in this example). With both methods, the total amount depreciated is equal to the initial investment minus the salvage value ($I - S$).

PROBLEM 3.8

An asset has an initial value of $88,000 and a salvage value of $22,000. It is estimated that the life of the asset is five years. Compute the straight-line depreciation and the sum-of-the-years-digits depreciation for this asset.

As you have noticed, the sum-of-the-years digits method offers accelerated depreciation. Since depreciation is subtracted from the years earnings to arrive at before-tax profits, the sum-of-the-years-digits method is usually preferable because it allows you to write off more of the asset in the earlier years. Of course, the greater the cost of capital or the effective interest rate, the more attractive an accelerated method like sum-of-the-years-digits depreciation becomes.

Next we will explore the declining-balance method of depreciation. The most commonly used declining-balance methods are *double declining balance, one-and-a-half declining balance,* and *one-and-a-quarter declining balance.* For these methods B is 2, 1.5, and 1.25. The next example investigates double declining balance.

EXAMPLE 3.9

Use double declining balance to depreciate the asset described in Example 3.8. This asset has an initial cost of $65,000 and a salvage value of $15,000. The life of the asset is four years.

Using the formula previously given for declining balance and the following table, we can determine the double-declining-balance depreciation for each year for the asset.

Year	Double Declining Balance	Book Value at the End of the Year
1	$\frac{2}{4}(\$65,000) = \$32,500$	$\$65,000 - \$32,500 = \$32,500$
2	$\frac{2}{4}(\$32,500) = \$16,250$	$\$32,500 - \$16,250 = \$16,250$
3	$\frac{2}{4}(\$16,250) = \$8125$	
	But the salvage value is $15,000. Therefore, we can depreciate only $1250, which will get us down to the salvage value.	
	Depreciation = $1250	$\$16,250 - \$1250 = \$15,000$
4	The depreciation is 0 because we are already at the salvage value	$\$15,000 - 0 = \$15,000$
Total:	$50,000	

As can be seen, only the book value changes in a declining-balance method. B and N are the same for each year. In this problem they are 2 and 4. In the first year, the depreciation is $32,500. The book value at the end of any year is the book value at the end of the previous year minus the depreciation for that year. The book value at the end of year 1 is $65,000 - $32,500 = $32,500. We used this book value to calculate the depreciation for the next year. This procedure continues until the book value reaches the salvage value; after that, the depreciation is zero. When the

(continued)

depreciation in later years is greater than double declining balance, it may be possible to switch to the straight-line method.

As you can see, double declining balance is a more accelerated depreciation method than the sum-of-the-years-digits method. If double declining balance is allowed, it is usually preferred over the sum-of-the-years-digits and straight-line depreciation.

PROBLEM 3.9

Depreciate the asset described in Problem 3.8 using one-and-a-half declining balance. This asset has an initial cost of $88,000, a salvage value of $22,000, and a useful life of five years.

Although the declining-balance method always appears to be more attractive, there are situations in which straight-line or sum-of-the-years-digits depreciation is the preferred approach. For example, you can use double declining balance on a company vehicle, but after it has been depreciated to its salvage value, you normally can make no further deductions. On the other hand, if you use straight line, you can usually deduct an allowance per mile after the vehicle has depreciated to its salvage value. The number of miles the vehicle is to be driven after it has depreciated to its salvage value is one factor that you must consider before deciding which depreciation method to use. For other assets, there are regulations that may change over time. These regulations require careful analysis before you decide upon a depreciation method.

In making investment decisions, you should take depreciation and tax into account. Thus, it is advisable to base the investment strategies on the after-tax returns.

EXAMPLE 3.10

The expected net income before depreciation and taxes for Klastorin's Kleaners for the next 5 years is: $32,000, $34,000, $38,000, $43,000 and $45,000. The firm's tax rate is 50 percent, or 0.5. Ted Klastorin is considering different depreciation methods. As in Problem 3.8, the equipment has an initial value of $88,000, a salvage value of $22,000, and a useful life of five years. How much tax will Klastorin pay each year if he uses straight-line depreciation? Refer back to Problem 3.8 for depreciation data.

Expected Net Income Before Depreciation and Taxes	−	Straight-line Depreciation	=	Net Income Before Taxes	× 0.5 =	Tax
$32,000		$13,200		$18,800		$ 9,400
$34,000		$13,200		$20,800		$10,400
$38,000		$13,200		$24,800		$12,400
$43,000		$13,200		$29,800		$14,900
$45,000		$13,200		$31,800		$15,900

Total tax: $63,000

   Net income before taxes is the expected net income before depreciation and taxes minus the straight-line depreciation. The tax to be paid is this value times 50 percent, or 0.5.

PROBLEM 3.10

How much tax will Klastorin pay if he uses one-and-a-half declining balance? Refer to Problem 3.9 for depreciation data.

Expected Net Income Before Depreciation and Taxes	−	1.5-declining-balance Depreciation	=	Net Income Before Taxes	× 0.5 = Tax
$32,000					
$34,000					
$38,000					
$43,000					
$45,000					

Total tax:

Although it is complex to compute, the effect of taxes and depreciation on investment decisions is very important. All financial decisions should be made on an after-tax basis.

SUMMARY

In this unit we have investigated several methods of deciding among competing investment alternatives. The best methods use net present value and the internal rate of return. These approaches are not without fault. Investments with the same present value may have significantly different project lives. Furthermore, investments with the same net present value may have substantially different cash flows. In one investment, there may be tremendous cash outflows at the beginning and large postive cash inflows at the end of an investment. Some organizations may prefer investments with shorter lives and investments that do not have substantial negative cash flows at the beginning of the project, even though these projects have the highest net present value. Attempts to include these factors into the analysis notwithstanding, decision making is still an art.

Another limitation of the models presented in this unit is that they do not consider risk. They assume that all cash flows are known with certainty. This assumption may not be valid. Making decisions under conditions of risk and uncertainty is the subject of the next unit.

ANSWERS

3.1   The payback period for investment 1 is 4 years ($1000 + $1000 + $3000 + $15,000 = $20,000). The payback period for investment 2 is 3.5 years ($7000 + $6000 + $5000 + $4000 (0.5) = $20,000). Finally, the payback period for investment 3 is 4 years ($10,000 + $5000 + $3000 + $2000 = $20,000). According to the payback period criterion, investment 2 is the best investment because it has the lowest payback period. It is interesting that the payback periods for investment 1 and investment 3 are the same, even though the cash flows for the first 4 years follow completely different patterns. According to the payback criterion, these two investments are equally desirable. Most operations managers would prefer investment 3 to investment 1 because the returns in the first few years are much greater. This feature is one of the drawbacks of the payback period technique.

3.2 $$\text{Payback} = \frac{\$123,545 - \$44,560}{\$14,667} = 5.39 \text{ yr.}$$

3.3 $$P = \$890 = \frac{F}{(1 + i)^N} = \frac{\$1000}{(1 + 0.06)^2} = \frac{\$1000}{1.1236}$$

3.4   Looking in Table 3.1 for 8 percent and twelve years, we find a factor of 0.397. Thus, the present value is (0.397) $5600 = $2223.20. Another way of looking at this problem is that $2223.20 invested today at 8 percent will be worth $5600.00 in twelve years.

3.5   Looking in Table 3.2 for an interest rate of 6 percent and for four years, we find a factor of 3.465. Thus, the present value is

$$S = \$29,799 = R \times \text{(a factor from Table 3.2)} = \$8600 \, (3.465)$$

3.6   Since the cash flows for investment A are uniform and equal, you can use Table 3.2 to calculate the present value of the future cash flows. The factor 4.486 appears in Table 3.2 for an interest rate of 9 percent over 6 years. Thus, the present value of the future cash flows for investment A is (4.486)($19,000) = $85,234. Subtracting the initial investment from this value gives the net present value. The net present value for investment A is $85,234 − $61,000 = $24,234.

The net present value for investment B is found using Table 3.1 and the following table.

Year	Investment B Cash Flow	Present Value Factor (Table 3.1)	Investment B Present Values
1	$19,000	0.917	$17,423
2	$20,000	0.842	$16,840
3	$21,000	0.772	$16,212
4	$22,000	0.708	$15,576
5	$21,000	0.650	$13,650
6	$20,000	0.596	$11,920
7	$11,000	0.547	$6,017
		Total:	$97,638

Thus, the net present value is $97,638 − $74,000 = $23,638, so investment A is preferable to investment B because it has a higher present value.

3.7

Trial Number	Interest Rate (i)	Present Value Factor (Table 3.2)	Present Value of Cash Flow	Comments
1	7%	6.971	$111,536	*i* is too low
2	20%	3.837	$61,392	*i* is too high
3	18%	4.078	$65,248	*i* is too low but is very close

For practical purposes, the internal rate of return is 18 percent. We were very lucky; it took only three trials to find the approximate value of the internal rate of return. It is not uncommon to have to make more than ten trials before arriving at a good estimate.

3.8 For this asset, $(I - S)$ is $88,000 − $22,000 = $66,000. For the sum of the years digits, ΣN is needed. For this problem it is $1 + 2 + 3 + 4 + 5 = 15$. You can compute the depreciation for all five years with both methods using the following table.

Year	Straight Line	Sum of the years digits
1	$\dfrac{\$66,000}{5} = \$13,200$	$\$66,000 \left(\dfrac{5}{15}\right) = \$22,000$
2	$\dfrac{\$66,000}{5} = \$13,200$	$\$66,000 \left(\dfrac{4}{15}\right) = \$17,600$
3	$\dfrac{\$66,000}{5} = \$13,200$	$\$66,000 \left(\dfrac{3}{15}\right) = \$13,200$
4	$\dfrac{\$66,000}{5} = \$13,200$	$\$66,000 \left(\dfrac{2}{15}\right) = \$8800$
5	$\dfrac{\$66,000}{5} = \$13,200$	$\$66,000 \left(\dfrac{1}{15}\right) = \$4400$
Totals:	$66,000	$66,000

3.9

Year	1.5 Declining Balance	Book Value at the End of the Year
1	$\dfrac{1.5}{5}(\$88,000) = \$26,400$	$\$88,000 - \$26,400 = \$61,600$
2	$\dfrac{1.5}{5}(\$61,600) = \$18,480$	$\$61,600 - \$18,480 = \$43,120$
3	$\dfrac{1.5}{5}(\$43,120) = \$12,936$	$\$43,120 - \$12,936 = \$30,184$
4	$\dfrac{1.5}{5}(\$30,184) = \$9055.20$ (Use $8184)	$\$30,184 - \$8184 = \$22,000$
5	The depreciation is 0	$\$22,000 - 0 = \$22,000$

In year 4, the depreciation is computed to be $9055.20. If this value were used, however, the value of the asset would be below the book value. Thus, only $8184 can be depreciated in the fourth year. This figure will bring the value of the asset down to the book value in the fourth year. It also causes the depreciation for the fifth year to be zero.

3.10

Expected Net Income Before Depreciation and Taxes	−	1.5-declining-balance Depreciation	=	Net Income Before Taxes × 0.5	=	Tax
$32,000		$26,400		$5,600		$2,800
$34,000		$18,480		$15,520		$7,760
$38,000		$12,936		$25,064		$12,532
$43,000		$8,184		$34,816		$17,408
$45,000		0		$45,000		$22,500

Total tax: $63,000

Although the total taxes are the same, the taxes are lower in the first few years for the one-and-a-half declining balance method. For the first year, Klastorin pays $6600 less in taxes using one-and-a-half declining balance. This savings he can reinvest in his business or place it in a bank to earn dividends. If Klastorin sells the equipment after two years, he will save $9240 = ($9400 + $10,400) − ($2800 + $7760) in income tax. If he sells the equipment for more than the book value, he will have to pay a capital gains tax on the difference.

HOMEWORK PROBLEMS

3-1. Last week, Ball Manufacturers, located in Arizona, decided to acquire a new piece of manufacturing equipment. This new equipment has an initial cost of $30,000. The only question remaining in Joe Sullivan's mind is whether or not to purchase the rebuilding contract along with the new equipment. The rebuilding contract would result in an expenditure of $10,000 in the fifth year of the investment. This would result in an additional $4,000 of positive cash flow due to reduced maintenance costs and better quality products in year 6, year 7, and year 8. Joe would like to make an analysis of whether or not to sign the rebuilding contract with the supplier. He has chosen eight years over which to make his decision. Without the rebuild, the cash flow for the eight years, starting with year 1, would be as follows: $10,000, $11,000, $12,000, $12,000, $8,000, $7,000, $6,000, and $5,000. Currently, the effective interest rate is 8%. Should Joe sign the contract to rebuild the equipment in year 5?

3-2. The expected net income before depreciation and taxes for a new building project is expected to be $60,000 for the first year. After that, there is expected to be a $1,000 per year increase for twenty years, which will result in an expected net income before depreciation and taxes of $80,000 in the 20th year. The initial cost of the building project is $500,000. At this time, the company is in a 48% tax bracket, and the salvage value is estimated to be $100,000. Determine the straight-line depreciation, the net income, the tax, and the after-tax income for this particular building project for 20 years. In addition, compute the total tax and the total after-tax income for this building project.

The manager of the building project is uncertain about the actual salvage value and its impact on tax and the after-tax income. Using a table, recompute the depreciation, the net income, the tax, and the after-tax figures for all twenty years of the building project, using a salvage value of $50,000 and a salvage value of $200,000. In addition, compute the total tax for twenty years and the total after-tax income for twenty years as well.

Unit 4

Decision Theory

Capital investment decisions such as those seen in Unit 3 usually assume that future cash flows are known with certainty. In the real world, however, salvage values, interest rates, product demand levels, machinery lifetimes, changes in technology, and a host of other factors create conditions of risk and uncertainty in decision making. Yet decisions must be made concerning investments in new buildings, equipment, and research, and actions must be taken to control inventory and to plan maintenance and scheduling.

Decision theory is a rational approach to the selection of the best alternative or course of action. There are typically three classifications in decision theory. They depend upon the degree of certainty of the possible outcomes or consequences facing the decision maker. The three types of decision models are:

1. *Decision making under certainty*—the decision maker knows with certainty the consequence or outcome of any alternative or decision choice. For example, a decision maker knows with complete certainty that a $100 deposit in a checking account will result in an increase of $100 in the balance of that account.
2. *Decision making under risk*—the decision maker knows the probability of occurrence of the outcomes or consequences for each choice. We may not know whether it will rain tomorrow, but we may know that the probability of rain is 0.3.
3. *Decision making under uncertainty*—the decision maker does not know the probability of occurrence of the outcomes for each alternative. For example, the probability that a Democrat will be president twenty years from now is not known.

In decision making under certainty, the decision maker knows the outcome of his actions, and he will choose the alternative that will maximize his well-being or will result in the best outcome. In decision making under risk, the decision maker will attempt to maximize his or her *expected* well-being. The decision approach typically employed is maximization of expected monetary value. The criteria for decision making under uncertainty that we will discuss in this unit include maximax, maximin, and equally likely.

FUNDAMENTALS OF DECISION MAKING

Regardless of the complexity of a decision or the sophistication of the technique used to analyze the decision, all decision makers are faced with alternatives and states of nature. The following terms will be used in this unit:

Terms:

Alternative—a course of action or a strategy that may be chosen by a decision maker (for example, not carrying an umbrella tomorrow).

State of Nature—an occurrence or a situation over which the decision maker has little or no control (for example, tomorrow's weather).

Symbols used in a decision table:

A—an alternative

S—a state of nature

Symbols used in a decision tree:

☐ —a decision node from which one of several alternatives may be selected

◯ —a state of nature node out of which one state of nature will occur

To present a manager's decision alternatives, we can develop *decision trees* and *decision tables* using the above symbols.

EXAMPLE 4.1

The Thompson Lumber Company is investigating the possibility of producing and marketing back-yard storage sheds. Undertaking this project would require the construction of either a large or a small manufacturing plant. The market for the product produced—storage sheds—could be either favorable or unfavorable. Thompson, of course has the option of not developing the new product line at all. A decision tree for this situation is presented in Figure 4.1.

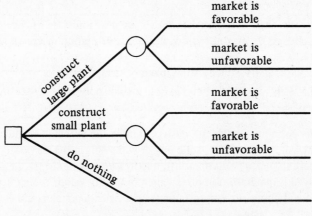

Figure 4.1. Thompson's Decision Tree

In constructing a decision tree, we must be sure that all alternatives and states of nature are in their correct and logical places and that we include *all* possible alternatives and states of nature.

EXAMPLE 4.2

We may also develop a decision table to help Thompson Lumber define its alternatives. Let

A_1 = the construction of a large plant

A_2 = the construction of a small plant

A_3 = do nothing

Also let

S_1 = a favorable market condition

S_2 = an unfavorable market condition

With these definitions, we can construct the following decision table.

States of Nature →		*Favorable Market*	*Unfavorable Market*
Alternatives ↓		S_1	S_2
Construct large plant	A_1		
Construct small plant	A_2		
Do nothing	A_3		

The body of the table is blank so that we can later fill in the consequences, usually expressed in dollar amounts, of given alternative and state of nature combinations. In Problem 4.1, develop a decision tree and decision table where the decision is to stock 5, 6, or 7 cases.

PROBLEM 4.1

Daily demand for cases of Royal Cola soda at Helen's Food Shop has always been 5, 6, or 7 cases. Develop a decision tree and a decision table that illustrate the decision alternatives as to whether to stock 5, 6, or 7 cases.

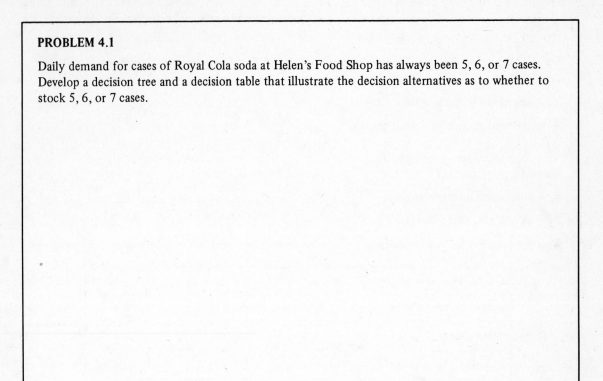

DECISION TABLES

For any alternative and a particular state of nature, there is a consequence or outcome, which is usually expressed as a monetary value. This is called a *conditional value*. We will start by investigating the conditional values for Thompson Lumber Company.

EXAMPLE 4.3

Refer to Example 4.2 and construct a decision table including conditional values based on the following information. With a favorable market, a large facility would give Thompson's a net profit of $200,000. If the market is unfavorable, a $180,000 net loss would occur. A small plant would result in a net profit of $100,000 in a favorable market, but a net loss of $20,000 would be encountered if the market was unfavorable.

(continued)

States of Nature →		*Favorable market*	*Unfavorable market*
Alternatives ↓		S_1	S_2
Construct large plant	A_1	$200,000	−$180,000
Construct small plant	A_2	$100,000	−$20,000
Do nothing	A_3	$0	$0

Note: It is important to include *all* alternatives, including "Do nothing."

Some problems require a few calculations before we can place conditional values in the decision table. This is true for the situation described in Problem 4.1. Example 4.4 shows how to compute conditional values and place them in a decision table.

EXAMPLE 4.4

In Problem 4.1, demand could be 5, 6, or 7 cases of Royal Cola per day. Thus 5, 6, or 7 cases should be stocked each day. Each case has a cost of $3.00 and a selling price of $6.00. Helen may return cases not sold at the end of the day to the supplier, who will refund the cost of each case except for a fee of $1.00 per case for handling and restorage. Develop the appropriate decision table.

1. The marginal profit of selling one case is the selling price minus the cost.

$$\text{Marginal profit} = \text{MP} = \$6 - \$3 = \$3$$

2. The marginal loss of not selling one case is the return cost of $1.00.

$$\text{ML} = \$1$$

3. For any alternative and state of nature combination, the conditional value is the marginal profit multiplied by the number of cases sold minus the marginal loss multiplied by the number of cases not sold.

$$\text{Conditional value} = (\text{MP}) \times (\text{cases sold}) - (\text{ML}) \times (\text{cases not sold})$$

The decision table, including conditional values, is as follows.

(continued)

State of Nature →		Demand is 5 cases	Demand is 6 cases	Demand is 7 cases
Alternatives ↓		S_1	S_2	S_3
Stock 5 cases	A_1	$15	$15	$15
Stock 6 cases	A_2	$14	$18	$18
Stock 7 cases	A_3	$13	$17	$21

PROBLEM 4.2

For a particular item, marginal profit is $4.00 and marginal loss is $2.00. Daily demand can vary from 0 to 5 items, and the number of items stocked may vary from 1 to 5 items each day. Construct a decision table for this problem. Let

$$A_i = \text{alternative of stocking } i \text{ items.}$$

$$S_i = \text{a daily demand of } i \text{ items}$$

States of Nature →		0	1	2	3	4	5
Alternatives (in units) ↓		S_0	S_1	S_2	S_3	S_4	S_5
Stock 1	A_1						
Stock 2	A_2						
Stock 3	A_3						
Stock 4	A_4						
Stock 5	A_5						

Each conditional value is obtained as follows:

$$\text{Conditional value} = (MP) \times (\text{units sold}) - (ML) \times (\text{units not sold})$$

It is also interesting to note that for any row, the conditional value increases by $6 = (4 + 2)$ until the demand is greater than the supply.

Before leaving the topic of conditional value, we will note that it is often convenient to use variables to represent conditional values. Let O_{ij} = the outcome, or conditional value, resulting from alternative A_i and state of nature S_j. Problem 4.2 can be symbolically represented as:

States of Nature →	S_0	S_1	S_2	S_3	S_4	S_5
Alternatives ↓						
A_1	O_{10}	O_{11}	O_{12}	O_{13}	O_{14}	O_{15}
A_2	O_{20}	O_{21}	O_{22}	O_{23}	O_{24}	O_{25}
A_3	O_{30}	O_{31}	O_{32}	O_{33}	O_{34}	O_{35}
A_4	O_{40}	O_{41}	O_{42}	O_{43}	O_{44}	O_{45}
A_5	O_{50}	O_{51}	O_{52}	O_{53}	O_{54}	O_{55}

For Problem 4.2, we would get

$$O_{10} = -2$$
$$O_{11} = \ 4$$
$$O_{12} = \ 4$$

and so on

Given a decision table with conditional values and probability assessments for all states of nature, we can determine the *Expected Monetary Value* (EMV) for each alternative. This figure represents the *average* return for each alternative if we could repeat the decision a large number of times. Picking that alternative which has the maximum EMV is one of the most popular decision criteria. For any alternative, we can compute EMV as follows:

$$\text{EMV}(A_i) = \sum_{j=1}^{n} O_{ij} P_j$$

where

$$\text{EMV}(A_i) = \text{the expected monetary value for alternative } i$$

$$P_j = \text{the probability of occurrence of state of nature } j$$

The following example reveals the computational procedure typically used to determine the maximum EMV.

EXAMPLE 4.5

Using the structure and data of Example 4.3 and the probability information contained in the following table, we can determine the EMV for each alternative that Thompson Lumber faces.

State of Nature →		Favorable market	Unfavorable market
Alternatives ↓		S_1	S_2
Large facility	A_1	$200,000	−$180,000
Small facility	A_2	$100,000	−$20,000
Do nothing	A_3	$0.00	$0.00
P_i →		0.5	0.5

P_{S_1} = probability of a favorable market = 0.5

P_{S_2} = probability of an unfavorable market = 0.5

1. EMV(A_1) = (0.5)($200,000) + (0.5)(−$180,000)

     = $10,000

2. EMV(A_2) = (0.5)($100,000) + (0.5)(−$20,000)

     = $40,000

3. EMV(A_3) = (0.5)($0) + (0.5)($0)

     = $0

The maximum EMV is seen in alternative A_2. Thus, according to the EMV decision criterion, we would build the small facility.

PROBLEM 4.3

Given the following information, choose the best alternative using the EMV method.

State of Nature →			
Alternatives ↓	S_1	S_2	S_3
A_1	$15	$15	$15
A_2	$14	$18	$18
A_3	$13	$17	$21
P_{Si} →	0.2	0.3	0.5

Under normal circumstances, when we can assess the probability of occurrence of each state of nature, the EMV decision criteria are appropriate. When we cannot assess these probabilities satisfactorily, we need other decision criteria. This type of problem demands decision making under uncertainty. The criteria that we will cover include:

1. *Maximax*—this criterion finds an alternative that *max*imizes the *max*imum outcome or consequence for every alternative. First, we find the maximum outcome within every alternative, and then we pick the alternative with the maximum number. Since this decision criterion locates the alternative with the *highest* possible *gain*, it has been called an "optimistic" decision criterion.
2. *Maximin*—this criterion finds the alternative that *max*imizes the *min*imum outcome or consequence for every alternative. First, we find the minimum outcome within every alternative, and then we pick the alternative with the maximum number. Since this decision criterion locates the alternative that has the *least* possible *loss*, it has been called a "pessimistic" decision criterion.
3. **Equally likely**—this decision criterion finds the alternative with the highest average outcome. We first calculate the average outcome for every alternative, which is the sum of all outcomes divided by the number of outcomes. Then we pick the alternative with the maximum number. The equally likely approach assumes that all probabilities of occurrence for the states of nature are equal and thus each state of nature is equally likely.

EXAMPLE 4.6

Given the following decision table, determine the maximax, maximin, and equally likely decision criteria.

States of Nature →	S_1	S_2
Alternatives ↓		
A_1	$200,000	−$180,000
A_2	$100,000	−$20,000
A_3	$0	$0

1.

States of Nature →	S_1	S_2	Maximum in row	Minimum in row	Row average
Alternatives ↓					
A_1	$200,000	−$180,000	($200,000)	−$180,000	$10,000
A_2	$100,000	−$20,000	$100,000	−$20,000	($40,000)
A_3	$0	$0	$0	($0)	$0
			Maximax↑	Maximin↑	Equally ↑ likely

2. The maximax choice is alternative A_1. This is the *max*imum of the *max*imum number within each row, or alternative.
3. The maximin choice is alternative A_3. This is the *max*imum of the *min*imum number within each row, or alternative.
4. The equally likely choice is A_2. This is the maximum of the average outcome of each alternative. This approach assumes that all outcomes for any alternative are *equally likely*.

PROBLEM 4.4

With the following information, determine the maximax, maximin, and the equally likely decision criteria.

(continued)

States of Nature → Alternatives ↓	S_1	S_2	S_3
A_1	$15	$15	$15
A_2	$14	$18	$18
A_3	$13	$17	$21

DECISION TREES

Decisions that lend themselves to display in a decision table also lend themselves to display in a decision tree. We should analyze some decisions, however, using decision trees. It is convenient to use a decision table in problems having one set of decisions and one set of states of nature. Many problems, however, include sequential decisions and states of nature. When there are two or more sequential decisions and later decisions are based on the outcome of prior ones, the decision tree approach becomes appropriate.

Although we may apply all previously discussed decision criteria, expected monetary value (EMV) is the most commonly used and usually the most appropriate criterion for decision tree analysis. One of the first steps in the analysis is to graph the decision tree and to specify the monetary consequences of all contingencies or outcomes for a particular problem.

EXAMPLE 4.7

A group of medical professionals is considering the construction of a private clinic. If the market is favorable, they could realize a net profit of $100,000. If the market is not favorable, they could lose $40,000. They have also been approached by a marketing research team that will perform a study of the market for an additional $5,000 The results of the study could be either favorable or unfavorable.

(continued)

They would like to construct a decision tree and indicate its appropriate conditional monetary values. The following definitions are helpful:

A_1 –hire the marketing research group
A_2 –do not hire the marketing research group
S_1 –the research, if the group is hired, is favorable
S_2 –the research, if the group is hired, is unfavorable
A_3 –build the clinic
A_4 –do not build the clinic
S_3 –the market is favorable, given the clinic is built
S_4 –the market is unfavorable, given the clinic is built
A_i –an alternative
S_i –a state of nature

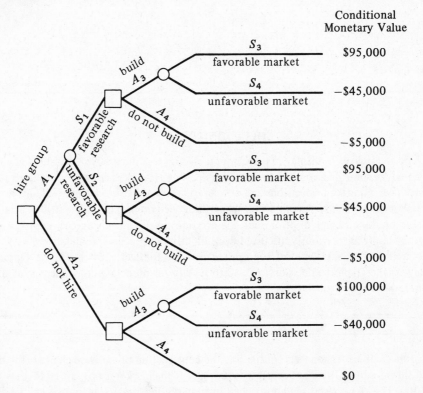

	Conditional Monetary Value
S_3 favorable market	$95,000
S_4 unfavorable market	–$45,000
	–$5,000
S_3 favorable market	$95,000
S_4 unfavorable market	–$45,000
	–$5,000
S_3 favorable market	$100,000
S_4 unfavorable market	–$40,000
	$0

In determining the conditional monetary value for each branch, we need to subtract $5,000 from those branches of the decision tree that embody A_1 (research), in other words, the top six terminal branches. We used the following convention:

(continued)

☐ —a decision

◯ —a state of nature

Perhaps the most difficult aspect of a decision tree problem is including *all* contingencies or outcomes. Thus, even if the marketing research is unfavorable, the doctors still have the option of building the clinic. They cannot assume that the information from the marketing research group is perfect, or even reliable, at this stage.

PROBLEM 4.5

Construct a decision tree and include the appropriate conditional monetary values for the following problem. The Thompson Lumber Company, first discussed in Example 4.1, can perform their own study at a cost of $10,000 to obtain additional marketing information. This information might help them in deciding whether to build a large plant, a small plant, or to not build any plant at all to produce backyard storage sheds. As discussed in Example 4.3, a large plant with a favorable market would net a profit of $200,000. If the market were unfavorable, a $180,000 loss would occur. A small plant would net a profit of $100,000 in a favorable market, but a net loss of $20,000 would occur if the market were unfavorable.

Let

A_1 = study.
A_2 = no study.
A_3 = large plant.
A_4 = small plant.
A_5 = do nothing.

S_1 = favorable study result.

S_2 = unfavorable study result.

S_3 = favorable market.

S_4 = unfavorable market.

After the conditional values have been determined for each possible outcome, or terminal branch, on the decision tree, the next step is to specify the probabilities of occurrence of each state of nature. Such probabilities can be assessed by the manager/decision maker. Then we can analyze the entire decision tree. Note that all probabilities appear in parentheses next to their appropriate states of nature on the decision tree.

EXAMPLE 4.8

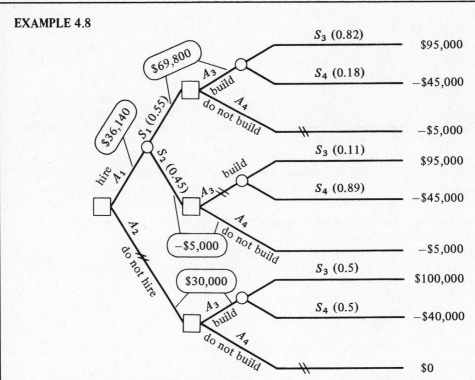

Figure 4.2. Decision Tree Reflecting Alternatives Facing Group of Medical Professionals

The solution of the decision displayed in Figure 4.2 is to hire the marketing research group (alternative A_1). If the research is favorable (state of nature S_1), the clinic should be built (alternative A_3). If the research is not favorable (state of nature S_2), the clinic should not be built (alternative A_4). The decision to hire the marketing research team and make a decision based on their findings has an expected value of $36,140. The expected value of not hiring the marketing research team and building the clinic has an expected value of $30,000. Thus, the best decision is to hire the research team and base the decision on their conclusions.

But how did we arrive at this decision? Where did the numbers come from? The solution will be discussed shortly, but first we should explain a few symbols and conventions.

(continued)

First of all, all probabilities are enclosed in parentheses; (0.82), (0.18), (0.11), and so on are all probabilities. Conditional monetary values appear at the end of the decision tree. The conditional monetary value of hiring the research team and building the clinic when the market for the clinic is favorable is $95,000. Likewise, −$45,000 is the conditional monetary value of hiring the marketing team and building the clinic when the market for the clinic is unfavorable. Now we are in a position to solve this problem.

The objective is to determine the expected value of A_1 and A_2. The only way to accomplish this goal is to start at the end of the decision tree and, working toward the beginning of the decision tree, calculate expected values. These values have been circled on the decision tree. For example, $69,800 is the expected value of A_3, given S_1. This is the top branch of the tree. In the analysis, EMV $(A_3|S_1)$ is the expected monetary value of A_3, given S_1. In general, EMV $(x|y)$ is the expected monetary value of x, given y. Looking at the top of the decision tree, you can see that the expected value of A_3 ($69,800) is greater than the expected value of $A_4(−$5000)$, given S_1. Thus, if we are at the top branch of the tree, we would always pick A_3. So A_4 at the top of the tree has been crossed off (||). In general, we cross off an alternative that we would not choose because it has a lower expected monetary value than another alternative. An explanation of how to analyze the above decision follows.

Working from the end of the tree, we will start calculating EMVs.

1. EMV$(A_3|S_1)$ = building given a favorable survey result

$$= (0.82)(\$95,000) + (0.18)(-\$45,000)$$

$$= \$77,900 - \$8100$$

$$= \$69,800$$

EMV$(A_4|S_1) = -\$5000$

Thus, if the research is favorable, we would want to build (A_3) with an expected return of $69,800.

2. EMV$(A_3|S_2)$ = building given an unfavorable survey result

$$= (0.11)(\$95,000) + (0.89)(-\$45,000)$$

$$= \$10,450 - \$40,050$$

$$= -\$29,600$$

EMV$(A_4|S_2) = -\$5000$

(continued)

Thus, if the research is unfavorable (S_2), we would always *not* build.

Note that $A_4|S_1$ and $A_3|S_2$ have been crossed out on the tree, and the EMV of the better alternatives have been placed by S_1 and S_2 and circled.

3. $EMV(A_3)$ = building without any research

$$= (0.5)(\$100,000) + (0.5)(-\$40,000)$$

$$= \$50,000 - \$20,000$$

$$= \$30,000$$

Since $EMV(A_4) = 0$, we would build if we decided *not* to acquire marketing research. Thus, $EMV(A_3) = EMV(A_2) = \$30,000$.

4. $EMV(A_1)$ = seeking marketing research information

$$= (0.55)(\$69,800) + (0.45)(-\$5000)$$

$$= \$38,390 - \$2250$$

$$= \$36,140$$

5. Since $EMV(A_1)$ is greater than $EMV(A_2)$, because $\$36,140 \geqslant \$30,000$, we should seek the marketing information. If the results are favorable, we will build; if the results are unfavorable, we will not build. This conclusion can be drawn from the decision tree, where all of the EMVs have been circled and arrows have been drawn to the appropriate alternative.

PROBLEM 4.6

The decision tree shown in Figure 4.3 reflects the decision facing the Thompson Lumber Company executives.

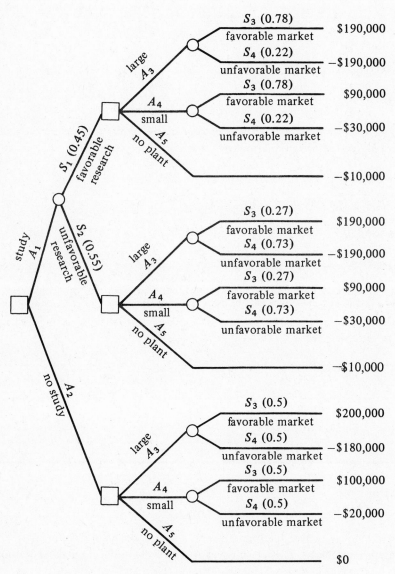

Figure 4.3. Thompson Lumber Company Decision Tree

(continued)

What do you recommend?

SUMMARY

Decision-making techniques discussed in this unit apply to a large number of different production and operations management problems. These techniques are especially useful for making decisions under risk and uncertainty. Investments in research and development, plant and equipment, and even new buildings and structures can be analyzed with these decision-making techniques. Problems in inventory control, aggregate planning, maintenance, scheduling, and production control are just a few possible applications of the decision techniques discussed in this unit. Whenever you face a decision that contains risk and chance, you can use these techniques to make good decisions.

ANSWERS

4.1   **Decision Tree**

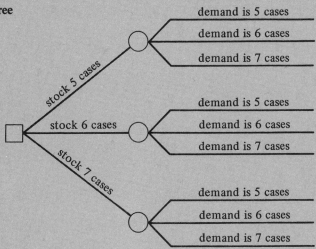

Decision Table

States of Nature →		*Demand is 5 cases*	*Demand is 6 cases*	*Demand is 7 cases*
Alternatives ↓		S_1	S_2	S_3
Stock 5 cases	A_1			
Stock 6 cases	A_2			
Stock 7 cases	A_3			

4.2

States of Nature →		0	1	2	3	4	5
Alternatives (in units) ↓		S_0	S_1	S_2	S_3	S_4	S_5
Stock 1	A_1	−$2	$4	$4	$4	$4	$4
Stock 2	A_2	−$4	$2	$8	$8	$8	$8
Stock 3	A_3	−$6	0	$6	$12	$12	$12
Stock 4	A_4	−$8	−$2	$4	$10	$16	$16
Stock 5	A_5	−$10	−$4	$2	$8	$14	$20

4.3

State of Nature → Alternatives ↓	S_1	S_2	S_3	EMV
A_1	$15	$15	$15	$15
A_2	$14	$18	$18	$17.2
A_3	$13	$17	$21	$18.2
P_{Si} →	0.2	0.3	0.5	

EMV $(A_1) = (0.2)(\$15) + (0.3)(\$15) + (0.5)(\$15) = \$15$

EMV $(A_2) = (0.2)(\$14) + (0.3)(\$18) + (0.5)(\$18) = \$17.2$

EMV $(A_3) = (0.2)(\$13) + (0.3)(\$17) + (0.5)(\$21) = \$18.2$

Thus alternative A_3, which has an EMV of $18.2, is the best alternative according to the EMV decision criteria. Also note that EMV values have been placed on the right side of the table.

4.4

States of Nature → Alternatives ↓	S_1	S_2	S_3	Maximum in row	Minimum in row	Row average
A_1	$15	$15	$15	$15	($15)	$15
A_2	$14	$18	$18	$18	$14	$16.67
A_3	$13	$17	$21	($21)	$13	($17)

Maximax↑   Maximin↑   Equally likely↑

Maximax is alternative A_3—optimistic.
Maximin is alternative A_1—pessimistic.
Equally likely is alternative A_3.

4.5

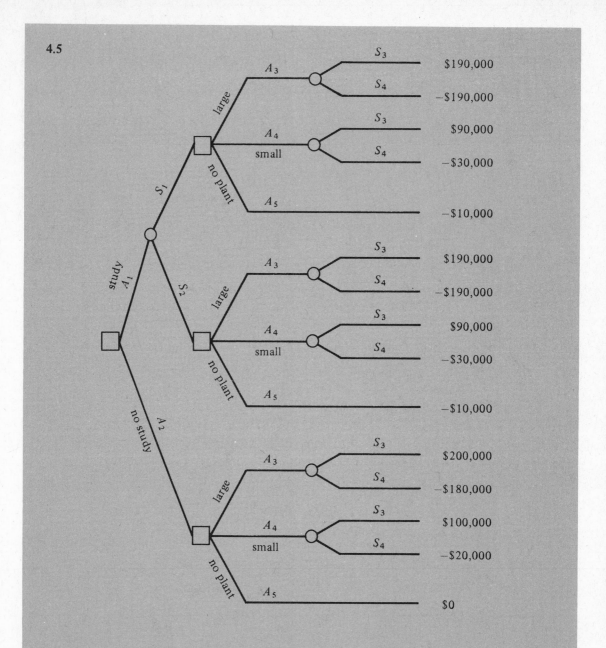

Because of the cost of the marketing study, you had to subtract $10,000 from the top ten terminal branches. As previously mentioned, you must include *all* possible alternatives and outcomes in their logical sequence.

4.6

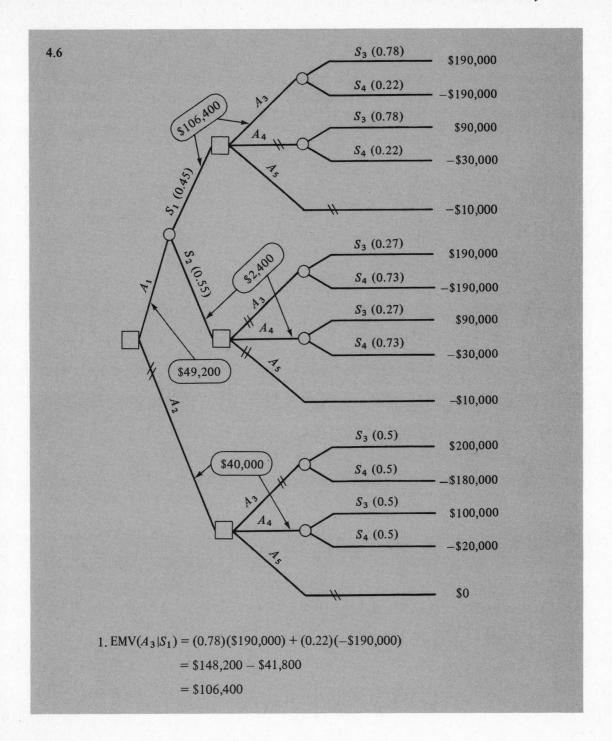

1. EMV$(A_3|S_1)$ = (0.78)($190,000) + (0.22)(−$190,000)

         = $148,200 − $41,800

         = $106,400

By inspection, EMV $(A_3|S_1)$ is the greatest expected value, given a favorable market.

2. $\text{EMV}(A_3|S_2) = (0.27)(\$190{,}000) + (0.73)(-\$190{,}000)$

$$= \$51{,}300 - \$138{,}700$$

$$= -\$87{,}400$$

$\text{EMV}(A_4|S_2) = (0.27)(\$90{,}000) + (0.73)(-\$30{,}000)$

$$= \$24{,}300 - \$21{,}900$$

$$= \$2{,}400$$

$\text{EMV}(A_5|S_2) = -\$10{,}000$

Thus, given an unfavorable market, build the small plant with an expected return of \$2400.

3. $\text{EMV}(A_3) = (0.5)(\$200{,}000) + (0.5)(-\$180{,}000)$

$$= \$100{,}000 - \$90{,}000$$

$$= \$10{,}000$$

$\text{EMV}(A_4) = (0.5)(\$100{,}000) + (0.5)(-\$20{,}000)$

$$= \$50{,}000 - \$10{,}000$$

$$= \$40{,}000$$

$\text{EMV}(A_5) = 0$

Thus, building a small plant is the best choice if the marketing research is not performed.

4. $\text{EMV}(A_1) = (0.45)(\$106{,}400) + (0.55)(\$2400)$

$$= \$47{,}880 + \$1320$$

$$= \$49{,}200$$

Thus, A_1 is preferable to A_2. The best choice is to seek marketing research information. If the research is favorable, build the large plant; but if the research is unfavorable, build the small plant. This choice, which maximizes EMV, has an expected return of \$49,200.

HOMEWORK PROBLEM

The group of medical professionals, first discussed in Example 4.7, are not sure about their original projections. Now, they think that if the medical demand is high that the M.D.s could realize a net profit of $130,000. If the market is not favorable, they could lose $50,000. They still estimate that their chance of success is 50–50. Construct a decision tree for this problem and determine what you would recommend to the medical professionals. Of course, they still have the option to do nothing.

Unit 5

Quality Control

To some individuals, a high-quality product is one that will last longer, is stronger, is built heavier, and, in general, is more durable than other products. In some cases, this is a good definition of a quality product, but sometimes these attributes may not represent high quality. Indeed, a high-quality circuit breaker or fuse is not one that will last longer during periods of high current or voltage. This characteristic would indicate a defective or low-quality circuit breaker or fuse. The quality of any product must be related to the degree to which the product or service is able to perform as it was intended. When we are able to measure the degree to which a product or service fulfills its purpose or objective, then we are in a position to control and regulate product quality. The purpose of a *quality control system* is to measure and regulate the degree to which a product or service meets specified standards.

In this unit, we will investigate two quality control systems: *acceptance sampling plans* and *control charts*. Acceptance sampling attempts to distinguish between acceptable and unacceptable products and services. Control charts attempt to determine if a product or service falls outside acceptable control limits, in which case it may not be functioning properly. These two systems are depicted in Figures 5.1A and 5.1B.

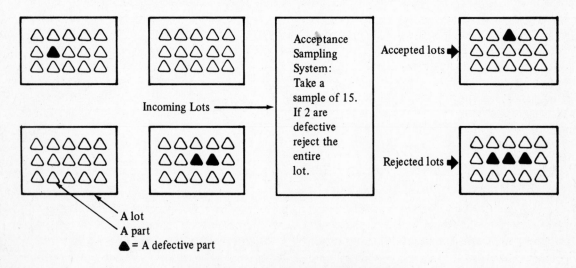

Figure 5.1A. Acceptance Sampling Plan

An acceptance sampling plan is shown in Figure 5.1A. In general, the objective of an acceptance sampling plan is to establish an inspection procedure that will distinguish between acceptable and unacceptable products or services. In Figure 5.1, the plan is to take a sample of fifteen items or parts. If two or more of these are defective, then the entire lot is rejected. What is done with the rejected lots varies from system to system. Sometimes every item in the rejected lot is inspected. This is called 100 percent inspection of the rejected lots. In other instances, the firm will return the lot to the supplier, and the supplier must straighten out the problem.

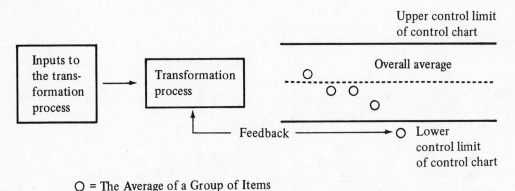

○ = The Average of a Group of Items

Figure 5.1B. Control Chart Systems

Figure 5.1B reveals the overall purpose of a control chart. Inputs or raw materials are transformed into useful products and services. For our discussion here, we will use the term "item" to represent one product or service. A control chart establishes upper and lower acceptable limits. If the average of a group of items falls outside the control limits, it usually means that the process is not functioning the way it should be. The upper and lower control-chart limits could be stated in temperature, pressure, pounds, length, number of sales calls made, number of patients seen, and so on. In a control chart, we set the upper and lower acceptable limits within which we expect to observe the product or service averages.

The remainder of this unit will explore how we can develop acceptance sampling plans and control charts. Under acceptance sampling, we will determine the size of the sample that must be inspected and the number of defective items or parts that would cause us to reject the entire lot. Under control charts, we will be setting upper and lower control limits. When the average of a group of items falls outside these limits, we will have reason to suspect that the process used to produce the products or services is out of adjustment or malfunctioning to some degree.

ACCEPTANCE SAMPLING

One way to guarantee the quality of incoming or outgoing parts or items is to inspect each one. This is called 100 percent inspection. Defective pieces are replaced or repaired. One hundred percent inspection can be very expensive, however. For these costly cases, a random sample may be selected and inspected. The quality of the random sample is used to judge the quality of all items in the lot. The lot of items is either accepted or rejected based on how many defects are found in the sample. This strategy is called *acceptance sampling*.

In a single sampling plan, the sample size n must be determined. Additionally, the maximum number of defects c allowed in an acceptable lot must be specified. Since the random sample may not reflect the true quality of the items, the risk of incorrectly classifying a lot must be carefully analyzed.

In acceptance sampling, usually two parties are involved: the producer of the product or service and the consumer of the product or service. In specifying a sampling plan, each party wants to avoid costly mistakes in accepting or rejecting a lot. The producer wants to avoid the mistake of having a good lot rejected because he usually has the responsibility of replacing all defects in the rejected lot or of paying for a new lot to be shipped to the supplier. On the other hand, the customer wants to avoid the mistake of accepting a bad lot because defects found in the accepted lot are usually the responsibility of the customer. These types of mistakes are shown in Figure 5.2.

Sampling conclusion

Actual condition	Lot is accepted by the sampling plan	Lot is rejected by the sampling plan
A good lot (AQL)	A favorable outcome	Producer's risk (α) ---------- Type I error
A bad lot (LTPD)	Consumer's risk (β) ---------- Type II error	A favorable outcome

Figure 5.2. The Outcome of an Acceptance Sampling Plan

In this figure,

AQL=the *acceptable quality level* in percent defective of a good lot. If an acceptable quality level is 20 defects in a lot of 2000 items or parts, then AQL is $20/2000 = 0.01 = 1\%$.

LTPD=the *lot tolerance percent defective* of a bad lot. If it is agreed upon that an unacceptable quality level is 100 defects in a lot of 2000, then the LTPD is $100/2000 = 0.05 = 5\%$.

(α) *Producer's risk*=the probability of making a type-I error or mistake. This is the probability of rejecting a good lot as seen in Figure 5.2. Of course, producers attempt to keep this risk or probability as low as possible. If the probability of rejecting a good lot is set at 0.02, then the producer's risk = $\alpha = 0.02$.

(β) *Consumer's risk*=the probability of making a type-II error or mistake. This is the probability of accepting a bad or defective lot. The consumer would like to keep this probability as low as possible. If the probability of accepting a bad lot is set at 0.1, then the consumer's risk = $\beta = 0.1$.

Once we have specific values for AQL, LTPD, α, and β, then we can compute or determine a sampling plan. With a single sample, we need to determine the sample size n and the acceptance number c. The acceptance number specifies the maximum number of allowable defects for an acceptable lot. When the number of defects is greater than c, then the lot is rejected.

Without the use of tables, the determination of n and c is not easy. Indeed, it is much easier to start with values for n and c and to then determine AQL, LTPD, α, and β. In fact, in the selection of a sampling plan, it is possible to determine the probability of accepting a lot of *any* percent defective in addition to AQL and LTPD lots. A graph of the probability of acceptance of a given lot versus the percent defective is called an *operating characteristic* (OC) *curve*. A curve of this type appears in Figure 5.3.

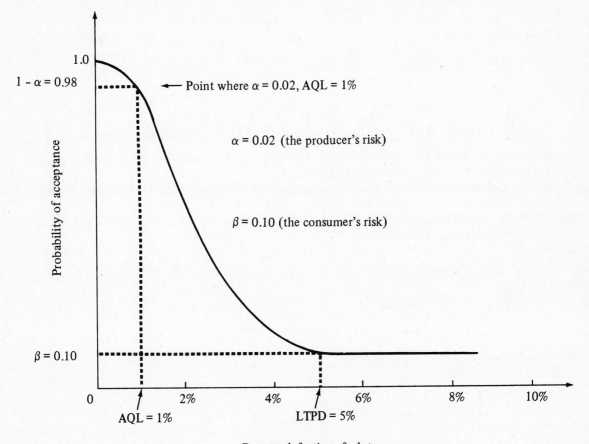

Percent defective of a lot.

Figure 5.3. Operating Characteristic (OC) Curve

The OC curve plays an important part in acceptance sampling. For each combination of n and c, there exists a unique OC curve. When n is small, as in Figure 5.4a, the OC curve is relatively flat. As n increases, the OC curve gets steeper (see Figure 5.4b), α and β decrease, and thus the sampling plan does a better job

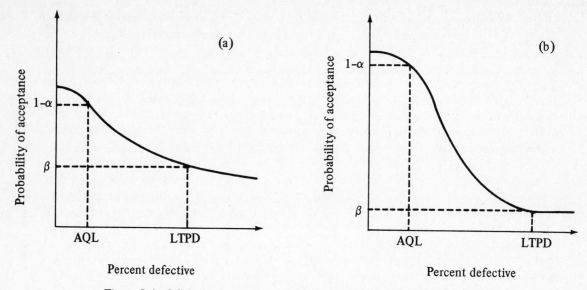

Figure 5.4. *OC Curve for Different Values of n with c Remaining Constant*

in discriminating between good and bad lots. As the sample size increases to 100 percent inspection, the producer's risk α and the consumer's risk β approach zero.

As c, the acceptance number, decreases, the consumer's risk β decreases while the producer's risk α increases. When c is zero, the consumer will accept only lots with zero defects in the sample. In this case, the consumer's risk of accepting a "bad" lot is indeed small. Decreasing c has a tendency to shift the OC curve closer to the origin as seen in Figure 5.5.

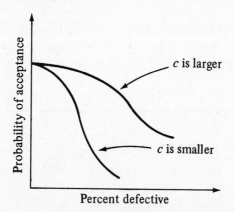

Figure 5.5. *OC Curve for Different Values*
of c with n Remaining Constant

Arriving at n and c is a delicate balance between cost and compromise. As n increases, the inspection cost increases. As c decreases, the risk shifts from the consumer to the producer.

Although it is possible to start with a sampling plan and develop an operating characteristic curve using probability distributions such as the hypergeometric, binomial, Poisson, and normal, this is not the objective of acceptance sampling. Instead we want to start with an OC curve and determine a sampling plan from it. Although there are several ways to accomplish this goal, we will use MIL-STD-105, a military standard sampling plan that has wide acceptance.

EXAMPLE 5.1

Ken Ramsing and Alan Eliason have been discussing quality control standards for years, and somehow they always manage to arrive at an understanding. Ken is the quality control manager for Electronic Distributors, Inc., a producer of electronic parts. Alan purchases parts from Ken's company and produces CB radios and electronic meters. Electronic Distributors is now manufacturing a new electronic part that Alan would like to use in his products. Alan estimates that he will need 550 of these new parts in the next six months. Furthermore, Alan insists that a lot with more than 5 percent defective parts is a defective lot (LTPD), and he wants the probability of accepting a bad lot (β) to be very low. Ken, on the other hand, wants the probability of accepting a good lot to be very high ($1 - \alpha$). Both Alan and Ken have agreed that a good lot is one that contains 1.5 percent defective parts or less (AQL). In quality control terms, LTPD is 5 percent, and AQL is 1.5 percent. Given this information, what sampling plan should be used? In other words, what should the sample size n be and what is the maximum number of allowable defects c in the sample? In addition, what is the producer's risk α and what is the consumer's risk β?

The first step is to determine n and c. This step requires the use of two tables. Table 5.1 gives you a letter as a function of the lot or batch size and the inspection level. For the problems in this unit, we will use general inspection level II. This level is used for most cases. Looking under General inspection level II and for a lot size of 550 units, we find the letter "J." This letter is used to find n and c in Table 5.2. To find the sample size, we locate the letter "J" in the Sample Size Code Letter (the first column of Table 5.2). Reading across to the second column, we see that the sample size is 80 units. Staying in the same row, where the code letter is J, we search the body of the table to find c. The top of the table shows acceptable quality levels. Find 1.5 and read down. The acceptance number c is 3. Re, the rejection number, is 4. Thus the sampling plan is to take a sample of 80 units. If 3 or fewer defects turn up, the lot is acceptable. If there are 4 or more defects, the lot is rejected.

The final step is to find the values of α and β for this particular sampling plan. Given AQL and LTPD, we go to Table 5.3 to find values for α and β. Furthermore, we can use Table 5.3 to construct the complete OC curve. The first column gives values for P_a, the probability, in percent, of a lot being accepted. The body of the table contains percent defective. By looking in the column for the acceptable quality level—in this case, AQL = 1.5—we find the percent defective (p) that corresponds to the probability of acceptance (P_a). When $p = 1.05$, $P_a = 99.0$ percent, or 0.99. When $p = 1.73$, $P_a = 95$ percent, or 0.95, and so forth. The probability of accepting a bad lot is β. For a bad lot, LTPD = 5 percent. We look for 5 in the column where AQL = 1.5. We see 4.57, which is close enough. This corresponds to a probability of acceptance P_a of 50 percent, or 0.5, so β is 0.5. The probability of rejecting a good lot is α, so $1 - \alpha$ is the probability of accepting a good lot. For a good lot in this example, AQL = 1.5. Staying in the same column, we find 1.73, which is close to 1.5. P_a is 95 percent, or 0.95. This is the probability of acceptance ($1 - \alpha$). Thus, $\alpha = 1 - 0.95 = 0.05$.

In this example we have found $n = 80$, $c = 3$, $\alpha = 0.05$, and $\beta = 0.5$.

Table 5.1. Sample Size Code Letters

Lot or Batch Size			Special Inspection Levels				General Inspection Levels		
			S-1	S-2	S-3	S-4	I	II	III
2	to	8	A	A	A	A	A	A	B
9	to	15	A	A	A	A	A	B	C
16	to	25	A	A	B	B	B	C	D
26	to	50	A	B	B	C	C	D	E
51	to	90	B	B	C	C	C	E	F
91	to	150	B	B	C	D	D	F	G
151	to	280	B	C	D	E	E	G	H
281	to	500	B	C	D	E	F	H	J
501	to	1,200	C	C	E	F	G	J	K
1,201	to	3,200	C	D	E	G	H	K	L
3,201	to	10,000	C	D	F	G	J	L	M
10,001	to	35,000	C	D	F	H	K	M	N
35,001	to	150,000	D	E	G	J	L	N	P
150,001	to	500,000	D	E	G	J	M	P	Q
500,001	and	over	D	E	H	K	N	Q	R

U.S. Department of Defense, MIL-STD 419, *Sampling Procedures and Tables for Inspection of Variables for Percent Defective*, U.S. Government Printing Office, Washington, D.C. 11957

Table 5.2. *Single Sampling Plans for Normal Inspection*

AQL (normal inspection)

Sample size code letter	Sample size	0.010		0.015		0.025		0.040		0.065		0.10		0.15		0.25		0.40		0.65		1.0		1.5		2.5		4.0		6.5		10		15		25		40		65		100		150		250		400		650		1000	
		c	Re	c	Re	c	Re	c	Re	c	Re	c	Re	c	Re	c	Re	c	Re	c	Re	c	Re	c	Re	c	Re	c	Re	c	Re	c	Re	c	Re	c	Re	c	Re	c	Re	c	Re	c	Re	c	Re	c	Re	c	Re	c	Re
A	2	↓		↓		↓		↓		↓		↓		↓		↓		↓		↓		↓		↓		↓		↓		↓		↓		0	1	1	2	2	3	3	4	5	6	7	8	10	11	14	15	21	22	30	31
B	3	↓		↓		↓		↓		↓		↓		↓		↓		↓		↓		↓		↓		↓		↓		↓		0	1	1	2	2	3	3	4	5	6	7	8	10	11	14	15	21	22	30	31	44	45
C	5	↓		↓		↓		↓		↓		↓		↓		↓		↓		↓		↓		↓		↓		↓		0	1	1	2	2	3	3	4	5	6	7	8	10	11	14	15	21	22	30	31	44	45	↑	
D	8	↓		↓		↓		↓		↓		↓		↓		↓		↓		↓		↓		↓		↓		0	1	1	2	2	3	3	4	5	6	7	8	10	11	14	15	21	22	30	31	44	45	↑		↑	
E	13	↓		↓		↓		↓		↓		↓		↓		↓		↓		↓		↓		↓		0	1	1	2	2	3	3	4	5	6	7	8	10	11	14	15	21	22	30	31	44	45	↑		↑		↑	
F	20	↓		↓		↓		↓		↓		↓		↓		↓		↓		↓		↓		0	1	1	2	2	3	3	4	5	6	7	8	10	11	14	15	21	22	30	31	44	45	↑		↑		↑		↑	
G	32	↓		↓		↓		↓		↓		↓		↓		↓		↓		↓		0	1	1	2	2	3	3	4	5	6	7	8	10	11	14	15	21	22	30	31	44	45	↑		↑		↑		↑		↑	
H	50	↓		↓		↓		↓		↓		↓		↓		↓		↓		0	1	1	2	2	3	3	4	5	6	7	8	10	11	14	15	21	22	30	31	44	45	↑		↑		↑		↑		↑		↑	
J	80	↓		↓		↓		↓		↓		↓		↓		↓		0	1	1	2	2	3	3	4	5	6	7	8	10	11	14	15	21	22	30	31	44	45	↑		↑		↑		↑		↑		↑		↑	
K	125	↓		↓		↓		↓		↓		↓		↓		0	1	1	2	2	3	3	4	5	6	7	8	10	11	14	15	21	22	30	31	44	45	↑		↑		↑		↑		↑		↑		↑		↑	
L	200	↓		↓		↓		↓		↓		↓		0	1	1	2	2	3	3	4	5	6	7	8	10	11	14	15	21	22	30	31	44	45	↑		↑		↑		↑		↑		↑		↑		↑		↑	
M	315	↓		↓		↓		↓		↓		0	1	1	2	2	3	3	4	5	6	7	8	10	11	14	15	21	22	30	31	44	45	↑		↑		↑		↑		↑		↑		↑		↑		↑		↑	
N	500	↓		↓		↓		↓		0	1	1	2	2	3	3	4	5	6	7	8	10	11	14	15	21	22	30	31	44	45	↑		↑		↑		↑		↑		↑		↑		↑		↑		↑		↑	
P	800	↓		↓		↓		0	1	1	2	2	3	3	4	5	6	7	8	10	11	14	15	21	22	30	31	44	45	↑		↑		↑		↑		↑		↑		↑		↑		↑		↑		↑		↑	
Q	1250	↓		↓		0	1	1	2	2	3	3	4	5	6	7	8	10	11	14	15	21	22	30	31	44	45	↑		↑		↑		↑		↑		↑		↑		↑		↑		↑		↑		↑		↑	
R	2000	↓		0	1	1	2	2	3	3	4	5	6	7	8	10	11	14	15	21	22	30	31	44	45	↑		↑		↑		↑		↑		↑		↑		↑		↑		↑		↑		↑		↑		↑	

Ac = acceptance number.
Re = rejtion number.

Source: MIL-STD-105D. *Sampling Procedures and Tables for Inspection by Attributes*, Department of Defense, April 29, 1963.

Table 5.3. OC Curve Values for Single Sampling Plans (Code Letter J)

AQL (normal inspection)

p (in defects per hundred units)

P_a	0.15	0.65	1.0	1.5	2.5	4.0	⊠	6.5	⊠	10	⊠	15
99.0	0.013	0.186	0.545	1.03	2.23	3.63	4.38	5.96	7.62	9.35	12.9	15.7
95.0	0.064	0.444	1.02	1.71	3.27	4.98	5.87	7.71	9.61	11.6	15.6	18.6
90.0	0.131	0.665	1.38	2.18	3.94	5.82	6.79	8.78	10.8	12.9	17.1	20.3
75.0	0.360	1.20	2.16	3.17	5.27	7.45	8.55	10.8	13.0	15.3	19.9	23.4
50.0	0.866	2.10	3.34	4.59	7.09	9.59	10.8	13.3	15.8	18.3	23.3	27.1
25.0	1.73	3.37	4.90	6.39	9.28	12.1	13.5	16.3	19.0	21.8	27.2	31.2
10.0	2.88	4.86	6.65	8.35	11.6	14.7	16.2	19.3	22.2	25.2	30.9	35.2
5.0	3.75	5.93	7.87	9.69	13.1	16.4	18.0	21.2	24.3	27.4	33.4	37.8
1.0	5.76	8.30	10.5	12.6	16.4	20.0	21.8	25.2	28.5	31.8	38.2	42.9
AQL	0.15	0.65	1.0	1.5	2.5	4.0	⊠	6.5	⊠	10	⊠	15

AQL (tightened inspection)

p (in percent defective)

P_a	0.15	0.65	1.0	1.5	2.5	4.0	⊠	6.5	⊠	10
99.0	0.013	0.188	0.550	1.05	2.30	3.72	4.50	6.13	7.88	9.75
95.0	0.064	0.444	1.03	1.73	3.32	5.06	5.98	7.91	9.89	11.9
90.0	0.132	0.666	1.38	2.20	3.98	5.91	6.91	8.95	11.0	13.2
75.0	0.359	1.202	2.16	3.18	5.30	7.50	8.62	10.9	13.2	15.5
50.0	0.863	2.09	3.33	4.57	7.06	9.55	10.8	13.3	15.8	18.3
25.0	1.72	3.33	4.84	6.31	9.14	11.9	13.3	16.0	18.6	21.3
10.0	2.84	4.78	6.52	8.16	11.3	14.2	15.7	18.6	21.4	24.2
5.0	3.68	5.80	7.66	9.39	12.7	15.8	17.3	20.3	23.2	26.0
1.0	5.59	8.00	10.1	12.0	15.6	18.9	20.5	23.6	26.5	29.5
AQL	0.25	1.0	1.5	2.5	4.0	6.5	⊠	10	⊠	

Source: MIL-STD-105D, Sampling Procedures and Tables for Inspection by Authorities, Department of Defense, April 19, 1963.

PROBLEM 5.1

High-level ohm resistors come in lots of 2000 each. If AQL is 2.5, what is the sampling plan? Determine values only for n and c.

PROBLEM 5.2

The lot size for a particular item is 1000, and AQL is 1 percent. Determine n and c. If LTPD is 10 percent, determine values for α and β.

In most sampling plans, when a lot is rejected, the entire lot is inspected and all of the defective items are replaced. Use of this replacement technique improves the average outgoing quality, in terms of percent defective. In fact, given (1) any sampling plan that replaces all defective items encountered and (2) the true incoming percent defective for the lot, it is possible to determine the average outgoing quality (AOQ) in percent defective. Here is the equation for AOQ:

$$AOQ = \frac{(P_d)\,(P_a)\,(N-n)}{N}$$

where

P_d = the true percent defective of the lot

P_a = the probability of accepting the lot

N = the number of items in the lot

n = the number of items in the sample

EXAMPLE 5.2

The percent defective from an incoming lot is 3 percent. An OC curve showed the probability of acceptance to be 0.55. Given a lot size of 2000 and a sample of 100, what is the average outgoing quality in percent defective?

$$\text{AOQ} = \frac{(P_d)(P_a)(N - n)}{N}$$

$$= \frac{(0.03)(0.55)(2000 - 100)}{2000}$$

$$= 0.016$$

Thus, an acceptance sampling plan changes the quality of the lots in percent defective from 0.03 to 0.016, on the average. Acceptance sampling significantly increases the quality of the inspected lots.

PROBLEM 5.3

In an acceptance sampling plan developed for lots containing 1000 units, the sample size n is 85 and c is 3. The percent defective of the incoming lots is 2 percent and the probability of acceptance, which was obtained from an OC table, is 0.64. What is the average outgoing quality?

In most cases, we do not know the value of P_a; we must determine it from the particular sampling plan. The fact that we seldom know the true incoming percent defective presents another problem. What is done in most cases is to assume several different incoming percent defective values. Then we can determine the average outgoing quality for each value.

EXAMPLE 5.3

What is the AOQ for the acceptance sampling plan developed in Example 5.1 if the quality of the incoming lots in percent defective is 1.5 percent? What is AOQ when the incoming percent defective is 5 percent?

(continued)

In Example 5.1, we found that the sample size would be 80 units for a lot size of 550 units. Furthermore, we determined P_a at both percent defective levels. As you recall, the acceptable quality level, AQL, was 1.5 and we determined that $P_a = 0.95$. The LTPD for this example was 5 percent, and the P_a at that level was found to be 0.5. With this information, we can determine the average outgoing quality for both incoming percent defective levels.

$$\text{AOQ (at 1.5\%)} = \frac{(0.015)(0.95)(550 - 80)}{550} = 0.012$$

$$\text{AOQ (at 5\%)} = \frac{(0.05)(0.5)(550 - 80)}{550} = 0.021$$

In terms of the acceptance sampling plan developed in Example 5.1, if the incoming quality is 1.5 percent defective, the outgoing quality will be 1.2 percent on the average. On the other hand, if the incoming quality is 5 percent defective, then the outgoing quality will be 2.1 percent defective, on the average.

PROBLEM 5.4

Referring to Problem 5.2, determine the average outgoing quality at each of the following incoming quality levels:

1. The incoming quality is 1 percent defective.
2. The incoming quality is 2 percent defective.
3. The incoming quality is 5 percent defective.
4. The incoming quality is 10 percent defective.

Did you notice how AOQ changed for different percent defectives? When the percent defective of the incoming lots is either very high or very low, the percent defective of the outgoing lots is low. AOQ at 1 percent was 0.0087, and AOQ at 10 percent was 0.001. For moderate levels of the incoming percent defective, AOQ is higher: AOQ at 5 percent was 0.012. Thus AOQ is low for small values of the incoming percent defective. As the incoming percent defective increases, the AOQ increases up to a point. Then, for increasing incoming percent defective, AOQ decreases. This relationship can be seen in Figure 5.6.

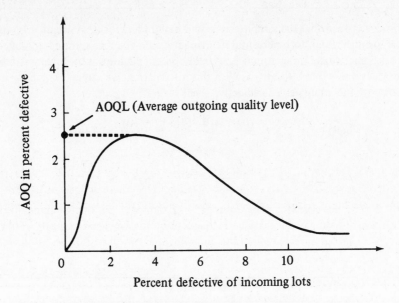

Figure 5.6 AOQ Versus Percent Defective of Incoming Lots

DOUBLE AND MULTIPLE SAMPLING

Thus far in this unit we have explored acceptance sampling plans that use a single sample in deciding whether to accept or reject an incoming lot. With a single sample, it is not uncommon to have a sample size of 80 or 125, as you saw in the previous examples and problems. There are many situations, however, in which a sample this large would be extremely expensive. If you were testing jet engines, for example, testing 125 might be unreasonable. To overcome this problem, it is possible to use a *double sampling plan,* which provides three possible actions after the first sample has been taken: (1) accept the lot, (2) reject the lot, or (3) take a second sample. In the second sample, your action will be to accept or reject the lot. Double sampling extends to *multiple sampling,* in which as many as seven samples can be taken. Of course, the advantage of double or multiple sampling is to reduce the size of the first or second sample. Normally, we can decide to accept or reject after the first or second sample. Although operations management texts typically do not cover double and multiple sampling plans, the procedure is almost identical to the procedure for finding a single sampling plan.

One other extension of double and multiple sampling is *sequential sampling.* This technique allows us to make a decision after every item or part has been inspected. Sequential sampling is like multiple sampling, in which the sample size *n* is one item or part.

Acceptance sampling is an excellent way of screening incoming lots. When the defective parts are replaced with good parts, acceptance sampling helps to increase the quality of the lots by reducing the outgoing percent defective. We explored this concept with AOQ.

Another purpose of quality control is to detect problems and to take corrective action. In a manufacturing operation, for example, when parts or items continually do not meet the specification, it may be appropriate to inspect the manufacturing process itself. Perhaps a machine needs adjustment or perhaps a piece of equipment is not operating properly. How do we know when to suspect a problem or an incorrectly adjusted machine? When an item doesn't meet specification, how do we know whether it is just a random occurrence or whether something is wrong with the process? Control charts help to answer these and related questions.

CONTROL CHARTS FOR AVERAGES AND RANGES

The basic idea behind a control chart is to set upper and lower limits on the aspect of the process you want to control. These upper and lower limits can be in units of temperature, pressure, weight, and so on. Then we take samples of the output of the process and plot the average of these samples on a chart that has the upper limit and lower limit on it. If the average of one of the samples falls outside of the upper or lower limit, the process is carefully checked. A typical control chart appears in Figure 5.7. Each point or dot on

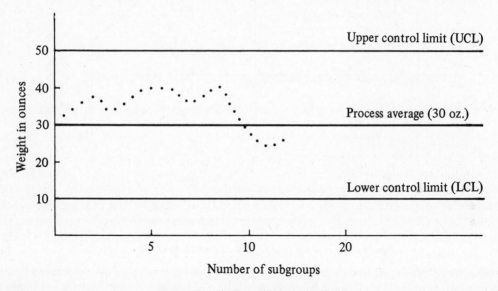

Figure 5.7. A Sample Control Chart

the chart represents the average of one sample. Although the size of the sample differs, usually five items or parts make up one sample. Thus, one point is usually the average of about five items or parts. The process average, which is 30 ounces in Figure 5.7, is usually the average of the averages of the samples over a long period of time.

When the average of the samples falls within the upper and lower control limits on the chart, the process is considered "in control"; otherwise, the process is "out of control" or "out of adjustment." We have discussed how to compute the process average by taking the average of the averages of the samples, but how do we determine the control limits (UCL and LCL)?

We made it clear that one point on the control chart is the average of one given sample. This rule is the key to control charts, and it also gives us the ability to set upper and lower limits. In a statistics class, you may have learned about the *Central Limit Theorem.* In general terms, this theorem states that regardless of the distribution of the universe, in this case the process, the distribution of average values $\overline{X}$ from this universe or process will tend to follow a normal curve as the sample size tends toward infinity. Fortunately, even if n is fairly small, the distributions of the averages will still roughly follow a normal curve. To refresh your memory, Figure 5.8 shows a typical normal distribution.

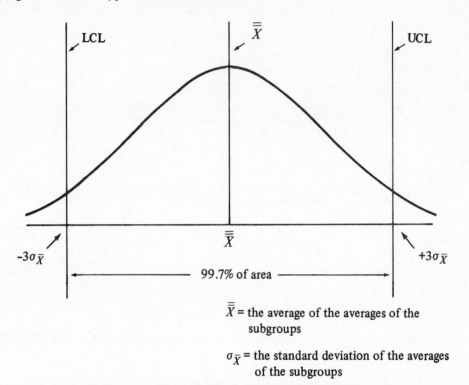

$\overline{\overline{X}}$ = the average of the averages of the subgroups

$\sigma_{\overline{X}}$ = the standard deviation of the averages of the subgroups

Figure 5.8. The Normal Distribution and Control Limits

One property of the normal curve is that about 99.7 percent of the area under the curve falls within ±3 standard deviations of the distribution average. Thus, if we set our control limits at +3 and −3 standard deviations, as suggested in Figure 5.8, then 99.7 percent of the time the average of the samples will fall inside these bounds if the process doesn't change. If a point on the control chart falls outside of the control limits, then we are 99.7 percent sure that the process has changed. This is the theory behind control charts.

One way of computing the upper and lower control limits is

$$\text{UCL}_{\overline{X}} = \overline{\overline{X}} + 3\sigma_{\overline{X}}$$

$$\text{LCL}_{\overline{X}} = \overline{\overline{X}} - 3\sigma_{\overline{X}}$$

where $\overline{\overline{X}}$ = the average of the averages of the subgroups and $\sigma_{\overline{X}}$ = the standard deviation of the averages of the subgroups.

If we have the true process average and the standard deviation of the sample averages, it is possible to determine the upper and lower control chart limits. But even estimating the standard deviation of the averages of the samples is a bothersome task. Furthermore, we would not expect an inspector, who may never have had a statistics course, to estimate the standard deviation of the sample averages. Thus, using the above equations is usually cumbersome and impractical. Instead, by making a few assumptions, we can use the average *range* of the samples. Doing so, we get the following equations for the upper and lower control limits:

$$UCL_{\bar{X}} = \bar{\bar{X}} + A\bar{R}$$

$$LCL_{\bar{X}} = \bar{\bar{X}} - A\bar{R}$$

where

$\bar{R}$ = the average range of the samples

A = a value from Table 5.4

$\bar{\bar{X}}$ = the average of the averages of the samples

EXAMPLE 5.4

Squibb Root Beer bottles soft drinks labeled "net weight 16 ounces." An overall process average of 16.01 ounces has been found by taking several batches of samples, where each sample contained five bottles. The average range of the process is 0.25 ounces. Determine the upper and lower control limits for averages for this process.

Looking in Table 5.4 for a sample size of 5 in the mean factor A column, we find the number 0.577. Thus the upper and lower control chart limits are

$$
\begin{aligned}
UCL_{\bar{X}} &= \bar{\bar{X}} + A\bar{R} \\
&= 16.01 + (0.577)(0.25) \\
&= 16.01 + 0.144 \\
&= 16.154 \\
LCL_{\bar{X}} &= \bar{\bar{X}} - A\bar{R} \\
&= 16.01 - 0.144 \\
&= 15.866
\end{aligned}
$$

The upper control limit is 16.154, and the lower control limit is 15.866.

Table 5.4. Factors for Computing Control Chart Limits

Sample Size n	Mean Factor A	Upper Range B	Lower Range C
2	1.880	3.268	0
3	1.023	2.574	0
4	0.729	2.282	0
5	0.577	2.114	0
6	0.483	2.004	0
7	0.419	1.924	0.076
8	0.373	1.864	0.136
9	0.337	1.816	0.184
10	0.308	1.777	0.223
12	0.266	1.716	0.284
14	0.235	1.671	0.329
16	0.212	1.636	0.364
18	0.194	1.608	0.392
20	0.180	1.586	0.414
25	0.153	1.541	0.459

Source: Reprinted by permission of American Society for Testing Materials, copyright. Taken from Special Technical Publication 15–C, "Quality Control of Materials," pp. 63 and 72, 1951.

PROBLEM 5.5

The manufacturer of precision parts for drill presses produces round shafts for use in the construction of drill presses. The average diameter of a shaft is 0.56 inch. The inspection samples contain 6 shafts each. The average range of these samples is 0.006 inch. Determine the upper and lower control chart limits.

In the foregoing example and problem, you determined the upper and lower control limits for the process average. In addition to being concerned with the process average, many operations managers are interested in the process dispersion or variability. Even though the process average is under control, the variability of the process may not be. For example, something may have worked itself loose in a piece of equipment. As a result, the average of the samples may remain the same, but the variation within the samples could be entirely too large. For this reason, it is very common to find a control chart for ranges in order to monitor the process variability, as well as a control chart for the process average, which monitors the process average. The theory behind the control charts for ranges is the same for the process average. Limits are established that contain ±3 standard deviations of the distribution for the average range $\bar{R}$. With a few simplifying assumptions, we can set the upper and lower control limits for ranges.

$$UCL_R = B\bar{R}$$

$$LCL_R = C\bar{R}$$

where

$$UCL_R = \text{upper control chart limit for the range}$$
$$LCL_R = \text{lower control chart limit for the range}$$
$$B \text{ and } C = \text{values from Table 5.4}$$

EXAMPLE 5.5

The average *range* of a process is 53 pounds. If the sample size is 5, determine the upper and lower control chart limits.

Looking in Table 5.4 for a sample size of 5, we find that $B = 2.114$ and that $C = 0$. The range control chart limits are

$$UCL_R = B\bar{R}$$

$$= (2.114)(53 \text{ pounds})$$

$$= 112.042 \text{ pounds}$$

$$LCL_R = C\bar{R}$$

$$= (0)(53 \text{ pounds})$$

$$= 0$$

PROBLEM 5.6

Determine the upper and lower control limits for ranges for Squibb Root Beer (see Example 5.4).

PROBLEM 5.7

Nocaf Drinks, Inc., a producer of decaffeinated coffee, bottles Nocaf. Each bottle should have a net weight of 4 ounces. The machine that fills the bottles with coffee is new, and the operations manager wants to make sure that it is properly adjusted. The manufacturer of the machine has stated that the process average should be 4.05 ounces and that the average range should be 0.31 when the machine is properly adjusted. The operations manager takes a sample of 7 bottles and records the average and range in ounces for each sample. The data for the first 8 samples is in the following table. Note that every sample consists of 7 bottles.

Sample Number	Sample Range	Sample Average
1	0.41	4.00
2	0.55	4.16
3	0.44	3.99
4	0.48	4.00
5	0.56	4.17
6	0.62	3.93
7	0.54	3.98
8	0.44	4.01

Is the machine properly adjusted and in control?

There are other indicators besides control chart limits that suggest that a process is out of control. Some operations managers, for example, consider a process out of control if seven or more points in a row fall above or below the average value of the control chart. Thus, even if the ranges in one of the samples did not exceed the upper control chart limit in Problem 5.7, we might consider the process to be out of control because all eight ranges fall above the predicted average of 0.31.

CONTROL CHARTS FOR ATTRIBUTES

So far we have investigated control charts for the process average and range. In some processes, however, our concern might be percent defective. For example, how many light bulbs are defective in a given lot, how many letters in a batch of correspondence contain typing errors, or how many computer cards per 100 produced are wrongly key punched? Again, we would want to establish control chart limits, this time for percent defectives. Although it is beyond the scope of this book to derive these control chart limits, they are given below (for 99.7% confidence limits):

$$\text{UCL}_p = p + 3\sqrt{\frac{pq}{n}}$$

$$\text{LCL}_p = p - 3\sqrt{\frac{pq}{n}}$$

where

UCL_p = upper control chart limit

LCL_p = lower control chart limit

p = fraction defective in the sample taken

$q = 1 - p$

n = total number of items in the sample

EXAMPLE 5.6

In the last 200 items, the percent defective has been 0.04. Determine the upper and lower control limits for the process.

$$\text{UCL}_p = p + 3\sqrt{\frac{pq}{n}}$$

$$= 0.04 + 3\sqrt{\frac{(0.04)(0.96)}{200}}$$

$$= 0.04 + 3(0.014)$$

$$= 0.04 + 0.042$$

(continued)

$$= 0.082$$

$$\text{LCL}_p = 0.04 - 0.042$$

$$= 0 \text{ (since we can't have a negative percent defective)}$$

PROBLEM 5.8

Altman Electronics, Inc., makes resistors, and among the last 100 resistors inspected, the percent defective has been 0.05. Determine the upper and lower control limits for this process.

ANSWERS

5.1   From Table 5.1 we obtain a sample size code letter of K for a lot of 2000 and a general inspection level of II. In Table 5.2 we see that the sample size is 125 resistors, the acceptance number is 7, and the rejection number is 8. The sampling plan is to take a sample of 125 units and to accept the sample if there are 7 or fewer defects. In other words, $n = 125$ and $c = 7$.

5.2   1. The sample size code letter found in Table 5.1 is J.
2. Knowing that AQL $= 1$, you could find $n = 80$ and $c = 2$ in Table 5.2.
3. In Table 5.3, 10.1 is close to 10 for LTPD in the column where AQL $= 1$, so $\beta = 1.0\% = 0.01$.
4. In Table 5.3, 1.03 is close to 1 for AQL, so $\alpha = 1 - 0.95 = 0.05$.

5.3
$$\text{AOQ} = \frac{(0.02)(0.64)(1000 - 85)}{1000} = 0.012$$

5.4   1.
$$\text{AOQ at 1\%} = \frac{(0.01)(0.95)(1000 - 80)}{1000} = 0.0087$$

2.
$$\text{AOQ at 2\%} = \frac{(0.02)(0.75)(1000 - 80)}{1000} = 0.0138$$

3.
$$\text{AOQ at 5\%} = \frac{(0.05)(0.25)(1000 - 80)}{1000} = 0.012$$

4.
$$\text{AOQ at 10\%} = \frac{(0.10)(0.01)(1000 - 80)}{1000} = 0.001$$

The only difficulty in this problem is finding P_a for the different percent defective levels. This step was done with the aid of Table 5.3. Since AQL was set at 1 percent, we must look in the column under 1.0 in Table 5.3 for the appropriate percent defectives. We find 1.03, which is close to 1 percent. Reading across in the same row, we get 95.0 percent, or 0.95, for the probability of acceptance. 2.16 is close to 2 percent, and P_a at this level is 75.0%, or 0.75. 4.84 is close to 5 percent, and P_a is 0.25. Finally, 10.1 is close to 10 percent, and P_a at this level is 1.0 percent, or 0.01.

5.5   The mean factor A, from Table 5.4 where the sample size is 6, is seen to be 0.483. With this factor, you can obtain the upper and lower control limits.

$$\begin{aligned}
\text{UCL} &= 0.56 + (0.483)(0.006) \\
&= 0.56 + 0.0029 \\
&= 0.5629
\end{aligned}$$

$$\text{LCL} = 0.56 - 0.0029$$

$$= 0.5571$$

5.6   As you recall from Example 5.4, the average range of the sample is 0.25 ounce and the number of items in one sample is 5. Thus the control chart for ranges is

$$\text{UCL}_R = (2.114)(0.25 \text{ ounce})$$

$$= 0.5285 \text{ ounce}$$

$$\text{LCL}_R = (0)(0.25 \text{ ounce})$$

$$= 0$$

5.7

$$\text{UCL}_X = 4.05 + (0.373)(0.31)$$

$$= 4.05 + .116$$

$$= 4.166$$

$$\text{LCL}_X = 4.05 - (.116)$$

$$= 3.934$$

$$\text{UCL}_R = (1.864)(0.31)$$

$$= .578$$

$$\text{LCL}_R = (0.136)(0.31)$$

$$= .042$$

It appears that the process average is in control, but the sample ranges are not (see sample number 6). Indeed, all of the ranges are above the average range of 0.31 set by the manufacturer. Thus, some part of the machine is out of adjustment. There is too much variability or dispersion in the process. Perhaps a loose or missing part is causing this problem.

5.8

$$\text{UCL}_p = 0.05 + 3\sqrt{\frac{(0.05)(0.95)}{100}}$$

$$= 0.05 + 3(0.0218)$$

$$= 0.05 + 0.0654$$

$$= 0.1154$$

$$\text{LCL}_p = 0.05 - 0.0654$$

$$= 0 \, (\text{since the percent defective can't be negative})$$

HOMEWORK PROBLEMS

5-1. For the last two months, Rhonda Radner has been concerned about the number 5 machine at the West Factory. In order to make sure that the number 5 machine is operating correctly, samples are taken, and the average and range for each sample is computed. Each sample consists of 12 items produced from the machine. Recently 12 samples were taken, and for each sample, the sample range and sample average was computed. The sample range and sample average were 1.1 and 46 for the first sample, 1.31 and 45 for the second sample, .91 and 46 for the third sample, and 1.1 and 47 for the fourth sample. After the fourth sample, the sample averages increased. For the fifth sample, the range was 1.21 and the average was 48; for sample number 6 it was .82 and 47; for sample number 7, it was .86 and 50; and for the eighth sample, it was 1.11 and 49. After the eighth sample, the sample average continued to increase, never getting below 50. For sample number 9, the range and average were 1.12 and 51; for sample number 10, they were .99 and 52; for sample number 11, they were .86 and 50: and for sample number 12, they were 1.2 and 52.

While Rhonda's boss wasn't overly concerned about the process, Rhonda was. During installation, the supplier set an average of 47 for the process with an average range of 1.0. It was Rhonda's feeling that something was definitely wrong with machine number 5. Do you agree?

5-2. Because of the poor quality of various semiconductor products used in their manufacturing process, Microlaboratories have decided to develop a quality control program. Because the semiconductor parts they get from suppliers are either good or defective, George Haverty has decided to develop control charts for attributes. The total number of semiconductors in every sample is 200. Furthermore, George would like to determine the upper control chart limit and the lower control chart limit for various values of the fraction defective (p) in the sample taken. To allow more flexibility, he has decided to develop a table that lists values for $p, q,$ UCL, and LCL. The values for p should range from .01 to .1, incrementing by .01 each time.

Unit 6

Forecasting

Forecasts are basically just estimates of future activities: the technique of forecasting aims to reduce the uncertainty that surrounds those activities.

Forecasting future sales of products and the need for parts or components is an extremely important topic in production–operations management. The better management is able to estimate the future, the better it will be able to prepare for it.

Demand forecasting is particularly important in production–operations management because it is the input to scheduling and to inventory production control activities. Although it usually indicates the overall level of production, forecasting might also indicate what products should be produced, in what quantities, and when they should be produced.

There are many ways to forecast demand. In numerous firms (especially smaller ones) the entire process is subjective, involving seat-of-the-pants methods, intuition, and years of experience. The surprising thing is that, under certain circumstances, this may just be management's best approach. This is especially so when firsthand knowledge of changes in sales patterns is readily available from owners, managers, or marketing representatives.

The popular *delphi technique* is a procedure designed to formalize individual opinions. Delphi is an iterative way of asking experts to develop forecasts individually, comparing them, returning them to the experts for revised opinions, and repeating the procedure until a consensus has been reached.

Another important quantitative means of forecasting demand is *regression* and *correlation analysis*. With regression and correlation, variables are studied to see if one seems to cause or influence another's behavior. For this reason, regression is generally referred to as a *causal* method.

Time series methods, including moving averages, exponential smoothing and trend projection, are still other mathematical approaches to forecasting. These techniques entail examining patterns of demand over time and projecting that pattern into the future.

There is no single forecasting method that is always superior. One organization may find regression effective, another firm may use several approaches, and a third may combine quantitative and subjective techniques. Whatever tool works best for a firm is the one that it should use.

MOVING AVERAGES: A TIME SERIES MODEL

Time series models such as moving averages, weighted moving averages, exponential smoothing, and trend projections all use historical data as a starting point in forecasting. Let us begin with the simplest of these models, the *moving averages* technique.

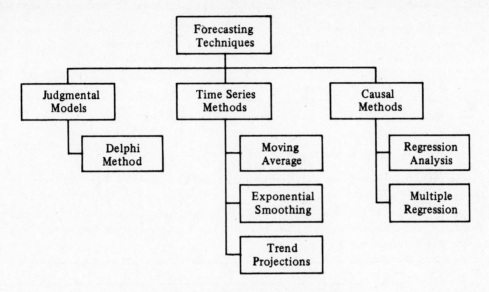

Figure 6.1. Major Forecasting Methods

Moving averages are useful if we can assume that market demands will stay fairly steady over time. A four-month moving average is found by simply summing the demand during the past four months and dividing by 4. With each passing month, the most recent month's data is added to the sum of the previous three months' data, and the earliest month is dropped. This tends to smooth out irregularities or seasonal fluctuations in a data series.

Mathematically, the moving average (which serves as an estimate of the next period's demand) is expressed as

$$\text{Moving average} = \frac{\Sigma \text{ demand in previous } n \text{ periods}}{n}$$

where n is the number of periods in the moving average—for example, 4 months, 5 months, or 6 months, respectively, for a 4-, 5-, or 6-period moving average.

EXAMPLE 6.1

Storage shed sales at Wallace Garden Supply are shown in the middle column below. A three-month moving average appears on the right.

(continued)

Month	Actual Shed Sales	Three-month Moving Average
Jan.	10	
Feb.	12	
Mar.	13	
Apr.	16	$(10 + 12 + 13)/3 = 11\ 2/3$
May	19	$(12 + 13 + 16)/3 = 13\ 2/3$
June	23	$(13 + 16 + 19)/3 = 16$
July	26	$(16 + 19 + 23)/3 = 19\ 1/3$
Aug.	30	$(19 + 23 + 26)/3 = 22\ 2/3$
Sept.	28	$(23 + 26 + 30)/3 = 26\ 1/3$
Oct.	18	$(26 + 30 + 28)/3 = 28$
Nov.	16	$(30 + 28 + 18)/3 = 25\ 1/3$
Dec.	14	$(28 + 18 + 16)/3 = 20\ 2/3$

A *weighted moving average* makes an adjustment to the regular moving average, usually in order to place more emphasis on recent values. This makes the technique more responsive to trends, since latter periods may be more heavily weighted. Deciding which weights to use requires some experience and a bit of luck. Choice of weights is somewhat arbitrary since there is no set formula to determine them. If the latest month or period is weighted too heavily, the forecast might reflect a large and unusual change in the demand or sales pattern too quickly.

A weighted moving average may be expressed mathematically as

$$\text{Weighted moving average} = \frac{\Sigma(\text{weight for period } n)(\text{demand in period } n)}{\Sigma \text{ weights}}$$

EXAMPLE 6.2

Wallace's Garden Supply (see Example 6.1) decides to forecast storage shed sales by weighting the past three months as follows:

Weights Applied	Period
3	Last month
2	2 months ago
1	3 months ago

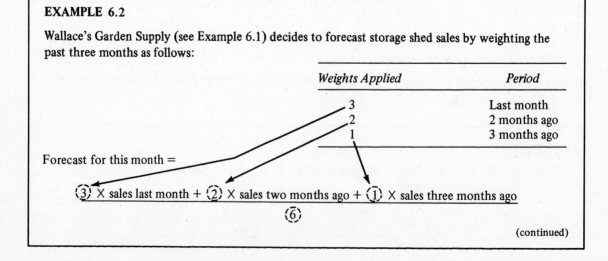

Forecast for this month =

$$\frac{③ \times \text{sales last month} + ② \times \text{sales two months ago} + ① \times \text{sales three months ago}}{⑥}$$

(continued)

The results of this weighted average forecast are shown in the table below.

Month	Actual Shed Sales	Three-month Weighted Moving Averages
Jan.	10	
Feb.	12	
Mar.	13	
Apr.	16	$[(3 \times 13) + (2 \times 12) + (10)]$ /6 = 12 1/6
May	19	$[(3 \times 16) + (2 \times 13) + (12)]$ /6 = 14 1/3
June	23	$[(3 \times 19) + (2 \times 16) + (13)]$ /6 = 17
July	26	$[(3 \times 23) + (2 \times 19) + (16)]$ /6 = 20 1/2
Aug.	30	$[(3 \times 26) + (2 \times 23) + (19)]$ /6 = 23 5/6
Sept.	28	$[(3 \times 30) + (2 \times 26) + (23)]$ /6 = 27 1/2
Oct.	18	$[(3 \times 28) + (2 \times 30) + (26)]$ /6 = 28 1/3
Nov.	16	$[(3 \times 18) + (2 \times 28) + (30)]$ /6 = 23 1/3
Dec.	14	$[(3 \times 16) + (2 \times 18) + (28)]$ /6 = 18 2/3

In this particular forecasting situation, you can see that weighting the latest month more heavily provides a much more accurate projection.

PROBLEM 6.1

Data collected on the yearly demand for 50-pound bags of fertilizer at Wallace's Garden Supply are shown below. Develop a three-year moving average to forecast sales. Then estimate demand again with a weighted moving average in which sales in the most recent year are given a weight of 2 and sales in the other two years are each given a weight of 1. Which method do you think is best?

(continued)

Year	Demand for Fertilizer (in thousands of bags)	Three-year Moving Averages	Weighted Three-year Moving Averages
1968	4	—	—
1969	6	—	—
1970	4	—	—
1971	5		
1972	10		
1973	8		
1974	7		
1975	9		
1976	12		
1977	14		
1978	15		

Both simple and weighted moving averages are effective in smoothing out sudden fluctuations in the demand pattern in order to provide stable estimates. Moving averages do, however, have two problems. For one thing, they cannot pick up trends very well. Since they *are* averages, they will always stay within past levels and will not predict a change to a higher or lower level. The second problem is that moving averages require extensive record keeping of past data.

EXPONENTIAL SMOOTHING: A SECOND TIME SERIES MODEL

Exponential smoothing is a time series forecasting method that is easy to use and efficiently handled by computers. Although it is a type of moving average technique, it involves very *little* record keeping of past data. We can write the basic exponential-smoothing formula as follows:

New forecast = last period's forecast + α (last period's actual demand
    − last period's forecast)

Or, this can be written mathematically as:

$$F_t = F_{t-1} + \alpha(A_{t-1} - F_{t-1})$$

where α is a weight (or smoothing constant) that has a value between zero and one. The concept is not as complex as it might seem. The latest estimate of demand is equal to our old estimate adjusted by a fraction of the difference between the last period's actual demand and the old estimate.

The smoothing constant α can be changed to give more weight to recent data (when it is high) or more weight to past data (when it is low). For example, when $\alpha = 0.5$ it can be shown mathematically that the new forecast is based almost entirely on demand in the last three periods. When $\alpha = 0.1$, the forecast places little weight on recent demand and takes *many* periods (about 19) of historic values into account.

EXAMPLE 6.3

In January, a car dealer predicted a February demand for 142 Ford Fairmonts. Actual February demand was 153 autos. Using a smoothing constant of $\alpha = 0.20$, we can forecast the March demand using the exponential smoothing model. Substituting into the formula, we obtain

$$\text{New forecast (for March demand)} = 142 + 0.2\,(153 - 142)$$

$$= 144.2$$

Thus, the demand forecast for Ford Fairmonts in March is 144.

PROBLEM 6.2

Suppose actual demand for Ford Fairmonts in March was 136. Referring to Example 6.3, forecast the demand for April using the exponential smoothing model with a constant of $\alpha = 0.20$.

PROBLEM 6.3

The Port of Galveston unloaded quantities of a particular grain from ships during 1982 and 1983 as shown in the following table.

Year and Quarter	Tonnage Unloaded	Forecast
1982:I	180	175
II	168	
III	159	
IV	175	
1983:I	190	
II	205	
III	180	
IV	182	
1984:I	?	

(continued)

Compute the quarterly forecasts of grain tonnage using the exponential smoothing model. Assume that the forecast of grain unloaded in the first quarter of 1982 was 175 tons. Use a smoothing weight of $\alpha = 0.10$.

PROBLEM 6.4

Quarterly forecasts for data given in Problem 6.3 are shown below as obtained with a smoothing weight of $\alpha = 0.50$.

Year and Quarter	Tonnage Unloaded	Forecast
1982:I	180	175
II	168	178
III	159	173
IV	175	166
1983:I	190	170
II	205	180
III	180	193
IV	182	186
1984:I	?	184

(a) Does this increase in the α weight make the forecasting system more or less sensitive to changes in quarterly tonnage? Why?
(b) If the tonnage unloaded was mainly affected by random market demands for grain and only slightly by systematic changes in demand, should a high or low value of α be used?

PROBLEM 6.5

Sales of Cool-Man air conditioners have grown steadily during the past five years (see table). The sales manager had predicted in 1978 that 1979 sales would be 410 air conditioners. Using exponential smoothing with a weight of $\alpha = 0.30$, develop forecasts for 1980 through 1984.

Year	Sales	Forecast
1979	450	410
1980	495	
1981	518	
1982	563	
1983	584	
1984	?	

The simple form of exponential smoothing that we have examined does have one disadvantage. Just like other moving average methods, it does not pick up trends in data very well. Fortunately, more advanced exponential-smoothing models often have built in trend correction factors.

EXPONENTIAL SMOOTHING WITH TREND ADJUSTMENT

To illustrate a more complex exponential smoothing model, let us consider one that adjusts for trend. The idea is to compute a simple exponential smoothing forecast as above and then adjust for positive or negative lag in trend. The formula is:

$$\text{Forecast including trend } (FIT_t) = \text{New forecast } (F_t) + \text{Trend correction } (T_t)$$

To smooth out the trend, the equation for the trend correction uses a smoothing constant, β, in the same way the simple exponential model uses α. T_t is computed by:

$$T_t = T_{t-1} + \beta(F_t - F_{t-1})$$

where T_t = smoothed trend for period t

T_{t-1} = smoothed trend for one period earlier

β = trend smoothing constant that we select

F_t = simple exponential smoothed forecast for period t

F_{t-1} = forecast for one period earlier

There are three steps to compute a trend-adjusted forecast.

Step 1. Compute a simple exponential forecast for time period t (F_t).

Step 2. Compute the trend by using the equation

$$T_t = T_{t-1} + \beta(F_t - F_{t-1})$$

To start step 2 for the first time, an initial trend value must be inserted (either by a good guess or by observed past data). After that, trend is computed.

Step 3. Calculate the trend adjusted exponential smoothing forecast (FIT_t) by this formula:

$$FIT_t = F_t + T_t$$

EXAMPLE 6.4

A large Spokane manufacturer uses exponential smoothing to forecast demand for a pollution control equipment product. It appears that a trend is present.

(continued)

Month	Demand
1	12
2	17
3	20
4	19
5	24
6	26
7	31
8	32
9	36

Smoothing constants are assigned the values of $\alpha = .2$ and $\beta = .4$. Assume the initial forecast for month 1 was 11 units.

Step 1. Forecast for month 2 (F_2) = Forecast for month 1 (F_1) + α (Month 1 demand − Forecast for month 1)

$$F_2 = 11 + .2(12 - 11) = 11.0 + 0.2 = 11.2 \text{ units}$$

Step 2. Compute the trend present. Assume an initial trend adjustment of zero, i.e., $T_1 = 0$.

$$T_2 = T_1 + \beta(F_2 - F_1)$$
$$T_2 = 0 + .4(11.2 - 11.0)$$
$$= .08$$

Step 3. Compute the forecast including trend (*FIT*)

$$FIT_2 = F_2 + T_2$$
$$FIT_2 = 11.2 + .08$$
$$= 11.28 \text{ Units}$$

We will do the same calculations for the third month also.

Step 1. $F_3 = F_2 + \alpha$ (Demand in month 2 − F_2)
$F_3 = 11.2 + .2(17 - 11.2) = 12.36$

Step 2. $T_3 = T_2 + \beta (F_3 - F_2)$
$T_3 = .08 + .4(12.36 - 11.2) = .54$

Step 3. $FIT_3 = F_3 + T_3$
$FIT_3 = 12.36 + .54 = 12.90$

So the simple exponential forecast (without trend) for month 2 was 11.2 units while the trend-adjusted forecast was 11.28 units. In month 3, the simple forecast was 12.36 units, while the trend-adjusted forecast was 12.90 units. Naturally, different values of T_1 and β can produce even better estimates.

PROBLEM 6.6

Continue forecasting trend-adjusting demands for the manufacturer in Example 6.4. After computing FIT_4 through FIT_9, prepare a graph comparing Actual Demand, Forecast without trend (F_t), and Forecast Including Trend (FIT_t).

TREND PROJECTIONS: A THIRD TIME SERIES MODEL

The last time series forecasting method we will discuss is trend projection. This technique fits a straight line to a series of historical data points, and then projects the line into the future.

One quick way to visualize the historical trend is the use of a *scatter diagram*. We label the horizontal (X) axis of a two-dimensional graph as "time" and the vertical (Y) axis as sales, demand, or whatever variable we propose to forecast. Example 6.5 helps illustrate the relationship between time and sales of radios for a wholesaler.

EXAMPLE 6.5

Wacker Distributors tabulated annual sales for two of its products—radios and stereos—over the past ten years as shown:

Year	Radios	Stereos
1	300	110
2	310	100
3	320	120
4	330	140
5	340	170
6	350	150
7	360	160
8	370	190
9	380	200
10	390	190

One simple way to examine these historical data and perhaps use them to establish a forecast is to draw a scatter diagram for each product. Figure 6.2 shows the scatter diagram of radio sales. This picture of the relationship between sales of a product and time is useful in spotting trends or cycles.

Figure 6.2 shows radio sales increasing at a constant rate of 10 radios each year. If we extend the line left to the vertical axis, we would see that sales would be 290 in year 0. The equation

$$\text{Sales} = 290 + 10 \, (\text{year})$$

best describes this relationship between sales and time. A reasonable estimate of radio sales in year 11 is 400 and in year 12 is 410 radios.

(continued)

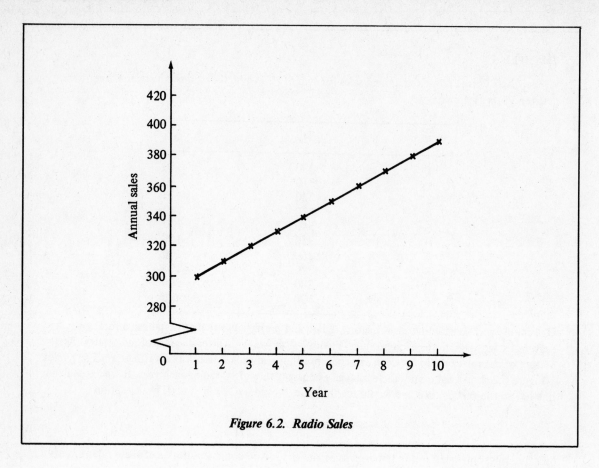

Figure 6.2. Radio Sales

PROBLEM 6.7

Now try drawing the scatter diagram for Wacker's stereo sales from the data given in Example 6.5. What happens when you attempt to place a trend line among the data points?

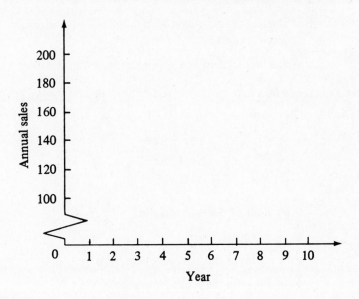

If we decide to develop a linear trend line by a precise statistical method, as opposed to "eyeballing" the line as in Problem 6.7, the *least squares method* may be applied. This approach yields an equation that describes the straight line of best fit.

A least squares line is described in terms of its y intercept (the height at which it intercepts the y axis) and its slope (the angle of the line). If we can compute the y intercept and slope, we can express the line with the following equation:

$$\hat{y} = a + bx$$

where

$\hat{y}$ (called "*y* hat") = computed value of the variable to be predicted (called the dependent variable)

a = y axis intercept

b = slope of the regression line (or the rate of change in *y* for given changes in *x*)

x = the independent variable (which is *time* in this case).

Statisticians have developed equations that we can use to find the values of *a* and *b* for any regression line. The slope *b* is found by

$$b = \frac{\Sigma xy - n\bar{x}\,\bar{y}}{\Sigma x^2 - n\bar{x}^2}$$

where

b = slope of the regression line

Σ = summation sign

x = values of the independent variable

y = values of the dependent variable

$\bar{x}$ = the average of the values of the *x*'s

$\bar{y}$ = the average of the values of the *y*'s

n = the number of data points or observations

We can compute the *y* intercept *a* as follows:

$$a = \bar{y} - b\bar{x}$$

Example 6.6 shows how to apply these concepts.

EXAMPLE 6.6

Shown below are data on the demand for electrical generators from a midwestern manufacturer over the period 1977–83. Let us fit a straight-line trend to these data and forecast 1984 sales.

Year	Electrical Generators Sold
1977	74
1978	79
1979	80
1980	90
1981	105
1982	142
1983	122

With a series of data over time, we can minimize the computations by transforming the values of the x variable (time) to simpler numbers that sum to zero. Thus, in this case, we can designate 1977 as year -3, 1978 as year -2, and so on.

Year	Time Period x	Generator Sales y	x^2	xy
1977	-3	74	9	-222
1978	-2	79	4	-158
1979	-1	80	1	-80
1980	0	90	0	0
1981	$+1$	105	1	105
1982	$+2$	142	4	284
1983	$+3$	122	9	366
	$\Sigma x = 0$	$\Sigma y = 692$	$\Sigma x^2 = 28$	$\Sigma xy = 295$

When $\Sigma x = 0$, then it follows that $\bar{x} = \Sigma x / n = 0$, and the formulas for a and b simplify to

$$b = \frac{\Sigma xy - n\bar{x}\,\bar{y}}{\Sigma x^2 - n\bar{x}^2} = \frac{\Sigma xy - 0}{\Sigma x^2 - 0}$$

$$= \frac{\Sigma xy}{\Sigma x^2}$$

(continued)

or in this case,

$$b = \frac{295}{28} = 10.54$$

$$a = \bar{y} - b\bar{x} = \bar{y} - 0 = \bar{y}$$

or

$$a = \frac{\Sigma y}{7} = \frac{692}{7} = 98.86$$

Hence, the regression equation is

$$\hat{y} = 98.86 + 10.54x$$

To project sales in 1984, we first denote the year 1984 in our new coding system—in this case, $x = +4$.

$$\hat{y} \text{ (sales in 1984)} = 98.86 + 10.54(4)$$

$$= 141.02, \text{ or } 141 \text{ generators}$$

We can estimate sales for 1985 by inserting $x = +5$ in the same equation:

$$\hat{y} \text{ (sales in 1985)} = 98.86 + 10.54(5)$$

$$= 151.56, \text{ or } 152 \text{ generators}$$

PROBLEM 6.8

Room registrations in the Jerusalem Towers Plaza Hotel have been recorded for the past nine years. Management would like to determine the mathematical trend of guest registration in order to project future occupancy. This estimate would help the hotel determine whether a future expansion will be needed. Given the time series data below, develop a regression equation relating registrations to time. Then forecast 1987 registrations.

(continued)

Year	Transformed Year x	Room Registrations (in thousands)	x^2	xy
1975		17		
1976		16		
1977		16		
1978		21		
1979		20		
1980		20		
1981		23		
1982		25		
1983		24		

When working with time series data such as those in Example 6.6 and Problem 6.8, we may find that the series happens to contain an even number of years. If we have six years, as an example, the earliest year would be coded as −2.5 and the following years would be −1.5, −0.5, +0.5, +1.5, and +2.5. Then again $\Sigma x = 0$.

SEASONAL VARIATIONS IN DATA

Time series forecasting such as that in Example 6.6 and Problem 6.8 involves looking at the *trend* of data over a series of time observations. Sometimes, however, recurring variations at certain seasons of the year make a *seasonal* adjustment in the trend line forecast necessary. Demand tor coal and fuel oil, for example, usually peaks during cold winter months. Demand for golf clubs or suntan lotion may be highest in summer. Analyzing data in monthly or quarterly terms usually makes it easy for a statistician to spot seasonal patterns. Seasonal indices can then be developed by several common methods. Let's see how indices that have already been prepared can be applied to adjust trend line forecasts.

EXAMPLE 6.7

Management of Shore's Department Store has used time series regression to forecast retail sales for the next four quarters. The sales estimates are $100,000, $120,000, $140,000, and $160,000 for the respective quarters. Seasonal indices for the four quarters have been found to be 1.30, 0.90, 0.70, and 1.15, respectively.

To compute a seasonalized or adjusted sales forecast, we just multiply each seasonal index times the appropriate trend forecast.

$$\hat{y}_{\text{seasonal}} = \text{index} \times \hat{y}_{\text{trend forecast}}$$

Hence,

$$\text{for Quarter I:} \quad \hat{y}_{\text{I}} = (1.30)(\$100,000) = \$130,000$$

$$\text{Quarter II:} \quad \hat{y}_{\text{II}} = (0.90)(\$120,000) = \$108,000$$

$$\text{Quarter III:} \quad \hat{y}_{\text{III}} = (0.70)(\$140,000) = \$98,000$$

$$\text{Quarter IV:} \quad \hat{y}_{\text{IV}} = (1.15)(\$160,000) = \$184,000$$

PROBLEM 6.9

Quarterly demand for Jaguar XKE's at a certain New York auto dealer are forecast with this equation:

$$\hat{y} = 10 + 3x$$

where

$$
\begin{array}{rll}
x = \text{quarters} \quad - & \text{Quarter I of 1978} & = 0 \\
& \text{Quarter II of 1978} & = 1 \\
& \text{Quarter III of 1978} & = 2 \\
& \text{Quarter IV of 1978} & = 3 \\
& \text{Quarter I of 1979} & = 4 \\
& \text{and so on.} &
\end{array}
$$

$\hat{y}$ = quarterly demand

The demand for sports cars is seasonal and the indices for Quarters I, II, III, and IV are 0.80, 1.00, 1.30, and 0.90 respectively.

Forecast demand for each quarter of 1980. Then seasonalize each forecast to adjust for quarterly variations.

CAUSAL FORECASTING METHODS: REGRESSION ANALYSIS

Causal forecasting models usually consider several variables that are related to the variable being predicted. Once these related variables have been found, a statistical model is built and used to forecast the variable of interest. This approach is more powerful than the time series methods that use only the historical values of the forecasted variables.

Many factors can be considered in a causal analysis. For example, the sales of a product might be related to the firm's advertising budget, the price charged, competitor's prices and strategies, or even the economy and unemployment rates. In this case, sales would be called the *dependent variable,* while the other variables would be *independent variables.* The most common way of quantifying causal forecasting models is *regression analysis.*

We can use the same mathematical model we employed in the least squares method of trend projection to perform a regression analysis. *Y* will still be the dependent variable that we want to forecast. But now the independent variable, *x,* needs no longer be time.

EXAMPLE 6.8

Triple A Construction Company renovates old homes in Albany. Over time, the company has found that their dollar volume of renovation work is dependent on the Albany area payroll. The following table lists Triple A's revenues and the amount of money earned by wage earners in Albany during the years 1978–1983.

y *Triple A's Sales* *($000,000)*	*x* *Local Payroll* *($000,000,000)*
2.0	1
3.0	3
2.5	4
2.0	2
2.0	1
3.5	7

Triple A management wants to establish a mathematical relationship that will help it predict sales. First, they need to determine whether there is a straight-line (linear) relationship between area payroll and sales, so they plot the known data on a scatter diagram.

(continued)

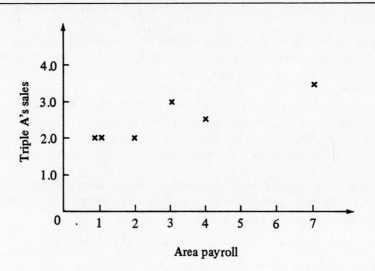

It appears from the six data points that there is a slight, positive relationship between the independent variable of payroll and the dependent variable of sales. As payroll increases, Triple A's sales tend to be higher.

We can find a mathematical equation by using the least squares regression approach.

Sales y	*Payroll* x	x^2	xy
2.0	1	1	2.0
3.0	3	9	9.0
2.5	4	16	10.0
2.0	2	4	4.0
2.0	1	1	2.0
3.5	7	49	24.5
$\Sigma y = 15.0$	$\Sigma x = 18$	$\Sigma x^2 = 80$	$\Sigma xy = 51.5$

$$\bar{x} = \frac{\Sigma x}{6} = \frac{18}{6} = 3$$

$$\bar{y} = \frac{\Sigma y}{6} = \frac{15}{6} = 2.5$$

(continued)

$$b = \frac{\Sigma xy - n\bar{x}\,\bar{y}}{\Sigma x^2 - n\bar{x}^2} = \frac{51.5 - (6)(3)(2.5)}{80 - (6)(3^2)} = 0.25$$

$$a = \bar{y} - b\bar{x} = 2.5 - (0.25)(3) = 1.75$$

The estimated regression equation, therefore, is

$$\hat{y} = 1.75 + 0.25x$$

or

$$\text{Sales} = 1.75 + 0.25 \text{ payroll}$$

If the local Chamber of Commerce predicts that the Albany area payroll will be $6 hundred million next year, we can estimate sales for Triple A with the regression equation.

$$\text{Sales (in \$000,000)} = 1.75 + 0.25(6) = 1.75 + 1.50$$

$$= 3.25$$

or

$$\text{Sales} = \$325,000$$

The final part of Example 6.8 illustrates a central weakness of causal forecasting methods like regression. Even when we have computed a regression equation, it is necessary to provide a forecast of the independent variable x—in this case, payroll—before estimating the dependent variable y for the next time period. Although not a problem for all forecasts, you can imagine the difficulty of determining future values of *some* common independent variables (such as unemployment rates, gross national product, price indices, etc.).

PROBLEM 6.10

The operations manager of a musical instrument distributor feels that demand for bass drums may relate to the number of television appearances by the popular rock group Green Shades during the previous month. The manager has collected the data shown in the following table.

Demand for Bass Drums	Green Shades TV Appearances
3	3
6	4
7	7
5	6
10	8
8	5

(a) Graph these data to see whether a linear equation might accurately describe the relationship between the group's television appearances and the sales of bass drums each month.

(continued)

(b) Use the least squares regression method to derive a forecasting equation.

(c) What would you estimate bass drum sales would have been if the Green Shades had performed on TV nine times last month?

CORRELATION COEFFICIENT FOR REGRESSION LINES

The regression equation is one way of expressing the nature of the relationship between two variables. The equation and curve show how one variable depends upon the value and changes in another variable.

Another way to evaluate the relationship between two variables is to compute the *coefficient of correlation*. This measure expresses the degree of strength of the linear relationship. It is usually identified as *r* and can be any number between +1 and −1. Figure 6.3 illustrates what different values of *r* might look like.

The coefficient of correlation measures the percent of variation in *y* explained by the regression line. To compute *r* we use much the same data needed earlier to calculate *a* and *b* for the regression line. The rather lengthy equation for *r* is

$$r = \frac{n\Sigma xy - \Sigma x \Sigma y}{\sqrt{[n\Sigma x^2 - (\Sigma x)^2][n\Sigma y^2 - (\Sigma y)^2]}}$$

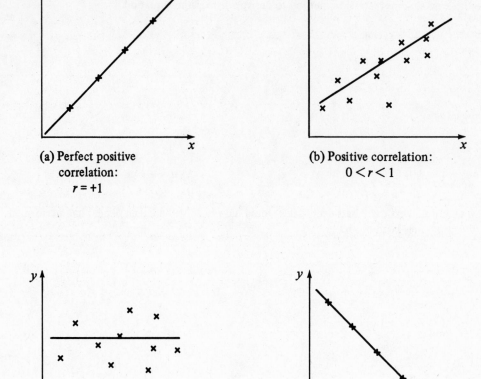

(a) Perfect positive
    correlation:
    $r = +1$

(b) Positive correlation:
    $0 < r < 1$

(c) No correlation:
    $r = 0$

(d) Perfect negative
    correlation:
    $r = -1$

Figure 6.3. Four Values of the Correlation Coefficient

EXAMPLE 6.9

In Example 6.2 we looked at the relationship between Triple A Construction Company's renovation sales and payroll in Albany. To compute the coefficient of correlation for the data shown, we need only add one more column of calculations (for y^2) and then apply the equation for r.

y	x	x^2	xy	y^2	
2.0	1	1	2.0	4.0	
3.0	3	9	9.0	9.0	New
2.5	4	16	10.0	6.25	Column
2.0	2	4	4.0	4.0	
2.0	1	1	2.0	4.0	
3.5	7	49	24.5	12.25	
$\Sigma y = 15.0$	$\Sigma x = 18$	$\Sigma x^2 = 80$	$\Sigma xy = 51.5$	$\Sigma y^2 = 39.5$	

$$r = \frac{(6)(51.5) - (18)(15.0)}{\sqrt{[(6)(80) - (18)^2][(6)(39.5) - (15.0)^2]}} = \frac{309 - 270}{\sqrt{(156)(12)}} = \frac{39}{\sqrt{1872}}$$

$$= \frac{39}{43.3}$$

$$= 0.901$$

This r of 0.901 appears to be a significant correlation and helps to confirm the closeness of the relationship of the two variables.

PROBLEM 6.11

A University of Alabama study to determine the correlation between bank deposits and consumer price indices in Birmingham, Alabama, revealed the following (based on $n = 5$ years of data):

$$\Sigma x = 15$$
$$\Sigma x^2 = 55$$
$$\Sigma xy = 70$$
$$\Sigma y = 20$$
$$\Sigma y^2 = 130$$

(continued)

Find the coefficient of correlation. What does it imply to you?

Problem 6.12 asks you to apply *both* the regression and correlation techniques to form a more complete analysis.

PROBLEM 6.12

The accountant at O. H. Hall Coal Distributors, Inc., notes that the demand for coal seems to be tied to an index of weather severity developed by the National Weather Bureau. That is, when weather was extremely cold in the U. S. over the past five years (and hence the index was high), coal sales were high. The accountant proposes that one good forecast of next year's coal demand could be made by developing a regression equation and then consulting the *Farmer's Almanac* to see how severe next year's winter will be. For the data shown below, derive a least squares regression and compute the coefficient of correlation for the data.

Coal sales (in million of tons) (y)	Weather Index (x)
4	2
1	1
4	4
6	5
5	3

(continued)

Although the coefficient of correlation is the most commonly used measure to describe the relationship between two variables, another measure does exist. It is called the *coefficient of determination*. This is simply the square of the coefficient of correlation, namely, r^2. The value of r^2 will always be a positive number in the range of $0 \leqslant r^2 \leqslant 1$. The coefficient of determination is the percent of variation in the dependent variable y that the regression equation explains.

MULTIPLE REGRESSION ANALYSIS

Multiple regression is a practical extension of the model we just observed. For example, if Triple A Construction (in Examples 6.8 and 6.9) wanted to include average annual interest rates in its model to forecast renovation sales, the proper equation would be:

$$\hat{y} = a + b_1 x_1 + b_2 x_2$$

where
$\hat{y}$ = the dependent variable, sales

$a = y$ intercept

x_1 and x_2 = values of the two independent variables,
area payroll and interest rates, respectively

The mathematics of multiple regression becomes quite complex (and is usually tackled by computer), so we leave the formulas for a, b_1, and b_2 to statistics textbooks.

EXAMPLE 6.10

The new multiple regression line for Triple A Construction, calculated by our computer is:

$$\hat{y} = 1.80 + .30x_1 - 5.0x_2$$

we also find that the new coefficient of correlation is .96, implying the inclusion of the variable, x_2, interest rates, adds even more strength to the linear relationship.

We can now estimate Triple A's sales if we substitute in values for next year's payroll and interest rate. If Albany's payroll will be $600 million and the interest rate will be .12 (12%), sales will be forecast as:

$$\text{Sales (\$100,000's)} = 1.80 + .30(6) - 5.0(0.12)$$
$$= 1.8 + 1.8 - 0.6$$
$$= 3.00$$

or

$$\text{Sales} = \$300,000$$

PROBLEM 6.13

If the interest rate in Albany drops to 8%, but the payroll drops to $500 million, how will Triple A Construction's sales be impacted? Refer to Example 6.10.

FORECAST ERRORS

Some forecasting techniques, such as the moving average and exponential smoothing techniques, require that the forecaster use judgment in making the forecast. Moving average requires a determination of the number of periods to be averaged, and the exponential smoothing technique requires the determination of the smoothing constant, α. Furthermore, forecasters must select from one of many techniques in making the best forecast. The overall objective is to increase the accuracy of the forecast by minimizing the difference between the forecasted values and the actual or observed values. Three of the techniques that are used to determine forecasting accuracy are:

1. Mean absolute deviations (MAD).
2. Mean squared error (MSE).
3. Mean absolute percent error (MAPE).

MAD is the average of the absolute differences between the forecasted values and the observed values. MSE is the average of the squared differences between forecasted and observed values, and MAPE is the absolute difference between the forecasted and observed values expressed as a percentage of the observed values.

As an example, let us refer to the Port of Galveston forecasts, shown earlier as Problems 6.3 and 6.4. In Problem 6.3, port management considered an exponential smoothing constant of $\alpha = 0.10$. In Problem 6.4, you were given the results of an $\alpha = 0.50$ constant. Using MAD, which one would be better?

EXAMPLE 6.11

The data for $\alpha = 0.1$ is tabled below

Year and Quarter	Tonnage Unloaded	Forecast	Absolute Deviation
1982-I	180	175.00	5.0
1982-II	168	175.50	7.5
1982-III	159	174.75	15.75
1982-IV	175	173.18	1.82
1983-I	190	173.36	16.64
1983-II	205	175.02	29.98
1983-III	180	178.02	1.98
1983-IV	182	178.22	3.78
1984-I	?	178.60	

The total absolution deviation = 82.45. Thus, MAD = 82.45/8 = 10.31

PROBLEM 6.14

Your job is to compute the MAD for the $\alpha = 0.5$ data in the following table.

Year and Quarter	Tonnage Unloaded	Forecast	Absolute Deviation
1982-I	180	175	
1982-II	168	178	
1982-III	159	173	
1982-IV	175	166	
1983-I	190	170	
1983-II	205	180	
1983-III	180	193	
1983-IV	182	186	
1984-I	?	184	

Which smoothing constant is preferred?

ANSWERS

6.1

Year	Demand	Three-year Moving Averages	Weighted Three-year Moving Averages
1968	4		
1969	6		
1970	4		
1971	5	$(4 + 6 + 4)/3 = 4\ 2/3$	$[(2\times4) + 6 + 4]/4 = 4\ 1/2$
1972	10	$(6 + 4 + 5)/3 = 5$	$[(2\times5) + 4 + 6]/4 = 5$
1973	8	$(4 + 5 + 10)/3 = 6\ 1/3$	$[(2\times10) + 5 + 4]/4 = 7\ 1/4$
1974	7	$(5 + 10 + 8)/3 = 7\ 2/3$	$[(2\times8) + 10 + 5]/4 = 7\ 3/4$
1975	9	$(10 + 8 + 7)/3 = 8\ 1/3$	$[(2\times7) + 8 + 10]/4 = 8$
1976	12	$(8 + 7 + 9)/3 = 8$	$[(2\times9) + 7 + 8]/4 = 8\ 1/4$
1977	14	$(7 + 9 + 12)/3 = 9\ 1/3$	$[(2\times12) + 9 + 7]/4 = 10$
1978	15	$(9 + 12 + 14)/3 = 11\ 2/3$	$[(2\times14) + 12 + 9]/4 = 12\ 1/4$

Note: *4* = sum of the weights in denominator.

The *weighted* moving average appears to be slightly more accurate in its annual forecasts.

6.2   New forecast (for April demand) $= 144.2 + 0.2(136 - 144.2)$

$$= 142.6, \text{ or } 143 \text{ autos}$$

6.3

Year and Quarter	Forecast
1982:I	175.00
II	$175.50 = 175.00 + 0.10\ (180 - 175)$
III	$174.75 = 175.50 + 0.10\ (168 - 175.50)$
IV	$173.18 = 174.75 + 0.10\ (159 - 174.75)$
1983:I	$173.36 = 173.18 + 0.10\ (175 - 173.18)$
II	$175.02 = 173.36 + 0.10\ (190 - 173.36)$
III	$178.02 = 175.02 + 0.10\ (205 - 175.02)$
IV	$178.22 = 178.02 + 0.10\ (180 - 178.02)$
1984:I	$178.60 = 178.22 + 0.10\ (182 - 178.22)$

6.4   (a) An increase in α makes the forecasting system more sensitive. The larger the value of the smoothing constant, the more weight we give to last period's actual demand in computing the new forecast.

(b) We would use a relatively low value of α because the system should not be sensitive to random changes in demand.

6.5

Year	Forecast
1979	410.0
1980	$422.0 = 410 + 0.3\,(450 - 410)$
1981	$443.9 = 422 + 0.3\,(495 - 422)$
1982	$466.1 = 443.9 + 0.3\,(518 - 443.9)$
1983	$495.2 = 466.1 + 0.3\,(563 - 466.1)$
1984	$521.8 = 495.2 + 0.3\,(584 - 495.2)$

6.6

Month	Actual Demand	Forecast, F_t (without trend)	Trend	Adjusted FIT_t
1	12	11.00	0	—
2	17	11.20	.08	11.28
3	20	12.36	.54	12.90
4	19	13.89	1.15	15.04
5	24	14.91	1.56	16.47
6	26	16.73	2.29	19.02
7	31	18.58	3.03	21.61
8	32	21.07	4.03	25.09
9	36	23.25	4.90	28.15

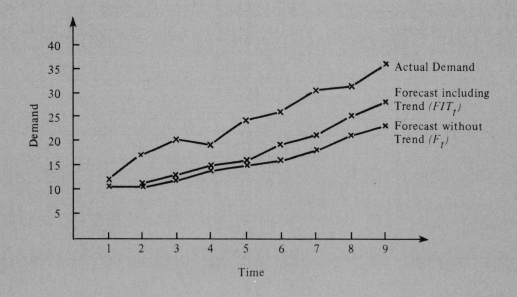

Time

6.7

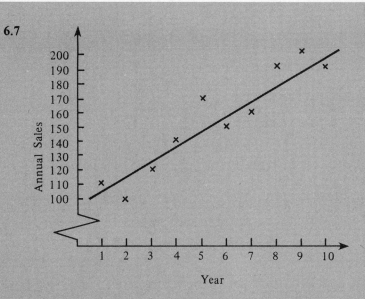

The trend line may not be perfectly accurate because of variation each year. But stereo sales do appear to have been increasing over the past ten years. If we had to forecast future sales, we would probably pick a larger figure each year.

6.8

Year	Transformed Year x	Registrants y (in thousands)	x^2	xy
1975	−4	17	16	−68
1976	−3	16	9	−48
1977	−2	16	4	−32
1978	−1	21	1	−21
1979	0	20	0	0
1980	+1	20	1	20
1981	+2	23	4	46
1982	+3	25	9	75
1983	+4	24	16	96
	$\Sigma x = 0$	$\Sigma y = 182$	$\Sigma x^2 = 60$	$\Sigma xy = 68$

$$b = \frac{\Sigma xy}{\Sigma x} = \frac{68}{60}$$

$$= 1.13$$

$$a = \bar{y} = \frac{\Sigma y}{n} = \frac{182}{9}$$

$$= 20.22$$

$\hat{y}$ (registrations) $= 20.22 + 1.13x$

The projection of guest registrations in 1987 (which is $x = +8$ in the coding system used) is

$$\hat{y} = 20.22 + 1.13(8)$$

$$= 29.26, \text{ or } 29,260 \text{ guests in } 1987.$$

6.9   Quarter II of 1979 is coded $x = 5$; Quarter III of 1979, $x = 6$; and Quarter IV of 1979, $x = 7$. Hence, Quarter I of 1980 is coded $x = 8$; Quarter II, $x = 9$; and so on.

$\hat{y}$ (1980 Quarter I) $= 10 + 3(8)$ $= 34$ Adjusted forecast $= (0.80)(34) = 27.2$

$\hat{y}$ (1980 Quarter II) $= 10 + 3(9)$ $= 37$ Adjusted forecast $= (1.00)(37) = 37$

$\hat{y}$ (1980 Quarter III) $= 10 + 3(10) = 40$ Adjusted forecast $= (1.30)(40) = 52$

$\hat{y}$ (1980 Quarter IV) $= 10 + 3(11) = 43$ Adjusted forecast $= (0.90)(43) = 38.7$

6.10   (a) The observations do not form a perfect straight line but approach linearity over the range shown.

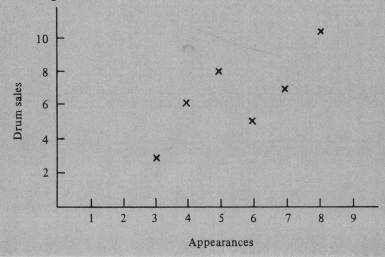

(b)

Demand for Drums y	TV Appearances x	x^2	xy
3	3	9	9
6	4	16	24
7	7	49	49
5	6	36	30
10	8	64	80
8	5	25	40
$\Sigma y = 39$	$\Sigma x = 33$	$\Sigma x^2 = 199$	$xy = 232$

$n = 6$ pairs of observations

$\bar{x} = 33/6$

$\bar{y} = 39/6$

$b = \dfrac{\Sigma xy - n\bar{x}\bar{y}}{\Sigma x^2 - n\bar{x}^2} = \dfrac{232 - (6)(33/6)(39/6)}{199 - (6)(33/6)^2}$

$= 1$

$a = \bar{y} - b\bar{x} = 39/6 - (1)(33/6) = 6/6$

$= 1$

Therefore $\hat{y} = 1.0 + 1.0x$

(c) If $x = 9$ performance by the Green Shades, then estimated sales are

$$\hat{y} = 1.0 + 1.0(9) = 1.0 + 9.0 = 10 \text{ drums}$$

6.11 $r = \dfrac{(5)(70) - (15)(20)}{\sqrt{[(5)(55) - (15)^2]\ [(5)(130) - (20)^2]}} = \dfrac{(50)}{\sqrt{(50)(250)}} = \dfrac{1}{\sqrt{5}}$

$= 0.447$

This result indicates that only a moderate but positive amount of correlation exists between the two variables.

6.12

y	x	x^2	xy	y^2
4	2	4	8	16
1	1	1	1	1
4	4	16	16	16
6	5	25	30	36
5	3	9	15	25
$\Sigma y = 20$	$\Sigma x = 15$	$\Sigma x^2 = 55$	$\Sigma xy = 70$	$\Sigma y^2 = 94$

$$\overline{x} = \frac{\Sigma x}{n} = \frac{15}{5}$$

$$= 3$$

$$\overline{y} = \frac{\Sigma y}{n} = \frac{20}{5}$$

$$= 4$$

$$b = \frac{70 - (5)(3)(4)}{55 - (5)(9)} = \frac{70 - 60}{55 - 45} = \frac{10}{10}$$

$$= 1$$

$$a = \overline{y} - b\overline{x} = 4 - (1)(3)$$

$$= 1$$

Thus, $\hat{y} = 1 + 1x$ is the regression line.

$$r = \frac{(5)(70) - (15)(20)}{\sqrt{[(5)(55) - (15)^2] \; [(5)(94) - (20)^2]}}$$

$$= +0.845$$

The high value of r implies a fairly strong correlation between the weather index (x) and the demand for coal (y).

6.13 $\hat{y} = 1.80 + .30(5) - 5.0(.08)$

$= 1.8 + 1.5 - 0.4 = 2.9$

Sales $= \$290,000$

6.14   Deviations from $\alpha = .05$ are 5, 10, 14, 9, 20, 25, 13, 4

Total absolute deviation $= 100$

MAD $= 100/8 = 12.5$

Based on this analysis, a smoothing constant of 0.1 is preferred over 0.5. Its MAD is smaller.

HOMEWORK PROBLEMS

6-1. Sales of Cool-Man air conditioners have grown steadily during the past five years.

Year	Sales
1976	450
1977	495
1978	518
1979	563
1980	584
1981	?

a. The sales manager had predicted in 1975 that 1976 sales would be 410 air conditioners. Using exponential smoothing with an alpha weight of $\alpha = 0.30$, develop forecasts for 1977 through 1981.
b. Use a three-month moving average forecasting model to forecast the sales of Cool-Man air conditioners.
c. Using the trend projection method, develop a forecasting model for the sales of Cool-Man air conditioners.
d. Would you use exponential smoothing with a smoothing constant of 0.3, a three-month moving average, or regression to predict the sales of Cool-Man air conditioners?

6-2. A lifeguard who took this course last year decided to see if she could predict the number of swimmers at the pool from the temperature. Here are the data she collected over a five day period:

Temperature (°F)	Swimmers
92	286
85	260
101	310
97	294
93	290

a. Using temperature as the independent (X) variable, develop a regression equation after finding: $\Sigma X, \Sigma X^2, \Sigma Y, \Sigma XY, \overline{X}, \overline{Y}, a + b$.
b. Use this equation to predict the number of swimmers when temperatures hit: 85, 93, and 101.
c. Explain why two of the three predictions don't exactly equal the actual figures.
d. Compute ΣY^2 and the coefficient of correlation. Explain, in general terms, the meaning of this correlation.

Unit 7

Inventory Analysis

Inventory analysis has always been a concern of top management. In many companies, inventory is one of the most expensive and important assets. Often it represents as much as 40 percent of the total invested capital in an industrial organization. Because of the size of the investment and its importance to the overall functioning of the firm, good inventory management is crucial. On one hand, companies will try to reduce the cost of inventory by reducing the amount of inventory on hand. On the other hand, however, it is necessary to realize that customer dissatisfaction can increase significantly due to low inventory levels and stockouts. Inventories are a prerequisite of workable systems of production, distribution, and marketing of goods.

Regardless of the complexity of inventory decisions and their associated mathematical models, there are three important decisions that apply to each current or potential item in inventory. These decisions are:

1. When to place an order for an item
2. How much of an item to order
3. What types of items to order

To state the problem in simple terms, a manager must decide "when," "how much," and "what" to order.

The major objective of the inventory decision is to minimize the total inventory cost. At the beginning of this chapter, we will consider only ordering and carrying costs. Ordering costs consist of all the costs associated with placing an order. They include the costs of supplies and ordering forms, order processing, clerks, and so on. *Carrying costs* are those costs associated with holding or carrying inventory over time. Carrying costs include the cost of storage, insurance, spoilage, theft, opportunity cost, and so on.

The inventory models discussed in the beginning of this unit assume that demand and lead time are known and constant and that no quantity discounts are available. When this is the case, the most significant costs are the cost of placing an order and the cost of holding inventory items over a period of time. Hence, in making inventory decisions, it will be the overall objective to minimize the sum of the carrying and ordering costs.

One of the most common inventory decisions is to determine what quantity will minimize the sum of the ordering cost and the carrying cost. As the quantity ordered increases, the total number of orders placed per year will decrease. Thus, as the quantity ordered increases, the annual ordering cost will decrease. But as the order quantity increases, the carrying cost will also increase due to the costs of maintaining larger average inventories. Figure 7.1 graphically shows the relationship between the order quantity and the carrying and ordering costs. Looking at the graph, you can see the total cost and the order quantity that will minimize the total cost. The order quantity that produces the minimum total cost is called the *optimal order quantity* (Q^*) or the *economic order quantity* (EOQ). It answers the question of "how much to order."

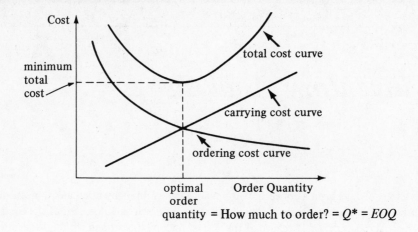

Figure 7.1. Relationship Between Order Quantity and Costs

If you assume that demand and lead time, which is the time it takes to obtain the order after placing it, are known and constant and that no quantity discounts are available, inventory usage over time is simple to plot (see Figure 7.2). We start at an inventory level of zero. When we receive an order for Q^* units, the

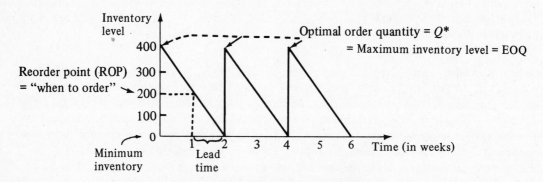

Figure 7.2. Inventory Usage over Time

inventory level jumps to Q^*. Then, inventory is used at a constant rate, and eventually it will drop to zero again. But when should we place an order to make sure that we never run out of inventory? Look at Figure 7.2. Most production-operations managers establish a reorder point (ROP) in units. When the inventory level drops to the reorder point, they place an order. If the lead time is one week, and inventory units are sold at a rate of 200 units per week, the ROP is $1 \times 200 = 200$ units.

This figure reveals the optimal order quantity and reorder point: Q^* is 400 units and ROP is 200 units. Thus, whenever the inventory level drops below 200 units, an order is placed for 400 units. In one week (the lead time), the new order of 400 units arrives as the inventory level drops to zero.

We have answered the questions "How much to order?" and "When to order?" graphically, but we can also determine them algebraically. First we will find the economic order quantity (EOQ) Q^*.

ECONOMIC ORDER QUANTITY

One useful quantity in EOQ analysis is the *average inventory level*, which is one-half the maximum inventory level. The first problem will be to express the average inventory level algebraically.

PROBLEM 7.1

Let the variable Q represent the quantity of units ordered. Assuming a constant uniform demand, determine the average inventory level. Assuming a unit purchase price of P, determine the average dollar value of inventory.

In Figure 7.1, the optimum order quantity was the point that minimized the total cost, where total cost is the sum of ordering cost and carrying cost. Referring to Figure 7.1, you can see that the optimal order quantity is at the point where the ordering cost is equal to the carrying cost. We will use this fact in future problems. Instead of graphically determining optimal inventory levels, let us now develop equations that will solve directly for the optimum. The necessary steps are:

1. Develop an expression for ordering cost.
2. Develop an expression for carrying cost.
3. Set ordering cost equal to carrying cost.
4. Solve the equation for the desired optimum.

EXAMPLE 7.1

Using the following variables, determine ordering and carrying costs and solve for Q^*:

$$Q \;=\; \text{number of pieces per order}$$

$$Q^* \;=\; \text{optimum number of pieces per order}$$

$$D \;=\; \text{annual demand in units, for the inventory item}$$

$$O_c \;=\; \text{ordering cost for each order}$$

$$C_c \;=\; \text{carrying cost per unit per year}$$

(continued)

---

1. Ordering cost   =   (no. of orders placed/yr.) (order cost/order)

               = $\left(\dfrac{\text{annual demand}}{\text{no. units in each order}}\right)$ (order cost/order)

               = $\left(\dfrac{D}{Q}\right)(O_c)$

               = $\dfrac{D}{Q}\,O_c$

2. Carrying cost   =   (average inventory level) (carrying cost/unit/year)

               = $\left(\dfrac{\text{order quantity}}{2}\right)$ (carrying cost/unit/year)

               = $\left(\dfrac{Q}{2}\right)(C_c)$

               = $\dfrac{Q}{2}\,C_c$

3. Optimal order quantity is found when order cost = carrying cost, namely,

$$\frac{D}{Q}\,O_c = \frac{Q}{2}\,C_c$$

4. To solve for Q^*, simply cross-multiply terms and isolate Q on the left of the equals sign.

$$2DO_c = Q^2 C_c$$

$$Q^2 \;=\; \frac{2DO_c}{C_c}$$

$$Q^* \;=\; \sqrt{\frac{2DO_c}{C_c}}$$

Inventory carrying costs for many businesses and industries are often expressed as an annual percentage of the unit cost or price. In these cases, there is another variable in the equation.

Let I be the annual inventory carrying charge as a percent of price. The cost of storing one unit of inventory for the year, C_c, is given by $C_c = IP$, where P is the unit price of an inventory item. In this case, Q^* can be expressed as

$$Q^* = \sqrt{\frac{2DO_c}{IP}}$$

Some books use the unit cost instead of the unit price. There I would be the annual carrying charge as a percent of cost. Here we will use unit price instead of unit cost.

Now that we have derived equations for the optimal order quantity Q^*, it is possible to solve inventory problems directly.

EXAMPLE 7.2

Sumco, a company that sells pump housings to other manufacturers, would like to reduce its inventory cost by determining the optimal number of pump housings to obtain per order. The annual demand is 1000 units, the ordering cost is $10 per order, and the average carrying cost per unit per year is $.50. Using these figures, we can calculate the optimal number of units per order.

1. $Q^* = \sqrt{\dfrac{2DO_c}{C_c}}$

2. $Q^* = \sqrt{\dfrac{2(1000)(10)}{0.50}}$

3. $Q^* = \sqrt{40,000}$

4. $Q^* = 200$ units

PROBLEM 7.2

Sumco would also like to determine the optimum number of units per order for pump input generators. The annual demand is 4900 units, the ordering cost is $50 per order, the price is $500 per unit, and the annual carrying cost expressed as a percentage of unit price is 20 percent. What is the optimum number of units per order?

$$Q^* = \sqrt{\qquad\qquad}$$

$$Q^* =$$

We can determine the expected number of orders placed during the year (N) and the expected time between order (T) as follows:

$$\text{Expected number of orders} = N = \frac{\text{demand}}{\text{order quantity}} = \frac{D}{Q^*} = \sqrt{\frac{DC_c}{2O_c}}$$

Expected time between orders $= T =$ number of working days in a year, divided by N

PROBLEM 7.3

The Xemex Computer Corporation purchases 8000 transistors each year for use in the minicomputers it manufactures. The unit cost of each transistor is $10, and the cost of carrying one transistor in inventory for a year is $3. Ordering cost is $30 per order.

What are the optimal order quantity, the expected number of orders placed each year, and the expected time between orders? Assume that Xemex operates a 200-day working year.

As mentioned earlier in this unit, the total annual inventory cost is the sum of the ordering and carrying costs.

$$\text{Total annual cost} = \text{ordering cost} + \text{carrying cost}$$

In terms of the variables in the model, we can express the total cost TC as:

$$TC = \frac{D}{Q} O_c + \frac{Q}{2} C_c$$

PROBLEM 7.4

Using the information given in Problem 7.3, find the total annual inventory cost for the ordering policy you calculated to be optimal.

PROBLEM 7.5

In the preceding problem, you computed the total annual inventory cost TC for the optimal order quantity Q^*. Q^* was 400 units. If 400 units is the optimal order quantity that minimizes total costs, then any other order quantity will result in a higher total cost. Calculate the total cost for order quantities of 410 units and 390 units.

TC (at 410 units)   =

　　　　　　　　　　 =

TC (at 390 units)   =

　　　　　　　　　　 =

Often the total inventory cost expression is written to include the actual cost of the material purchased. Since we assumed in Problem 7.3 that the annual demand and the price per transistor were known values (8000 transistors per year and $10), total annual cost should include purchase cost. Material cost does not depend on the particular order policy found to be optimal, since, regardless of how many units are ordered each year, we still incur an annual material cost of $DP = (8000)(\$10) = \$80,000$. (Later in this unit, we will discuss the case in which this may not be true, namely, when a "quantity discount" is available to the customer who orders a certain amount each time.)

REORDER POINTS

Now that we have decided how much to order, we shall look at the second inventory question, "When to order?" Most simple inventory models assume that receipt of an order is instantaneous. In other words, we assume that a firm will wait until its inventory level for a particular item reaches zero before placing an order and that it will receive the items in stock immediately. As you know, however, the time between the placing and receipt of an order, called the lead time or delivery time, is often a few days or even a few weeks. Thus, the when-to-order decision is usually expressed in terms of a *reorder point,* the inventory level at which an order should be placed.

The reorder point ROP is given as:

$$ROP = (\text{demand per day}) (\text{lead time for a new order in days})$$

$$= dL$$

This equation for ROP assumes that demand is uniform and constant. When such is not the case, safety stock should be added (see Unit 8).

The demand per day d is found by dividing the annual demand D by the number of working days in a year:

$$d = \frac{D}{\text{number of working days}}$$

EXAMPLE 7.3

Xemex's demand for transistors is 8000 per year. The firm operates a 200-day working year. On the average, delivery of an order takes 3 working days. We calculate the reorder point for transistors as follows:

$$d = \text{daily demand} = \frac{D}{\text{number of working days}} = \frac{8000}{200}$$

$$= 40$$

$$ROP = \text{reorder point} = dL = 40 \text{ units/day} \times 3 \text{ days}$$

$$= 120 \text{ units}$$

Hence, when the inventory stock of transistors drops to 120, an order should be placed. The order will arrive 3 days later, just as the firm's stock is depleted to zero.

PROBLEM 7.6

Annual demand for the notebook binders at Jessie Cohen's Stationery Shop is 10,000 units. Jessie operates her business 200 days per year and finds that deliveries from her supplier generally take 5 working days.

Calculate the reorder point for the notebook binders that she stocks.

PRODUCTION INVENTORY MODELS

In the previous inventory models we assumed that the entire inventory order was received at one time. There are times, however, when the firm may receive its inventory over a period of time. Such cases require a different model, one that does not require the instantaneous receipt assumption. This model is applicable when inventory continuously flows or builds up over a period of time after an order has been placed or when units are produced and sold simultaneously. Under these circumstances, we must take into account the daily production (or inventory flow) rate and the daily demand rate. Figure 7.3 shows inventory levels as a function of time.

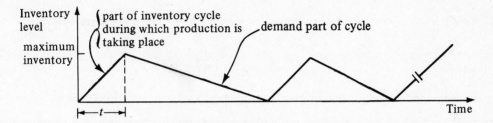

Figure 7.3. Change in Inventory Levels over Time

Because this model is especially suitable for the production environment, it is commonly called the *Production run model.* It is useful when inventory continuously builds up over time and the traditional economic order quantity assumptions are valid. We derive this model by setting ordering costs or setup costs equal to carrying costs and solving for the appropriate variable. Example 7.4 develops the expression for carrying cost.

EXAMPLE 7.4

Using the following symbols, determine the expression for annual inventory carrying cost for the production run model:

$$Q \;=\; \text{number of pieces per order}$$

$$C_c \;=\; \text{carrying cost per unit per year}$$

$$p \;=\; \text{daily production rate}$$

$$d \;=\; \text{daily demand rate, or usage rate}$$

$$t \;=\; \text{length of the production run in days}$$

1. Annual inventory carrying cost = (average inventory level) $\times$ (carrying cost per unit per year)
   = (average inventory level) $\times$ C_c
2. Average inventory level = (maximum inventory level)/2

(continued)

---

3. Maximum inventory level = (total produced during the production run) − (total used during the production run) = $pt - dt$.

But Q = total produced = pt, and thus $t = Q/p$. Therefore,

$$\text{Maximum inventory level} = p\left(\frac{Q}{p}\right) - d\left(\frac{Q}{p}\right) = Q - \frac{d}{p}Q$$

$$= Q(1 - \frac{d}{p})$$

4. Annual inventory carrying cost (or simply carrying cost) = $\dfrac{\textit{maximum inventory level}}{2}(C_c)$

$$= \frac{Q}{2}\left[1 - \left(\frac{d}{p}\right)\right]C_c$$

PROBLEM 7.7

Using the expression for carrying cost given in Example 7.4 and the expression for ordering cost from Example 7.1, solve for the optimal number of pieces per order by equating ordering cost and carrying cost.

Ordering cost (from Example 7.1) =

Carrying cost (from Example 7.4) =

$Q*$ = optimum number of pieces per order

$Q*$ =

Compare the result in Problem 7.7 to the result of Example 7.1. Note the inclusion of the factor $[1 - (d/p)]$ in the equation in Problem 7.7.

We can use the equation for $Q*$ to solve for the optimum order or production quantity when inventory continuously flows in over time.

EXAMPLE 7.5

Given the following values, solve for the optimum number of units per order.

Annual demand $= D = 1000$ units

Setup cost $= O_c = \$10$

Carrying cost $= C_c = \$.50$ per unit per year

Daily production rate $= p = 8$ units daily

Daily demand rate $= d = 6$ units daily

$$1. \quad Q^* = \sqrt{\frac{2DO_c}{C_c[1 - (d/p)]}}$$

$$2. \quad Q^* = \sqrt{\frac{2(1000)(10)}{0.50\,[1 - (6/8)]}}$$

$$= \sqrt{\frac{20,000}{0.50(1/4)}} = \sqrt{160,000}$$

$$= 400$$

You may want to compare this solution with the answer in Example 7.2. Eliminating the instantaneous receipt assumption, where $p = 8$ and $d = 6$, has resulted in an increase in Q^* from 200 in Example 7.2 to 400. Also note that

$$d = \frac{D}{\text{number of days the plant is in operation}}$$

PROBLEM 7.8

Solve for Q^* where

Annual demand $= 1000$ units

Setup cost $= \$20$ per setup

Carrying cost $= \$1$ per unit per year

Daily production rate $= 9$ units daily

(continued)

Daily demand rate = 8 units daily

$$Q^* = \sqrt{}$$

$$Q^* =$$

We can also calculate Q^* when annual data is available. When annual data is used, we can express Q^* as

$$Q^* = \sqrt{\frac{2DO_c}{C_c[1-(D/P)]}}$$

D = annual demand rate

P = annual production rate

PROBLEM 7.9

Goco, Inc., has an annual demand rate of 1000 units and an average annual production rate of 2000 units. Setup cost is $10 and carrying cost is $1.00. What is the optimal number of units to be produced?

$$Q^* = \sqrt{}$$

$$Q^* =$$

BACK-ORDER INVENTORY MODELS

In other inventory models we have not allowed inventory shortages, that is, insufficient stock to meet current demand. There are many situations in which planned shortages or stockouts may be advisable. This is the case especially for expensive items that have high carrying costs. Car dealerships and appliance stores rarely stock every model for this reason.

In this section, we will assume that stockouts and back-ordering are allowable. The model is called the *back-order,* or *planned shortages, inventory model.* The assumptions for this model are the same as for previous models. In addition, however, we will assume that sales will not be lost due to a stockout. We will use the same variables, with the addition of B_c, the cost of back-ordering one unit for one year. Thus,

$$Q \quad = \text{ number of pieces per order}$$

$$D \quad = \text{ annual demand in units}$$

$$C_c \quad = \text{ carrying cost per unit per year}$$

$$O_c \quad = \text{ ordering cost for each order}$$

$$B_c \quad = \text{ back-ordering cost per unit per year}$$

$$S \quad = \text{ remaining units after the back-order is satisfied}$$

$$Q - S \quad = \text{ amount back-ordered}$$

Figure 7.4 shows the inventory level as a function of time.

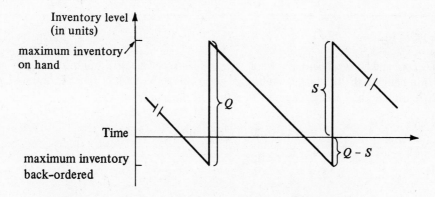

Figure 7.4. Change in Inventory over Time with Back-orders

The total cost must include the cost of being out of stock (back-ordering cost):

$$T_c = \text{ordering cost} + \text{carrying cost} + \text{back-ordering cost}$$

We can use calculus to solve for Q^* and S^* once the total cost is expressed using the above variables. The results are as follows:

$$Q^* \quad = \text{optimum order size in units}$$

$$= \sqrt{\left(\frac{2O_cD}{C_c}\right)\left(\frac{C_c + B_c}{B_c}\right)}$$

$$S^* \quad = \text{optimum remaining units after back-ordering}$$

$$= \sqrt{\left(\frac{2O_cD}{C_c}\right)\left(\frac{B_c}{B_c + C_c}\right)}$$

or

$$S^* \quad = Q^*\left(\frac{B_c}{B_c + C_c}\right)$$

and

$$Q^* - S^* \quad = \text{optimum amount back-ordered in units}$$

$$= Q^* - Q^*\left(\frac{B_c}{B_c + C_c}\right)$$

or

$$Q^* - S^* \quad = Q^*\left(1 - \frac{B_c}{B_c + C_c}\right)$$

EXAMPLE 7.6

Richmond Tool and Die Company is a wholesaler of high-speed electric drill bits. Data for one model that the firm handles, the G-28 titanium bit, are given below. We wish to find the optimum order size for the G-28 bit and the optimum number of bits to be back-ordered.

$$D \quad = 20,000 \text{ drill bits per year}$$

$$C_c \quad = \$2$$

$$O_c \quad = \$15$$

$$B_c \quad = \$10$$

1. $Q^* = \sqrt{\left(\frac{2O_cD}{C_c}\right)\left(\frac{C_c + B_c}{B_c}\right)}$

(continued)

2. $Q^* = \sqrt{\left(\dfrac{2(15)(20,000)}{2}\right)\left(\dfrac{2+10}{10}\right)} = \sqrt{300,000\left(\dfrac{12}{10}\right)}$

$= \sqrt{360,000}$

3. $Q^* = 600$ units per order

4. $Q^* - S^* = Q^*\left(1 - \dfrac{B_c}{B_c + C_c}\right)$

5. $Q^* - S^* = 600\left(1 - \dfrac{10}{10+2}\right) = 100$ units back-ordered each inventory cycle

---

PROBLEM 7.10

Given the following information, determine values for Q^* and S^*

$$D = 10,000 \text{ units}$$
$$C_c = \$1$$
$$O_c = \$10$$
$$B_c = \$2$$
$$Q^* =$$
$$S^* =$$

PROBLEM 7.11

Ace's Home Center allows back-ordering on most of its major appliances, including dishwashers. The annual demand for one type of dishwasher is 100. It costs approximately $10 to place an order and the annual carrying cost is $4 per year per unit. Back-ordering cost is approximately $5. What is the optimal order quantity and what is the optimal number of remaining units after the back order has been satisfied?

$$Q^* = \sqrt{}$$

$$Q^* =$$

$$S^* =$$

$$S^* =$$

QUANTITY DISCOUNT MODELS

To obtain a higher sales volume, many businesses offer reduced product costs for large purchases. These discounts are typically referred to as *quantity discounts*. Given the opportunity to purchase large quantities at a reduced product cost, the manager must decide between the *economic* order quantity ($Q_E = \sqrt{2DO_c/C_c}$) and the quantity *discount* (Q_D). The overall approach is to find which option, Q_E or Q_D, minimizes total costs, which must now include the product cost. Thus the objective is to minimize

$$T_c = \text{total cost} = \text{ordering cost} + \text{carrying cost} + \text{product cost}$$

$$= \frac{D}{Q} O_c + \frac{QC_c}{2} + \text{product cost}$$

where product cost is usually expressed as annual demand D multiplied by the unit price *P*, or *DP*. By following four steps we can decide whether or not to take the quantity discount:

1. Calculate Q_E.
2. Calculate total cost using Q_E.
3. Calculate total cost using Q_D.
4. The optimum order quantity will be the quantity with the lowest cost—either Q_E or Q_D.

EXAMPLE 7.7

Given the following data, determine whether or not the quantity discount should be taken:

$$D = 500 \text{ units}$$

$$O_c = \$4.90$$

$$C_c = \$1$$

$$P = \$10$$

If inventory is purchased in lots of 80 units, the discount price will be $8 per unit.

$$P_D = \text{discount price}$$

$$= \$8$$

$$Q_D = \text{discount quantity}$$

$$= 80 \text{ units}$$

(continued)

1. Calculate Q_E.

$$Q_E = \sqrt{\frac{2DO_c}{C_c}}$$

$$= \sqrt{\frac{2(500)(4.9)}{1}} = \sqrt{4900}$$

$$= 70 \text{ units}$$

2. Calculate total cost for $Q = Q_E = 70$.

$$T_c = \frac{D}{Q} O_c + \frac{QC_c}{2} + PD = \frac{500}{70} 4.9 + \frac{70(1)}{2} + 10(500)$$

$$= 5070$$

3. Calculate total cost for $Q_D = 80$.

$$T_c = \frac{500}{80} \times 4.9 + \frac{80(1)}{2} + 8(500)$$

$$= 4071$$

4. Choose the lowest total cost quantity. In this example, the optimum order quantity is $Q^* = Q_D = 80$ units.

PROBLEM 7.12

Should the quantity discount be taken, given the following data on a hardware item stocked by the Hilliard Brothers Paint Store.

$$D = 2000 \text{ units}$$

$$O_c = \$10$$

$$C_c = \$1$$

$$P = \$1$$

(continued)

$$P_D = \text{discount price} = \$.75$$

$$Q_D = \text{discount quantity} = 2000 \text{ units}$$

1. $Q_E = \sqrt{}$

    $Q_E =$

2. T_c where $Q = Q_E =$

    $T_c =$

3. T_c where $Q = Q_D =$

    $T_c =$

4. Optimum order quantity is _____ $= Q\_\_$

PROBLEM 7.13

The regular price of a tape deck component is $20. On orders of 75 units or more, the price is discounted to $18.50. On orders of 100 units or more, the discount price is to $15.75. At present, Sound Business, Inc., a manufacturer of stereo components, has an inventory carrying cost of $1 per

(continued)

600

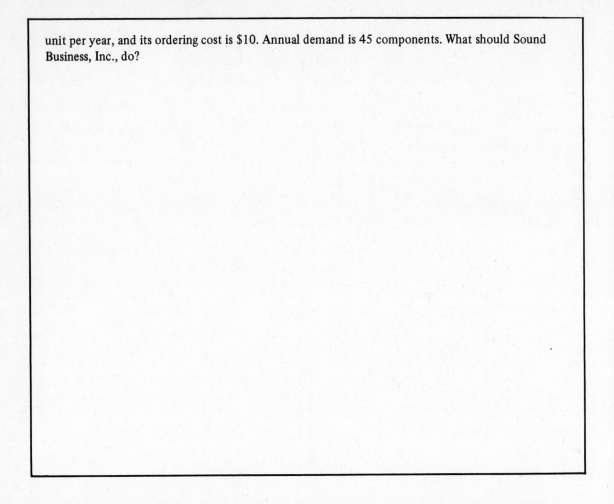

unit per year, and its ordering cost is $10. Annual demand is 45 components. What should Sound Business, Inc., do?

In the example and problems above we assumed that carrying costs stay the same when the discount is applied. Because the discount reduces the capital invested (from $10 to $8 per unit in Example 7.7), the per unit holding cost ($1 in that case) will probably be reduced by a small amount. If it appears that the carrying cost will change significantly, then a correction must be accounted for.

PROBABILISTIC INVENTORY MODELS

All of the inventory models we have discussed so far make the assumption that the demand for a product is constant and uniform. In this unit we will relax this assumption. The following inventory models apply when product demand is not known but can be specified by means of a probability distribution. These types of models are called *probabilistic inventory models.*

One of the most important concerns of management faced with uncertain demand is the possibility of a stockout. One approach is to carry extra units in inventory, or *safety stock,* to avoid this possibility. It involves adding the number of units of safety stock as a buffer to the reorder point. As you recall,

$$\text{Reorder point} \quad = \text{ROP} = dL$$

$$d \ = \ \text{daily demand}$$

$$L \ = \ \text{order lead time, or the number of working days} \\ \text{it takes to deliver an order}$$

The inclusion of safety stock (ss) changes the expression to

$$\text{ROP} = dL + \text{ss}$$

The amount of safety stock depends on the cost of incurring a stockout and the cost of carrying the extra inventory.

EXAMPLE 7.8

ABCO, Inc., has determined that its reorder point is $50(dL)$ units. Its carrying cost per unit per year is \$5 and stockout cost is \$40 per unit. ABCO has experienced the following probability distribution for inventory demand during the reorder period. The optimum number of orders per year is 6.

(continued)

Number of Units		Probability
	30	0.2
	40	0.2
ROP →	50	0.3
	60	0.2
	70	0.1
		1.0

How much safety stock should ABCO keep on hand?

The overall objective is to find the safety stock that minimizes the total additional inventory carrying costs and stockout costs on an annual basis. The annual carrying cost is simply the carrying cost multiplied by the units added to the ROP. For example, a safety stock of 20 units, which implies that the new ROP with safety stock is 70(= 50 + 20) raises the annual carrying cost by $5(20)=$100.

The stockout cost is more difficult to compute. For any safety stock level, it is the expected cost of stocking out. We can compute it by multiplying the number of units short by the probability by the stockout cost by the number of times per year the stockout can occur (or the number of orders per year). Then we add stockout costs for each possible stockout level for a given ROP. For zero safety stock, a shortage of 10 units will occur if demand is 60, and a shortage of 20 units will occur if the demand is 70. Thus the stockout costs for zero safety stock are:

(10 units short)(0.2)($40/stockout)(6 possible stockouts per year) + (20 units short)(0.1)($40)(6).

The following table summarizes the total costs for each alternative.

Safety Stock	Additional Carrying Cost	Stockout Cost	Total Cost
20	(20)($5) = $100	0	$100
10	(10)($5) = $50	(10)(0.1)($40)(6) = $240	$290
0	0	(10)(0.2)($40)(6) + (20)(0.1)($40)(6) = $960.00	$960

The safety stock with the lowest total cost is 20 units. This safety stock changes the reorder point to 50 + 20 = 70 units.

PROBLEM 7.14

A product is ordered once each year and the reorder point without safety stock (dL) is 100 units. Inventory carrying cost is $10 per unit per year, and the cost of a stockout is $50 per unit per year. Given the following demand probabilities during the reorder period, how much safety stock should be carried?

Demand During Reorder Period	Probability
0	0.1
50	0.2
ROP → 100	0.4
150	0.2
200	0.1

Safety Stock	Carrying Cost	Stockout Cost	Total Cost

When it is difficult or impossible to determine the cost of being out of stock, a manager may decide to follow a policy of keeping enough safety stock on hand to keep the number of stockouts to a minimum. The following example assumes that demand during the reorder period follows a normal curve.

EXAMPLE 7.9

The Hinsdale Company carries an inventory item that has a normally distributed demand during the reorder period. The mean (average) demand is 350 units and the standard deviation is 10. Hinsdale wants to follow a policy that results in stockouts occurring 5 percent of the time. How much safety stock should the firm maintain?

(continued)

The following figure may help you to visualize the example:

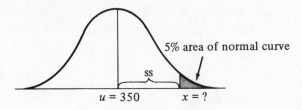

5% area of normal curve

ss

$u = 350$ $x = ?$

u = mean demand = 350 units

σ = standard deviation = 10

x = mean demand + safety stock

ss = safety stock = $x - u$

$$Z = \frac{x - u}{\sigma}$$

We use the properties of a standardized normal curve to get a Z value for an area under the normal curve of 0.95 (or $1 - 0.05$). Using a normal table (see Appendix A), we find a Z value of 1.65. Also

$$Z = \frac{x - u}{\sigma} = \frac{ss}{\sigma}$$

$$= 1.65 = \frac{ss}{\sigma}$$

Solving for safety stock gives:

$$ss = 1.65(10)$$

$$= 16.5 \text{ units}$$

PROBLEM 7.15

What safety stock should Inlux Corporation maintain if mean sales are 80 during the reorder period, the standard deviation is 7, and Inlux can tolerate stockouts 10 percent of the time?

(continued)

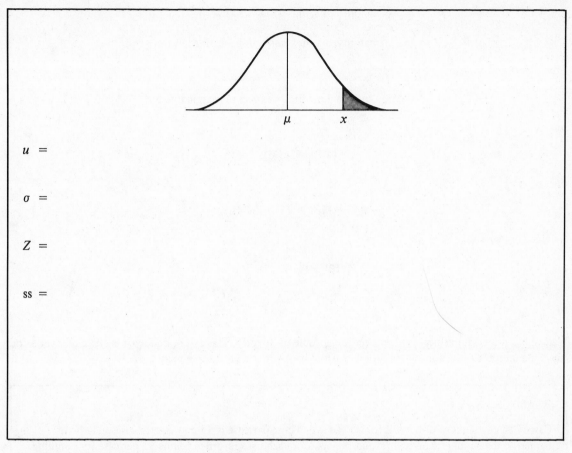

$u \ =$

$\sigma \ =$

$Z \ =$

ss $=$

Thus far we have seen how some probabilistic inventory models can help to determine safety stock and reorder points under conditions of uncertainty. Yet the operations manager faces many discrete stocking alternatives in which the demand for the product varies according to a probability distribution. As discussed in Unit 4, decision tables and trees are useful when a manager faces many alternatives and states of nature. For some types of inventory problems, shortcut methods exist. One such method is marginal analysis.

MARGINAL ANALYSIS

For many large inventory models, using a decision table to determine an optimal stocking policy would be tedious and cumbersome. With 20 possible demand values, for example, we would need a 20 × 20 decision table. Fortunately, there is an easier method for dealing with the problem if we can determine the marginal profit (MP) and a marginal loss (ML). Given any inventory level, we would add an additional unit to our inventory level only if its expected marginal profit equals or exceeds its expected marginal loss. This relationship can be expressed symbolically as follows:

$$P = \text{the probability of selling } \textit{at least} \text{ one additional unit}$$

$$= \text{the probability that demand will be at this level or greater}$$

The relationship is

$$\text{Expected marginal profit} \geq \text{expected marginal loss}$$

or

$$E(\text{MP}) \geq E(\text{ML})$$

or

$$P(\text{MP}) \geq (1 - P)(\text{ML})$$

Solving for P, we get

$$P(\text{MP}) + P(\text{ML}) \geq \text{ML}$$

or

$$P \geq \frac{\text{ML}}{\text{MP} + \text{ML}}$$

We can use this relationship to solve inventory problems directly. This type of analysis is especially good for one-time inventory decisions when reordering and back-ordering are not possible.

EXAMPLE 7.10

Cases of a particular product sell for $6 each. The cost per case is $3 and unsold cases may be re-turned to the supplier who will refund the cost for each case returned minus $1 per case for handling and storage. The probability distribution of demand is as follows:

Demand	Probability that Demand Will Be at This Level
5	0.2
6	0.3
7	0.5

1. From the previously developed relationship, we know that

$$P \geq \frac{\text{ML}}{\text{ML} + \text{MP}}$$

(continued)

2. The next step is to determine P. As you recall, P is the probability that demand will be at this level or greater. We can compute this *cumulative* probability as follows

Demand	Probability that Demand Will Be at This Level	Probability that Demand Will Be at This Level or Greater
5	0.2	$1.0 \geqslant .25$
6	0.3	$0.8 \geqslant .25$
7	0.5	$0.5 \geqslant .25$

$$\text{ML} = \text{marginal loss}$$

$$= \$1$$

$$\text{MP} = \text{marginal profit} = \$6 - \$3$$

$$= \$3$$

Thus

$$P \geqslant \frac{1}{1 + 3}$$

$$\geqslant 0.25$$

3. We keep adding additional units as long as the $P \geqslant \text{ML}/(\text{ML} + \text{MP})$ relationship holds.
   If we stock 7 units, our marginal profit will be greater than our marginal loss:

$$P \text{ at 7 units} \geqslant \frac{\text{ML}}{\text{ML} + \text{MP}}$$

$$0.5 \geqslant 0.25$$

Thus the optimal policy is to stock 7 units.

PROBLEM 7.16

Daily demand for lots of an item has the following probability distribution.

Demand (in lots)	Probability that Demand Will Be at this Level
0	0.2
1	0.3
2	0.4
3	0.1

A lot costs $8 and sells for $10. Unsold lots may be returned for a refund, but there is a $1 charge for handling. Determine the optimal stocking policy for the item.

PROBLEM 7.17

For a given product, ML = $4 and MP = $1. What stocking policy would you recommend in regard to the following demand distribution?

Demand (in units)	Probability that Demand Will Be at This Level
0	0.05
1	0.05
2	0.05
3	0.1
4	0.15
5	0.15
6	0.2
7	0.10
8	0.05
9	0.05
10	0.03
11	0.02
	1.00

ANSWERS

7.1
$$\text{Average inventory level} = Q/2$$

$$\text{Average dollar level} = \frac{PQ}{2}$$

The unit purchase price has also been called the unit cost C. In this case, the average dollar level becomes $CO/2$. In this book, we will use P.

7.2
$$Q^* = \sqrt{\frac{2DO_c}{IP}} = \sqrt{\frac{2(4900)(50)}{(0.20)(500)}} = \sqrt{4900}$$

$$= 70 \text{ units}$$

7.3
$$Q^* = \sqrt{\frac{2DO_c}{C_c}} = \sqrt{\frac{2(8000)(30)}{3}}$$

$$= 400 \text{ units}$$

$$N = \frac{D}{Q^*} = \frac{8000}{400}$$

$$= 20 \text{ orders}$$

N also can be calculated directly, as follows:

$$N = \sqrt{\frac{DC_c}{2O_c}} = \sqrt{\frac{8000(3)}{2(30)}} = \sqrt{400}$$

$$= 20 \text{ orders}$$

$$\text{Time between orders} = T = \frac{\text{no. working days}}{N} = \frac{200}{20}$$

$$= 10 \text{ days}$$

Hence, an order for 400 transistors is placed every 10 days. Presumably, then, 20 orders are placed each year.

7.4
$$\text{TC} = \frac{D}{Q} O_c + \frac{Q}{2} C_c$$

Since $Q*$ was found to be 400 units in Problem 7.3,

$$TC = \frac{(8000)(30)}{400} + \frac{(400)(3)}{2} = 600 + 600$$

$$= \$1200$$

7.5 $$TC \text{ (at 410 units)} = \frac{(8000)(30)}{(410)} + \frac{(410)(3)}{2}$$

$$= \$1200.37$$

$$TC \text{ (at 390 units)} = \frac{(8000)(30)}{(390)} + \frac{(390)(3)}{2}$$

$$= \$1200.38$$

The total cost is higher. The optimal order quantity that minimizes total cost is 400 units. Note too, that the cost difference is not that significant. Consequently minor errors or deviations probably do not drastically increase the total inventory cost.

7.6 $$d = \frac{10,000}{200}$$

$$= 50 \text{ units/day}$$

$$ROP = dL = (50 \text{ units/day})(5 \text{ days})$$

$$= 250 \text{ units}$$

Thus, Jessie should reorder when her stock of notebook binders reaches 250.

7.7   1. Order cost $= (D/Q)O_c$

2. Carrying cost $= \frac{1}{2}C_cQ[1 - (d/p)]$

3. Set ordering cost equal to carrying cost to obtain $Q*$:

$$\frac{D}{Q*}O_c = \frac{1}{2}C_cQ*[1 - (d/p)]$$

4. Solve for $Q*$:

$$Q*^2 = \frac{2DO_c}{C_c[1-(d/p)]}$$

$$Q* = \sqrt{\frac{2DO_c}{C_c[1-(d/p)]}}$$

7.8 $$Q* = \sqrt{\frac{2(1000)(20)}{1(1-(8/9)]}} = \sqrt{\frac{40,000}{1/9}} = \sqrt{360,000}$$

$$= 600$$

7.9   1. $$Q* = \sqrt{\frac{2DO_c}{C_c[1-(D/P)]}}$$

2. $$Q* = \sqrt{\frac{2(1000)(10)}{1[1-(1000/2000)]}} = \sqrt{\frac{20,000}{1/2}} = \sqrt{40,000}$$

$$= 200 \text{ units}$$

7.10   1. $$Q* = \sqrt{\left[\frac{2(10)(10,000)}{1}\right]\left(\frac{1+2}{2}\right)} = \sqrt{200,000\left(\frac{3}{2}\right)}$$

$$= \sqrt{300,000}$$

2. $Q* = 547$

3. $$S* = 547\left(\frac{2}{2+1}\right)$$

4. $S* = 365$

7.11   1. $$Q* = \sqrt{\frac{2(10)(100)}{4}\left(\frac{4+5}{5}\right)} = \sqrt{500\left(\frac{9}{5}\right)}$$

$$= \sqrt{900}$$

2. $Q* = 30 \text{ dishwashers}$

3. $S^* = 30\left(\dfrac{5}{4+5}\right)$

4. $S^* = 17$ dishwashers

7.12   1. $Q_E = \sqrt{\dfrac{2(2000)(10)}{1}}$

   $= 200$

2. T_c at $Q_E = \dfrac{2000}{200}\,10 + \dfrac{200(1)}{2} + 2000(1) = 100 + 100 + 2000$

   $= \$2200$

3. T_c at $Q_D = \dfrac{2000}{2000}\,10 + \dfrac{2000(1)}{2} + 2000(0.75) = 10 + 1000 + 1500$

   $= \$2510$

4. Optimum order quantity that minimizes total cost is Q_E:

$$Q_E = 200 \text{ units}$$

$$T_c \text{ for } Q_E = \$2200$$

7.13   1. $Q_E = \sqrt{\dfrac{2(10)(45)}{1}} = 30$ tape deck components

2. T_c at $Q_E = \dfrac{45}{30}(10) + \dfrac{30(1)}{2} + 20(45)$

   $= \$930$

3. T_c at 75 units $= \dfrac{45}{75}(10) + \dfrac{75}{2}(1) + 18.50(45) = 6 + 37.5 + 832.5$

   $= \$876$

$$T_c \text{ at 100 units} = \frac{45}{100}(10) + \frac{100}{2}(1) + 15.75(45) = 4.5 + 50 + 708.75$$

$$= \$763.25$$

4. The optimum order quantity that minimizes total inventory cost Q_D at 100 units is

$$Q^* = 100 \text{ units}$$

$$T_c = \$763.25$$

Since the annual demand is 45 units and Q^* is 100 units, an order is placed about every two years.

7.14

Safety Stock	Carrying Cost	Stockout Cost	Total Cost
0	0	(50)(0.2)($50)(1) + (100)(0.1)($50)(1) = $1000	$1000
50	(50)(10) = $500	(50)(0.1)($50)(1) = $250	$750
100	(100)(10) = $1000	0	$1000

The safety stock that minimizes total cost is 50 units. The reorder point becomes 100 units + 50 units = 150 units.

7.15

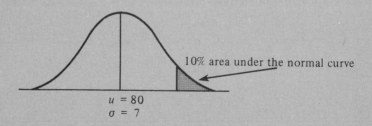

10% area under the normal curve

$u = 80$
$\sigma = 7$

1. Z at an area of 0.9 (or $1 - 0.10$) = 1.28 from Appendix A

2. $Z = 1.28 = \dfrac{x - u}{\sigma} = \dfrac{\text{ss}}{\sigma}$

3. $\text{ss} = 1.28\sigma$

4. $\text{ss} = 1.28(7) = 8.96$ units, or 9 units

7.16   1. $P \geqslant \dfrac{ML}{ML + MP}$

$ML = \$1$

$MP = \$10 - \$8 = \$2$

$P \geqslant \dfrac{\$1}{\$1 + \$2} = \dfrac{1}{3}$

$\geqslant 0.333$

2. The next step is to determine P.

Demand (in lots)	Probability that Demand Will Be at This Level	Probability that Demand Will Be at This Level or Greater
0	0.2	$(0.2+0.3+0.4+0.1) = 1.0 \geqslant 0.333$
1	0.3	$(0.3+0.4+0.1) = 0.8 \geqslant 0.333$
2	0.4	$(0.4+0.1) = 0.5 \geqslant 0.333$
3	0.1	$(0.1) = 0.1$ not $\geqslant 0.333$

3. Again, we will keep adding lots as long as the marginal profit of adding that one lot is greater than or equal to the marginal loss, as reflected in the relationship $P \geqslant ML/(MP + ML)$. Thus, in this problem, the optimal policy is to *stock 2 lots*.

7.17   1. $P \geqslant \dfrac{ML}{ML + MP} = \dfrac{\$4}{\$4 + \$1}$

$\geqslant 0.8$

(continued)

2. The next step is to determine P.

Demand (in units)	Probability that Demand Will Be at This Level	Probability that Demand Will Be at This Level or Greater
0	0.05	1.0 $\geqslant 0.8$
1	0.05	0.95 $\geqslant 0.8$
2	0.05	0.90 $\geqslant 0.8$
→ 3	0.1	0.85 $\geqslant 0.8$
4	0.15	0.75
5	0.15	0.60
6	0.2	0.45
7	0.10	0.25
8	0.05	0.15
9	0.05	0.10
10	0.03	0.05
11	0.02	0.02
	1.00	

3. The optimal policy is to stock 3 units.

HOMEWORK PROBLEMS

7.1. The demand for Rocky Flier football dolls is 10,000 dolls per year. The cost to place an order is $20 per order, and the carrying cost is $2.00 per doll per year.

a. Compute the order quantity.

b. Compute the order quantity when back ordering is allowed and the back ordering cost is $40 per doll per year.

c. Compute the order quantity when back ordering is allowed and the back ordering cost is $100 per doll per year.

d. Compute the order quantity when back ordering is allowed and the back ordering cost is $500 per doll per year.

e. Compute the order quantity when back ordering is allowed and the back ordering cost is $1,000 per doll per year.

f. What happens to the order quantity as the back ordering cost increases?

g. What assumptions are made with the back ordering model?

7.2. Georgia Products offers the following discount schedule for its four-by-eight-foot sheets of quality plywood.

Order	Unit Cost
9 sheets or less	$18.00
10 to 50 sheets	$17.50
More than 50 sheets	$17.25

Home Sweet Home Company orders plywood from Georgia Products. Home Sweet Home has an ordering cost of $45.00. The carrying cost is 20 percent, and the annual demand is 100 sheets. What do you recommend? (Note that the formula for Q^* on the top of p. 129 must now be used. Why?)

Unit 8

Material Requirements and Capacity Planning

In Unit 7, we investigated traditional inventory control techniques. In this unit we will explore two related concepts—material requirements planning and capacity requirements planning. We will start with material requirements planning.

MATERIALS REQUIREMENTS PLANNING (MRP)

In all of the inventory models discussed in Unit 7, we have assumed the demand for one item was independent of the demand for other items. For example, the demand for refrigerators is usually independent of the demand for dishwashers. Many inventory problems, however, are interrelated. The demand for one item is dependent on the demand for another item. Consider a manufacturer of small power lawn mowers. The demand for lawn mower wheels and spark plugs depends on the demand for lawn mowers. Four wheels and one spark plug go into each finished lawn mower. Usually when the demand for different items is dependent, the relationship between the items is known and constant. Thus you should forecast the demand for the final products and compute the requirements for component parts.

As in the previously discussed inventory models, the major questions to answer are "How much to order?" and "When to order?" But dependent demand can make inventory scheduling and planning very complex indeed. In these situations, you can rely on material requirements planning (MRP). Some of the benefits of MRP are:

1. Increased customer service and satisfaction
2. Reduced inventory costs
3. Better inventory planning and scheduling
4. Higher total sales
5. Faster response to market changes and shifts
6. Reduced inventory levels without reduced customer service

Although most MRP systems are computerized, the analysis is straightforward and similar from one computerized system to the next. A material structure tree and a material requirements plan are common elements of most systems. The following example reveals how to develop them.

EXAMPLE 8.1

The first step is to develop the material structure tree. Demand for product A is 50 units. Each unit of A requires 2 units of B and 3 units of C. Now, each unit of B requires 2 units of D and 3 units of E. Furthermore, each unit of C requires 1 unit of E and 2 units of F. Thus the demand for B, C, D, E, and F is completely dependent on the demand for A. Given this information, we can construct a material structure tree for the related inventory items:

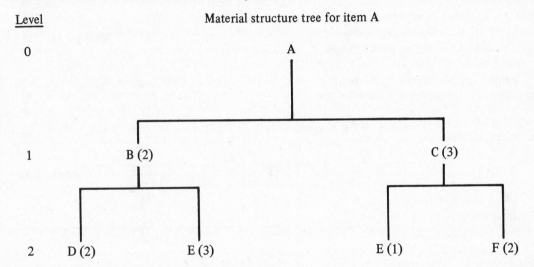

The structure tree has three levels: 0, 1, and 2. Items above any level are called *parents,* and items below any level are called *components.* There are three parents: A, B, and C. Each parent item has at least one level below it. Items B, C, D, E, and F are components because each item has at least one level above it. In this structure tree, B and C are both parents and components. The number in parentheses indicates how many units of that particular item are needed to make the item immediately above it. Thus B (2) means that it takes 2 units of B for every unit of A, and F (2) means that it takes 2 units of F for every unit of C.

Once we have developed the material structure tree, we can determine the number of units of each item required to satisfy demand. This information is displayed in the following table:

Part B:	2 × number of A's =	(2)(50) =	100
Part C:	3 × number of A's =	(3)(50) =	150
Part D:	2 × number of B's =	(2)(100) =	200
Part E:	3 × number of B's + 1 × number of C's =	(3)(100) + (1)(150) =	450
Part F:	2 × number of C's =	(2)(150) =	300

(continued)

Thus for 50 units of A, we will need 100 units of B, 150 units of C, 200 units of D, 450 units of E, and 300 units of F. Of course, we could have determined these numbers directly from the material structure tree by multiplying the numbers along the branches times the demand for A, which is 50 units for this problem. For example, the number of units of D needed is simply $(2)(2)(50) = 200$ units.

The next step is to construct a *gross material requirements plan.* This is a time schedule that shows when an item must be ordered from suppliers when there is no inventory on hand or when the production of an item must be started in order to satisfy the demand for the finished product by a particular date. Let's assume that one company produces all of the items in the foregoing list. It takes one week to make A, two weeks to make B, one week to make C, one week to make D, two weeks to make E, and three weeks to make F. Using this information, we can construct the gross material requirements plan and draw up a production schedule that will satisfy the demand of 50 units of A by a future date, as shown in Table 8.1.

Table 8.1. Gross Material Requirements Plan for 50 Units of A

	Week 1	2	3	4	5	6	Lead Time
A: Required date						50	
Order release					50		1 week
B: Required date					100		
Order release			100				2 weeks
C: Required date					150		
Order release				150			1 week
D: Required date			200				
Order release		200					1 week
E: Required date			300	150			
Order release	300	150					2 weeks
F: Required date				300			
Order release	300						3 weeks

The interpretation of the table is as follows: If you want 50 units of A at week 6, you must start the manufacturing process in week 5. Thus, in week 5, you will need 100 units of B and 150 units of C. These two items take two weeks and one week to produce (see lead times). Production of B should start in week 3, and C should start in week 4 (see order release figures for these items). Working backward, we can perform the same computations for all of the other items. The material rquirements plan graphically reveals when production of each item should begin and end in order to have 50 units of A at week 6.

PROBLEM 8.1

The demand for product S is 100 units. Each unit of S requires 1 unit of T and 0.5 units of U. Each unit of T requires 1 unit of V, 2 units of W, and 1 unit of X. Finally, each unit of U requires 0.5 units of Y and 3 units of Z. One firm manufactures all items. It takes two weeks to make S, one week to make T, two weeks to make U, two weeks to make V, three weeks to make W, one week to make X, two weeks to make Y, and one week to make Z. Construct a material structure tree and a gross material requirements plan for the dependent inventory items. Identify all levels, parents, and components.

So far, we have considered gross material requirements. In other words, we have assumed that there is no inventory on hand. When there is inventory on hand, you must calculate the actual, or net, requirements to avoid overstocking or overordering. In considering on-hand inventory, it is important to realize that the items actually contain subassemblies or parts. If the gross requirement for lawn mowers is 100 units and there are 20 lawn mowers on hand, the net requirement for lawn mowers is 80 (or 100 − 20). But each lawn mower on hand contains 4 wheels and 1 spark plug. As a result, the requirement for wheels drops by 80 wheels (20 lawn mowers on hand × 4 wheels/lawn mower), and the requirement for spark plugs drops by 20 (20 × 1). Thus, if there is inventory on hand for a parent item, the requirements for the parent item and all its components decrease because stored inside each lawn mower are all the components for lower-level parts.

EXAMPLE 8.2

In Example 8.1 we developed a structure tree and a gross requirements plan. Given the following on-hand inventory, we will now construct a net requirements plan.

Item	On-hand Inventory
A	10
B	15
C	20
D	10
E	10
F	5

Using these data, we can develop a net material requirements plan, which includes gross requirements, on-hand inventory, net requirements, planned-order receipt, and planned-order release for each item. We begin with A and work backward through the other items. Table 8.2 shows the net material requirements plan for product A.

(continued)

Table 8.2. Net Material Requirements Plan

Item	Inventory	1	2	3	4	5	6	Lead Time
				Week				
A	Gross						50	1 week
	On hand:10						10	
	Net						40	
	Order receipt						40	
	Order release					40		
B	Gross					80^A		2 weeks
	On hand:15					15		
	Net					65		
	Order receipt					65		
	Order release			65				
C	Gross					120^A		1 week
	On hand:20					20		
	Net					100		
	Order receipt					100		
	Order release				100			
D	Gross			130^B				1 week
	On hand:10			10				
	Net			120				
	Order receipt			120				
	Order release		120					
E	Gross			195^B	100^C			2 weeks
	On hand:10			10	0			
	Net			185	100			
	Order receipt			185	100			
	Order release	185	100					
F	Gross				200^C			3 weeks
	On hand:5				5			
	Net				195			
	Order receipt				195			
	Order release	195						

The net requirements plan is constructed like the gross requirements plan. Starting with item A, we work backword to determine net requirements for all items. To do these computations we constantly refer to the structure tree and lead times. The gross requirement for A is 50 units in week 6. Ten items are on hand, and thus the net requirements and planned-order receipt both are 40 items in

(continued)

week 6. Because of the one-week lead time, the planned-order release is 40 items in week 5 (see the arrow connecting the order receipt and other release). Look down column 5 and refer to the structure tree in Example 8.4. Eighty (2 X 40) items of B and 120 (3 X 40) items of C are required in week 5 in order to have a total of 50 items of A in week 6. The letter "A" to the right of the gross figure for item B and C means that this demand for B and C was generated as a result of the demand for the parent, A. Performing the same type of analysis for B and C yields the net requirements for D, E, and F. Note the on-hand inventory in row E week 4. It is zero because the on-hand inventory (10 units) was used to make B in column 3.

PROBLEM 8.2

Construct a net material requirements plan from the data in Problem 8.1 and the following on-hand inventory.

Item	On-hand Inventory
S	20
T	20
U	10
V	30
W	30
X	25
Y	15
Z	10

In Example 8.2 and Problem 8.2, we considered only one product and demand value. Fifty units of A were required in week 6 in Example 8.2, and 100 units of S were required in week 7 in Problem 8.2. Normally there is a demand for many products over time. For each product, management must prepare a master production schedule (see Table 8.3). We work each amount in the master production schedule through the net material requirements plan, as we did for 50 units of A and 100 units of S. The result is a much larger net material requirements plan.

Table 8.3. Master Production Schedule for A and S

Gross Requirements for Product A										
Week	6	7	8	9	10	11	12	13	14	and so on
Amount	50		100	47	60		110	75		

Gross Requirements for Product S										
Week	7	8	9	10	11	12	13	14	15	16	and so on
Amount	100	200	150			60	75		100		

Material requirements planning is not a static technique. Once you have established the material structure tree (also called the "bill of materials") and material requirements plan, you can modify them when changes in time requirements and in the production process occur. Thus, if one of the production time estimates was one week less than it should have been, you can add that week to the material requirements plan. If a technological breakthrough allows the construction of one of the intermediate inventory items with fewer parts, then you can alter the material structure tree and the material requirements plan accordingly. Regardless of the reason or cause of any changes, you can manipulate the model to reflect them. Thus you can always have an up-to-date schedule or plan that depicts when to begin production of all the intermediate inventory items to be sure of satisfying the demand for the finished product on time.

Performing the modifications suggested above as a result of a changing inventory system is cumbersome to do by hand. Indeed, it is likely that several errors will result when the dependent items are complex. Can you imagine how difficult it would be to construct a material structure tree or a material requirements plan for an automobile? It would take you forever, and making changes would be impossible. In general, MRP systems are computerized. The computerized programs, however, perform the same types of calculations that we have demonstrated in this unit. Furthermore, some MRP computer programs activate other computer programs that perform other applications. Sales ordering, invoicing, billing, purchasing, production scheduling, capacity planning, and warehouse management are a few examples. A central strength of MRP is its timely and accurate *replanning* capability. Due to scrappages, missed receiving dates, cancellations, and so on, it is not uncommon to run the MRP program about once a week. With MRP the operations manager can react to the real world.

So far, we have only considered one end-product. In the examples, this was Product A. For most manufacturing companies, there are normally two or more end-products that use some of the same parts or components. All of the end-products must be incorporated into a single net material requirements plan. This is handled in the next example and problem.

EXAMPLE 8.3

In the MRP examples, we developed a net material requirements plan for Product A. Now, we will show you how to modify the net material requirements plan when a second end-product is introduced. The second end-product will be called AA. The material structure tree for product AA is shown below:

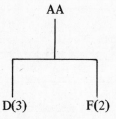

AA

D(3)   F(2)

Let's assume that we need 10 units of AA. With this information, we can compute the gross requirements for AA. This is done below:

Part D: 3 × number of AA's = 3 × 10 = 30

Part F: 2 × number of AA's = 2 × 10 = 20

In order to develop a net material requirements plan, we will need to know the lead time for AA. Let's assume that it is 1 week. We will also assume that we will need 10 units of AA in week 6, and that we have no units of AA on hand. Now, we are in a position to modify the net materials requirement plan for Product A to include AA. This is done in Table 8.3.

(continued)

Table 8.3   Net Material Requirements Plan, including AA

Item	Inventory	Week 1	2	3	4	5	6	Lead Time
AA	Gross						10	1 week
	On hand: 0						0	
	Net						10	
	Order receipt						10	
	Order release					10		
A	Gross						50	1 week
	On hand: 10						10	
	Net						40	
	Order receipt						40	
	Order release					40		
B	Gross					80^A		2 weeks
	On hand: 15					15		
	Net					65		
	Order receipt					65		
	Order release			65				
C	Gross					120^A		1 week
	On hand: 20					20		
	Net					100		
	Order receipt					100		
	Order release				100			
D	Gross			130^B		30^{AA}		1 week
	On hand: 10			10		0		
	Net			120		30		
	Order receipt			120		30		
	Order release		120		30			
E	Gross			195^B	100^C			2 weeks
	On hand: 10	0		10	0			
	Net			185	100			
	Order receipt			185	100			
	Order rlease	185	100					
F	Gross				200^C	20^{AA}		3 weeks
	On hand: 5				5	0		
	Net				195	20		
	Order receipt				195	20		
	Order release	195	20					

(continued)

Look at the top row of Table 8.3. As you can see, we have a gross requirement of 10 units of AA in week 6. Since we don't have any units of AA on hand, the net requirement is also 10 units of AA. Because it takes 1 week to make AA, the order release of 10 units of AA is in week 5. This means that we will start making AA in week 5 and have the finished units in week 6.

Because we start making AA in week 5, we must have 30 units of D and 20 units of F in week 5. See the rows for D and F in Table 8.3. The lead time for D is one week. Thus, we must give the order release in week 4 to have the finished units of D in week 5. You should note that there was no inventory on hand for D in week 5. The original 10 units of inventory of D that we started with was used in week 5 to make B, which was subsequently used to make A. We also need to have 20 units of F in week 5 in order to produce 10 units of AA by week 6. Again, we have no on-hand inventory of F in week 5. The original 5 units we started with was used in week 4 to make C, which was subsequently used to make A. The lead time for F is 3 weeks. Thus, the order release for 20 units of F must be in week 2. See the F row in Table 8.3.

The previous example shows how the inventory requirements of two products can be reflected in the same net materials requirements plan. Some manufacturing companies can have over 100 end-products that must be coordinated in the same net material requirements plan. Although this can be very complicated, the same principles we used in this example are employed. It is nice to know that several computer programs have been developed to handle large and complex manufacturing operations.

In addition to using MRP to handle end-products and finished goods, MRP can also be used to handle spare parts and components. This is important because most manufacturing companies sell these spare parts and components for maintenance. The net material requirements plan should also reflect these spare parts and components. This concept is explored in the next problem.

PROBLEM 8.3

In addition to 100 units of S, there is also a demand for 20 units of U, which is a component of S. The 20 units of U are needed for maintenance purposes. These units are needed one week before S, in week 6. Modify the net material requirements plan to reflect this component.

CAPACITY PLANNING

Capacity is the maximum output of a system at any given point in time. An automobile manufacturer, for example, can state its capacity in the total number of cars that can be produced at a particular point in time. Capacity is normally expressed as a rate, such as the number of automobiles that can be produced per week, per month, or per year. For most manufacturing companies, measuring capacity can be straight-forward. It is simply the maximum number of units that can be produced at a specific point in time. For service organizations, determining capacity can be more difficult. What is the capacity of a medical clinic, a church, or an alcohol abuse program? These service organizations do not grind out products. They provide a service that can be difficult to measure. In these cases, capacity can be measured in terms of the maximum input available at a specific point in time. This input can include the number of employees, the funds that are available, and equipment that can be used in providing the service.

Capacity planning and material requirements planning are interrelated topics. In some cases, the results of a net material requirements plan is not feasible. There is not enough capacity to implement it. Therefore, adjustments have to be made to the material requirements plan and future emphasis is needed in planning for capacity expansion. Developing one comprehensive model or approach that optimizes both the material requirements plan and the capacity plan would be very difficult, and therefore, most organizations perform these important functions together, but using separate techniques.

In the rest of this section, we will investigate the concepts and techniques of capacity planning in more detail. First, we will lay the groundwork for capacity planning in general. Several fundamental concepts and techniques will be presented. Then, we will investigate specific techniques that can be used to actually perform capacity planning. These techniques include forecasting, decision-tree analysis, and the transportation approach. Forecasting and decision-tree analysis have been covered in previous units. The transportation approach will be covered in a future unit. Therefore, we will only show you how to set up a typical transportation problem. The actual solution of these problems will be delayed until the transportation approach is covered in Unit 11.

Economies-of-scale is an important concept at the center of most capacity planning decisions. The heart of any capacity planning decision is to determine the maximum capacity at future points in time. If the future capacity is too small, there will be lost opportunity. On the other hand, a large facility or too much capacity can result in an unused investment and a waste of financial resources. In general, large facilities mean lowered unit cost. This concept is called economies-of-scale. This means that the larger the facility, the more economical it is to produce a particular product. This overall concept is shown in Figure 8.1.

As mentioned previously, capacity can be measured in units of output or units of input as related to the productive system—the number of pieces produced, tons of output, financial resources expended, and the total work time available. Many organizations use total work time available as a measure of overall capacity.

The design capacity of an organization is the maximum capacity that can be achieved. Few companies operate at the design capacity level. This would be like running your personal automobile as fast as it could go at all times. The result would be wasted fuel, unsafe operating conditions, and the great likelihood of blown engines and other mechanical problems. For the same reasons, most organizations operate their facilities at a rate under the design capacity. The actual capacity utilized might be 80 percent of the design capacity. This concept is called the percentage of utilization. It can be computed from the following formula:

$$\text{Utilization} = \frac{\text{Optimal Output}}{\text{Design Capacity}}$$

Another consideration is system efficiency. Depending upon how facilities are implemented and their subsequent operation, it may be difficult or impossible to reach 100 percent efficiency. As many new car owners know, the actual mileage they obtain may be far below the stated mileage published by the car manufacturer. Typically, system efficiency is expressed as a percentage of the design capacity. Without a knowledge of system efficiency and utilization, it is impossible to compute the rated capacity. The rated capacity is a measure of the maximum usable capacity of a particular facility. It will always be less than or equal to the design capacity. The equation used to compute rated capacity in terms of hours per week is given below:

$$\begin{pmatrix} \text{Rated} \\ \text{Capacity} \end{pmatrix} = \begin{pmatrix} \text{Number of} \\ \text{Machines} \end{pmatrix} \begin{pmatrix} \text{Machine} \\ \text{Hours} \end{pmatrix} \begin{pmatrix} \text{Utilization} \end{pmatrix} \begin{pmatrix} \text{System} \\ \text{Efficiency} \end{pmatrix}$$

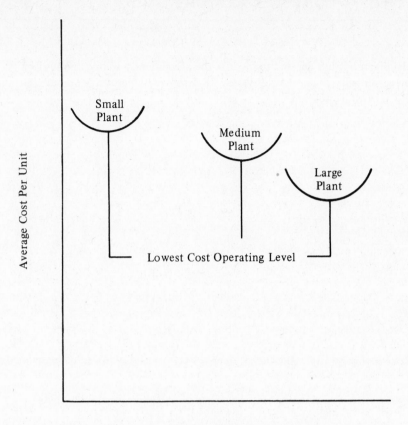

Figure 8.1. Economies of Scale

EXAMPLE 8.4

The North Atlantic Manufacturing Company has a facility for processing petroleum products. The facility has a system efficiency of 90 percent, and the utilization is 80 percent. Three subfacilities are used to process the petroleum products. The facilities operate seven days a week and three 8-hour shifts per day. What is the rated capacity?

In order to compute the rated capacity, we must multiply the number of subfacilities times the number of machine hours times the utilization times the system efficiency. Currently, there are three subfacilities. Each facility is used seven days a week, three shifts a day. Therefore, each subfacility is utilized for 168 hours per week ($168 = 7 \times 3$ shifts per day $\times 8$ hours per shift). With this information, the rated capacity can be determined. This is done as follows:

$$\text{Rated Capacity} = (3)(168)(.8)(.9) = 363 \text{ hours/week}$$

PROBLEM 8.4

North Atlantic Manufacturing has decided to increase their facilities by adding one subfacility. Doing this, however, will reduce their overall system efficiency to 85 percent. Compute the new rated capacity under this situation.

Determining future capacity requirements can be a very complicated procedure. One of the most important factors is future demand for goods and services. In some cases, future demand can be predicted with a high degree of certainty. Under these cases, deterministic procedures, including forecasting, financial analysis, and break-even analysis can be employed. In other cases, future demand for goods and services can be highly variable and uncertain. Under these circumstances, probabilistic models, including decision theory, can be employed. First, we will investigate the situation where demand for goods and services can be predicted with a respectable amount of precision.

When demand for goods and services can be forecasted with a high degree of precision, determining capacity requirements can be straightforward. It normally requires two phases. During the first phase, future demand is forecasted. During the second phase, this forecast is used to determine future capacity requirements.

When future demand can be predicted with accuracy, the first phase is to make a demand forecast. Forecasting techniques were described in detail in a previous unit. If you have not covered this unit, or if you have not studied this material recently, you may wish to review the unit on forecasting before proceeding any further.

EXAMPLE 8.5

During the last several years, demand for petroleum products from North Atlantic Manufacturing has been steady and predictable. Furthermore, there has been a direct relationship between barrels of petroleum products processed and rated capacity expressed in hours per week. This has allowed the executives of North Atlantic Manufacturing to forecast rated capacity with a fair degree of accuracy. Furthermore, North Atlantic Manufacturing has found that a simple moving average using three periods has been successful. North Atlantic Manufacturing has compiled the following data that it would like to use to forecast future demand for rated capacity. This is shown below:

Month	Rated Capacity Hours/Week
Jan	500
Feb	510
Mar	514
Apr	520
May	524
June	529

With the above data, it is possible to project rated capacity into the future.

PROBLEM 8.5

In a previous unit on forecasting, you were shown how to develop a moving average forecast, using a 3 period average technique. With the data presented in the above example, compute the forecasted capacity for North Atlantic Manufacturing for the month of July.

The previous example and problem reveal the use of only one forecasting technique. In addition to a simple moving average, there are many other techniques, including regression analysis, weighted moving average, and exponential smoothing. Furthermore, it is possible to compare various forecasting techniques to determine the most accurate one for a particular application. This can be done using scatter diagrams and a number of other techniques. You are encouraged to review the forecasting unit in this book or to investigate forecasting in more detail in a quantitative analysis book, such as *Quantitative Analysis* by the authors and published by Allyn and Bacon for further discussion.

Once the rated capacity has been forecasted, the next step is to determine the types of facilities to be employed to satisfy these future demand requirements. The overall concept is shown in Figure 8.2.

As seen in Figure 8.2, future demand has been forecasted to increase at a fairly constant rate. Figure 8.2 also reveals how new capacity can be planned for future demand growth. As seen in Figure 8.2, new capacity is acquired at the beginning of year one. This capacity will be sufficient to handle increased demand until the beginning of year two. At the beginning of year two, new capacity is again acquired which will allow the organization to meet demand to the beginning of the year three. This process can be continued indefinitely into the future.

The capacity plan shown in Figure 8.2 is only one of an almost limitless number of plans to satisfy future demand. In this figure, new capacity was acquired at the beginning of year one and at the beginning of year two. It would also be possible to acquire one large facility at the beginning of year one that would satisfy demand until the beginning of year three. This is shown in Figure 8.3.

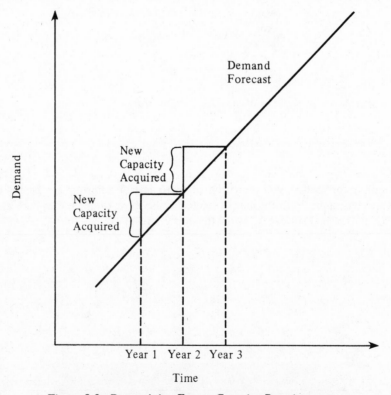

Figure 8.2. Determining Future Capacity Requirements

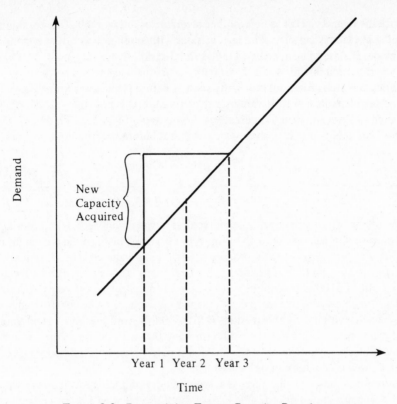

Figure 8.3. Determining Future Capacity Requirements

In Figure 8.3, new capacity is acquired during the beginning of year one which will satisfy future demand until the beginning of year three. Figure 8.2 and Figure 8.3 reveal only two possible alternatives. In some cases, deciding between alternatives can be relatively easy. The total cost of each alternative can be computed and the alternative with the least total cost is selected. In other cases, determining the capacity of future facilities can be much more complicated. Some companies use break-even analysis and select the alternative with the shortest break-even period. Other companies perform detailed and sophisticated financial analysis. This financial analysis can compare net present value or the internal rate of return. These concepts were presented in previous units, and therefore they will not be discussed in more detail. In most cases, there are numerous subjective factors that are difficult to quantify and measure. These factors include the potential of technological obsolescence, future developments in productive systems, building restrictions, capital restrictions work-force limitations and problems, local, state, and federal laws and regulations, and so on.

When future demand for goods and services, and therefore rated capacity, are subject to fluctuation, deterministic procedures are normally not adequate. In these cases, we must look at probabilistic models to solve capacity requirements problems. Typically, the decision will be what size facility to build to meet future demand. In some cases, no new facilities should be acquired. The major variable deals with demand factors and the overall market favorability for the goods and services being produced. In some cases, it is possible to categorize the future market as being either favorable or unfavorable. One technique that has been used successfully in making capacity planning decisions with an uncertain future is decision theory. Decision theory includes the use of both decision tables and decision trees.

Decision theory was discussed in Unit 4. This particular technique lays out alternatives and various states of nature. For capacity planning situations, the state of nature typically is future demand or market favorability. With probability values for the various states of nature, it is possible to make decisions that maximize the expected value of the various alternatives. If you haven't had decision theory, or if you have covered it some time ago, you may wish to review this unit before proceeding to the next example and problem.

EXAMPLE 8.6

Southern Hospital Supplies, a company that manufactures hospital bandages, is considering capacity expansion. Their major alternatives are to do nothing, build a small plant, build a medium plant, or build a large plant. The new facility would produce a new type of bandage, and currently the potential or marketability for this product is unknown. If a large plant is constructed and a favorable market exists, a profit of $100,000 could be realized. On the other hand, a large plant would result in a $90,000 loss with an unfavorable market. If a medium plant were to be constructed, a $60,000 profit would be realized with a favorable market. A $10,000 loss would result from an unfavorable market. A small plant, on the other hand, would return $40,000 with favorable market conditions. If the market conditions were unfavorable, the hospital supply company would only lose $5,000. Of course, there is always the option of doing nothing.

Recent market research indicates that there is a .4 probability of a favorable market, which means that there is a .6 probability of an unfavorable market. With this information, it is possible to select the alternative that will result in the highest or maximum expected monetary value. This can be done using either a decision tree or a decision table.

PROBLEM 8.6

Using the techniques you learned in Unit 4 on decision theory, solve the capacity problem given in the above example.

(continued)

Another decision related to capacity planning is facility location. Where should new capacity be placed? One objective of locating future capacity is to minimize total costs, including transportation and manufacturing costs. In a future unit, on facility location and transportation models, you will learn how to locate new capacity in such a way as to minimize total costs. Factory and warehouse capacities along with unit transportation costs are required. Furthermore, unit production costs and other related costs are needed. With this information, it is possible to employ several alternative transportation models. The model that yields the lowest total cost will indicate the desired location for new facilities. Because this technique is covered in detail in a future unit, it will not be discussed in more detail here.

ANSWERS

8.1   Level   Material structure tree

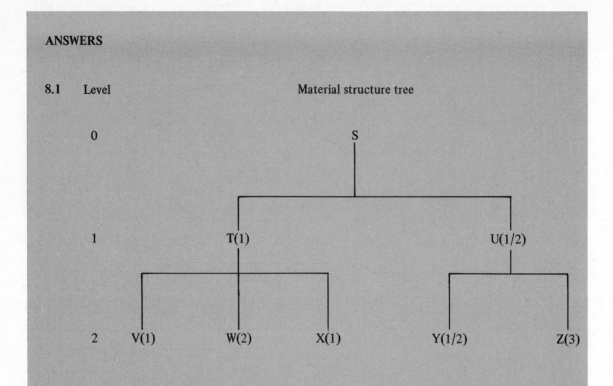

Part T: (1)(100)   = 100 units

Part U: (1/2)(100) = 50 units

Part V: (1)(100)   = 100 units

Part W: (2)(100)   = 200 units

Part X: (1)(100)   = 100 units

Part Y: (1/2)(50)   = 25 units

Part Z: (3)(50)   = 150 units

Parent items are S, T, and U. Component items are T, U, V, W, X, Y, and Z.

(continued)

Gross Material Requirements Plan

	Week							Lead Time
	1	2	3	4	5	6	7	
S: Required date							100	2 weeks
Order release					100			
T: Required date					100			1 week
Order release				100				
U: Required date					50			2 weeks
Order release			50					
V: Required date				100				2 weeks
Order release		100						
W: Required date				200				3 weeks
Order release	200							
X: Required date				100				1 week
Order release			100					
Y: Required date			25					2 weeks
Order release	25							
Z: Required date			150					1 week
Order release		150						

8.2   Net Material Requirements Plan

Item Inventory		Week 1	2	3	4	5	6	7	Lead Time
S	Gross							100	2 weeks
	On hand: 20							20	
	Net							80	
	Order receipt							80	
	Order release					80			
T	Gross					80^S			1 week
	On hand: 20					20			
	Net					60			
	Order receipt					60			
	Order release				60				
U	Gross					40^S			2 weeks
	On hand: 10					10			
	Net					30			
	Order receipt					30			
	Order release			30					
V	Gross				60^T				2 weeks
	On hand: 30				30				
	Net				30				
	Order receipt				30				
	Order release		30						
W	Gross				120^T				3 weeks
	On hand: 30				30				
	Net				90				
	Order receipt				90				
	Order release	90							
X	Gross				60^T				1 week
	On hand: 25				25				
	Net				35				
	Order receipt				35				
	Order release			35					
Y	Gross			15^U					2 weeks
	On hand: 15			15					
	Net			0					
	Order receipt			0					
	Order release	0							
Z	Gross			90^U					1 week
	On hand: 10			10					
	Net			80					
	Order receipt			80					
	Order release		80						

8.3 Net Material Requirements Plan

Item Inventory		1	2	3	4	5	6	7	Lead Time
S	Gross							100	2 weeks
On hand: 20								20	
	Net							80	
	Order receipt							80	
	Order release					80			
T	Gross					80^S			1 week
On hand: 20						20			
	Net					60			
	Order receipt					60			
	Order release				60				
U	Gross					40^S	20		2 weeks
On hand: 10						10	0		
	Net					30	20		
	Order receipt					30	20		
	Order release			30	20				
V	Gross				60^T				2 weeks
On hand: 30					30				
	Net				30				
	Order receipt				30				
	Order release		30						
W	Gross				120^T				3 weeks
On hand: 30					30				
	Net				90				
	Order receipt				90				
	Order release	90							
X	Gross				60^T				1 week
On hand: 25					25				
	Net				35				
	Order receipt				35				
	Order release			35					
Y	Gross			15^U	10^U				2 weeks
On hand: 15				15	0				
	Net			0	10				
	Order receipt			0	10				
	Order release	0	10						
Z	Gross			90^U	60^U				1 week
On hand: 10				10	0				
	Net			80	60				
	Order receipt			80	60				
	Order release		80	60					

8.4   System efficiency   = .85

Utilization   = .80

No. of Subfacilities   = 4

No. of subfacility hours = 168

$$\text{Rated capacity} = (4)(168)(.80)(.85)$$

$$= 457 \text{ hours/week}$$

8.5

Month	Rated Capacity (Hours/Week)	Forecasted Rated Capacity
Jan.	500	
Feb.	510	
Mar.	514	
Apr.	520	508 = (500 + 510 + 514)/3
May	524	516 = (510 + 514 + 520)/3
June	529	519 = (514 + 520 + 524)/3
July		524 = (520 + 524 + 529)/3

The demand for July is 524 hours/week.

8.6

Alternative ↓ \\ States of Nature →	Favorable Market	Unfavorable Market	EMV
Large Plant	$100,000	$−90,000	$−14,000
Medium Plant	$ 60,000	$−10,000	$18,000
Small Plant	$ 40,000	$ −5,000	$13,000
Do Nothing	0	0	0
Probability	.4	.6	

Maximum EMV is the medium plant. The expected monetary value (EMV) is $18,000.

HOMEWORK PROBLEMS

8.1. Jerry Young is thinking about opening a bicycle shop in his hometown. Jerry loves to take his own bike on fifty-mile trips with his friends, but he believes that any small business should only be started if there is a good chance of making a profit. Jerry can open a small shop, a large shop, or no shop at all. Because there will be a five-year lease on the building that Jerry is thinking about using, he wants to make sure that he makes the correct decision. Jerry is also thinking about hiring his old marketing professor to conduct a marketing research study. If the study is conducted, the results could be either favorable or unfavorable. Develop a decision tree for Jerry.

Jerry Young has done some analysis about the probability of the bicycle shop. If Jerry builds the large bicycle shop, he will earn $60,000 if the market is favorable, but he will lose $40,000 if the market is unfavorable. The small shop will return a $30,000 profit in a favorable market and a $10,000 loss in an unfavorable market. At the present time, he believes that there is a 50–50 chance that the market will be favorable. His old marketing professor will charge him $5,000 for the marketing research. It is estimated that there is a .6 probability that the survey will be favorable. Furthermore, there is a .9 probability that the market will be favorable given a favorable outcome from the study. However, the marketing professor has warned Jerry that there is only a .12 probability of a favorable market if the marketing research results are not favorable. Jerry is confused. What should he do?

8.2. Currently, Cascade Manufacturing uses three machines in their manufacturing process. The current number of machine hours available is 168, the utilization is 80%, and the system efficiency is 90%. Paul Peterson is considering the addition of new machines and the impact it will have on the rated capacity. If an additional machine is obtained, which would give Paul a total of 4 machines, the system efficiency will drop to 85%. With a fifth machine, system efficiency will drop to 80%; with a sixth machine, system efficiency will drop to 75%; and with a seventh machine, system efficiency will drop to 70%. Compute the rated capacity for 3, 4, 5, 6, and 7 machines, respectively.

Linear Programming: Applications and the Graphical Solution

Linear programming (LP) is a mathematical technique designed to help production and operations managers in their planning and decision making. In general, it is popular with organizations that want to make most effective use of their resources. Resources typically include machinery, manpower, money, time, warehouse space, and raw materials. A few examples of problems in which LP has been successfully applied in a management setting are:

1. Development of a production schedule that will satisfy future demands for a firm's product and at the same time *minimize* total production and inventory costs.
2. Selection of the product mix in a factory to make best use of machine and labor-hours available while *maximizing* the firm's profit.
3. Determination of grades of petroleum products to yield the *maximum* profit.
4. Selection of different blends of raw materials in feed mills to produce finished feed combinations at *minimum* cost.
5. Determination of a distribution system that will *minimize* total shipping cost from several warehouses to various market locations.
6. Allocation of a limited advertising budget among radio, TV, and newspaper spots in order to *maximize* advertising effectiveness.

All LP problems, as you can see, seek to maximize or minimize some quantity (usually profit or cost). We refer to this property as the *objective* of an LP problem. The second property that LP problems have in common is the presence of restrictions, or *constraints*, that limit the degree to which we can achieve our objective. We want, therefore, to maximize or minimize a quantity (the objective function) subject to limited resources (the constraints).

FORMULATING LINEAR PROGRAMMING PROBLEMS

A very common linear programming problem is the *product mix problem*. Two or more products are usually formed using limited resources, such as personnel and machines. The profit that the firm seeks to maximize is based on the profit contribution per unit of each product. The company would like to determine how many units of each product it should produce so as to maximize overall profit, given its limited resources.

EXAMPLE 9.1

Dress-Rite, a clothing manufacturer that produces men's shirts and pajamas, has two primary resources available: sewing-machine time (in the sewing department) and cutting-machine time (in the cutting department). Over the next month, Dress-Rite can schedule up to 280 hours of work on sewing machines and up to 450 hours of work on cutting machines. Each shirt produced requires 1 hour of sewing time and 1.5 hours of cutting time. Outputting each pair of pajamas requires 0.75 hours of sewing time and 2 hours of cutting time.

Our goal here is to develop relationships to describe these restrictions. One general relationship is that the amount of resource *used* is less than or equal to the amount of resource *available*. In the case of the sewing department, for example, the total time used is

(1 hour/shirt) × (number of shirts produced) + (0.75 hour/pajama) × (number of pajamas produced)

To express the LP constraints for this problem mathematically, we let

$$X_1 = \text{number of shirts produced}$$

$$X_2 = \text{number of pajamas produced}$$

Then,

First Constraint: $1X_1 + 0.75X_2 \leq 280$ hours of sewing-machine time available—our first scarce resource

Second Constraint: $1.5X_1 + ②X_2 \leq 450$ hours of cutting-machine time available—our second scarce resource

Note: This means that each pair of pajamas takes 2 hours of the cutting resource.

EXAMPLE 9.2

In Example 9.1, Dress-Rite established two constraints that will keep the company from exceeding the machine time available for production. But the company wants to determine the product mix (of shirts and pajamas) that will maximize its profits. Its accounting department analyzes cost and sales figures and states that each shirt produced will yield a $4 contribution to profit and that each pair of pajamas will yield a $3 contribution to profit.

This information can be used to create the LP *objective function* for this problem.

(continued)

Objective function: maximize total contribution to profit $= \$4X_1 + \$3X_2$

where

$$X_1 = \text{number of shirts produced}$$

$$X_2 = \text{number of pajamas produced}$$

EXAMPLE 9.3

Electro Corporation manufactures two electrical products: air conditioners and fans. The assembly processes are similar in that both require a certain amount of wiring and drilling. Each air conditioner takes 4 hours of wiring and 2 hours of drilling. Each fan must go through 2 hours of wiring and 1 hour of drilling. During the next production period, 240 hours of wiring time and up to 100 hours of drilling time are available. Each air conditioner sold yields a profit of $27; each fan brings $15 profit. Electro would like to formulate this production mix situation as a linear programming problem. Let

$$X_1 = \text{number of air conditioners to be produced}$$

$$X_2 = \text{number of fans to be produced}$$

Objective function: maximize profit $= \$27X_1 + \$15X_2$

First Constraint: $4X_1 + 2X_2 \leqslant 240$ hours of wiring time available

Second Constraint: $2X_1 + 1X_2 \leqslant 100$ hours of drilling time available

Constraints added to ensure nonnegative solutions: $X_1 \geqslant 0$ and $X_2 \geqslant 0$.

Without these simple constraints on each X_i, it might be possible for a solution to tell us to produce a negative number of one of the products.

We see in the preceding examples that each linear programming problem contains (1) an objective function, (2) certain constraints (resulting from limited resources) that keep the firm from producing unlimited quantities and hence making unlimited profits, and (3) certain interactions among variables, namely, the more units of one product produced the less the firm can make of other products.

PROBLEM 9.1

The Thompson Tub Company manufactures two lines of bathtubs, called Model A and Model B. Every tub requires a blend of steel and zinc. The company has available a total of 25,000 pounds of steel and 6500 pounds of zinc. Each Model A bathtub requires a mixture of 130 pounds of steel and 20 pounds of zinc, and each yields a profit to the firm of $85. Each Model B tub brings a profit of $70; each requires 100 pounds of steel and 30 pounds of zinc. Formulate these data as a linear programming problem with an objective function and constraints.

PROBLEM 9.2

The Outdoor Furniture Corporation manufactures two products: benches and picnic tables for use in yards and parks. The firm has two main resources: its carpenters (labor force) and a supply of redwood for use in the furniture. During the next production period, 1200 hours of manpower are available under a union agreement. The firm also has a stock of 5000 pounds of quality redwood. Each bench that Outdoor Furniture produces requires 4 labor-hours and 10 pounds of redwood; each picnic table takes 7 labor-hours and 35 pounds of redwood. Completed benches yield a profit of $9 each, and tables a profit of $20 each. Formulate this information as a LP problem.

It is possible for a problem to include many more variables, or products, as we shall see shortly. It is possible also to have more than two constraints even in a simple LP problem. Constraints may involve not only less-than-or-equal-to ($\leqslant$) inequalities, but equalities ($=$) and greater-than-or-equal-to ($\geqslant$) inequalities as well.

EXAMPLE 9.4

Referring back to Example 9.3, we are informed that Electro Corporation's management wants to reformulate their LP production mix problem. In particular, management has become very sensitive to wasted, or unused, time on an expensive new drilling machine and wants *all* 100 hours of available time used in production. The firm also decides that to ensure an adequate supply of air conditioners for a contract, they should manufacture *at least* 25 air conditioners. Since there was an oversupply of fans during the previous period, management also insists that *no more than* 70 fans be produced. We can use this new information to reformulate the constraints of Example 9.3.

Objective function: Maximize profit $= \$27X_1 + \$15X_2$ (no change)

Wiring time constraint: $4X_1 + 2X_2 \leqslant 240$ (no change)

Drilling time constraint: $2X_1 + 1X_2 = 100$ (now an equality)

Air conditioner minimum constraint: $X_1 \geqslant 25$ (new greater-than-or-equal-to ($\geqslant$) constraint)

Fan maximum constraint: $X_2 \leqslant 70$ (new fan constraint)

PROBLEM 9.3

MSA Computer Corporation manufactures two models of minicomputers, the Alpha 6 and the Beta 8. The firm employs five workers, each of whom puts in 160 hours per month on the assembly line. Management insists on maintaining full employment during next month's operations. It requires 18 labor-hours to assemble each Alpha 6 computer and 25 labor-hours to assemble each Beta 8 model. MSA would like to see at least 10 Alpha 6's produced but no more than 20 Beta 8's during the

(continued)

production period. Alpha 6's generate $1200 profit per unit, and Beta 8's yield $1800 each. Formulate an LP problem using these data.

GRAPHICAL REPRESENTATION OF CONSTRAINTS

In order to determine the optimal solution to a linear programming problem, we must first identify a set, or region, of feasible solutions. When there are only two variables in the problem, as in the previous examples and problems, we can plot the constraints on a two-dimensional graph. The variable X_1 is usually treated as the horizontal axis and the variable X_2 as the vertical axis. Because of the nonnegativity constraints (i.e., $X_1 \geqslant 0, X_2 \geqslant 0$), we are always working in the first (or northeast) quadrant of the graph.

EXAMPLE 9.5

The Flair Furniture Company produces inexpensive tables and chairs. It has formulated the following LP problem:

$$\text{Maximize profit} = \$7X_1 + \$5X_2$$

subject to

$$\text{Constraint A: } 4X_1 + 3X_2 \leqslant 24 \text{ (first resource)}$$

$$\text{Constraint B: } 2X_1 + 1X_2 \leqslant 10 \text{ (second resource)}$$

$$X_1 \geqslant 0, X_2 \geqslant 0$$

(continued)

where X_1 stands for the number of tables produced and X_2 stands for the number of chairs produced.

We would like to graphically represent the constraints of this problem. The first step is to convert the constraint *inequalities* into *equalities* (or equations); that is,

$$\text{Constraint A: } 4X_1 + 3X_2 = 24$$

$$\text{Constraint B: } 2X_1 + 1X_2 = 10$$

The equation for constraint A is plotted in Figure 9.1a and constraint B in Figure 9.1b

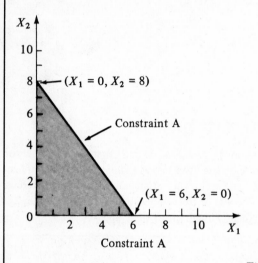
Constraint A

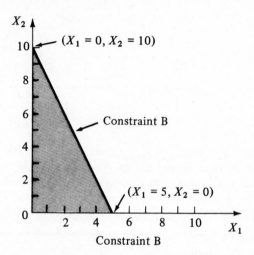
Constraint B

Figure 9.1.

To plot the line in Figure 9.1a, all we need to do is to find the points at which the line $4X_1 + 3X_2 = 24$ intersects the X_1 and X_2 axes. When $X_1 = 0$ (the location where the line touches the X_2 axis), it implies that $3X_2 = 24$ or that $X_2 = 8$. Likewise, when $X_2 = 0$, we see that $4X_1 = 24$ and that $X_1 = 6$. Thus constraint A is bounded by the line running from $(X_1 = 0, X_2 = 8)$ to $(X_1 = 6, X_2 = 0)$. The shaded area represents all points that satisfy the original *inequality*.

(continued)

Constraint B is illustrated similarly in Figure 9.1b. When $X_1 = 0$, then $X_2 = 10$ and when $X_2 = 0$, then $X_1 = 5$. Constraint B then is bounded by the line between $(X_1 = 0, X_2 = 10)$ and $(X_1 = 5, X_2 = 2)$. The shaded area represents the original inequality.

Figure 9.2 shows both constraints together. The shaded region is the part that satisfies both restrictions.

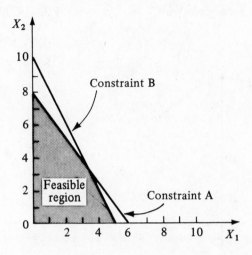

Figure 9.2. Feasible Region for the Flair Furniture Company

The shaded region in Figure 9.2 is called the *area of feasible solutions,* or simply the *feasible region.* This region must satisfy *all* conditions specified by the program's constraints and thus is the region where all constraints overlap. Any point in the region would be a *feasible solution* to the Flair Furniture Company problem. Any point outside the shaded area would represent an *infeasible solution.* Hence, it would be feasible to manufacture three tables and two chairs $(X_1 = 3, X_2 = 2)$, but it would violate the constraints to produce seven tables and four chairs. This can be seen by plotting these points on the above graph.

PROBLEM 9.4

Graphically represent the following constraints and their feasible region.

First constraint: $2X_1 + 1X_2 \leqslant 40$

Second constraint: $X_1 + 3X_2 \leqslant 30$

$X_1 \geqslant 0, X_2 \geqslant 0$

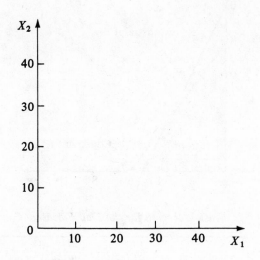

PROBLEM 9.5

Graph the following constraints and indicate the area of feasible solutions.

$$\text{Constraint A: } 5X_1 + 2X_2 \leqslant 250$$

$$\text{Constraint B: } 1X_1 + 2X_2 \leqslant 150$$

$$\text{Constraint C: } \qquad X_1 \leqslant 40$$

$$X_1 \geqslant 0, X_2 \geqslant 0$$

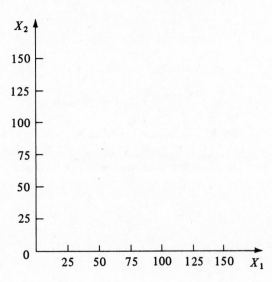

THE CORNER-POINT SOLUTION METHOD

There are several approaches to take in finding the optimal solution once you have graphically established the feasible region. The simplest one conceptually is called the *corner-point method*. The mathematical theory behind linear programming states that the optimal solution to any problem (that is, the values of

X_i that yield the maximum profit or minimum cost) will lie at a corner point, or extreme point, of the feasible region. Hence, it is necessary only to find the values of the variables at each corner, for the maximum profit or optimal solution will lie at one of them.

EXAMPLE 9.6

Let us solve the problem graphed in Example 9.5 using the corner-point method. The Flair Furniture Company LP formulation is repeated here:

Maximize profit = $\$7X_1 + \$5X_2$

subject to

$$\text{Constraint A: } 4X_1 + 3X_2 \leqslant 24$$

$$\text{Constraint B: } 2X_1 + 1X_2 \leqslant 10$$

$$X_1 \geqslant 0, X_2 \geqslant 0$$

As we saw in Figure 9.2, the feasible region is a four-sided polygon with four corners, or extreme points. These point are labeled "a," "b," "c," and "d" in Figure 9.3. To find the (X_1, X_2) values producing the maximum profit, we first find the coordinates of each corner and test their profit levels.

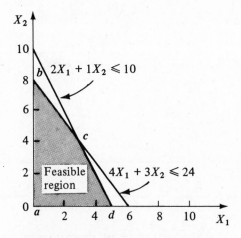

*Figure 9.3. Corner Points in the Flair
Furniture Problem*

(continued)

Point a: $X_1 = 0, X_2 = 0$ Profit $= \$7(0) + \$5(0) = \quad 0$

Point b: $X_1 = 0, X_2 = 8$ Profit $= \$7(0) + \$5(8) = \$40$

Point d: $X_1 = 5, X_2 = 0$ Profit $= \$7(5) + \$5(0) = \$35$

We skipped corner point c momentarily because in order to accurately establish its coordinates, we must solve for the intersection of the two constraint lines. To do so, we apply the method of *simultaneous equations* to the two lines,

$$4X_1 + 3X_2 = 24 \quad \text{and} \quad 2X_1 + 1X_2 = 10$$

This means that we will try to eliminate either of the two variables, and solve for the other. We may do so by multiplying the second equation by -2 [which is $-2(2X_1 + 1X_2 = 10)$] and by adding it to the first equation. Hence,

$$4X_1 + 3X_2 = 24$$

$$\underline{-4X_1 - 2X_2 = -20}$$

$$1X_2 = 4$$

When $X_2 = 4$, then $4X_1 + 3(4) = 24$, which implies $4X_1 = 12$ or $X_1 = 3$. Now we can evaluate point c.

Point c: $(X_1 = 3, X_2 = 4)$ Profit $= \$7(3) + \$5(4) = \$41$

Because point c produces the highest profit of any corner point, the product mix $X_1 = 3$ tables and $X_2 = 4$ chairs is the optimal solution to Flair Furniture's problem. This solution will result in a profit of \$41.

PROBLEM 9.6

The objective function corresponding to the LP constraints in Problem 9.4 is:

$$\text{Maximize profit} = \$9X_1 + \$7X_2$$

The problem's constraints, you may recall, were

$$2X_1 + 1X_2 \leqslant 40$$

$$X_1 + 3X_2 \leqslant 30$$

Solve for the optimal solution using the corner-point method.

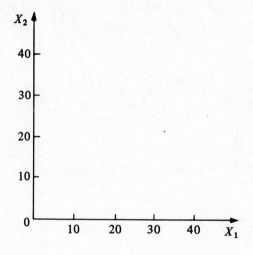

PROBLEM 9.7

Use the corner-point method to solve Problem 9.5 for its optimal solution. The objective function is:

$$\text{Maximize profit} = 2X_1 + 3X_2$$

The constraints are:

$$5X_1 + 2X_2 \leqslant 250$$

$$1X_1 + 2X_2 \leqslant 150$$

$$1X_1 \leqslant 40$$

$$X_1 \geqslant 0, X_2 \geqslant 0$$

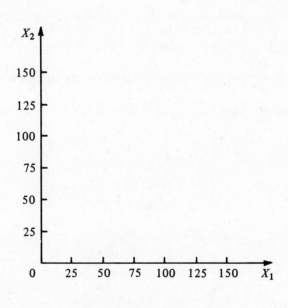

Note *that although the optimal solution to Example 9.6 and Problems 9.6 and 9.7 fell at a corner point located at the intersection of two constraint equations, this is by no means always the case. The optimal solution could just as easily be at a corner bordering on the X_1 or X_2 axis (such as points b or d in Example 9.6). The location depends upon the values of the objective function coefficients..*

MINIMIZATION PROBLEMS IN LP

Many linear programming problems involve *minimizing* an objective, such as cost, instead of maximizing a profit function. Basically, we can apply the same graphical approach to the solution of these types of problems.

EXAMPLE 9.7

Wacker Chemicals, Inc., produces two types of photo-developing fluids. The first, a black-and-white picture chemical, costs Wacker $2500 per ton to produce. The second, a color photo chemical, costs $3000 per ton.

Based upon an analysis of current inventory levels and outstanding orders, Wacker's production manager has specified that at least 30 tons of the black-and-white chemical and at least 20 tons of the color chemical must be produced during the next month. In addition, the manager notes that an existing inventory of a highly perishable raw material needed in both chemicals must be used within 30 days. In order to avoid wasting the expensive raw material, Wacker must produce a total of at least 60 tons of the photo chemicals in the next month.

We may formulate this information as a minimization LP problem. Let

$$X_1 = \text{number of tons of black-and-white picture chemical produced}$$

$$X_2 = \text{number of tons of color picture chemical produced}$$

$$\text{Minimize cost} = \$2500X_1 + \$3000X_2$$

subject to

$$X_1 \geqslant 30 \text{ tons of black-and-white chemical}$$

$$X_2 \geqslant 20 \text{ tons of color chemical}$$

$$X_1 + X_2 \geqslant 60 \text{ total tonnage}$$

$$X_1, X_2 \geqslant 0 \text{ nonnegativity requirements}$$

EXAMPLE 9.8

To solve Example 9.7 graphically, we construct the problem's feasible region:

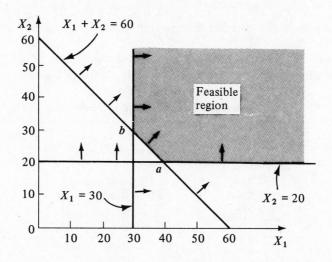

Minimization problems are often unbounded outward (that is, on the right side and on the top), but this characteristic causes no problem in solving them. As long as they are bounded inward (on the left side and the bottom), we can establish corner points. The optimal solution will lie at one of the corners.

In this case, there are only two corner points, **a** and **b**. It is easy to determine that at point **a**, $X_1 = 40$ and $X_2 = 20$ and that at point **b**, $X_1 = 30$ and $X_2 = 30$. The optimal solution is found at the point yielding the lowest total cost.

$$\text{Total cost at } \mathbf{a} = 2500X_1 + 3000X_2$$

$$= 2500(40) + 3000(20)$$

$$= \$160,000$$

$$\text{Total cost at } \mathbf{b} = 2500X_1 + 3000X_2$$

$$= 2500(30) + 3000(30)$$

$$= \$165,000$$

The lowest cost to Wacker Chemicals, Inc., is at point **a**. Hence the production manager should produce 40 tons of the black-and-white chemical and 20 tons of the color photo chemical.

PROBLEM 9.8

The Holiday Meal Turkey Ranch is considering buying two different types of turkey feed. Each feed contains, in varying proportions, some or all of the three nutritional ingredients essential for fattening turkeys. Brand X feed costs the ranch $.02 per pound. Brand Z costs $.03 per pound. The rancher would like to determine the lowest-cost diet that meets the minimum monthly intake requirement for each nutritional ingredient.

The following table contains relevant information about the composition of Brand X and Brand Z feeds, as well as the minimum monthly requirement for each nutritional ingredient per turkey.

Composition of Each Pound of Feed

Ingredient	Brand X Feed	Brand Z Feed	Minimum Monthly Requirement
A	5 oz.	10 oz.	90 oz.
B	4 oz.	3 oz.	48 oz.
C	0.5 oz.	0	1.5 oz.
Cost/lb.	$.02	$0.03	

Formulate an LP problem for the turkey ranch.

PROBLEM 9.9

Draw the feasible solution region for the constraints that you set in Problem 9.8, calculate the cost at each corner point, and indicate the value of the optimal solution.

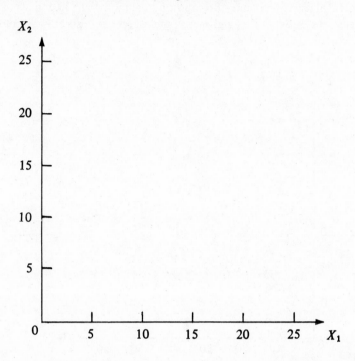

PROBLEM 9.10

The Sweet Smell Fertilizer Company markets bags of manure labeled "not less than 60 pounds dry weight." The manure is a combination of compost and sewage wastes. To provide a quality fertilizer, each bag should contain at least 30 pounds of compost but no more than 40 pounds of sewage. Each pound of compost costs Sweet Smell $.05 and each pound of sewage costs $.04. Formulate and solve this LP problem.

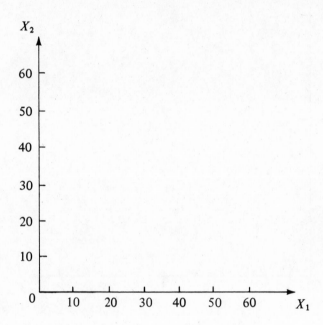

LINEAR PROGRAMMING APPLICATIONS

With the experience you gained earlier in this unit formulating relatively simple LP problems, you are now ready to tackle some larger ones. The foregoing examples and problems each contained just two variables (X_1 and X_2). Unfortunately, most real-world problems contain many more variables and cannot be solved graphically. (The graphical approach is valid only when the LP model has exactly two variables—which correspond to the two axes on a graph). In Unit 10 we will talk about a new method, the simplex algorithm, for handling larger problems. But right now, let us use the principles already developed to formulate a few, more complex problems. The practice you will get by "paraphrasing" the following LP situations should help develop your skills for applying linear programming to other common production and operations situations.

Problem 9.11 involves another *production mix* decision. Limited resources must be allocated among various products that a firm produces. The firm's overall objective is to manufacture the selected products in such quantities as to maximize total profits.

PROBLEM 9.11

The Failsafe Electronics Corporation primarily manufactures four highly technical products, which it supplies to aerospace firms that hold NASA contracts. Each of the products must pass through the following departments before they are shipped: wiring, drilling, assembly, and inspection. The time requirements (in hours) for each unit produced and its corresponding profit value are summarized in this table:

| | Department | | | | Unit |
Product	Wiring	Drilling	Assembly	Inspection	Profit
XJ201	0.5	3	2	0.5	$9
XM897	1.5	1	4	1.0	$12
TR29	1.5	2	1	0.5	$15
BR788	1.0	3	2	0.5	$11

The production time available in each department each month and the minimum monthly production requirement to fulfill contracts are as follows:

Department	Capacity (in hours)	Product	Minimum Production Level
Wiring	1500	XJ201	150
Drilling	1700	XM897	100
Assembly	2600	TR29	300
Inspection	1200	BR788	400

(continued)

The production manager has the responsibility of specifying production levels for each product for the coming month. Help him by setting up the constraints and objective function for Failsafe's problem.

Problem 9.12 is an example of the *diet problem,* which was originally used by hospitals to determine the most economical diet for patients. Known in agricultural applications as the *feed mix problem,* the diet problem involves specifying a food or feed ingredient combination that will satisfy stated nutritional requirements at a minimum cost level.

PROBLEM 9.12

The Feed 'N Ship Ranch fattens cattle for local farmers and ships them to meat markets in Kansas City and Omaha. The owners of the ranch seek to determine the amounts of cattle feed to buy to satisfy minimum nutritional standards and, at the same time, minimize total feed costs.

The feed mix may contain three grains in the following proportions *per pound of feed*:

| | Feed | | |
Ingredient	Stock X	Stock Y	Stock Z
A	3 oz.	2 oz.	4 oz.
B	2 oz.	3 oz.	1 oz.
C	1 oz.	0 oz.	2 oz.
D	6 oz.	8 oz.	4 oz.

(continued)

The cost per pound of grains X, Y, and Z is $.02, $.04, and $.025, respectively. The minimum requirement per cow per month is 64 ounces of ingredient A, 80 ounces of ingredient B, 16 ounces of ingredient C, and 128 ounces of ingredient D.

The ranch faces one additional restriction—it can obtain only 500 pounds of Stock Z per month from the feed supplier, regardless of its need. Since there are usually 100 cows at the Feed 'N Ship Ranch at any given time, this constraint limits the amount of Stock Z for use in the feed of each cow to no more than 5 pounds, or 80 ounces, per month.

Formulate this information as a linear programming problem.

One of the most important areas of linear programming application is *production scheduling.* Solving a production scheduling problem allows the production manager to set up an efficient, low-cost production schedule for his product over several production periods. Basically, the problem resembles the common product-mix model for each period in the future. Production levels must allow the firm to meet demand for its product within manpower and inventory limitations. The objective is either to maximize profit or to minimize the total cost (production plus inventory).

EXAMPLE 9.9 and PROBLEM 9.13

The Simone Appliance Company is thinking of manufacturing and selling trash compactors on an experimental basis over the next six months. The manufacturing costs and selling prices of the compactors are projected to vary from month to month. Table 9.1 gives these forecast costs and prices.

(continued)

Table 9.1. Manufacture Costs and Selling Price

Month	Manufacturing Cost	Selling Price (during month)
Jul.	$60	—
Aug.	$60	$80
Sept.	$50	$60
Oct.	$60	$70
Nov.	$70	$80
Dec.	—	$90

All compactors manufactured during any month are shipped out in one large load at the end of that month. The firm can sell as many units as it produces, but its operation is limited by the size of its warehouse, which holds a maximum of 100 compactors.

Simone's production manager, Tom White, needs to determine the number of compactors to manufacture and sell each month in order to maximize the firm's profit. Simone has no compactors on hand at the beginning of July and wishes to have no compactors on hand at the end of the test period in December.

To formulate this LP problem, Tom White lets

$X_1, X_2, X_3, X_4, X_5, X_6$ = number of units *manufactured* during July (first month), August (second month), etc.

$Y_1, Y_2, Y_3, Y_4, Y_5, Y_6$ = number of units *sold* during July, August, etc.

He notes that because the company starts with no compactors (and because it takes one month to gear up and ship out the first batch), it cannot sell any units in July (that is, $Y_1 = 0$). Also, since it wants zero inventory at the end of the year, manufacture during the month of December must be zero (that is, $X_6 = 0$).

Profit for Simone Appliances is sales minus purchase cost. Hence Tom White's objective function is

$$\text{Maximize profit} = 80Y_2 + 60Y_3 + 70Y_4 + 80Y_5 + 90Y_6$$

$$- (60X_1 + 60X_2 + 50X_3 + 60X_4 + 70X_5)$$

The first part of this expression is the sales price times the units sold each month. The second part is the manufacture cost; namely, the costs from Table 9.1 times the units manufactured.

To set up the constraints, White needs to introduce a new set of variables: $I_1, I_2, I_3, I_4, I_5, I_6$. These

(continued)

represent the inventory at the end of a month (after all sales have been made and after the amount produced during the month has been stacked in the warehouse). Thus,

$$
\begin{array}{cccccc}
\text{inventory at} & & \text{inventory at} & & \text{current} & & \text{this month's} \\
\text{end of this} & = & \text{end of} & + & \text{month's} & - & \text{sales} \\
\text{month} & & \text{previous month} & & \text{production} & &
\end{array}
$$

For July, this is $I_1 = X_1$, since there is neither previous inventory nor sales. For August,

$$I_2 = I_1 + X_2 - Y_2$$

Completion of this problem requires ten more constraints. Establishing them is a job that we leave to *you*! First, set up four constraints to represent the remaining months (September through December). Then, set up six constraints to guarantee that storage at the warehouse never exceeds its capacity of 100 units.

PROBLEM 9.14

Al Simone, president of the Simone Appliance Company, examines his production manager's LP formulation (Problem 9.13) and turns red with fury. "Dummy," he screams at Tom White, "that objective function isn't going to maximize our profit at all! It doesn't take into account our inventory carrying costs."

(continued)

Poor Tom! What he evidently failed to recall was that there is a cost, called the *inventory carrying cost*, associated with holding a unit of inventory in stock.

After Simone calms down, he and White estimate that, on a monthly basis, inventory carrying cost per trash compactor is $.90. Furthermore, they assume that monthly ending inventories are an acceptable approximation of the average inventory levels during the month.

Given this assumption and the above information, rewrite the complete objective function for the Simone Appliance Company.

The above production scheduling problem is somewhat simplified relative to real-world dynamic problems. If several products were manufactured and sold, however, instead of only one, and if constraints on cash available and production rates were added, the problem would indeed become difficult.

ANSWERS

9.1   Let

$$X_1 = \text{number of Model A bathtubs produced}$$

$$X_2 = \text{number of Model B bathtubs produced}$$

Maximize profit $= 85X_1 + 70X_2$
subject to the constraints

$$130X_1 + 100X_2 \leqslant 25{,}000 \text{ (pounds of steel)}$$

$$20X_1 + \ 30X_2 \leqslant \ 6500 \text{ (pounds of zinc)}$$

$$X_1 \geqslant \ 0, X_2 \geqslant \ 0 \text{ (nonnegativity constraints)}$$

9.2   The data can be summarized in tabular form:

	Bench	Table	Amount Available
Resource 1: Manpower	4	7	1200 hours
Resource 2: Redwood	10	35	5000 pounds
Profit contribution per unit	$9	$20	

Let

$$X_1 = \text{number of benches produced}$$

$$X_2 = \text{number of tables produced}$$

Maximize profit $= 9X_1 + 20X_2$
subject to

$$4X_1 + \ 7X_2 \leqslant 1200$$

$$10X_1 + 35X_2 \leqslant 5000$$

$$X_1 \geqslant 0 , X_2 \geqslant 0$$

9.3   Let

$$X_1 = \text{number of Alpha 6 minicomputers assembled}$$

$$X_2 = \text{number of Beta 8 minicomputers assembled}$$

Objective function: Maximize profit $= 1200X_1 + 1800X_2$

First constraint: $18X_1 + 25X_2 = 800$ (total labor-hours available during month
$= 5$ workers $\times$ 160 hours each)

Second constraint: $X_1 \geqslant 10$ (produce at least 10 Alphas)

Third constraint: $X_2 \leqslant 20$ (produce no more than 20 Betas)

$$X_1 \geqslant 0, \ X_2 \geqslant 0$$

9.4   Computation for points at which constraints intersect the X_1 and X_2 axes:

First constraint: $2X_1 + X_2 \leqslant 40$
When $X_1 = 0$, $1X_2 = 40$, then $X_2 = 40$; when $X_2 = 0$, $2X_1 = 40$, then $X_1 = 20$.

Second constraint: $1X_1 + 3X_2 \leqslant 30$
When $X_1 = 0$, $3X_2 = 30$, then $X_2 = 10$; when $X_2 = 0$, $1X_1 = 30$, then $X_1 = 30$.

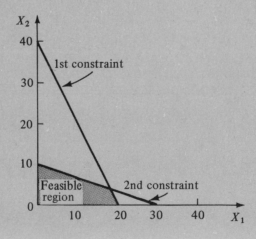

9.5   Computing end points of each constraint:

Constraint A: $5X_1 + 2X_2 \leqslant 250$
When $X_1 = 0$, $2X_2 = 250$, then $X_2 = 125$; when $X_2 = 0$, $5X_1 = 250$, then $X_1 = 50$.

Constraint B: $1X_1 + 2X_2 \leqslant 150$
When $X_1 = 0$, $2X_2 = 150$, then $X_2 = 75$; when $X_2 = 0$, $1X_1 = 150$, then $X_1 = 150$.

Constraint C: $X_1 \leqslant 40$
This is the vertical line $X_1 = 40$. It does not depend on what the value of X_2 is.

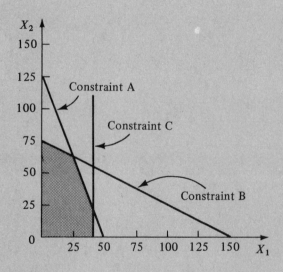

9.6

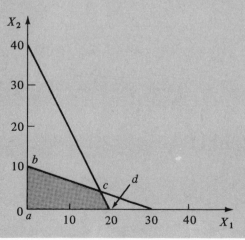

(continued)

Corner point a: $(X_1 = 0, X_2 = 0)$ Profit $= 0$

Corner point b: $(X_1 = 0, X_2 = 10)$ Profit $= 9(0) + 7(10) = \$70$

Corner point d: $(X_1 = 20, X_2 = 0)$ Profit $= 9(20) + 7(0) = \$180$

Corner point c is obtained by solving equations $2X_1 + 1X_2 = 40$ and $X_1 + 3X_2 = 30$ simultaneously. Multiply the second equation by -2 and add it to the first.

$$2X_1 + 1X_2 = 40$$

$$\underline{-2X_1 - 6X_2 = -60}$$

$$-5X_2 = -20$$

Thus, $X_2 = 4$.

$$X_1 + 3(X_2 = 4) = 30 \quad \text{or} \quad X_1 + 12 = 30 \quad \text{or} \quad X_1 = 18$$

Corner point c: $(X_1 = 18, X_2 = 4)$ Profit $= 9(18) + 7(4) = \$190$

Hence the optimal solution is

$$X_1 = 18, X_2 = 4 \quad \text{Profit} = \$190$$

9.7   This problem has five corner points to evaluate.

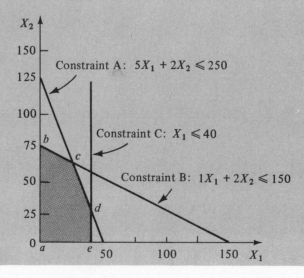

(continued)

Corner point a: $(X_1 = 0, X_2 = 0)$ Profit = 0

Corner point b: $(X_1 = 0, X_2 = 75)$ Profit = $2(0) + 3(75) = \$225$

Corner point e: $(X_1 = 40, X_2 = 0)$ Profit = $2(40) + 3(0) = \$80$

Corner point c is at the intersection of $5X_1 + 2X_2 = 250$ and $1X_1 + 2X_2 = 150$. We can simply subtract the second equation from the first (or vice versa) to eliminate the X_2 variable.

$$5X_1 + 2X_2 = 250$$

$$\underline{-1X_1 - 2X_2 = -150}$$

$$4X_1 \qquad = 100$$

Thus, $X_1 = 25$. Since $5X_1 + 2X_2 = 250$, then $5(25) + 2X_2 = 250$ and $2X_2 = 125$ or $X_2 = 62.5$.

Corner point c: $(X_1 = 25, X_2 = 62.5)$ Profit = $2(25) + 3(62.5) = \$237.50$

Finally, corner point d is at the intersection of the equations $X_1 = 40$ and $5X_1 + 2X_2 = 250$. Since we know that $X_1 = 40$, then $5(40) + 2X_2 = 250$ or $X_2 = 25$.

Corner point d: $(X_1 = 40, X_2 = 25)$ Profit = $2(40) + 3(25) = \$155$

The optimal solution is, then, at point c, namely, $X_1 = 25$, $X_2 = 62.5$; Profit = $\$237.50$.

9.8   Let

X_1 = number of pounds of Brand X feed purchased

X_2 = number of pounds of Brand Z feed purchased

Objective function: Minimize cost = $\$0.02X_1 + \$0.03X_2$

First constraint: $5X_1 + 10X_2 \geqslant 90$ ounces of ingredient A per month

Second constraint: $4X_1 + 3X_2 \geqslant 48$ ounces of ingredient B per month

Third constraint: $0.5X_1 \qquad \geqslant 1.5$ ounces of ingredient C per month

$$X_1 \geqslant 0, \quad X_2 \geqslant 0$$

9.9

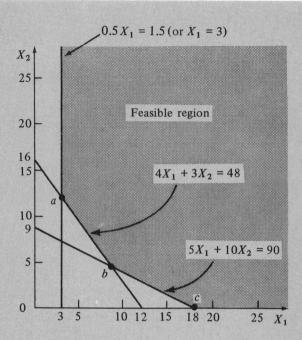

Using the corner-point method, we determine the coordinates of each of the three corner points and then calculate the cost at each.

For point a, we find the coordinates at the intersection of $X_1 = 3$ and $4X_1 + 3X_2 = 48$. Substitute $X_1 = 3$ into the latter equation to obtain $4(3) + 3X_2 = 48$, which implies $3X_2 = 36$, or $X_2 = 12$. Thus,

$$\text{Point a:} \quad (X_1 = 3, X_2 = 12) \quad \text{Cost} = \$0.02(3) + \$0.03(12) = \$.42$$

For point b, we solve equations $4X_1 + 3X_2 = 48$ and $5X_1 + 10X_2 = 90$ simultaneously. (Multiply the first equation by −5, the second equation by 4, and add them together.)

$$\text{Point b:} \quad (X_1 = 8.4, X_2 = 4.8) \quad \text{Cost} = \$0.02(8.4) + \$0.03(4.8) = \$.312$$

$$\text{Point c:} \quad (X_1 = 18, X_2 = 0) \quad \text{Cost} = \$0.02(18) + \$0.03(0) \quad = \$.36$$

Minimum cost is at $X_1 = 8.4$ pounds of Brand X and $X_2 = 4.8$ pounds of Brand Z (per turkey per month) for a cost of $.312 per turkey.

9.10 Let

$$X_1 = \text{number of pounds of compost in each bag}$$

$$X_2 = \text{number of pounds of sewage waste in each bag}$$

Minimize cost = $\$.05X_1 + \$.04X_2$
subject to

$$X_1 + X_2 \geqslant 60 \text{ pounds minimum per bag}$$

$$X_1 \geqslant 30 \text{ pounds of compost per bag}$$

$$X_2 \leqslant 40 \text{ pounds of sewage per bag}$$

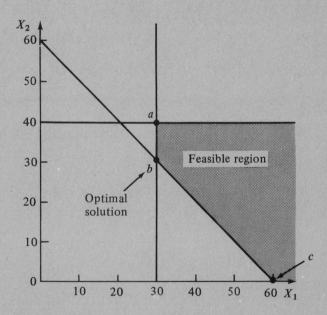

Corner point a: $(X_1 = 30, X_2 = 40)$ Cost = $\$.05(30) + \$.04(40) = \$3.10$

Corner point b: $(X_1 = 30, X_2 = 30)$ Cost = $\$.05(30) + \$.04(30) = \$2.70$

Corner point c: $(X_1 = 60, X_2 = 0)$ Cost = $\$.05(60) + \$.04(0) = \$3.00$

9.11   Let

$$X_1 = \text{number of units of XJ201 produced}$$

$$X_2 = \text{number of units of XM 897 produced}$$

$$X_3 = \text{number of units of TR 29 produced}$$

$$X_4 = \text{number of units of BR788 produced}$$

Maximize profit $= 9X_1 + 12X_2 + 15X_3 + 11X_4$
subject to

$$0.5X_1 + 1.5X_2 + 1.5X_3 + 1X_4 \leqslant 1500 \text{ hours of wiring available}$$

$$3X_1 + 1X_2 + 2X_3 + 3X_4 \leqslant 1700 \text{ hours of drilling available}$$

$$2X_1 + 4X_2 + 1X_3 + 2X_4 \leqslant 2600 \text{ hours of assembly available}$$

$$0.5X_1 + 1X_2 + 0.5X_3 + .5X_4 \leqslant 1200 \text{ hours of inspection}$$

$$X_1 \qquad\qquad\qquad \geqslant 150 \text{ units of XJ201}$$

$$X_2 \qquad\qquad \geqslant 100 \text{ units of XM897}$$

$$X_3 \qquad \geqslant 300 \text{ units of TR 29}$$

$$X_4 \geqslant 400 \text{ units of BR788}$$

$$X_1, X_2, X_3, X_4 \geqslant 0$$

9.12   Let

$$X_1 = \text{number of pounds of Stock X purchased per cow each month}$$

$$X_2 = \text{number of pounds of Stock Y purchased per cow each month}$$

$$X_3 = \text{number of pounds of Stock Z purchased per cow each month}$$

(continued)

Minimum cost $= 0.02X_1 + 0.04X_2 + 0.025X_3$
subject to

Ingredient A requirement: $3X_1 + 2X_2 + 4X_3 \geqslant 64$

Ingredient B requirement: $2X_1 + 3X_2 + 1X_3 \geqslant 80$

Ingredient C requirement: $1X_1 + 0X_2 + 2X_3 \geqslant 16$

Ingredient D requirement: $6X_1 + 8X_2 + 4X_3 \geqslant 128$

Stock Z limitation: $\qquad\qquad X_3 \leqslant 80$

$$X_1, X_2, X_3 \geqslant 0$$

9.13 Constraints for the remaining months are as follows:

September: $I_3 = I_2 + X_3 - Y_3$

October: $I_4 = I_3 + X_4 - Y_4$

November: $I_5 = I_4 + X_5 - Y_5$

December: $I_6 = I_5 - Y_6$

Constraints for the storage capacity are

$I_1 \leqslant 100$

$I_2 \leqslant 100$

$I_3 \leqslant 100$

$I_4 \leqslant 100$

$I_5 \leqslant 100$

$I_6 = 0$ (in order to end up with zero inventory at the end of December)

9.14 Maximize profit $= 80Y_2 + 60Y_3 + 70Y_4 + 80Y_5 + 90Y_6 - (60X_1 + 60X_2 + 50X_3$
$+ 60X_4 + 70X_5) - (0.9I_1 + 0.9I_2 + 0.9I_3 + 0.9I_4 + 0.9I_5)$

HOMEWORK PROBLEMS

9-1. The advertising agency promoting the new Breem dishwashing detergent wants to get the best exposure possible for the product within the $100,000 advertising budget ceiling placed upon it. To do so, the agency needs to decide how much of the budget to spend on each of its two most effective media: (1) television spots during the afternoon hours and (2) large ads in the city's Sunday newspaper. Each television spot costs $3,000; each Sunday newspaper ad costs $1,250. The expected exposure, based on industry ratings, is 35,000 viewers for each TV commercial and 20,000 readers for each newspaper advertisement. The agency director, Mavis Early, knows from experience that it is important to use both media in order to reach the broadest spectrum of potential Breem customers. She decides that at least five, but no more than twenty-five television spots should be ordered; and that at least ten newspaper ads should be contracted. How many times should each of the two media be used to obtain maximum exposure while staying within the budget? Use the graphic method to solve.

9-2. This is the slack time of year and we would actually like to shut down the plant, but if we laid off our core employees they would probably go to work for our competitor. We could keep our core (full time year-round) employees busy by making 10,000 round tables per month, or by making 20,000 square tables per month (or some ratio thereof). We do, however, have a contract with a supplier to buy precut table tops for 5,000 square tables per month. Handling and storage costs per round table will be $10, while these costs would be $8 per square table. Draw a graph, algebraically describe the constraint inequations and the objective function, identify the points bounding the feasible solution area, find the cost at each point and the optimum solution. Let X_1 equal the thousands of round tables per month and X_2 equal the thousands of square tables per month.

Linear Programming: The Simplex Method

Most real-world linear programming problems have more than two variables and, thus, are too large for graphical solution. A procedure called the *simplex method* may be used to find the optimal solution to multi-variable problems. The simplex method is actually an algorithm (or a set of instructions) with which we examine corner points in a methodical fashion until we arrive at the best solution—highest profit or lowest cost. Computer programs exist to solve LP problems with as many as several thousand variables, but it is useful to understand the mechanics of the algorithm.

CONVERTING THE CONSTRAINTS TO EQUATIONS

The first step of the simplex method requires that we convert each inequality constraint in an LP formulation into an equation. Less-than-or-equal-to constraints ($\leq$) can be converted to equations by adding *slack variables,* as illustrated in Example 10.1.

EXAMPLE 10.1

In Unit 9, we formulated the Flair Furniture Company's product mix problem as follows, using linear programming:

$$\text{Maximize profit} = \$7X_1 + \$5X_2$$

subject to LP constraints

$$2X_1 + 1X_2 \leq 10$$

$$4X_1 + 3X_2 \leq 24$$

where X_1 equals the number of tables produced and X_2 equals the number of chairs produced.

   To convert these inequality constraints to equalities, we add slack variables S_1 and S_2 to the left side of the inequality.

(continued)

The first constraint becomes

$$2X_1 + 1X_2 + S_1 = 10$$

and the second becomes

$$4X_1 + 3X_2 + S_2 = 24$$

To include all variables in each equation (a requirement of the next simplex step), we add slack variables not appearing in each equation with a coefficient of zero. The equations then appear as

$$2X_1 + 1X_2 + 1S_1 + 0S_2 = 10$$

$$4X_1 + 3X_2 + 0S_1 + 1S_2 = 24$$

Since slack variables represent unused resources (such as time on a machine or labor-hours available), they yield no profit but we must add them to the objective function with zero profit coefficients. Thus, the objective function becomes

$$\text{Maximize profit} = \$7X_1 + \$5X_2 + \$0S_1 + \$0S_2$$

PROBLEM 10.1

Convert the following LP problem (first seen as Problem 9.6) into the proper simplex form by adding slack variables.

$$\text{Maximize profit} = \$9X_1 + \$7X_2$$

subject to

$$2X_1 + 1X_2 \leqslant 40$$

$$X_1 + 3X_2 \leqslant 30$$

PROBLEM 10.2

Add slack variables to convert the following inequalities into equations and indicate their effect on the objective function.

$$\text{Maximize profit} = \$3X_1 + \$5X_2$$

subject to

$$X_2 \leqslant 6$$

$$3X_1 + 2X_2 \leqslant 18$$

SETTING UP THE FIRST SIMPLEX TABLEAU

To simplify handling the equations and objective function in an LP problem, we place all of the coefficients into a tabular form. We can express the two constraint equations of Example 10.1 as:

Solution Mix	Quantity (RHS)	X_1	X_2	S_1	S_2
S_1	10	2	1	1	0
S_2	24	4	3	0	1

The numbers on the right-hand side (RHS) of the equality appear at the left of the table for convenience. The numbers $(2, 1, 1, 0)$ and $(4, 3, 0, 1)$ represent the coefficients of the first equation and second equation, respectively.

As in the graphical approach of Unit 9, we begin the solution at the origin, where $X_1 = 0$, $X_2 = 0$, and profit $= 0$. The values of the two other variables, S, and S_2, then, must be nonzero. Since $2X_1 + 1X_2 + 1S_1 = 10$, we see that $S_1 = 10$. Likewise, $S_2 = 24$. These two slack variables comprise the initial solution mix— as a matter of fact, their values are found in the quantity column next to each variable. Since X_1 and X_2 are not in the solution mix, their initial values are automatically equal to zero.

Some production-operations management books call this initial solution a *basic feasible solution* and describe it in vector, or column, form as

$$\begin{bmatrix} X_1 \\ X_2 \\ S_1 \\ S_2 \end{bmatrix} = \begin{bmatrix} 0 \\ 0 \\ 10 \\ 24 \end{bmatrix}$$

Variables in the solution mix, which is often called the *basis* in LP terminology, are referred to as *basic variables*. In this example, the basic variables are S_1 and S_2. Variables not in the solution mix—or basis— (X_1 and X_2, in this case) are called *nonbasic variables*. Of course, if the optimal solution to this LP problem turned out to be $X_1 = 3, X_2 = 4, S_1 = 0$, and $S_2 = 0$, or in vector form,

$$\begin{bmatrix} X_1 \\ X_2 \\ S_1 \\ S_2 \end{bmatrix} = \begin{bmatrix} 3 \\ 4 \\ 0 \\ 0 \end{bmatrix}$$

then X_1 and X_2 would be the final basic variables, while S_1, and S_2 would be the nonbasic variables.

EXAMPLE 10.2

Table 10.1 shows the complete initial simplex tableau for Example 10.1.

Table 10.1. Completed Initial Simplex Tableau

| $C_j \rightarrow$ | Solution Mix | Quantity (RHS) | $7 | $5 | $0 | $0 |
			X_1	X_2	S_1	S_2
$0	S_1	10	2	1	1	0
$0	S_2	24	4	3	0	1
	Z_j	$0 (total profit)	$0	$0	$0	$0
	$C_j - Z_j$		$7	$5	$0	$0

The terms and rows that you have not seen before are:

(continued)

C_j: Profit contribution per unit of each variable. C_j applies to both the top row and first column. In the row, it indicates the unit profit for all variables in the LP objective function. In the column, C_j indicates the unit profit for each variable *currently* in the solution mix.

Z_j: In the quantity column, Z_j provides the total contribution (gross profit in this case) of the given solution. In the other columns (under the variables) it represents the gross profit *given up* by adding one unit of this variable into the current solution. The Z_j value for each column is found by multiplying the C_j of the row by the number in that row and jth column and summing.

The calculations for the values of Z_j in Table 10.1 are as follows:

$$Z_j \text{ (for total profit)} = 0(10) + 0(24) = 0$$

$$Z_j \text{ (for column } X_1) = 0(2) + 0(4) = 0$$

$$Z_j \text{ (for column } X_2) = 0(1) + 0(3) = 0$$

$$Z_j \text{ (for column } S_1) = 0(1) + 0(0) = 0$$

$$Z_j \text{ (for column } S_2) = 0(0) + 0(1) = 0$$

$C_j - Z_j$: This number represents the net profit (that is, the profit gained minus the profit given up), which will result from introducing one unit of each product (variable) into the solution. It is not calculated for the quantity column. To compute these numbers, we simply subtract the Z_j total from the C_j value at the very top of each variable's column.

The calculations for the net profit per unit ($C_j - Z_j$) row in this example are:

	Column			
	X_1	X_2	S_1	S_2
C_j for column:	$7	$5	0	0
Z_j for column:	0	0	0	0
$C_j - Z_j$ for column:	$7	$5	0	0

It was obvious to us when we computed a profit of $0 that this initial solution was not optimal. Examining numbers in the $C_j - Z_j$ row of Table 10.1, we see that total profit can be increased by $7 for each unit of X_1 (tables) and by $5 for each unit of X_2 (chairs) added to the solution mix. A negative number in the $C_j - Z_j$ row would tell us that profits would *decrease* if the corresponding variable were added to the solution mix. An optimal solution is reached in the simplex method when the $C_j - Z_j$ row contains no positive numbers. Such is not the case in our initial tableau.

PROBLEM 10.3

Set up an initial simplex tableau for the data in Problem 10.1.

$$\text{Maximize profit} = \$9X_1 + \$7X_2 + \$0S_1 + \$0S_2$$

subject to

$$2X_1 + 1X_2 + 1S_1 + 0S_2 = 40$$

$$1X_1 + 3X_2 + 0S_1 + 1S_2 = 30$$

$C_j \rightarrow$						
$\downarrow$	Solution Mix	Quantity				
	Z_j					
	$C_j - Z_j$					

PROBLEM 10.4

Set up an initial simplex tableau for the LP problem formulated in Problem 10.2.

$$\text{Maximize profit} = \$3X_1 + \$5X_2 + \$0S_1 + \$0S_2$$

subject to

$$0X_1 + 1X_2 + 1S_1 + 0S_2 = 6$$

$$3X_1 + 2X_2 + 0S_1 + 1S_2 = 18$$

(continued)

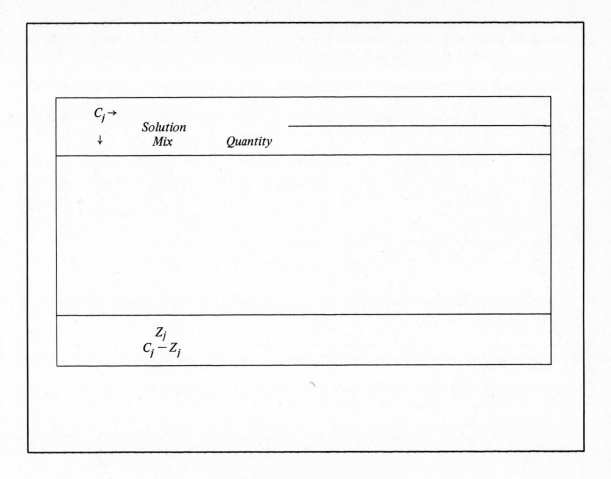

SIMPLEX SOLUTION PROCEDURES

Once we have completed an initial tableau, we proceed through a series of five steps to compute all of the numbers we need for the next tableau. The calculations are not difficult, but they are sufficiently complex that the smallest arithmetic error can produce a very wrong answer.

We will first list the five steps and then apply them in determining the second and third tableaux for the data in Example 10.2.

1. Determine which variable to enter into the solution mix next. Identify the column—hence, the variable—with the largest positive number in the $C_j - Z_j$ row of the previous tableau. This step means that we will now be producing some of the product contributing the greatest additional profit per unit.
2. Determine which variable to replace. Since we have just chosen a new variable to enter into the solution mix, we must decide which variable currently in the solution to remove to make room for it. To do so, we divide each amount in the quantity column by the corresponding number in the column selected in step 1. The row with the *smallest nonnegative number* calculated in this fashion will be replaced in the

next tableau (this smallest number, by the way, gives the maximum number of units of the variable that we may place in the solution). This row is often referred to as the *pivot row*, and the column identified in step 1 called the *pivot column*. The number at the intersection of the pivot row and column is the *pivot number.*

3. Compute new values for the pivot row. To find them, we simply divide every number in the row by the *pivot number.*

4. Compute new values for each remaining row. (In our sample problems there have been only two rows in the LP tableau, but most larger problems have many more rows.) All remaining row(s) are calculated as follows:

$$(\text{New row numbers}) = (\text{numbers in old row}) - \left[\left(\begin{array}{c} \text{number in old row} \\ \text{above or below} \\ \text{pivot number} \end{array} \right) \times \left(\begin{array}{c} \text{corresponding number in} \\ \text{the new row, i.e., the} \\ \text{row replaced in step 3} \end{array} \right) \right]$$

5. Compute the Z_j and $C_j - Z_j$ rows, as demonstrated in the initial tableau. If all numbers in the $C_j - Z_j$ row are zero or negative, we have found an optimal solution. If this is not the case, we must return to step 1.

All of these computations are best illustrated by way of an example—and best understood by way of several practice problems.

EXAMPLE 10.3

The initial simplex tableau competed in Table 10.1 of Example 10.2 is repeated below. We will follow the five steps just given to reach an optimal solution to the LP problem.

			$7	$5	$0	$0
$C_j \rightarrow$	Solution Mix	Quantity	X_1	X_2	S_1	S_2
$0 S_1	10	②	1	1	0	←pivot row
$0 S_2	24	4	3	0	1	
				pivot number		
Z_j	$0		$0	$0	$0	$0
$C_j - Z_j$			$7	$5	$0	$0

1st tableau

↑
pivot column
(maximum $C_j - Z_j$ values)

(continued)

Step 1. Variable X_1 will enter the solution next because it has the highest contribution to profit value, $C_j - Z_j$. Its column becomes the pivot column.

Step 2. Divide each number in the quantity column by the corresponding number in the X_1 column: $10/2 = 5$ for the first row and $24/4 = 6$ for the second row. The smaller of these numbers— 5—identifies the pivot row, the pivot number, and the variable to be replaced. The pivot row is identified above by an arrow and the pivot number is circled. Variable X_1 replaces variable S_1 in the solution mix column, as shown in the second tableau.

Step 3. Replace the pivot row by dividing every number in it by the pivot number ($10/2 = 5$, $2/2 = 1$, $1/2 = 1/2$, $1/2 = 1/2$, $0/2 = 0$). This new version of the entire pivot row appears below.

C_j	Solution Mix	Quantity	X_1	X_2	S_1	S_2
$7	X_1	5	1	1/2	1/2	0

Step 4. Calculate the new values for the S_2 row.

$$\begin{pmatrix} \text{Number in} \\ \text{new } S_2 \text{ row} \end{pmatrix} = \begin{pmatrix} \text{number in} \\ \text{old } S_2 \text{ row} \end{pmatrix} - \left[\begin{pmatrix} \text{number below pivot} \\ \text{number in old row} \end{pmatrix} \times \begin{pmatrix} \text{corresponding number} \\ \text{in the new } X_1 \text{ row} \end{pmatrix} \right]$$

4	=	24	−	[(4)	×	(5)]
0	=	4	−	[(4)	×	(1)]
1	=	3	−	[(4)	×	(½)]
−2	=	0	−	[(4)	×	(½)]
1	=	1	−	[(4)	×	(0)]

C_j	Solution Mix	Quantity	X_1	X_2	S_1	S_2
$7	X_1	5	1	1/2	1/2	0
0	S_2	4	0	1	−2	1

(continued)

Step 5:   Calculate the Z_j and $C_j - Z_j$ rows.

$$Z_j \text{ (for total profit)} = \$7(5) + 0(4) = \$35$$

$$Z_j \text{ (for } X_1 \text{ column)} = \$7(1) + 0(0) = \$7 \qquad C_j - Z_j = \$7 - \$7 = 0$$

$$Z_j \text{ (for } X_2 \text{ column)} = \$7(1/2) + 0(1) = \$7/2 \qquad C_j - Z_j = \$5 - \$7/2 = \$3/2$$

$$Z_j \text{ (for } S_1 \text{ column)} = \$7(1/2) + 0(-2) = \$7/2 \qquad C_j - Z_j = \ 0 - \$7/2 = -\$7/2$$

$$Z_j \text{ (for } S_2 \text{ column)} = \$7(0) + 0(1) = 0 \qquad C_j - Z_j = \ 0 - 0 = 0$$

2nd tableau

$C_j \rightarrow$	Solution Mix	Quantity	$7	$5	$0	$0
$\downarrow$			X_1	X_2	S_1	S_2
$7	X_1	5	1	1/2	1/2	0
$0	S_2	4	0	(1)	-2	1	$\leftarrow$ pivot row
				pivot number		
	Z_j	$35 (total profit)	$7	$7/2	$7/2	$0
	$C_j - Z_j$		$0	$3/2	-$7/2	$0

$\uparrow$
pivot column

Since not all numbers in the $C_j - Z_j$ row of this latest tableau are zero or negative, the foregoing solution (i.e., $X_1 = 5$, $S_2 = 4$, $X_2 = 0$, $S_1 = 0$; profit = \$35) is not optimal and we proceed to a third tableau and repeat the five steps.

Step 1.   Variable X_2 will enter the solution next by virtue of the fact that its $C_j - Z_j = 3/2$ is the largest (and only) positive number in the row. Thus, for every unit of X_2 that we start to produce, the objective function will increase in value by \$3/2, or \$1.50.

Step 2.   The pivot row becomes the S_2 row because the ratio $4/1 = 4$ is smaller than the ratio $5/(1/2) = 10$.

Step 3.   Replace the pivot row by dividing every number in it by the (circled) pivot number. Since every number is divided by one, there is no change.

Step 4.   Compute the new values for the X_1 row.

(continued)

$$\begin{pmatrix} \text{Number in} \\ \text{new } X_1 \text{ row} \end{pmatrix} = \begin{pmatrix} \text{number in} \\ \text{old } X_1 \text{ row} \end{pmatrix} - \left[\begin{pmatrix} \text{number above} \\ \text{pivot number} \end{pmatrix} \times \begin{pmatrix} \text{corresponding number} \\ \text{in new } X_2 \text{ row} \end{pmatrix} \right]$$

3	=	5	−	[(1/2)	×	(4)]
1	=	1	−	[(1/2)	×	(0)]
0	=	1/2	−	[(1/2)	×	(1)]
3/2	=	1/2	−	[(1/2)	×	(−2)]
−1/2	=	0	−	[(1/2)	×	(1)]

Step 5. Calculate the Z_j and $C_j - Z_j$ rows.

Z_j (for total profit) $= \$7(3) + \$5(4) = \$41$

Z_j (for X_1 column) $= \$7(1) + \$5(0) = \$7$ $C_j - Z_j = \$7 - 7 = \$0$

Z_j (for X_2 column) $= \$7(0) + \$5(1) = \$5$ $C_j - Z_j = \$5 - 5 = \$0$

Z_j (for S_1 column) $= \$7(3/2) + \$5(-2) = \$1/2$ $C_j - Z_j = \$0 - 1/2 = -\$1/2$

Z_j (for S_2 column) $= \$7(-1/2) + \$5(1) = \$3/2$ $C_j - Z_j = \$0 - 3/2 = -\$3/2$

| $C_j \rightarrow$ | Solution Mix | Quantity | $\$7$ | $\$5$ | $\$0$ | $\$0$ |
$\downarrow$			X_1	X_2	S_1	S_2
$\$7$	X_1	3	1	0	3/2	−1/2
$\$5$	X_2	4	0	1	−2	1
	Z_j	$\$41$	$\$7$	$\$5$	$\$1/2$	$\$3/2$
	$C_j - Z_j$		$\$0$	$\$0$	$-\$1/2$	$-\$3/2$

Since every number in the third tableau's $C_j - Z_j$ row is zero or negative, we have reached an optimal solution. That solution is: $X_1 = 3$ (tables), and $X_2 = 4$ (chairs), $S_1 = 0$ (slack in first resource), $S_2 = 0$ (slack in second resource) and profit $= \$41$.

It is interesting to compare the step-by-step solutions found in each simplex tableau above with the graphical corner-point solutions we found in the last unit.

PROBLEM 10.5

The first tableau for the LP problem shown as Problem 10.1 is repeated below. Use the simplex method to find an optimal solution.

$C_j \rightarrow$	Solution Mix	Quantity	$9 X_1	$7 X_2	0 S_1	0 S_2
0	S_1	40	2	1	1	0
0	S_2	30	1	3	0	1
	Z_j	0	0	0	0	0
	$C_j - Z_j$		$9	$7	0	0

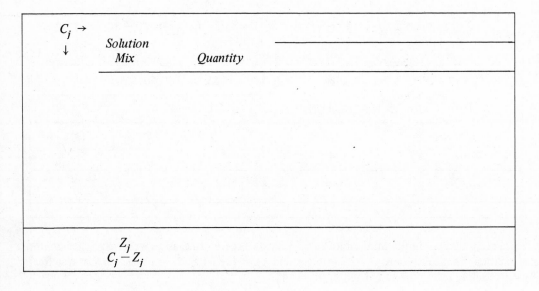

$C_j \rightarrow$	Solution Mix	Quantity				
	Z_j					
	$C_j - Z_j$					

(continued)

$C_j \rightarrow$	Solution Mix	Quantity				
$\downarrow$						
	Z_j					
	$C_j - Z_j$					

PROBLEM 10.6

Use the simplex algorithm to find the optimal values for X_1, X_2, S_1, S_2, and profit for Problem 10.2. The initial tableau is given below.

$C_j \rightarrow$	Solution Mix	Quantity	$3	$5	0	0
$\downarrow$			X_1	X_2	S_1	S_2
0	S_1	6	0	1	1	0
0	S_2	18	3	2	0	1
	Z_j	0	0	0	0	0
	$C_j - Z_j$		$3	$5	0	0

(continued)

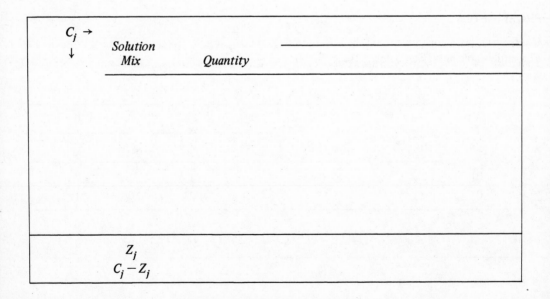

SUMMARY OF SIMPLEX STEPS FOR MAXIMIZATION PROBLEMS

The steps involved in using the simplex method to help solve an LP problem in which the objective function is to be maximized can be summarized as follows:

1. Choose the variable with the greatest positive $C_j - Z_j$ to enter the solution.
2. Determine the row to be replaced by selecting the one with the smallest (nonnegative) quantity-to-pivot-column ratio.
3. Calculate the new values for the pivot row.
4. Calculate the new values for the other row(s).
5. Calculate the C_j and $C_j - Z_j$ values for this tableau. If there are any $C_j - Z_j$ numbers greater than zero, return to step 1.

SHADOW PRICES

Example 10.3 and the problems that you have just solved lead us to the subject of shadow prices. Exactly how much should a firm be willing to pay to make additional resources available? Is one more hour of machine time worth $.50 or $1 or $5? Is it worthwhile to pay workers an overtime rate to stay one extra hour each night in order to increase production output? The worth of additional resources is valuable management information.

Fortunately, this information is available to us in the final simplex tableau of an LP problem. An important property of the $C_j - Z_j$ row is that the *negatives of the numbers in its slack variables (S_j) columns* provide what we call *shadow prices*. A shadow price is the value of one additional unit of a resource in the form of one more hour of machine time or labor time or other scarce resource.

EXAMPLE 10.4

Sparky's Electronic Products, Inc., produces gidgets (X_1) and widgets (X_2) and formulates these constraints:

$$2X_1 + 1X_2 \leq 40 \text{ hours of time available on drilling machine}$$

$$1X_1 + 3X_2 \leq 30 \text{ hours of time available on grinding machine}$$

Its objective function is

$$\text{Maximize profit} = \$9X_1 + \$7X_2$$

Sparky's solves this LP problem using the simplex algorithm. The final tableau appears below.

(continued)

$C_j \rightarrow$	Solution Mix	Quantity	$9	$7	0	0
$\downarrow$			X_1	X_2	S_1	S_2
$9	X_1	18	1	0	3/5	−1/5
$7	X_2	4	0	1	−1/5	2/5
	Z_j	$190	$9	$7	$4	$1
	$C_j - Z_j$		0	0	−$4	−$1

The objective function increases by $4 if an additional hour is available for drilling machines

This tableau indicates that the optimal solution is $X_1 = 18$, $X_2 = 4$, $S_1 = 0$, $S_2 = 0$ and profit = $190, where S_1 represents slack time on the drilling machine and S_2 represents slack time on the grinding machine.

Sparky is considering renting a second drilling machine at a cost to him of $2.50 per hour. Should he do so? The answer is *yes*—the shadow price of the drilling machine resource is $4. Thus, Sparky will *net* $1.50 for every additional hour he rents.

PROBLEM 10.7

Sparky discovers that he can also rent a second grinding machine for only $1.75 per hour. Should he do so?

PROBLEM 10.8

The following is the final simplex tableau of an LP problem that has three constraints and four real variables.

$C_j \rightarrow$	Solution Mix	Quantity	$4	$6	$3	$1	0	0	0
$\downarrow$			X_1	X_2	X_3	X_4	S_1	S_2	S_3
3	X_3	125	1/20	0	1	1/2	3/10	0	−1/5
0	S_2	425	39/12	0	0	−1/2	−1/2	1	0
6	X_2	25	39/60	1	0	1/2	−1/10	0	3/5
	Z_j	$525	$81/20	$6	$3	$9/2	$3/10	0	$3
	$C_j - Z_j$		−$1/20	0	0	−$7/2	−$3/10	0	−$3

What are the values of each of the shadow prices? What meaning does a zero shadow price have and how can it occur?

MINIMIZATION PROBLEMS

We can solve minimization problems in an almost identical manner as the maximization problems tackled earlier in this unit. One significant difference involves the $C_j - Z_j$ row. Since our objective is now to minimize costs, the new variable to enter the solution in each tableau (the pivot column) will be the one with the *largest negative* number in the $C_j - Z_j$ row. Thus, we will be choosing the variable that decreases costs the most. In minimization problems, an optimal solution is reached when all numbers in the $C_j - Z_j$ row are zero or *positive*—just the opposite of the maximization case.

In solving minimization problems we must also bring in additional variables. Since minimization problems involve greater-than-or-equal-to constraints (which must be treated differently than the less-than-or-equal-to constraints that typify maximization problems), a special procedure is necessary. The interested student should pick up a management science or operations research text for details. All other simplex steps, reviewed here, remain the same.

1. Choose the variable with the largest negative $C_j - Z_j$, to enter the solution.
2. Determine which row to replace by selecting the one with the smallest (nonnegative) quantity-to-pivot-column ratio.
3. Calculate new values for the pivot row.
4. Calculate new values for the other rows.
5. Calculate the C_j and $C_j - Z_j$ values for this tableau. If any $C_j - Z_j$ numbers are *less* than zero, return to step 1.

SOLVING LP PROBLEMS BY COMPUTER

Large-scale LP problems, which you may be called upon to formulate some day, could, with some long and careful computations, be solved by hand by following the steps of the simplex algorithm. It is, indeed, important to understand how that algorithm works. Unfortunately, the only good way to master the algorithm is to solve several problems by hand. Once you comprehend the mechanics of the simplex technique, however, it should not be necessary to struggle with the manual method again.

Almost every university and many medium-to-large business and government organizations have access to computers and "canned programs" (prewritten programs) that are capable of solving enormous linear programming problems. Although each firm's computer is slightly different, the approach to solving LP problems is basically the same. The format of the input data and the level of detail provided in output may differ from computer to computer, but a person who is experienced in dealing with computerized LP algorithms can easily adjust to minor variations.

In this section, we will demonstrate the entire process—from instructions for data input to output analysis—of running a typical LP computer program. The program illustration is called LINPRO. Written in the BASIC computer language, it was run on a DECSYSTEM 10 Time-sharing computer.

Students who want to run LINPRO generally need exact instructions as to how to enter the appropriate data via their time-sharing terminals. A separate program, called DESCRB, does nothing more than describe how to use LINPRO. By asking the computer to type DESCRB, the user receives the following set of instructions.

```
TYPE DESCRB-TUK
100    THESE INSTRUCTIONS ARE FOR 'LINPRO***
110
120
130    LINPRO*** USES THE TWO-PHASE SIMPLEX METHOD.
140
150
160    ENTER DATA STARTING AT LINE 10000:
170
180    HOWEVER, FIRST - ARRANGE YOUR CONSTRAINTS SO THAT THE
190    'LESS THAN' INEQUALITIES PRECEDE THE STRICT EQUALITIES,
200    WHICH, IN TURN, PRECEDE THE 'GREATER THAN' INEQUALITIES.
210
220    THEN - TYPE IN AS DATA THE COEFFICIENTS OF THE
230    CONSTRAINTS, ROW BY ROW.
240    DO NOT INCLUDE COEFFICIENTS FOR SLACK, SURPLUS,
250    OR ARTIFICIAL VARIABLES.
```

```
260
270     NEXT - TYPE IN AS DATA THE 'B' VECTOR (THE CONSTANTS,
280     OR RIGHT-HAND SIDES OF THE CONSTRAINTS) IN THE SAME ORDER
290     AS THE ROWS WERE TYPED ABOVE.
300     THESE VALUES MUST BE NON-NEGATIVE.
310
320     FINALLY - TYPE IN AS DATA THE COEFFICIENTS OF THE
330     OBJECTIVE FUNCTION.
340
350
360     AT RUN TIME YOU WILL BE ASKED TO:
370
380     INPUT WHETHER YOU ARE MAXIMIZING THE OBJECTIVE FUNCTION
390     (AS YOU PUT IT IN DATA), OR MINIMIZING IT.
400
410     INPUT THE NUMBER OF CONSTRAINTS AND VARIABLES IN YOUR PROGRAM,
420     RESPECTIVELY.
430
440     INPUT THE NUMBER OF 'LESS THAN' INEQUALITIES, STRICT
450     EQUALITIES, AND 'GREATER THAN' INEQUALITIES - IN THAT ORDER.
460
470
480     REMEMBER TO ALWAYS TYPE ZEROS WHEN APPLICABLE...
490
500
510     OUTPUT INCLUDES THE FOLLOWING ELIMINATABLE FEATURES:
520
530     THE INITIAL TABLEAU            -- LINE 860
540     THE FINAL TABLEAU             -- LINE 1550
550     THE BASIS BEFORE EACH ITERATION -- LINE 910
560
570     IF YOU DO NOT WANT ANY OF THESE FEATURES,
580     ELIMINATE THE INDICATED LINE - BEFORE RUN TIME.
```

Now consider the following linear programming problem:

$$\text{Maximize profit} = 4X_1 + 4X_2 + 7X_3$$

subject to

$$1X_1 + 7X_2 + 4X_3 \leqslant 100$$

$$2X_1 + 1X_2 + 7X_3 \leqslant 110$$

$$8X_1 + 4X_2 + 1X_3 \leqslant 100$$

We will solve this problem by running LINPRO. Note that all user responses to the computer are underlined on the printout that follows. The notes that we have added to the right of the computer's work explain important information. When you reach the final line of output, you will realize why the computer has become an invaluable tool in production and operations management and in managerial decision making.

```
OLD FILE NAME--LINFRO

READY
10000 DATA 1,7,4 ⎱
10010 DATA 2,1,7 ⎰──→ constraint coefficients
10020 DATA 8,4,1 ⎰
10030 DATA 100,110,100 ⎱──→ right-hand-side values
10040 DATA 4,4,7 ⎰──→ objective function coefficients
RUN


LINFRO        16:30        06-SEP-77



IF MAX, THEN TYPE:'1'; IF MIN, TYPE:'-1' ?1
TYPE:  NUMBER OF CONSTRAINTS, VARIABLES ?3,3
TYPE:  LESS THANS, EQUALITIES, GREATER THANS ?3,0,0
```

YOUR VARIABLES 1 THROUGH 3
SLACK VARIABLES 4 THROUGH 6

The computer has assigned the variables X_1, X_2, and X_3 to represent *real* problem variables and X_4, and X_5, and X_6 to stand for the slack variables needed in the simplex LP approach.

This is the initial tableau generated by the computer. Data are arranged in a slightly different format than we used earlier, but you will probably recognize the changes. The right-hand-side values, for example, are actually in the rightmost column here, whereas we placed them on the left in our simplex tableaux. The only other modification appears in the bottom row of the tableau. The values computed are not $C_j - Z_j$ but $Z_j - C_j$ (a computer quirk!) and hence the first variable to enter the solution will be the one with the *largest negative* value in the row—in this case, X_3 from the third column.

```
TABLEAU AFTER 0 ITERATIONS
 1   7   4   1   0   0   100

 2   1   7   0   1   0   110

 8   4   1   0   0   1   100

-4  -4  -7   0   0   0   0
```

```
BASIS BEFORE ITERATION 1
VARIABLE      VALUE
4             100
5             110
6             100
```

Initial basic feasible solution given is $X_4 = 100$, $X_5 = 110$, $X_6 = 100$ (all slack variables). Real variables X_1, X_2, and X_3 are equal to 0. The term "basis," we note again, is the same as our solution mix.

```
BASIS BEFORE ITERATION 2
VARIABLE      VALUE
4             37.1429
3             15.7143
6             84.2857
```

Variables in the solution at the end of one iteration are X_3 (real), X_4 (slack), and X_6 (slack). In this iteration, X_3 entered the solution because of its $C_j - Z_j$ value, noted above.

```
BASIS BEFORE ITERATION 3
VARIABLE      VALUE
2             5.77778
3             14.8889
6             62
```

Another real variable, X_2, has just entered the solution mix. The only slack variable remaining is X_6.

ANSWERS:

VARIABLE	VALUE
2	5.95442
3	12.5926
1	7.94872

Final solution: $X_2 = 5.95$
$X_3 = 12.59$
$X_1 = 7.94$

DUAL VARIABLES:

COLUMN	VALUE
4	0.307692
5	0.786325
6	0.264957

These are the shadow prices mentioned earlier. The value, for example, of one additional unit of the first resource (represented by the first slack variable, X_4) is \$.307.

OBJECTIVE FUNCTION VALUE = 143.761
IN 3 ITERATIONS

The optimal profit is \$143.76.

TABLEAU AFTER 3 ITERATIONS

0	1	0	0.153846	-8.83191E-2	2.84900E-3	5.95442
0	0	1	0	0.148148	-0.037037	12.5926
1	0	0	-7.69231E-2	2.56410E-2	0.128205	7.94872
0	0	0	0.307692	0.786325	0.264957	143.761

Final simplex tableau.

TIME: 1.56 SECS.   Time it took the computer to perform all of the above calculations!

To see how well you can interpret other outputs in the computerized LP problem, try to answer Problem 10.9.

PROBLEM 10.9

Let us assume that the example just given involved a manufacturing problem concerning three products (X_1, X_2, and X_3). Each of these products requires a certain amount of time on three different machines. Hence, we can think of the first constraint ($1X_1 + 7X_2 + 4X_3 \leqslant 100$) as representing a time limit of 100 available hours on machine number 1. The second machine has 110 hours available, and the third machine (represented by the third constraint) also provides 100 hours of production time.

(a) Before the third iteration of the simplex method, which machine still has unused time available?

(b) In the final solution, is there any unused time available on any of the three machines?

(continued)

(c) What would it be worth to the firm to make an additional hour of time available on the third machine?

(d) How much would the firm's profit increase if an extra 10 hours of time were available on the second machine at no extra cost?

ANSWERS

10.1

$$\text{Maximize profit} = 9X_1 + 7X_2 + 0S_1 + 0S_2$$

$$\text{subject to } 2X_1 + 1X_2 + 1S_1 + 0S_2 = 40$$

$$1X_1 + 3X_2 + 0S_1 + 1S_2 = 30$$

10.2

$$\text{Maximize profit} = 3X_1 + 5X_2 + 0S_1 + 0S_2$$

$$\text{subject to } 0X_1 + 1X_2 + 1S_1 + 0S_2 = 6$$

$$3X_1 + 2X_2 + 0S_1 + 1S_2 = 18$$

10.3

$C_j \rightarrow$ $\downarrow$	Solution Mix	Quantity	$9 X_1	$7 X_2	0 S_1	0 S_2
0	S_1	40	2	1	1	0
0	S_2	30	1	3	0	1
	Z_j	0	0	0	0	0
	$C_j - Z_j$		9	7	0	0

10.4

$C_j \rightarrow$ $\downarrow$	Solution Mix	Quantity	$3 X_1	$5 X_2	0 S_1	0 S_2
0	S_1	6	0	1	1	0
0	S_2	18	3	2	0	1
	Z_j	0	0	0	0	0
	$C_j - Z_j$		$3	$5	0	0

10.5   The correct second and third tableaux and some of their calculations appear below. The optimal solutions, given in the third tableau, are : $X_1 = 18$, $X_2 = 4$, $S_1 = 0$, $S_2 = 0$, and profit = $190.

Steps 1 and 2. To go from the first to the second tableaux, we note that the pivot column (in the first tableau) is X_1, which has the highest $C_j - Z_j$ value, $9. The pivot row is S_1 since 40/2 is less than 30/1, and the pivot number is 2.

Step 3.   The new X_1 row is found by dividing each number in the old S_1 row by the pivot number, namely, $40/2 = 20$, $2/2 = 1$, $1/2 = 1/2$, $1/2 = Y_2$, and $0/2 = 0$.

Step 4.   The new values for the S_2 row are computed as follows:

$$\begin{pmatrix} \text{Number in new} \\ S_2 \text{ row} \end{pmatrix} = \begin{pmatrix} \text{number in old} \\ S_2 \text{ row} \end{pmatrix} - \left[\begin{pmatrix} \text{number below} \\ \text{pivot number} \end{pmatrix} \times \begin{pmatrix} \text{corresponding number} \\ \text{in new } X_1 \text{ row} \end{pmatrix} \right]$$

10	=	30	−	[(1)	×	(20)]
0	=	1	−	[(1)	×	(1)]
5/2	=	3	−	[(1)	×	(1/2)]
−1/2	=	0	−	[(1)	×	(1/2)]
1	=	1	−	[(1)	×	(0)]

Step 5.   The following new Z_j and $C_j - Z_j$ rows are formed:

Z_j (profit) $= \$9(20) + 0(10) = \$180$

Z_j (for X_1) $= \$9(1) + 0(0) = \$9$ $C_j - Z_j = \$9 - \$9 = 0$

Z_j (for X_2) $= \$9(1/2) + 0(5/2) = \$9/2$ $C_j - Z_j = \$7 - 9/2 = \$5/2$

Z_j (for S_1) $= \$9(1/2) + 0(-1/2) = \$9/2$ $C_j - Z_j = \ 0 - 9/2 = -\$9/2$

Z_j (for S_2) $= \$9(0) + 0(1) = 0$ $C_j - Z_j = \ 0 - 0 = 0$

$C_j \rightarrow$			$9	$7	0	0	
$\downarrow$	Solution Mix	Quantity	X_1	X_2	S_1	S_2	
$9	X_1	20	1	1/2	1/2	0	
0	S_1	10	0	(5/2)	−1/2	1	← Pivot Row
	Z_j	$180	$9	$9/2	$9/2	0	
	$C_j - Z_j$		0	$5/2	−$9/2	0	

Pivot Column

(continued)

The above solution is not optimal and you must perform steps 1-5 again. The new pivot column is X_2, the new pivot row is S_1 and 5/2 (circled above) is the new pivot number.

| $C_j \rightarrow$ | Solution Mix | Quantity | $9 | $7 | 0 | 0 |
			X_1	X_2	S_1	S_2
$9	X_1	18	1	0	3/5	−1/5
$7	X_2	4	0	1	−1/5	2/5
	Z_j	$190	$9	$7	$4	$1
	$C_j - Z_j$		0	0	−$4	−$1

10.6 The optimal solution, found at the end of three complete tableaux, indicates that $X_1 = 2$, $X_2 = 6, S_1 = 0, S_2 = 0$, and profit $= \$36$.

| $C_j \rightarrow$ | Solution Mix | Quantity | $3 | $5 | 0 | 0 |
			X_1	X_2	S_1	S_2
$5	X_2	6	0	1	1	0
0	S_2	6	3	0	−2	1
	Z_j	$30	0	$5	$5	0
	$C_j - Z_j$		$3	0	−$5	0

| $C_j \rightarrow$ | Solution Mix | Quantity | $3 | $5 | 0 | 0 |
			X_1	X_2	S_1	S_2
$5	X_2	6	0	1	1	0
$3	X_1	2	1	0	−2/3	1/3
	Z_j	$36	$3	$5	$3	$1
	$C_j - Z_j$		0	0	−$3	−$1

10.7   No! The profit added for each additional hour of grinding machine made available is only $1. Since this shadow price is less than the $1.75-per-hour cost, he will lower his total profit if he rents the machine.

10.8

Resource Source	Value of an Additional Hour
First constraint (S_1)	$.30
Second constraint (S_2)	0
Third constraint (S_3)	$ 3

The second resource has a zero shadow price because not all of the resource is currently being used: 425 units are still available. It would hardly pay to buy more of the resource.

10.9   (a) Machine number 3, represented by slack variable X_6, still has 62 hours of unused time.
(b) There is no unused time according to the optimal solution. All three slack variables have been removed from the basis and have zero values.
(c) The shadow price of the third machine is the value of the dual variable in column 6. Hence, an extra hour of time on machine number 3 is worth $.26.
(d) For *each* extra hour of time made available at no cost on machine number 2, profit will increase by $.786. Thus, 10 hours of time will be worth $7.86.

HOMEWORK PROBLEMS

10-1. Each coffee table produced by Meising Designers nets the firm a profit of $9. Each bookcase yields a $12 profit. Meising's firm is small, and its resources limited. During any given production period (of 1 week), 10 gallons of varnish and 12 lengths of high-quality redwood are available. Each coffee table requires approximately 1 gallon of varnish and 1 length of redwood. Each bookcase takes 1 gallon of varnish and 2 lengths of wood. Formulate Meising's production mix decision as a linear programming problem, and solve using the simplex method. How many tables and bookcases should be produced each week? What will the maximum profit be?

10-2. a. Set up an initial simplex tableau, given the following two constraints and objective function:

$$1X_1 + 4X_2 \leqslant 24$$

$$1X_1 + 2X_2 \leqslant 16$$

$$\text{Maximize profit} = \$3X_1 + \$9X_2$$

You will have to add slack variables.
b. Briefly list the iterative steps necessary to solve the problem in part (a) above.
c. Determine the next tableau from the one you developed in part (a). Determine whether or not it is an optimum solution.
d. If necessary, develop another tableau and determine whether or not it is an optimum solution. Interpret this tableau.
e. Start with the same initial tableau from part (a) but use X_1 as the first pivot column. Continue to iterate it (a total of twice) until you reach an optimum solution.

Facility Location and Transportation Models

One of the most important decisions a firm can make is where to locate a new warehouse, factory, sales office, or service facility. The location of key facilities has a direct impact on the cost of product distribution. In many industries, one of the largest costs of operation is the transportation of goods.

Several analytic techniques have been developed to assist firms in location analysis. The *transportation method* determines the best pattern of shipments from several points of supply (sources) to points of demand (destinations) so as to minimize total transportation and production costs. The *factor weighting method* assigns a weight to each location decision factor based on its importance to management. Typical factors are availability of power, raw materials and transportation, zoning regulations, pollution standards, local tax structures, and labor costs. *Locational break-even analysis* uses the "break-even" approach of Unit 2 for cost comparison of alternative facility locations.

THE TRANSPORTATION MODEL

The transportation model answers the specific question of which sources (such as factories) in an organization should supply which destinations (such as warehouses). Usually, we have a given capacity of goods at each source and a given requirement for the goods at each destination. This is illustrated in Figure 11.1.

After we explain how the transportation model works, we will show you how to apply it in a facility location decision problem.

Although *linear programming* can also be used to solve transportation problems, more efficient, special-

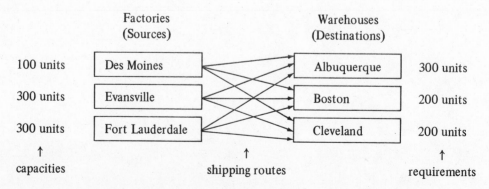

Factories (Sources)　　　　　Warehouses (Destinations)

100 units	Des Moines		Albuquerque	300 units
300 units	Evansville		Boston	200 units
300 units	Fort Lauderdale		Cleveland	200 units

↑ capacities　　　↑ shipping routes　　　↑ requirements

Figure 11.1. Example of a Transportation Problem

purpose algorithms have been developed. As in the simplex algorithm, they involve finding an initial feasible solution and then making step-by-step improvements until an optimal solution is reached. Unlike the simplex method, the transportation model is fairly simple to compute.

To begin the analysis of a transportation problem, management must determine the cost of shipping from each source to each destination. Such data are usually presented in tabular form, like Table 11.1 for the case of the Executive Furniture Corporation, a manufacturer of office desks.

The next step is to set up a transportation table; its purpose is to conveniently summarize all relevant data in a concise manner and to keep track of algorithm computations. Using the information from the Executive Furniture Corporation example displayed in Figure 11.1 and Table 11.1, we can construct a transportation table and label its various components (see Table 11.2).

Table 11.1. Transportation Costs per Desk for Executive Furniture Corporation

From \ To	Albuquerque	Boston	Cleveland
Des Moines	$5	$4	$3
Evansville	$8	$4	$3
Fort Lauderdale	$9	$7	$5

Table 11.2. Transportation Table for Executive Furniture Corporation

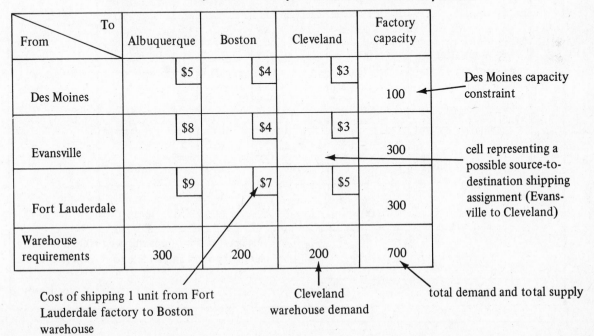

From \ To	Albuquerque	Boston	Cleveland	Factory capacity	
Des Moines	$5	$4	$3	100	← Des Moines capacity constraint
Evansville	$8	$4	$3	300	← cell representing a possible source-to-destination shipping assignment (Evansville to Cleveland)
Fort Lauderdale	$9	$7	$5	300	
Warehouse requirements	300	200	200	700	

Cost of shipping 1 unit from Fort Lauderdale factory to Boston warehouse

Cleveland warehouse demand

total demand and total supply

DEVELOPING AN INITIAL SOLUTION—THE NORTHWEST-CORNER RULE

Once we have arranged the data in tabular form, we must establish an initial feasible solution to the problem. One systematic procedure, known as the *northwest-corner rule,* requires that we start in the upper left-hand cell (or northwest corner) of the table and allocate units to shipping routes as follows:

1. Exhaust the supply (factory capacity) of each row before moving down to the next row.
2. Exhaust the (warehouse) requirements of each column before moving to the next column on the right.
3. Check that all supply and demands are met.

EXAMPLE 11.1

We can use the northwest-corner rule to find an initial feasible solution to the Executive Furniture Corporation problem shown in Table 11.2. It takes five steps in this example to make the initial shipping assignments:

1. Assign 100 units from Des Moines to Albuquerque (exhausting Des Moines supply).
2. Assign 200 units from Evansville to Albuquerque (exhausting Albuquerque's demand).
3. Assign 100 units from Evansville to Boston (exhausting Evansville's supply).
4. Assign 100 units from Fort Lauderdale to Boston (exhausting Boston's demand).
5. Assign 200 units from Fort Lauderdale to Cleveland (exhausting Cleveland's demand and Fort Lauderdale's supply).

From \ To	Albuquerque (A)	Boston (B)	Cleveland (C)	Factory capacity
Des Moines (D)	$5 100	$4	$3	100
Evansville (E)	$8 200	$4 100	$3	300
Fort Lauderdale (F)	$9	$7 (100)	$5 200	300
Warehouse requirements	300	200	200	700

Means that the firm is shipping 100 units along the Fort Lauderdale to Boston route.

(continued)

We can easily compute the cost of this shipping assignment.

Total Cost of This Initial Solution

| Route | | Units | | Total |
From	To	Shipped	Cost per Unit	Cost
D	A	100	$5	$ 500
E	A	200	$8	1600
E	B	100	$4	400
F	B	100	$7	700
F	C	200	$5	1000
			Total:	$4200

The solution given above is feasible since it satisfies all demand and supply constraints. We would be very lucky if this solution yielded the minimal transportation cost for the problem, however. It is more likely that we shall have to employ one of the iterative procedures designed to help reach an optimal solution. First, try to use this method to solve Problem 11.1.

PROBLEM 11.1

The management of Executive Furniture Corporation decided to expand the production capacity at its Des Moines factory and to cut back production at its other factories. It also recognizes a shifting market for its desks and revises the requirements at its three warehouses.

New Warehouse Requirements	New Factory Capacities
Albuquerque (A): 200 desks	Des Moines (D): 300 desks
Boston (B): 200 desks	Evansville (E): 150 desks
Cleveland (C): 300 desks	Fort Lauderdale (F): 250 desks

Shipping costs remain the same (see Example 11.1).

(continued)

Use the northwest-corner rule to establish an initial feasible shipping schedule and calculate its cost.

Table for Checking Unused Routes

From \ To				

THE STEPPING-STONE METHOD

The stepping-stone method is an iterative technique for moving from an initial feasible solution to an optimal solution. It is used to evaluate the cost-effectiveness of shipping goods via transportation routes *not* currently in the solution. We test each unused cell, or square, in the transportation table by asking the following question: "What would happen to total shipping costs if *one* unit of our product (for example, one desk) were tentatively shipped on an unused route?" We conduct this test as follows:

1. Select an unused square to evaluate.
2. Beginning at this square, trace a closed path back to the original square via squares that are currently being used (only horizontal and vertical moves are permissible).
3. Beginning with a plus (+) sign at the unused square, place alternate minus (−) signs and plus signs on each corner square of the closed path just traced.

4. Calculate an *improvement index* by adding together the unit cost figures found in each square containing a plus sign and then subtracting the unit costs in each square containing a minus sign.
5. Repeat steps 1–4 until you have calculated an improvement index for all unused squares. If all indices computed are greater than or equal to zero, you have reached an optimal solution. If not, it is possible to improve the current solution and decrease total shipping costs.

EXAMPLE 11.2

We can apply the stepping-stone method to the Executive Furniture Corporation data in Example 11.1 to evaluate unused shipping routes. The four currently unassigned routes are: Des Moines to Boston, Des Moines to Cleveland, Evansville to Cleveland, and Fort Lauderdale to Albuquerque.

Steps 1 and 2. Beginning with the Des Moines to Boston route, we first trace a closed path using only currently occupied squares (see the table on page 231) and then place alternate plus signs and minus signs in the corners of this path. We see that we can use only squares currently used for shipping to turn the corners of the route we're tracing. Hence, the path Des Moines–Boston to Des Moines–Albuquerque to Fort Lauderdale–Albuquerque to Fort Lauderdale–Boston to Des Moines–Boston would *not* be acceptable since the Fort Lauderdale–Albuquerque square is empty. It turns out that *only one* closed route is possible for each square we want to test. Once this one closed path is identified, we can begin assigning plus and minus signs to these squares in the path.

Step 3. How do we decide which squares get plus signs and which get minus signs? The answer is simple. Since we are testing the cost effectiveness of the Des Moines to Boston shipping route, we pretend we are shipping one desk from Des Moines to Boston. This is one more unit than we *were* sending between the two cities, so we place a plus sign in the box. But if we ship one *more* unit than before from Des Moines to Boston, we end up sending 101 desks out of the Des Moines factory. Because the Des Moines factory's capacity is only 100 units, we must ship one desk *less* from Des Moines to Albuquerque—this change prevents us from violating the limit constraint. To indicate that we have reduced the Des Moines to Albuquerque shipment, we place a minus sign in its box. Continuing along the closed path, we notice that we are no longer meeting the warehouse requirement for 300 units. In fact, if we reduce the Des Moines to Albuquerque shipment to 99 units, we must increase the Evansville to Albuquerque load by one unit, to 201 desks. Therefore, we place a plus sign in that box to indicate the increase. Finally, we note that if we assign 201 desks to the Evansville to Albuquerque route, then we must reduce the Evansville to Boston route by one unit, to 99 desks, in order to maintain the Evansville factory capacity constraint of 300 units. Thus, we insert a minus sign in the Evansville to Boston box. As a result, we have balanced demand and supply limitations among all four routes on the closed path.

(continued)

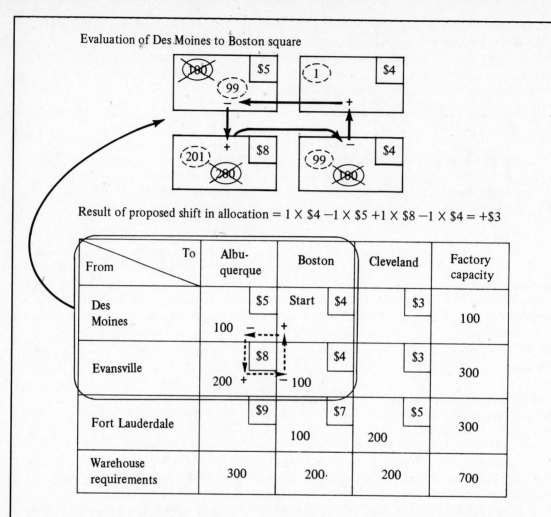

Evaluation of Des Moines to Boston square

Result of proposed shift in allocation = 1 × $4 − 1 × $5 + 1 × $8 − 1 × $4 = +$3

From \ To	Albu-querque	Boston		Cleveland	Factory capacity
Des Moines	$5 100	Start	$4	$3	100
Evansville	$8 200		$4 100	$3	300
Fort Lauderdale	$9	$7 100		$5 200	300
Warehouse requirements	300	200.		200	700

Step 4. We compute an improvement index for the Des Moines to Boston route by adding unit costs in squares with plus signs and subtracting costs in squares with minus signs. Hence,

$$\text{Des Moines to Boston index} = \$4 - \$5 + \$8 - \$4 = +\$3$$

This means that for every desk shipped via the Des Moines to Boston route, total transportation costs will *increase* by $3 over their current level.

Let us now examine the Des Moines to Cleveland unused route, one slightly more difficult to trace with a closed path. Again, you will notice that we turn each corner along the path only at squares on the existing route. The path can go *through* the Evansville to Cleveland box but cannot turn a corner and we cannot place a + or − sign there. We may use only an occupied square as a stepping stone.

(continued)

From \ To	(A) Albuquerque	(B) Boston	(C) Cleveland	Factory
(D) Des Moines	– $5 100	$4	Start + $3	100
(E) Evansville	+ $8 200	– $4 100	$3	300
(F) Fort Lauderdale	$9	+ $7 100	– $5 200	300
Warehouse requirements	300	200	200	700

Des Moines to Cleveland Index = $3 − $5 + $8 − $4 + $7 − $5 = $4

Thus, opening this route will also not lower total shipping costs.
The other two routes may be evaluated in a similar fashion:

Evansville to Cleveland index = $3 − $4 + $7 − $5 = $1   (closed path = EC − EB + FB − FC)

Fort Lauderdale to Albuquerque index = $9 − $7 + $4 − $8 = −$2
(closed path = FA − FB + EB − EA)

Because this last index is negative, a cost savings may be attained by making use of the (currently unused) Fort Lauderdale to Albuquerque route.

PROBLEM 11.2

The Hardrock Concrete Company has plants in three locations and is currently working on three major construction projects, located at different sites. The shipping cost per truckload of concrete, plant capacities, and project requirements are provided below.

(continued)

To From	Project A	Project B	Project C	Plant capacity
Plant 1	$10	$4	$11	70
Plant 2	$12	$5	$8	50
Plant 3	$9	$7	$6	30
Project requirements	40	50	60	150

Formulate an initial feasible solution to Hardrock's transportation problem using the northwest-corner rule. Then evaluate each unused shipping route by applying the stepping-stone method and computing all improvement indices.

Initial Solution

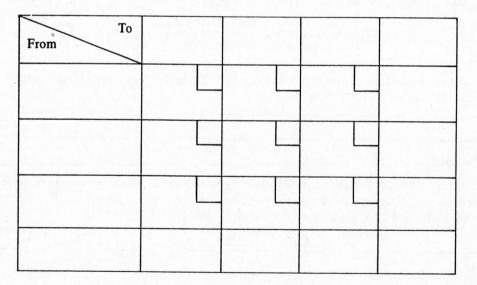

(continued)

Table for Checking Unused Routes.

From \ To				

In Example 11.2, we saw that a better solution is possible—due to the presence of a negative improvement index on one of the unused routes. Each negative index represents the amount by which total transportation costs could be decreased if one unit or product were shipped by that source-destination combination. The next step, then, is to choose that route (unused square) with the *largest negative improvement index*. We can then ship the maximum allowable number of units on that route and reduce the total cost accordingly. What is the maximum quantity that can be shipped on the new money-saving route? That quantity is found by referring to the closed path of plus signs and minus signs drawn for the route and selecting the *smallest number* found in those squares containing *minus signs*.

To obtain a new solution, we add that number to all squares on the closed path with plus signs and subtract it from all squares on the path assigned minus signs.

One iteration of the stepping-stone method is now complete. Again, we must test to see if it is optimal or whether we can make any further improvements. This is done by evaluating each unused square as described above.

EXAMPLE 11.3

To improve Executive Furniture's solution, we can use the improvement indices calculated in Example 11.2. The largest (and only) negative index is the Fort Lauderdale to Albuquerque route. We repeat the transportation table for the problem below.

From \ To	(A) Albuquerque	(B) Boston	(C) Cleveland	Factory
(D) Des Moines	100 $5	$4	$3	100
(E) Evansville	200 $8	100 $4	$3	300
(F) Fort Lauderdale	$9	− 100 $7	200 $5	300
Warehouse	300	200	200	700

The maximum quantity that may be shipped on the newly opened route (FA) is the smallest number found in squares containing minus signs—in this case, 100 units. Why 100 units? Since the total cost decreases by $2 per unit shipped, we know we would like to ship the maximum possible number of units. Previous stepping-stone calculations indicate that each unit shipped over the FA route results in an increase of one unit shipped from E to B and a decrease of one unit in both the

(continued)

amounts shipped from F to B (now 100 units) and from E to A (now 200 units). Hence, the maximum we can ship over the FA route is 100. This solution results in zero units being shipped from F to B. Now, we add 100 units (to the zero now being shipped) on route FA; then proceed to subtract 100 from route FB, leaving zero in that square (but still balancing the row total for F); then add 100 to route EB, yielding 200; and finally, subtract 100 from route EA, leaving 100 units shipped. Note that the new numbers still produce the correct row and column totals as required. The new solution is shown in the following table.

From \ To	(A) Albuquerque	(B) Boston	(C) Cleveland	Factory
(D) Des Moines	100 — $5	$4	$3	100
(E) Evansville	100 — $8	200 — $4	$3	300
(F) Fort Lauderdale	100 — $9	$7	200 — $5	300
Warehouse	300	200	200	700

Total shipping cost has been reduced by (100 units) $\times$ ($2 saved per unit) = $200 and is now $4000. This cost figure, of course, can also be derived by multiplying each unit shipping cost times the number of units transported on its route, namely

$$100(\$5) + 100(\$8) + 200(\$4) + 100(\$9) + 200(\$5) = \$4000$$

PROBLEM 11.3

Determine whether the new solution table presented in Example 11.3 contains the optimal transportation allocation for Executive Furniture. If not, compute an improved solution and test it for optimality.

From \ To	(A) Albuquerque	(B) Boston	(C) Cleveland	
(D) Des Moines				
(E) Evansville				
(F) Fort Lauderdale				

(continued)

From \ To	(A) Albuquerque	(B) Boston	(C) Cleveland	
(D) Des Moines				
(E) Evansville				
(F) Fort Lauderdale				

DEMAND NOT EQUAL TO SUPPLY

A common situation in real-world problems is the case where total demand is not equal to total supply. We can handle these "unbalanced" problems easily with the solution procedures discussed above if we first introduce *dummy sources* or *dummy destinations*. In the event that total supply is greater than total demand, we create a dummy destination, where demand exactly equals the surplus. If total demand is greater than total supply, we introduce a dummy source (factory) with a supply equal to the excess of demand over supply. In each case, we assign cost coefficients of zero each square on the dummy location or route.

EXAMPLE 11.4

Executive Furniture increases the rate of production of desks in its Des Moines factory to 250. To reformulate this unbalanced problem, we refer back to the data presented in Example 11.1. We use the northwest-corner rule to find the initial feasible solution.

From \ To	(A) Albuquerque	(B) Boston	(C) Cleveland	Dummy	Factory capacity	
(D) Des Moines	$5 250	$4	$3	0	250	← new Des Moines capacity
(E) Evansville	$8 50	$4 200	$3 50	0	300	
(F) Fort Lauderdale	$9	$7	$5 150	0 150	300	
Warehouse requirements	300	200	200	150	850	

Total cost = 250($5) + 50($8) + 200($4) + 50($3) + 150($5) + 150(0) = $3350

PROBLEM 11.4

Sound Track Stereos assembles its high-fidelity stereophonic systems at three plants and distributes systems from three regional warehouses. The production capacities at each plant, demand at each warehouse, and unit shipping costs are presented below.

(continued)

To From	Warehouse A	Warehouse B	Warehouse C	Plant Supply
Plant W	$6	$4	$9	200
Plant X	$10	$5	$8	175
Plant Y	$12	$7	$6	75
Warehouse demand	250	100	150	500 450

Set up this transportation problem by adding a dummy plant—then use the northwest-corner rule to find an initial basic feasible solution.

To From				

DEGENERACY

In order to apply the stepping-stone method to a transportation problem, we must observe a rule pertaining to the number of shipping routes being used. That rule may be stated as follows: the number of occupied squares in *any* solution (initial or later) must be equal to the number of rows in the table plus the number of columns minus 1. Solutions that do not meet this rule are called *degenerate.*

Usually, degeneracy occurs when there are too few squares, or shipping routes, being used. As a result, it becomes impossible to trace a closed path for each unused square. You might observe that no problem discussed in this unit thus far has been degenerate. The original furniture problem, for example, had 5 assigned routes (3 rows or factories + 3 columns or warehouses − 1). Example 11.4, employing a dummy warehouse, had 6 assigned routes (3 rows + 4 columns − 1) and was not degenerate either.

To handle degenerate problems, we artifically create an occupied cell—that is, we place a zero (representing a fake shipment) in one of the unused squares and then treat that square as if it were occupied. The square chosen, it should be noted, must be in such a position as to allow all stepping-stone paths to be closed or traced.

EXAMPLE 11.5

Martin Shipping Company has three warehouses from which it supplies its three major retail customers in San José. Martin's shipping costs, warehouse supplies, and customer demands are presented in the transportation table below. To make the initial shipping assignments in the table we apply the northwest-corner rule.

From \ To	Customer 1	Customer 2	Customer 3	Warehouse supply
Warehouse 1	100 $8	$2	$6	100
Warehouse 2	0 $10	100 $9	20 $9	120
Warehouse 3	$7	$10	80 $7	80
Customer demand	100	100	100	300

The initial solution is *degenerate* because it violates the rule that the number of used squares must equal the number of rows plus the number of columns minus one. To correct the problem, we may place a zero in the unused square that represents the shipping route from warehouse 2 to customer 1. Now we can close all stepping-stone paths and compute improvement indices.

PROBLEM 11.5

After one iteration of the stepping-stone method, Wilson Paint's analysts produced the following transportation table.

From \ To	Warehouse 1	Warehouse 2	Warehouse 3	Factory capacity
Factory A	120 $8	$5	$6	120
Factory B	$15	80 $10	$14	80
Factory C	30 $3	$9	50 $10	80
Warehouse requirements	150	80	50	280

Cost = $2350

Complete one more full iteration of the stepping-stone method to produce an improved cost solution.

(continued)

From \ To				

FACILITY LOCATION ANALYSIS

The location of a new factory or warehouse is an issue of major financial importance to a firm. Ordinarily, several alternative locations must be considered and evaluated. Even though there is a wide variety of subjective factors to consider (including quality of labor supply, presence of labor unions, community attitude and appearance, utilities, recreational and educational facilities for employees), rational decisions are intended to minimize relevant costs.

The transportation method proves useful when considering each alternative facility location within the framework of one overall production-distribution system. Each new potential plant or warehouse will produce a different allocation of shipments, depending on its own production and shipping costs and the costs of each existing facility. The choice of a new location depends on which will yield the *minimum cost* for the *entire system.* This concept is illustrated in Example 11.6.

EXAMPLE 11.6

Ashley Auto Top Carriers currently maintains plants in Atlanta and Tulsa to supply major distribution centers in Los Angeles and New York. Because of an expanding demand, Ashley has decided to open a third plant and has narrowed the choice to one of two cities—New Orleans and Houston. Table 11.3 gives the pertinent production and distribution costs, as well as the plant capacities and distribution demands.

Table 11.3. Production Costs, Distribution Costs, Plant Capacities, and Market
Demands for the Ashley Auto Top Carriers

	From Plants	To Distribution Centers Los Angeles	New York	Normal Production	Unit Production Cost
Existing plants	Atlanta	$8	$5	600	$6
	Tulsa	$4	$7	900	$5
Proposed locations	New Orleans	$5	$6	500	$4 (anticipated)
	Houston	$4	($6)	500	$3 (anticipated)
	Forecast Demand	800	1200	2000	

Indicates distribution cost (shipping, handling, storage) will be $6 per carrier between Houston and New York

The important question that Ashley faces is: "Which of the new locations will yield a lower cost for the firm in combination with the existing plants and distribution centers?" To determine the answer, we need to solve two transportation problems, one for each possible combination. The

(continued)

location that shows a lower total cost of distribution and production to the existing system will be recommended.

We begin by setting up a transportation table that represents the opening of a third plant in New Orleans (see Table 11.4). We use the northwest-corner method to find an initial solution. The total cost of this first solution is seen to be $23,600. *You should note that the cost of each individual "plant to distribution center" route is found by adding the distribution costs* (in the body of Table 11.3) *to the respective unit production costs* (in the right-hand column of Table 11.3). Thus, the total production-plus-shipping cost of one auto top carrier from Atlanta to Los Angeles is $14 ($8 for shipping plus $6 for production).

Table 11.4. Ashley's Transportation Table for New Orleans Plant

From \ To	Los Angeles	New York	Production capacity
Atlanta	600 $14	$11	600
Tulsa	200 $9	700 $12	900
New Orleans	$9	500 $10	500
Demand	800	1200	2000

Total cost = (600 units × $14) + (200 units × $9) + (700 units × $12) + (500 units × $10)

= $8400 + $1800 + $8400 + $5000

= $23,600

Is this initial solution optimal? We employ the stepping-stone method to test it and to compute improvement indices for unused routes.

Improvement index for Atlanta to New York route = $11 (Atlanta to New York)
−$14 (Atlanta to Los Angeles)
+$ 9 (Tulsa to Los Angeles)
−$12 (Tulsa to New York)
= −$ 6

(continued)

Improvement index for New Orleans to Los Angeles route   = $9 (New Orleans to Los Angeles)
−$10 (New Orleans to New York)
+$12 (Tulsa to New York)
−$9 (Tulsa to Los Angeles)

= $2

Since the firm can save $6 for every unit it ships from Atlanta to New York, it will want to improve the initial solution and send as many as possible (600, in this case) on this currently unused route.

To From	Los Angeles	New York	Production capacity
Atlanta	$14	$11 600	600
Tulsa	$9 800	$12 100	900
New Orleans	$9	$10 500	500
Demand	800	1200	2000

You may want to confirm that total cost is now $20,000, a saving of $3500 over the initial solution. Now, we must test the two unused routes to see if their improvement indices are negative numbers.

Index for Atlanta to Los Angeles   = $14 − $11 + $12 − $9
= $6

Index for New Orleans to Los Angeles   = $9 − $10 + $12 − $9
= $2

Since both indices are greater than zero, we have reached an optimal solution using the New Orleans plant. If Ashley selects to open the *New Orleans plant,* the firm's total distribution *system cost will be $20,000.*

This information, however, provides only half the answer to Ashley's problem. You can help provide complete information and recommend a solution by solving Problem 11.6.

PROBLEM 11.6

In Example 11.6, Ashley Auto Top Carrier proposed opening a new plant in either New Orleans or Houston. The firm's management found that the total system cost (of production plus distribution) would be $20,000 if they chose the New Orleans site.

What would be the total cost if Ashley opened a plant in Houston? At which proposed location should Ashley open the new facility?

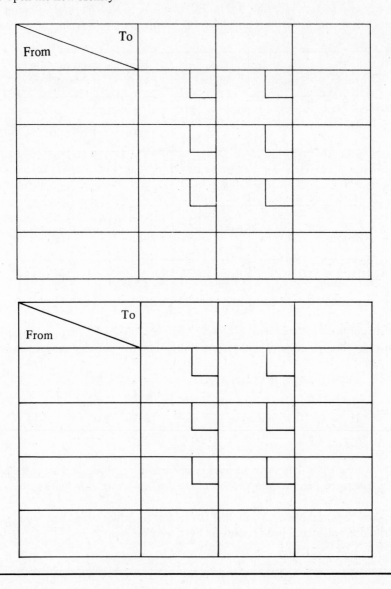

LOCATIONAL BREAK-EVEN ANALYSIS

Locational break-even analysis refers to the use of cost-volume analysis to make an economic comparison of location alternatives. By identifying fixed and variable costs and graphing them for each location, we can determine which one provides the lowest cost. Locational break-even analysis can be done mathematically or graphically. The graphic approach has the advantage of providing the range of volume over which each location is preferable.

The locational break-even method involves three steps:

1. Determine the fixed and variable cost for each location.
2. Plot the costs for each location, with costs on the vertical axis of the graph and annual volume on the horizontal axis.
3. Select the location that has the lowest total cost for the expected production volume.

EXAMPLE 11.7

A manufacturer of automobile carburators is considering three locations, Akron, Boston, and Chicago, for a new plant. Cost studies indicate that fixed costs per year at the sites are $30,000, $60,000, and $110,000, respectively, whereas variable costs are $75 per unit, $45 per unit, and $25 per unit, respectively. The expected selling price of the carburators produced is $120. The company wishes to find the most economical location for an expected volume of 2,000 units per year.

For each of the three locations, we can plot the fixed costs (those at a volume of zero units) and the total cost (fixed costs + variable costs) at the expected volume of output.

For Akron, Total cost (at volume of 2,000 units)

$$= \$30,000 + \$75(2,000)$$

$$= \$180,000$$

For Boston, Total cost $= \$\ 60,000 + \$45(2,000) = \$150,000$

For Chicago, Total cost $= \$110,000 + \$25(2,000) = \$160,000$

(continued)

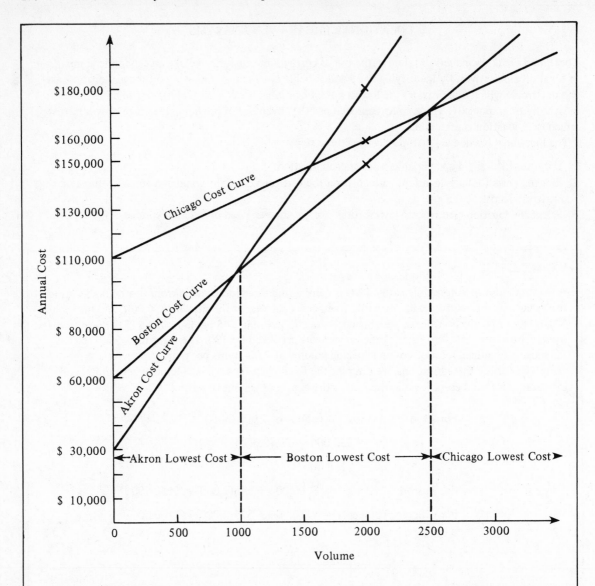

The graph shows that Boston provides the lowest cost location at the expected volume of 2,000 units per year. The expected profit is:

$$\text{Total Revenue} - \text{Total Cost} = \$120(2,000) - \$150,000 = \$90,000/\text{yr.}$$

The graph also tells us that for a volume of less than 1,000, Akron would be preferred and for a volume greater than 2,500, Chicago would yield the greatest profit.

PROBLEM 11.7

The fixed and variable costs for four potential plant sites for a ski equipment manufacturer are shown below:

Site	Fixed Cost per year	Variable Cost per unit
Atlanta	$125,000	$ 6
Burlington	75,000	$ 5
Cleveland	100,000	$ 4
Denver	50,000	$12

(a) Graph the total cost lines for the four potential sites.

(b) Over what range of annual volume is each location the preferable one (that with lowest expected cost)?

(c) If expected volume of the ski equipment is 5,000 units, which location would you recommend?

FACTOR RATING METHOD

Deciding where to locate a new facility usually includes several factors that management thinks are important. The *factor rating* method is popular because a variety of relevant criteria can be included in a given case. Managers can then consider the results of quantitative approaches, such as locational break-even analysis or the transportation method, together with the more qualitative factor rating approach in making a final decision.

There are six steps in the rating method.

1. Develop a list of relevant factors (such as location, community, power supply, labor force, etc.)
2. Assign a weight to each factor to reflect its relative importance in the company's objectives.
3. Develop a scale for each factor (e.g., 1–10 or 1–100 points).
4. Have management score each location on each factor, using the scale in step 3.
5. Multiply the scores times the weights for each factor and total the score for each location.
6. Make a recommendation based on the maximum point score, considering the results of quantitative approaches as well.

EXAMPLE 11.8

A western pharmaceutical firm has decided to expand its drug production in a new location. The expansion is due to limited capacity at its existing plant. The rating sheet below provides a list of factors that management has decided are important, their weightings, and the ratings for two possible sites, Tulsa and Denver.

Factor	Weight	Scores (out of 100) Tulsa	Denver	Weighted Scores Tulsa	Denver
Labor costs	.20	80	65	(.20)(80) = 16.0	(.2)(65) = 13.0
Closeness to Market	.25	60	70	(.25)(60) = 15.0	(.25)(70) = 17.5
Community	.30	75	90	(.30)(75) = 22.5	(.30)(90) = 27.0
Tax Structure	.10	85	80	(.10)(85) = 8.5	(.10)(80) = 8.0
Power Availability	.15	70	90	(.15)(70) = 10.5	(.15)(90) = 13.5
Totals	1.00			72.5	79.0

In this model, Tulsa's weighted factor score is 72.5 while Denver scores a higher 79.0. This suggests that Denver would be the preferred location for the new factory.

PROBLEM 11.8

Consolidated Refineries, headquartered in Baton Rouge, must decide among three Louisiana sites for the construction of a new oil processing center. The firm has selected the six factors listed below as a basis for evaluation and has assigned rating weights from one to five on each factor.

Factor No.	Factor Name	Rating Weight
1	Proximity to Mississippi River	5
2	Power source availability	3
3	Available work force	4
4	Distance from Baton Rouge	2
5	Community desirability	2
6	Equipment suppliers in area	3

Management rates each location on a 1–10 point basis as follows:

Factor No.	Location A	Location B	Location C
1	10	8	8
2	8	7	10
3	3	6	7
4	1	8	6
5	9	6	8
6	5	6	9

What site will be recommended?

ANSWERS

11.1

From \ To	A		B		C		Factory capacity
D	200	$5	100	$4		$3	300
E		$8	100	$4	50	$3	150
F		$9		$7	250	$5	250
Warehouse requirements	200		200		300		700

Total cost = 200($5) + 100($4) + 100($4) + 50($3) + 250($5)

= 1000 + 400 + 400 + 150 + 1250

= $3200

11.2

From \ To	A		B		C		Plant capacities
1	40	$10	30	$4		$11	70
2		$12	20	$5	30	$8	50
3		$9		$7	30	$6	30
Project requirements	40		50		60		150

(continued)

$$Cost = 40(\$10) + 30(\$4) + 20(\$5) + 30(\$8) + 30(\$6)$$

$$= \$1040$$

Using the stepping-stone method, the following improvement indices are computed:

Plant 1 to project C $= \$11 - \$4 + \$5 - \$8 = +\$4$
(closed path $= 1C$ to $1B$ to $2B$ to $2C$)

Plant 2 to project A $= \$12 - \$5 + \$4 - \$10 = +\$1$
(closed path $= 2A$ to $2B$ to $1B$ to $1A$)

Plant 3 to project A $= \$9 - \$6 + \$8 - \$5 + \$4 - \$10 = 0$
(closed path $= 3A$ to $3C$ to $2C$ to $2B$ to $1B$ to $1A$)

Plant 3 to project B $= \$7 - \$6 + \$8 - \$5 = \$4$
(closed path $= 3B$ to $3C$ to $2C$ to $2B$)

Since all indices are greater than or equal to zero, this initial solution provides the optimal transportation schedule, namely, 40 units from 1 to A, 30 units from 1 to B, 20 units from 2 to B, 30 units from 2 to C, and 30 units from 3 to C.

11.3   To test the solution table below for optimality, we must compute the improvement index for each unused square.

From \ To	A	B	C	Total Available
D	100 $5	$4	$3	100
E	100 $8	200 $4	$3	300
F	100 $9	$7	200 $5	300
Warehouse required	300	200	200	700

(continued)

Improvement indices:

$$\text{D to B} = \$4 - \$5 + \$8 - \$4 = +\$3 \quad \text{(closed path} = DB - DA + EA - EB)$$

$$\text{D to C} = \$3 - \$5 + \$9 - \$5 = +\$2 \quad \text{(closed path} = DC - DA + FA - FC)$$

$$\text{E to C} = \$3 - \$8 + \$9 - \$5 = -\$1 \quad \text{(closed path} = EC - EA + FA - FC)$$

$$\text{F to B} = \$7 - \$4 + \$8 - \$9 = +\$2 \quad \text{(closed path} = FB - EB + EA - FA)$$

Thus, an improvement can be made by shipping the maximum allowable number of units from E to C. Only the squares EA and FC will have minus signs in the closed path. Since the smallest number in these two squares is 100, we add 100 units to EC and FA and subtract 100 units from EA and FC. The new cost is $3900.

From \ To	A		B		C		Factory
D	100	$5		$4		$3	100
E		$8	200	$4	100	$3	300
F	200	$9		$7	100	$5	300
Warehouse	300		200		200		700

This table contains the optimal shipping assignments because each improvement index that can be computed at this point is greater than or equal to zero. Improvement indices for the table are:

$$\text{D to B} = \$4 - \$5 + \$9 - \$5 + \$3 - \$4 = \$2$$
$$\text{(closed path} = DB - DA + FA - FC + EC - EB)$$

$$\text{D to C} = \$3 - \$5 + \$9 - \$5 = \$2$$
$$\text{(closed path} = DC - DA + FA - FC)$$

(continued)

E to A = \$8 − \$9 + \$5 − \$3 = \$1
(closed path = EA − FA + FC − EC)

F to B = \$7 − \$5 + \$3 − \$4 = \$1
(closed path = FB − FC + EC − EB)

11.4

From \ To	A	B	C	Plant supply
W	\$6 200	\$4	\$9	200
X	\$10 50	\$5 100	\$8 25	175
Y	\$12	\$7	\$6 75	75
Dummy	0	0	0 50	50
Warehouse demand	250	100	150	500

Total cost = 200(\$6) + 50(\$10) + 100(\$5) + 25(\$8) + 75(\$6) + 50(0)

= \$2850

11.5   The table shown has a degenerate solution because only 4 square (less than the 3 + 3 − 1 required) are occupied. We can place a zero in square B1, square C2, square A2, or square B3 to allow unused paths to be closed. If square B1 is selected, the improvement indices for the four remaining unused squares can be computed as follows:

Index for A to 2 = \$5 − \$8 + \$15 − \$10 = \$2
(closed path = A2 − A1 + B1 − B2)

Index for A to 3 = \$6 − \$8 + \$3 − \$10 = −\$9
(closed path = A3 − A1 + C1 − C3)

(continued)

$$\text{Index for B to 3} = \$14 - \$15 + \$3 - \$10 = -\$8$$
$$\text{(closed path = B3 - B1 + C1 - C3)}$$

$$\text{Index for C to 2} = \$9 - \$10 + \$15 - \$3 = \$11$$
$$\text{(closed path = C2 - B2 + B1 - C1)}$$

It appears that Wilson should use the route from factory A to warehouse 3 and ship the maximum number of units permitted, namely, 50.

To From	Warehouse 1	Warehouse 2	Warehouse 3	Factory capacity
Factory A	$8 70	$5	$6 50	120
Factory B	$15	$10 80	$14	80
Factory C	$3 80	$9	$10	80
Warehouse requirements	150	80	50	280

$$\text{Cost} = 70(\$8) + 50(\$6) + 80(\$10) + 80(\$3)$$
$$= \$1900$$

This solution, also, is degenerate, but it decreases shipping costs by $450.

11.6   The MODI equations for each occupied square are, with $R_1 = 0$ to begin:

$$1.\ R_1 + K_1 = 10 \quad K_1 = 10$$

$$2.\ R_1 + K_2 = 4 \quad K_2 = 4$$

$$3.\ R_2 + K_2 = 5 \quad R_2 = 1$$

$$4.\ R_2 + K_3 = 8 \quad K_3 = 7$$

(continued)

11.6

From \ To	Los Angeles	New York	Production capacity
Atlanta	$14 600	$11	600
Tulsa	$9 200	$12 700	900
Houston	$7	$9 500	500
Demand	800	1200	2000

Total cost of initial solution = $8400 + $1800 + $8400 + $4500
= $23,100

Improvement index for Atlanta to New York = $11 − $14 + $9 − $12
= −$6

Improvement index for Houston to Los Angeles = $7 − $9 + $12 − $9
= $1

(continued)

To From	Los Angeles	New York	Production capacity
Atlanta	$14	$11 600	600
Tulsa	$9 800	$12 100	900
Houston	$7	$9 500	500
Demand	800	1200	2000

Total cost of improved solution = $19,500

Improvement indices for Atlanta to New York and Houston to Los Angeles routes are both positive at this point. Thus the solution is optimal. Upon comparing total costs for the Houston option ($19,500) to those for the New Orleans option ($20,000), we would recommend to Ashley that, all factors being equal, the firm should select the Houston site.

11.7   **a.**

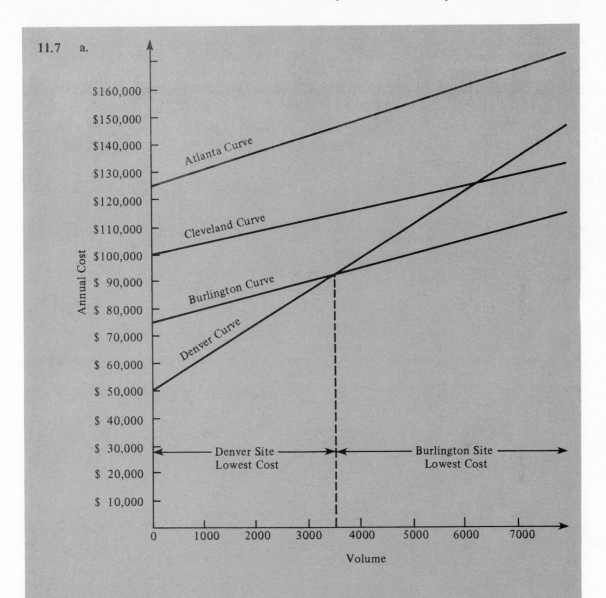

b. Denver is preferable over the range from 0–3,570, while Burlington is lowest cost at any volume over 3,570. Atlanta is never lowest in cost. Cleveland becomes the best site only when volume exceeds 25,000 units per year.

c. At volume = 5,000 units, Burlington is the least cost site.

11.8

Factor	Weight	Location A		Location B		Location C	
		Rating	Weighted Score	Rating	Weighted Score	Rating	Weighted Score
1	5	10	50	8	40	8	40
2	3	8	24	7	21	10	30
3	4	3	12	6	24	7	28
4	2	1	2	8	16	6	12
5	2	9	18	6	12	8	16
6	3	5	15	6	18	9	27
Total Weighted Scores			121		131		153

Based on the factor weighting method, site C would be selected.

Note that raw weights were used in computing these weighted scores (we just multiplied "weight" times "rating"). *Relative weights* could have been used instead by taking each factor weight and dividing by the sum of the weights (i.e., 19). Then factor 1's rate would be 5/19 = .26. Location C will still be selected.

HOMEWORK PROBLEMS

11-1. The Hardgrave Machine Company produces computer components at its plants in Cincinnati, Salt Lake City, and Pittsburgh. These plants have not been able to keep up with demand for orders at Hardgrave's four warehouses in Detroit, Dallas, New York, and Los Angeles. As a result, the firm has decided to build a new plant to expand its productive capacity. The two sites being considered are Seattle and Birmingham, Alabama; both cities are attractive in terms of labor supply, municipal services, and ease of factory financing.

The table below presents the production costs and output requirements for each of the three existing plants, demand at each of the four warehouses, and estimated production costs of the new proposed plants.

Hardgrave's Demand and Supply Data

Warehouse	Monthly Demand (units)	Production Plant	Monthly Supply	Cost to Produce One Unit
Detroit	10,000	Cincinnati	15,000	$48
Dallas	12,000	Salt Lake	6,000	$50
New York	15,000	Pittsburgh	14,000	$52
Los Angeles	9,000		35,000	
	46,000			

Supply needed from new plant = 46,000 − 35,000 = 11,000 units per month

Estimated Production Cost/Unit at Proposed Plants	
Seattle	$53
Birmingham	$49

(continued)

Transportation costs from each plant to each warehouse are summarized below:

Hardgrave's Shipping Costs

FROM \ TO	Detroit	Dallas	New York	Los Angeles
Cincinnati	$25	$55	$40	$60
Salt Lake	35	30	50	40
Pittsburgh	36	45	26	66
Seattle	60	38	65	27
Birmingham	35	30	41	50

Which of the new locations will yield the lowest cost for the firm in combination with the existing plants and warehouses?

11-2. The Krampf Lines Railway Company specializes in coal handling. On Friday, April 13, Krampf had empty cars at the following towns in the quantities indicated.

Town	Supply of Cars
Morgantown	35
Youngstown	60
Pittsburgh	25

By Monday, April 16, the following towns will need coal cars as follows:

Town	Demand for Cars
Coal Valley	30
Coaltown	45
Coal Junction	25
Coalsburg	20

Using a railway city-to-city distance chart, the dispatcher constructs a mileage table for the preceding towns. The result is:

	To			
From	*Coal Valley*	*Coaltown*	*Coal Junction*	*Coalsburg*
Morgantown	50	30	60	70
Youngstown	20	80	10	90
Pittsburgh	100	40	80	30

Minimizing total miles over which cars are moved to new locations, compute the best shipment of coal cars.

Aggregate Planning

Aggregate planning is concerned with planning the quantity and timing of production for the intermediate future, often from 3 months to 18 months ahead. Planners try to determine the best way to meet fore-casted product demand by adjusting production rates, manpower levels, inventory levels, overtime work, subcontracting rates, and other controllable variables. The goal of the process usually is to minimize costs over the planning period. Other objectives may be to minimize fluctuations in the work force or inventory level, or to keep a certain standard of service performance.

There are a variety of strategies that production planners may use in "pure" form or in combination.

1. Vary the size of the workforce by hiring or layoffs.
2. Vary the production rate by using overtime or idle time to increase or decrease capacity.
3. Vary the inventory levels—for example, produce inventory during low demand periods to meet high demand in future periods.
4. Subcontract to acquire temporary capacity.

Although each of these strategies could work well in adjusting to meet demand, a combination of them (called "mixed strategy") often works best.

We will describe several techniques that managers use in aggregate planning in this chapter. The most widely used and easy to visualize is called the *charting* or *graphical* method. More formal mathematical approaches, including the *transportation method* of linear programming, *linear decision rules,* and *hueristic methods* will also be discussed.

GRAPHICAL AND CHARTING TECHNIQUES

The graphical and charting techniques work with a few variables at a time to allow planners to compare projected demand with existing capacity. They are trial-and-error approaches that do not guarantee an optimal production plan.

In general, five steps are followed:

1. Determine the demand in each period.
2. Determine what the capacity is for regular time, overtime, and subcontracting each period.
3. Find the costs for labor and inventory holding.
4. Consider company policy that may apply to the workforce or stock level.
5. Develop alternative plans and examine their costs. These steps are illustrated in Examples 12.1 and 12.2.

EXAMPLE 12.1

A Philadelphia manufacturer of roofing supplies has developed monthly forecasts for an important product and presented the period January–June in Table 12.1. The demand per day is computed by simply dividing the expected demand by the number of working days each month.

Table 12.1

Month	Expected Demand	Production Days	Demand per day (Computed)
January	900	22	41
February	700	18	39
March	800	21	38
April	1,200	21	57
May	1,100	22	68
June	1,100	20	55
	6,200	124	

To illustrate the nature of the aggregate planning problem, the firm also draws a histogram (Figure 12.1) that charts the daily demand each month. The dotted line across the chart represents the production rate required to meet average demand. It is computed by:

$$\text{Average requirement} = \frac{\text{total expected demand}}{\text{number of production days}}$$

$$= \frac{6,200}{124} = 50 \text{ units/day}$$

(continued)

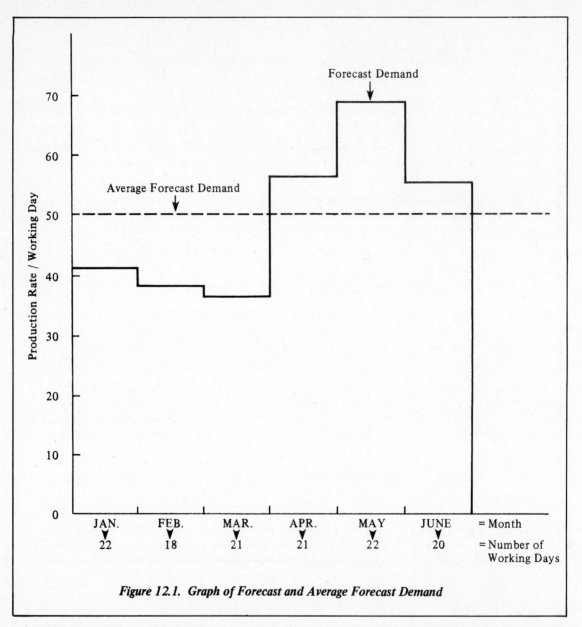

Figure 12.1. Graph of Forecast and Average Forecast Demand

The histogram in Figure 12.1 illustrates how the forecast differs from the average demand. Some strategies for meeting the forecast were listed earlier. The firm, for example, might hire and layoff workers as needed to yield a production rate that meets the average demand (as indicated by the dashed line). Or it might produce a steady rate of, say, 30 units and then subcontract excess demand to other roofing suppliers. A third plan might be to combine overtime work with some subcontracting to absorb demand. Example 12.2 illustrates two possible strategies.

EXAMPLE 12.2

One possible strategy (call it Plan 1) for the manufacturer described in Example 12.1 is to maintain a constant workforce throughout the six-month period. A second (Plan 2) is to maintain a constant workforce at a level necessary for the lowest demand month (March) and to meet all demand above this level by subcontracting. Table 12.2 provides cost information necessary for the analysis.

Table 12.2. Cost Information

Inventory Carrying Cost	$5/unit/month
Subcontracting Cost (marginal cost per unit above in-house manufacturing cost)	$10/unit
Average pay rate	$5/hour ($40/day)
Overtime pay rate	$7/hour above 8 hours
Man hours to produce a unit	1.6 hours/unit

ANALYSIS OF PLAN 1

In analyzing this approach, which assumes that 50 units are produced per day, we have a constant workforce, no overtime or idletime, use no safety stock, and use no subcontractors. The firm accumulates inventory during the slack period of demand, which is January through March, and depletes it during the higher demand warm season, April through June.

Month	Production at 50 units/day	Demand Forecast	Monthly Inventory Change	Ending Inventory
January	1,100	900	+200	200
February	900	700	+200	400
March	1,050	800	+250	650
April	1,100	1,200	−150	500
May	1,050	1,500	−400	100
June	1,000	1,100	−100	0
				1,850

Inventory carried to next month = 1,850 units.

Workforce required to produce 50 units/day = 10 men
(Since each unit requires 1.6 man hours to produce, each worker can make 5 units in an 8 hour day. Hence to produce 50 units, 10 workers are needed)

(continued)

ANALYSIS OF PLAN 2

A constant workforce is also maintained in this strategy, but set low enough to meet demand in March, the lowest month. To produce 38 units/day in-house, 7.6 workers are needed. (You can think of this as 7 full-time workers and one part-timer). All other demand is met by subcontracting. Subcontracting is thus required in every month. No inventory holding costs are incurred in Plan 2.

Since 6,200 units are required during the aggregate plan period, we must compute how many can be made by the firm and how many subcontracted for.

$$\text{In-house production} = 38 \text{ units/day} \times 124 \text{ production days}$$

$$= 4,712 \text{ units}$$

$$\text{Subcontract units} = 6,200 - 4,712 = 1,488 \text{ units}$$

Table 12.3. Cost Comparison of Plans 1 and 2

Cost	Plan 1 (Constant Workforce of 10 workers)	Plan 2 (Workforce of 7.6 workers plus subcontractors)
Inventory carrying cost	$9,250 (1,850 units carried × $5/unit)	$0
Regular labor cost	$49,600 (10 men × $40 day × 124 days)	$37,696 (7.6 men × $40 day × 124 days)
Overtime labor costs	$0	$0
Hiring or layoff costs	$0	$0
Subcontracting costs	$0	$14,880 (1,488 units × $10/unit)
Total Marginal Cost	$58,850	$52,576

Table 12.3 provides a cost comparison of Plans 1 and 2. Plan 2, with a total marginal cost of $52,576 is more attractive financially than Plan 1.

PROBLEM 12.1

The roofing supply manufacturer described in Examples 12.1 and 12.2 wishes to consider two additional planning strategies. Cost information in Table 12.2 is to be used.

In Plan 3, the firm wishes to maintain a constant workforce of 6 and to pay overtime to meet demand.

In Plan 4, a constant workforce is also desired, but at the higher level of 8. Overtime may be used whenever necessary to meet demand.

In Plan 5, a constant workforce of 7 is selected. The remainder of demand is filled by subcontracting work.

Compare Plans 3, 4 and 5. Which one is preferable? Is it better than Plans 1 or 2?

Of course, there are many other strategies that can be considered in a problem like this. Although charting is a popular management tool, its help is in evaluating strategies, not generating them. A systematic method that considers all costs and produces an effective solution is needed. Linear programming is one such approach.

THE TRANSPORTATION METHOD OF LINEAR PROGRAMMING

When aggregate planning problems are viewed as one of allocating operating capacity to meet the forecasted demand, they can be formulated in a linear programming format. The transportation method of LP (which was discussed in Unit 11) is not a trial and error approach like charting, but produces an optimal plan for minimizing costs. It is also flexible in that it can specify the regular and overtime production in each time period, the number of units to be subcontracted, extra shifts, and the carry over from period to period.

In Example 12.3, the supply consists of on-hand inventory and units produced by regular time, overtime, and subcontracting. Costs, in the upper right hand corner of each cell of the matrix, relate to units produced in a given period or units carried in inventory from an earlier period.

EXAMPLE 12.3

Harpell Radial Tire Company has developed the following data that relate to production, demand, capacity, and costs at its West Virginia plant.

	Sales Period		
	March	*April*	*May*
Demand	800	1,000	750
Capacity			
Regular time	700	700	700
Overtime	50	50	50
Subcontracting	150	150	130
Beginning Inventory	100 tires		
Costs			
Regular time	$40/tire		
Overtime	$50/tire		
Subcontract	$70/tire		
Carrying cost	$ 2 per tire per month.		

Table 12.4 illustrates the structure of the transportation table and an initial feasible solution. You should note the following:

1. Carrying costs are $2 per tire per month. Thus tires produced in one period and held one month will have a $2 higher cost. Since holding cost is linear, two months hold over costs $4.
2. Transportation problems require that supply equal demand. Hence, a dummy column called "unused capacity" has been added. Costs of not using capacity are zero.
3. The quantities in each column are the levels of inventory needed to meet demand requirements. We see that demand of 800 tires in March is met by using 100 tires from beginning inventory and 700 tires from regular time.

(continued)

Table 12.4

Supply from		Demand for				Total capacity available (supply)
		Period 1 (March)	Period 2 (April)	Period 3 (May)	Unused capacity (dummy)	
Beginning inventory		[0] 100	[2]	[4]	[0]	100
1	Regular time	[40] 700	[42]	[44]	[0]	700
	Overtime	[50]	[52] 50	[54]	[0]	50
	Subcontract	[70]	[72] 150	[74]	[0]	150
2	Regular time		[40] 700	[42]	[0]	700
	Overtime		[50] 50	[52]	[0]	50
	Subcontract		[70] 50	[72]	[0] 100	150
3	Regular time			[40] 700	[0]	700
	Overtime			[50] 50	[0]	50
	Subcontract			[70]	[0] 130	130
Demand		800	1,000	750	230	2,780

PROBLEM 12.2

A Washington, D.C. plant has developed the accompanying supply, demand, cost, and inventory data. The firm has a constant workforce and meets all of its demand. Allocate the production capacity to satisfy demand at a minimum cost. What is the cost of this plan?

Supply Capacity Available (in units)

Period	Regular Time	Overtime	Subcontract
1	300	50	200
2	400	50	200
3	450	50	200

Demand Forecast

Period	Demand (units)
1	450
2	550
3	750

Other Data
Initial inventory   50 units
Regular time cost per unit $50
Overtime cost per unit $65
Subcontract cost per unit $80
Carrying cost per unit per period $1

(continued)

Supply from		Demand for				Total capacity available (supply)
		Period 1	Period 2	Period 3	Unused capacity (dummy)	
Beginning inventory		0				
1	Regular time					
	Overtime					
	Subcontract					
2	Regular time					
	Overtime					
	Subcontract					
3	Regular time					
	Overtime					
	Subcontract					
Demand						

LINEAR DECISION RULE

The Linear Decision Rule (LDR) was developed in the 1950s by a group of researchers at the Carnegie Mellon University. LDR is an aggregate planning model that attempts to specify an optimum production rate and work force level over a specific period. It minimizes the total costs of payroll, hiring, layoffs, overtime and inventory through a series of quadratic cost curves. Using calculus, two *linear* equations are derived and then solved for the values that achieve minimum cost.

The exact nature of the cost equations is established by collecting data and fitting curves to that data. This can be difficult to do, however, and the real strength of the LDR approach is in setting a benchmark against which other models can be evaluated.

The general form of the decision rule equations used by the Carnegie researchers was:

$$P_t = (aF_t + bF_{t+1} + \cdots + lF_{t+11}) + mW_{t-1} + nI_{t-1} + p$$

$$W_t = (qF_t + \cdots + wF_{t+11}) + xW_{t-1} + yI_{t-1} + z$$

Where $a, b, \ldots, z$ = constants

P_t = production rate for the next month, t

W_{t-1} = workforce last month

I_{t-1} = ending inventory level last month

F_t = forecast for month t

EXAMPLE 12.4

This example illustrates the LDR model actually constructed by the Carnegie team. Data were collected from a paint factory for the years 1949 to 1954. Cost functions were determined from accounting data and subjective estimates.

The linear decision rules for the paint factory were:

(continued)

$$P_t = \begin{Bmatrix} +0.463\ F_t \\ +0.234\ F_{t+1} \\ +0.111\ F_{t+2} \\ +0.046\ F_{t+3} \\ +0.013\ F_{t+4} \\ -0.002\ F_{t+5} \\ -0.008\ F_{t+6} \\ -0.010\ F_{t+7} \\ -0.009\ F_{t+8} \\ -0.008\ F_{t+9} \\ -0.007\ F_{t+10} \\ -0.005\ F_{t+11} \end{Bmatrix} + 0.993\ W_{t-1} + 153 - 0.464\ I_{t-1}$$

$$W_t = 0.743\ W_{t-1} + 2.09 - 0.010\ I_{t-1} + \begin{Bmatrix} +0.0101\ F_t \\ +0.0088\ F_{t+1} \\ +0.0071\ F_{t+2} \\ +0.0054\ F_{t+3} \\ +0.0042\ F_{t+4} \\ +0.0031\ F_{t+5} \\ +0.0023\ F_{t+6} \\ +0.0016\ F_{t+7} \\ +0.0012\ F_{t+8} \\ +0.0009\ F_{t+9} \\ +0.0006\ F_{t+10} \\ +0.0005\ F_{t+11} \end{Bmatrix}$$

Comparing the LDR performance with that of the company's actual aggregate plans for a six year period, the researchers discovered that LDR improved performance by $173,000 per year.

Applying the LDR to other companies requires new data collection and the derivation of new decision rules. Once the process is in place, though, the production manager needs only to solve two simple equations at the beginning of each month.

PROBLEM 12.3

Assume you are in charge of production at the ABC Manufacturing Company. Your systems analysts have derived the constants $a, b, \ldots z$ for the LDR model and found that all are equal to 0.1. Production level last month was 250 units, the workforce consisted of 240 employees, and ending inventory was 100 units. Finally, your forecast of demand for each month in the future is 200 units.

Use the linear decision rule to set next month's production and workforce levels.

In Problem 12.3, the workforce, forecasts and inventory would be updated each month to produce a new aggregate plan for the next month.

HEURISTIC METHODS

A *heuristic decision rule* is a method that a manager applies based on his or her experiences in tackling a problem. Many decisions in the world of production and operations management are subject to "rules of thumb" that decision makers apply. Heuristics are popular in aggregate planning because of the restrictive nature of LDR and transportation methods in handling cost functions.

Management Coefficients Method
Developed by E.H. Bowman, this is a unique approach that builds a formal decision model around a manager's experience and performance. It uses a regression analysis of past production decisions made by managers. According to Bowman, managers' deficiencies were mostly inconsistencies in decision making. The management coefficients model attempts to minimize deviation from average behavior.

Search Decision Rule
The Search Decision Rule, developed by W.H. Taubert, is a pattern search algorithm that tries to find the minimum cost combination of various workforce and production levels. A computer is needed to make the thousands of systematic searches for points that produce a cost reduction. Search rules such as this do not yield optimal solutions, but are flexible enough to be used on any type of cost function. Because of this adaptability to the real world, Search Decision Rule is a widely used heuristic.

Parametric Production Planning
This approach, developed by C.H. Jones, also employs a search procedure to determine the coefficients for decision rules for production rate and workforce. Production and workforce equations similar to the LDR are established. This approach can be applied to most cost functions.

ANSWERS

12.1 Analysis of Plan 3

Employ 6 workers full-time and use overtime when necessary.

Regular production = 6 workers × 5 units/day × 124 days = 3720 units
Regular wages = 6 workers × $40/day × 124 days = $29,760

Overtime: 2480 units must be produced to meet total demand of 6200 units. To produce 2480 units requires (2480 × 1.6 hours/unit) 3968 hours

Overtime wages = 3968 hours × $7/hour = $27,776

Analysis of Plan 4

Employ 8 workers and use overtime when necessary. Carrying costs will be encountered now.

Month	Production at 40 units/day	Beginning of month inventory	Forecast Demand this month	Overtime Production Needed	Ending Inventory
Jan.	880	—	900	20	0
Feb.	720	0	700	0	20
Mar.	840	20	800	0	60
Apr.	840	60	1200	300	0
May	880	0	1500	620	0
June	800	0	1100	300	0
				1240 units	80 units

Carrying cost totals: 80 units × $5/unit/month = $400. To produce 1240 units at overtime rate (of $7/hour) requires 1,984 hours.

Overtime pay = $7/hour × 1,984 hours = $13,888
Regular pay: 8 workers × $40/day × 124 days = $39,680

Analysis of Plan 5

Constant workforce of 7 workers and subcontract remainder.
Regular production = 7 workers × 5 units/day × 124 days = 4340 units
Regular wage: $40 × 7 workers × 124 days = $34,720
Subcontract to produce : 6200 – 4340 = 1860 units
Subcontract cost = 1860 units × $10/unit = $18,600

Cost Comparison of Plans 3, 4, 5

Cost	Plan 3 (Workforce of 6 plus overtime)	Plan 4 (Workforce of 8 plus overtime)	Plan 5 (Workforce of 7 plus overtime)
Carrying Cost	$0	$400 (80 units carried × $5/unit)	$0
Regular Labor	$29,760 (6 workers × $40/day × 124 days)	$39,680 (8 workers × $40/day × 124 days)	$34,720 (7 workers × $40/day × 124 days)
Overtime	$27,776 (3968 hours × $7/hour)	$13,888 (1,984 hours × $7/hour)	$0
Hiring or firing	$0	$0	$18,600 (1860 units × $10/unit)
Subcontracting	$0	$0	
Total marginal costs	$57,536	$53,968	$53,320

Plan 2 is superior to Plans 1, 3, 4 and 5

12.2

Supply from		Demand for				Total capacity available (supply)
		Period 1	Period 2	Period 3	Unused capacity (dummy)	
Beginning inventory		50 [0]	— [1]	[2]	[0]	50
1	Regular time	300 [50]	[51]	[52]	[0]	300
	Overtime	50 [65]	[66]	[67]	[0]	50
	Subcontract	50 [80]	[81]	[82]	150 [0]	200
2	Regular time		400 [50]	[51]	[0]	400
	Overtime		50 [65]	[66]	[0]	50
	Subcontract		100 [80]	50 [81]	50 [0]	200
3	Regular time			450 [50]	[0]	450
	Overtime			50 [65]	[0]	50
	Subcontract			200 [80]	[0]	200
Demand		450	550	750	200	1,950

Cost of Plan

Period 1:   50($0) + 300($50) + 50($65) + 50($80) = $22,250

Period 2: 400($50) + 50($65) + 100($80)   = $31,250

Period 3:   50($81) + 450($50) + 50($65) + 200($80) = $45,800

Total Cost $99,300

12.3   ABC Co.'s production level next month should be:

$$P_t = [.1(200) + .1(200) + \cdots + .1(200)] + .1(240) + .1(100) + .1$$
$$= 274.1 \text{ units}$$

The firm's workforce level next month should be:

$$W_t = [.1(200) + .1(200) + \cdots + .1(200)] + .1(240) + .1(100) + .1$$
$$= 274.1 \text{ employees.}$$

Thus, this extremely simplified LDR says that next month's production should be 274 units and that 274 employees are needed. This means hiring an additional 34 workers.

HOMEWORK PROBLEM

The J. Mehta Company's production manager is planning for a series of one-month production periods for stainless steel sinks. The demand for the next four months is as follows:

Month	Demand for Stainless Steel Sinks
1	120
2	160
3	240
4	100

The Mehta firm can normally produce 100 stainless steel sinks in a month. This is done during regular production hours at a cost of $100 per sink. If demand in any one month cannot be satisfied by regular production, Mehta has three other choices: (1) he can produce up to 50 more sinks per month in overtime, but at a cost of $130 per sink; (2) he can purchase a limited number of sinks from a friendly competitor for resale (the maximum number of outside purchases over the four-month period is 450 sinks, at a cost of $150 each); or (3) he can fill the demand from his on-hand inventory. The inventory carrying cost is $10 per sink per month. Back orders are not permitted.

Inventory on-hand at the beginning of month 1 is 40 sinks.

Set up this "production smoothing" problem as a transportation problem to minimize cost. Use the northwest corner rule to find an initial level for production and outside purchases over the four-month period.

Unit 13

Product and Process Layout

The design of a production plant or, for that matter, any type of physical facility, requires that management consider the problem of layout. Layout decisions center about the best placement of machines (in a production setting), offices and desks (in a corporate setting), or service centers (in settings like hospitals or department stores). Management's goal is to lay out the system so that it operates at peak efficiency and effectiveness.

There are three basic layout patterns: process layout, product layout, and fixed-position layout. A *process layout* is one in which all machines that do the same job or all processes that are the same are grouped together in centers. These machine centers or departments perform special functions such as painting, sewing, heat treating, X-raying, bookkeeping, inspecting, shipping, and the like. A *product layout* is typified by the traditional automobile assembly line. The product moves along an assembly or conveyor line past a series of work stations. Workers and machines perform the required operations in sequence. A *fixed-position layout* is one in which the product remains stationary and all of the required workers and equipment come to the one work area. Good examples of the type of product for which fixed-position layout is appropriate are a submarine, a large missile, or a hydroelectric turbine.

Of these three layout formats only process layout and product layout have undergone extensive mathematical analysis. In this unit, we shall study the quantitative tools used by production and operations managers in tackling the layout problem. We might keep in mind, however, that unlike the straightforward mathematics of linear programming, waiting lines, forecasting and quality control, the layout and design of physical facilities is still as much an art as it is a science.

PROCESS LAYOUT

The process-oriented layout can simultaneously handle a wide variety of products or services. In fact, it is most efficient in processing products that have different forms or handling customers that have different needs, in other words, operations that do not justify an assembly-line setup. One classical example is a job shop that produces different products, each by a different sequence of operations. A product or order is produced in a batch, and the batch moves from one department to another in the particular sequence for that product. Figure 13.1 illustrates this process for two products. Another good example of the process layout is a hospital or clinic. A continuous inflow of patients, each with his or her own problem, requires routing through records areas, admissions, laboratories, operating rooms, intensive care area, pharmacies, nursing stations, and so on.

Advantages of process layout include greater flexibility in equipment and labor assignments and better utilization of machines. The breakdown of one machine, for example, need not halt an entire process

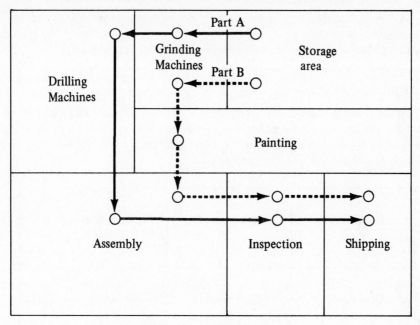

Figure 13.1. A Process Layout

because work can be transferred to others in the department. Process layout is also especially good for handling the manufacture of parts in small batches and for the production of a wide variety of parts in different sizes or forms.

The disadvantages of process layout come from the general-purpose use of the equipment. Orders take more time and money to move through the system because of material handling. In addition, labor skill requirements are higher, work-in-process inventories must be larger, and scheduling and coordinating are big problems.

In process layout planning, the most common approach is to arrange departments or work centers in the most economical locations. In many facilities, optimal placement in the most economical location means *minimizing material handling costs.* It entails placing departments with large interdepartmental flows of parts or people next to one another. Material handling cost in this approach depends upon: (1) the number of loads (or people) to be moved during some period of time between departments i and j and (2) the distance-related costs between departments.

Our objective can be expressed as follows:

$$\text{Minimize cost} = \sum_{i=1}^{n} \sum_{j=1}^{n} X_{ij} C_{ij}$$

where

n = total number of work centers or departments

i,j = individual departments

X_{ij} = number of loads moved from department i to department j

C_{ij} = cost to move a load between department i and department j

This formula, you may notice, assumes pick-up and set-down costs are constant. We consider only the distance-related handling costs.

The best way to understand the steps of process layout is to look at an example.

EXAMPLE 13.1

The ABC Company's management wants to arrange the six departments of its factory in a way that will minimize interdepartmental material handling costs. They make an initial assumption (to simplify the problem) that each department is 20 feet by 20 feet and that the building is 60 feet long and 40 feet wide. Figure 13.2 shows the available plant space.

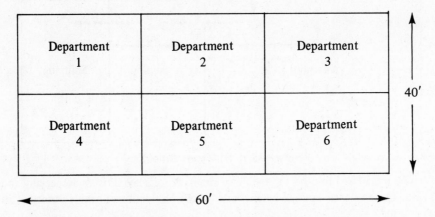

Figure 13.2. Building Dimensions and Possible Department Layout

The process layout procedure that they follow involves five steps.

Step 1.   *Construct a "from-and-to matrix"* showing the flow of parts or materials from department to department (see Table 13.1.)

(continued)

TABLE 13.1   Interdepartmental Flow of Parts

Department	Number of loads per week				
	1	2	3	4	5	6
1		50	100	0	0	20
2			30	50	10	0
3				20	0	100
4					50	0
5						0
6						

Step. 2. Develop an initial schematic diagram showing the sequence of departments through which parts will have to move. Try to place departments with a heavy flow of materials or parts next to one another (See Figure 13.3).

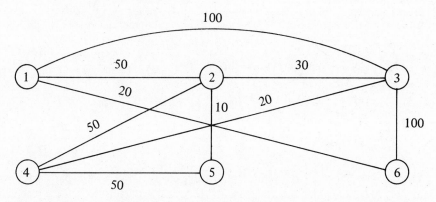

Figure 13.3. Interdepartmental Flow Graph Showing Number of Weekly Loads

Step 3. Determine the cost of this layout by using the material-handling cost equation shown earlier, that is,

$$\text{Cost} = \sum_i \sum_j X_{ij} C_{ij}$$

For this problem, the ABC Company assumes that a forklift carries all interdepartmental

(continued)

loads. The cost of moving one load between adjacent departments is estimated to be $1. Moving a load between nonadjacent departments costs $2. Hence, the handling cost between departments 1 and 2 is $50 ($1 × 50 loads), $200 between departments 1 and 3 ($2 × 100 loads), $40 between departments 1 and 6 ($2 × 20 loads), and so on. The total cost for the layout shown in Figure 13.3, then, is

$$
\begin{aligned}
\text{Cost} = \quad &\underset{\text{(1 and 2)}}{\$50} + \underset{\text{(1 and 3)}}{\$200} + \underset{\text{(1 and 6)}}{\$40} + \underset{\text{(2 and 3)}}{\$30} + \underset{\text{(2 and 4)}}{\$50} + \underset{\text{(2 and 5)}}{\$10} \\
&+ \underset{\text{(3 and 4)}}{\$40} + \underset{\text{(3 and 6)}}{\$100} + \underset{\text{(4 and 5)}}{\$50} \\
&= \$570
\end{aligned}
$$

Step 4. By trial and error (or by a more sophisticated computer program approach that we will discuss shortly), *try to improve this layout to establish a reasonably good arrangement of departments.*

Looking at Figure 13.3 and the cost calculations, it appears desirable to place departments 1 and 3 closer together. They currently are nonadjacent and the high volume of flow between them causes a large handling expense. Looking the situation over, we need to carefully check the effect of shifting departments and possibly raising (instead of lowering) overall costs.

One possibility is to switch departments 1 and 2. This exchange produces Figure 13.4, which shows that it is possible to reduce the cost to $480, a saving in material-handling costs of $90:

$$
\begin{aligned}
\text{Cost} = \quad &\underset{\text{(1 and 2)}}{\$50} + \underset{\text{(1 and 3)}}{\$100} + \underset{\text{(1 and 6)}}{\$20} + \underset{\text{(2 and 3)}}{\$60} + \underset{\text{(2 and 4)}}{\$50} + \underset{\text{(2 and 5)}}{\$10} \\
&+ \underset{\text{(3 and 4)}}{\$40} + \underset{\text{(3 and 6)}}{\$100} + \underset{\text{(4 and 5)}}{\$50} \\
&= \$480
\end{aligned}
$$

This, of course, is only one of a large number of possible changes. For a six-department problem there are actually 720 (or 6!) potential arrangements! In layout problems, we seldom reach an optimal solution—and instead may have to be satisfied with a "reasonable" one reached after a few trials.

Suppose the ABC Company is satisfied with the cost figure of $480 and the flow graph of Figure 13.4. The problem may not be solved yet. Often a fifth step is necessary.

Step 5. *Consider space or size requirements of each department;* that is, arrange the departments to fit the shape of the building and its nonmovable areas (such as the loading dock, washrooms, stairways). Often this step involves making certain that a very noisy, dusty, or

(continued)

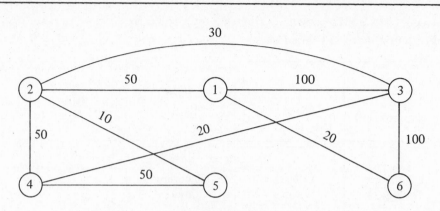

Figure 13.4. Second Interdepartmental Flow Graph

fume-producing department is not adjacent to offices or other departments upon which it may have a negative effect.

In the case of the ABC Company, space requirements are, as mentioned earlier, a simple matter (see Figure 13.5).

Department 2	Department 1	Department 3
Department 4	Department 5	Department 6

Figure 13.5. A Feasible Layout for the ABC Company

Now it is your turn! Using the concepts set forth in Example 13.1, try to resolve the layout difficulties in Problems 13.1 and 13.2

PROBLEM 13.1

The Snow-Bird Hospital is a small emergency-oriented facility located in a popular ski resort area in northern Michigan. Its new administrator, Mary Lord, decides to reorganize the hospital using the

(continued)

process layout method she studied in business school. The current layout of Snow-Bird's eight emergency departments is shown in Figure 13.6.

| Entrance/ Initial Processing | Exam Room 1 | Exam Room 2 | X-Ray | 10' |
| Laboratory Tests/EKG | Operating Room | Recovery Room | Cast-setting Room | 10' |

← 40' →

Figure 13.6. Snow-Bird Hospital Layout

The only physical restriction perceived by Ms. Lord is the need to keep the entrance and initial processing room in its current location. All other departments or rooms (each 10 feet square) can be moved if the layout analysis indicates it would be beneficial.

Mary's first step is to analyze records in order to determine the number of trips made by patients between departments in an average month; Table 13.2 gives these data. The objective, Ms. Lord

TABLE 13.2. Number of Patients Moving between Departments in One Month

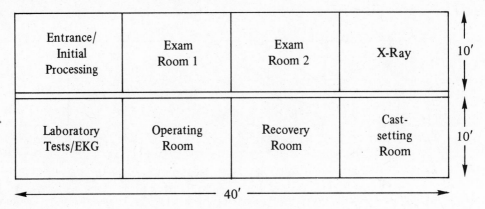

	1	2	3	4	5	6	7	8	Department
1		100	100	0	0	0	0	0	1 Entrance and initial processing
2			0	50	20	0	0	0	2 Examination room 1
3				30	30	0	0	0	3 Examination room 2
4					20	0	0	20	4 X-ray
5						20	0	10	5 Laboratory tests and EKG
6							30	0	6 Operating room
7								0	7 Recovery room
8									8 Cast-setting room

(continued)

decides, is to lay out the rooms so as to minimize the total distance walked by patients who enter for treatment. She writes her objective as

$$\text{Minimize patient movement} = \sum_{i=1}^{8} \sum_{j=1}^{8} X_{ij} C_{ij}$$

where

X_{ij} = number of patients per month (loads) moving from department i to department j

C_{ij} = distance in feet between departments i and j (which, in this case, is the equivalent of cost per load to move between departments)

Note that this is only a slight modification of the cost objective equation shown earlier.

Departments next to one another (such as entrance and examination room 1) are assumed to carry a walking distance of 10 feet. Diagonal departments are also considered adjacent and assigned a distance of 10 feet. Nonadjacent departments such as entrance and examination room 2 or entrance and recovery room are 20 feet apart, while nonadjacent rooms such as entrance and X-ray are 30 feet apart. (Hence, 10 feet is considered 10 units of cost, 20 feet is 20 units of cost, and 30 feet is 30 units of cost.)

Given the above information, redo the layout of Snow-Bird Hospital to improve its efficiency in terms of patient flow.

(continued)

(additional work space for Problem 13.1)

PROBLEM 13.2

Figure 13.7 shows an example of a poor facility layout. This organization loses time and money because of unnecessary personnel, information, and material movements. Without moving the production or shipping departments, see if you can reorganize the facility and create shorter communications distances.

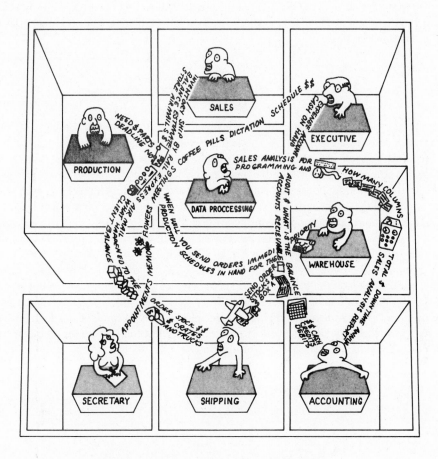

Figure 13.7. Poor Process-oriented Layout

Source: A. S. Volgyesi, "Space-age Approach to Space Allocation," reprinted from *Computer Decisions*, May, 1970, pp. 32, 35. Copyright 1970, Hayden Publishing Co.

The graphical approach we have been discussing is adequate for small problems. This method, often called Operations Sequence Analysis, does not suffice for larger problems, however. When twenty departments are involved in a layout problem, over 600 *trillion* different department configurations are possible. Fortunately, there are computer programs to handle layouts of up to forty departments. The best-known of these is called CRAFT (Computerized Relative Allocation of Facilities Technique), a program that produces "good" but not always "optimal" solutions. CRAFT is a search technique that systematically examines alternative departmental rearrangements to reduce the total material-handling cost. For further details as to the inputs and outputs of CRAFT, see the article "Allocating Facilities with CRAFT" in the March–April 1964 issues of *Harvard Business Review.* In addition, there are several other computer programs in the experimental stage.

PRODUCT LAYOUT

In a *product layout,* the product moves down a conveyor or *assembly line* and through a series of work stations until completed (see Figure 13.8). This is the way automobiles are assembled, television sets and ovens are produced, and soft drinks are bottled. Product-oriented layout typically uses more automated and specially designed equipment than is found in a process layout.

The central problem in product-layout planning is to balance the output capacity at each work station on the production line so that it is nearly the same, while obtaining the desired amount of the product. Management's goal is to create a smooth, continuous flow along the assembly line with a minimum of idle time at each person's work station. The term most often used to describe this process is *assembly-line balancing.*

The main advantage of product layout is the low manufacturing cost per unit usually associated with high-volume, standardized assembly lines. It also keeps material-handling costs low, reduces inventory in process, and facilitates the training and supervising of workers. These advantages usually outweigh the disadvantages of product layout, namely: (1) high-volume requirement because of the large investment needed to set up the assembly line; (2) work stoppage at one point that ties up the whole operation; and (3) lack of flexibility in handling a variety of products.

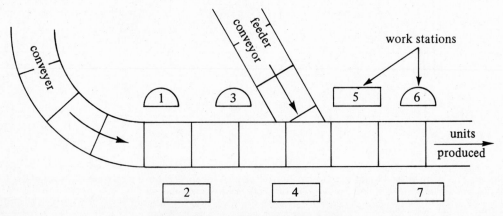

Figure 13.8. An Assembly-line Layout

Assembly line balancing. Line-balancing activities are usually undertaken to meet a certain required output from the line. In order to produce at a specified rate, management must know the time requirements for each assembly task (such as drilling a hole, tightening a nut, spray-painting a part, etc.). Management also needs to know the precedence relationship among the activities, that is, the sequence in which various tasks need be performed. Let us construct a precedence chart for the task data that follow.

EXAMPLE 13.2

We want to develop a precedence diagram for a product that requires a total assembly time of sixty-six minutes. The table that follows gives the tasks, assembly times, and sequence requirements for the product.

Task	Performance Time (in minutes)	Task Must Follow Task Listed Below	
A	10	—	
B	11	A	⎱ this means that tasks
C	5	B	⎰ B and E cannot be done
D	4	B	until task A has been
E	12	A	completed
F	3	C, D	
G	7	F	
H	11	E	
I	3	G, H	

The completed diagram looks like this:

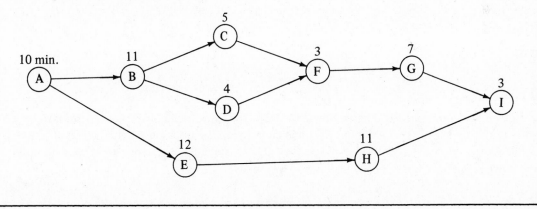

Once we have constructed a precedence chart summarizing the sequences and performance times, we turn to the job of grouping tasks into job stations to meet the specified production rate. This process involves three steps:

1. We take the demand (or production rate) per day and divide it into the productive time available per day (in minutes or seconds). This operation gives us what is called the *cycle time*, namely, the time the product is available at each work station:

$$\text{Cycle time} = \frac{\text{productive time per day}}{\text{demand per day}}$$

2. Calculate the theoretical *minimum number of work stations*. This is the total task-duration time divided by the cycle time. If we obtain a fraction, we round it up to the next whole number value:

$$\text{Minimum number of work stations} = \frac{\sum\limits_{i=1}^{m} \text{time for task } i}{\text{cycle time}}$$

where m is the number of assembly tasks.

3. We perform the line balance and assign specific assembly tasks to each work station. An efficient balance is one that will complete the required assembly, while following the specified sequence *and* keeping the idle time at each work station to a minimum. Example 13.3 illustrates this procedure.

EXAMPLE 13.3

Based on the precedence diagram and activity times given in Example 13.2 (repeated below), the firm determines that there are 480 productive minutes of work available per day. Furthermore, contracts require that 40 units be completed as output from the assembly line each day. Hence,

$$\text{Cycle time (in minutes)} = \frac{480 \text{ min.}}{40 \text{ units}}$$

$$= 12 \text{ minutes/unit}$$

$$\text{Minimum number of work stations} = \frac{\Sigma \text{ task times}}{\text{cycle time}} = \frac{66}{12}$$

$$= 5.5 \text{ or } 6 \text{ stations}$$

Figure 13.9 shows one solution that does not violate the sequence requirements and in which the tasks are grouped into six stations. To obtain it we moved appropriate activities into work stations that use as much of the available cycle time of twelve minutes as possible. The first work station consumes ten minutes and has an idle time of two minutes.

(continued)

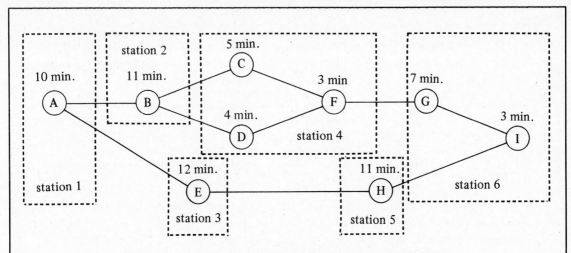

Figure 13.9. A Six-station Solution to Line-balancing Problem

The second work station uses eleven minutes, and the third consumes the full twelve minutes. Station 4 groups three small tasks and balances perfectly at twelve minutes. Station 5 has one minute of idle time, and station 6 (consisting of tasks G and I) has two minutes of idle time per cycle. Total idle time for this solution is six minutes per cycle.

We can compute the *efficiency* of a line balance by dividing the total task time by the product of the number of work stations assigned times the cycle time:

$$\text{Efficiency} = \frac{\Sigma \text{ task times}}{(\text{number of work stations}) \times (\text{cycle time})}$$

Management often compares different levels of efficiency for various numbers of work stations. In this way, the firm can determine the sensitivity of the line to changes in the production rate and work station assignments.

EXAMPLE 13.4.

We can calculate the balance efficiency for Example 13.3 as follows:

$$\text{Efficiency} = \frac{66 \text{ min.}}{(6 \text{ stations}) \times (12 \text{ min.})} = \frac{66}{72} = 91.7\%$$

Opening a seventh work station, for whatever reason, would decrease the efficiency of the balance to 78.6 percent:

$$\text{Efficiency} = \frac{66 \text{ min.}}{(7 \text{ stations}) \times (12 \text{ min.})} = 78.6\%$$

PROBLEM 13.3.

An assembly line whose activities are shown below has an eight-minute cycle time. Draw the precedence graph and find the minimum possible number of work stations. Then arrange the work activities into work stations so as to balance the line. What is the efficiency of this line balance?

Task	Performance Time (in minutes)	Task Must Follow This Task
A	5	—
B	3	A
C	4	B
D	3	B
E	6	C
F	1	C
G	4	D, E, F
H	2	G
	28	

PROBLEM 13.4

Suppose production requirements in Problem 13.3 increase and necessitate a reduction in cycle time from eight minutes to seven minutes. Balance the line once again using the new cycle time. Note that it is *not possible* to combine task times so as to group tasks into the minimum number of work stations. This condition occurs in actual balancing problems fairly often.

PROBLEM 13.5.

A manufacturer of electrical relays determines that the firm needs an output of 1400 completed relays per day. There are 420 minutes of productive time in each working day (which is equivalent to 25,200 seconds). Group the assembly-line activities into appropriate work stations and calculate the efficiency of the balance.

Task	Time (in seconds)	Must Follow Task
A	13	—
B	4	A
C	10	B
D	10	—
E	6	D
F	12	E
G	5	E
H	6	F, G
I	7	H
J	5	H
K	4	I, J
L	15	C, K

Large-scale line balancing problems, like large process layout problems, are often solved today by computers. Several different computer programs are available to handle the assignment of work stations on assembly lines with 100 (or more) individual work activities. Both the computer routine called COMSOAL (Computer Method for Sequencing Operations for Assembly Lines) and ASYBL$ (General Electric Assembly Line Configuration program) are widely used in larger problems to evaluate the thousands or millions of possible work station combinations much more efficiently than could ever be done by hand.

ANSWERS

13.1

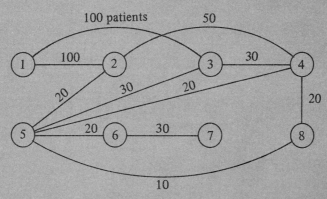

Using Snow-Bird's current layout, the total patient movement may be computed.

$$\text{Total movement} = \underset{\text{1 to 2}}{(100 \times 10')} + \underset{\text{1 to 3}}{(100 \times 20')} + \underset{\text{2 to 4}}{(50 \times 20')} + \underset{\text{2 to 5}}{(20 \times 10')} + \underset{\text{3 to 4}}{(30 \times 10')}$$

$$+ \underset{\text{3 to 5}}{(30 \times 20')} + \underset{\text{4 to 5}}{(20 \times 30')} + \underset{\text{4 to 8}}{(20 \times 10')} + \underset{\text{5 to 6}}{(20 \times 10')} + \underset{\text{5 to 8}}{(10 \times 30')}$$

$$+ \underset{\text{6 to 7}}{(30 \times 10')}$$

$$= 1000 + 2000 + 1000 + 200 + 300 + 600 + 600 + 200 + 200$$

$$+ 300 + 300$$

$$= 6700 \text{ feet}$$

There is no one "correct" solution, but you should be able to propose a new layout that will reduce this current figure of 6700 feet. Two useful changes, for example, are to switch rooms 3 and 5 and to interchange rooms 4 and 6. This change would result in the following schematic:

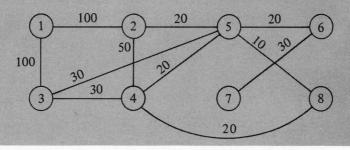

(continued)

Total movement $= (100 \times 10') + (100 \times 10') + (50 \times 10') + (20 \times 10') + (30 \times 10')$
           1 to 2   1 to 3   2 to 4   2 to 5   3 to 4

$+ (30 \times 20') + (20 \times 10') + (20 \times 20') + (20 \times 10') + (10 \times 10')$
           3 to 5   4 to 5   4 to 8   5 to 6   5 to 8

$+ (30 \times 10')$
     6 to 7

$= 1000 + 1000 + 500 + 200 + 300 + 600 + 200 + 400 + 200$

$+ 100 + 300$

$= 4800$ feet

Do you see any room for further improvement?

13.2

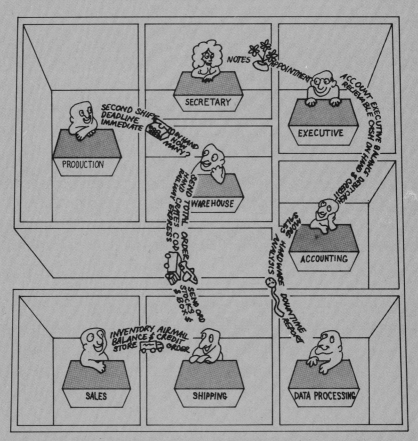

Good process-oriented layout

Source: A.S. Volgyesi, "Space-age Approach to Space Allocation," reprinted from *Computer Decisions,* May, 1970, pp. 32, 35. Copyright 1970, Hayden Publishing Co.

13.3   The theoretical minimum number of work stations is:

$$\frac{\Sigma t_i}{\text{cycle time}} = \frac{28 \text{ min.}}{8 \text{ min.}}$$

$$= 3.5 \text{ or } 4 \text{ stations}$$

The precedence graph and one good layout are shown below.

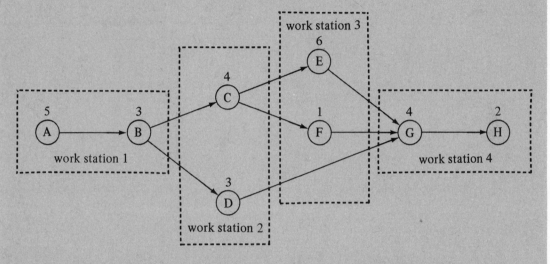

$$\text{Efficiency} = \frac{\text{total task time}}{(\text{number of work stations}) \times (\text{cycle time})} = \frac{28}{(4)(8)}$$

$$= 87.5\%$$

13.4

$$\text{Theoretical minimum number of stations} = \frac{28 \text{ min.}}{7 \text{ min.}}$$

$$= 4 \text{ stations}$$

The work activities may be grouped, however, into no fewer than five stations without violating precedence requirements.

(continued)

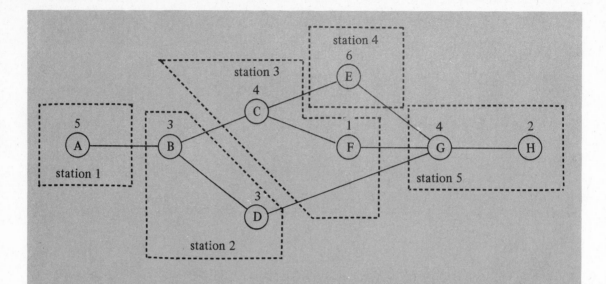

$$\text{Efficiency} = \frac{28}{(5)(7)} = \frac{28}{35}$$

$$= 80\%$$

Several other balances are also possible. One of them is to place A alone, tasks B and C together, D and F together, E by itself, and G and H together.

13.5

$$\text{Cycle time} = \frac{25,200 \text{ sec.}}{1400 \text{ units}}$$

$$= 18 \text{ sec./unit}$$

$$\text{Minimum number of work stations} = \frac{\Sigma t_i}{\text{cycle time}} = \frac{97 \text{ sec.}}{18 \text{ sec.}}$$

$$= 5.4 \text{ or } 6 \text{ stations}$$

(continued)

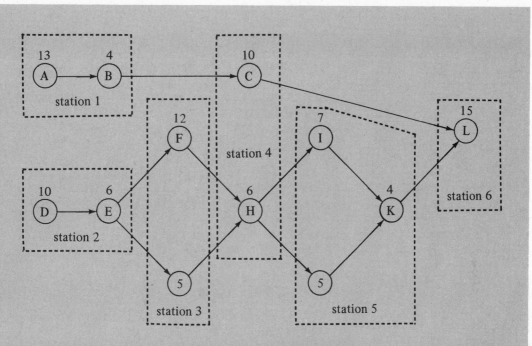

Total idle time = 11 seconds

$$\text{Balance efficiency} = \frac{97 \text{ sec.}}{(6 \text{ stations}) (18 \text{ sec.})}$$

$$= 89.8\%$$

HOMEWORK PROBLEM

A small western alarm clock manufacturer produces clocks that require a total assembly time of 76 minutes in eight tasks. The table that follows gives the tasks, assembly times, and sequence requirements for the clock.

Task	Performance Time (in minutes)	Immediate Predecessor Task
A	4	—
B	4	A
C	16	—
D	12	C
E	6	B
F	20	D,E
G	8	F
H	6	G

Total time   76 minutes

a. Draw a precedence diagram for the clock assembly.

b. Compute the cycle time needed to reach an output of 20 clocks per day. (The firm operates with eight-hour work days).

c. What is the minimum number of work stations required?

d. Assign specific assembly tasks to each work station to balance the line.

e. What is the efficiency of this line balance?

Unit 14

Work Measurement and Learning Curves

Despite dramatic advances in computer and equipment technology in the past twenty years, the most important factor in the production process is still labor. Effective management of the labor resource requires labor or production standards. These standards represent the amount of time it should take to perform specific job activities under normal working conditions. Standards serve many purposes. They help set up employee wage incentive plans, provide for performance comparisons, facilitate scheduling of jobs and machines, assist a firm in bidding on contracts and estimating delivery dates, and help in determining labor requirements.

How are labor or production standards set? In smaller firms they may be based simply on judgmental estimates, but in larger companies this measurement of human output and performance is the result of *work measurement techniques.* The three most important work-measurement methods used to set production standards are: (1) time studies, (2) predetermined time standards, and (3) work sampling. This unit covers each of these techniques.

Also part of the concept of setting labor or production standards is the learning curve. When human activities are done a number of times, they typically reflect improvement. The improvement in efficiency or productivity as a function of output is called the *learning curve effect.* This phenomenon, which has been documented in many applications (including airplane assembly, maintenance, construction, and machine shops), is addressed later in this unit.

TIME STUDIES

The classical stop-watch study, originally proposed by Frederick W. Taylor in 1881, is still the most widely used time-study method. To put it in simple terms, the time-study procedure involves taking a sample of one worker's performance and using it to set a standard for all workers. All that you need is a stop watch, pencil, paper, and the following seven steps:

1. Define the task to be studied.
2. Break down the task into precise elements (usually no more than a few seconds each).
3. Decide how many times to measure the task, that is, the number of cycles needed.
4. Time and record the elemental times and ratings of performance.

5. Compute the average cycle time. This is the arithmetic mean of all times measured, adjusted for unusual influences for each element.

$$\text{Average cycle time} = \frac{\Sigma \text{ times recorded to perform an element}}{\text{number of cycles observed}}$$

6. Compute the *normal time*. This measure includes consideration of a "performance rating" for the particular circumstances just observed.

$$\text{Normal time} = (\text{average cycle time}) \times (\text{rating factor})$$

The performance rating adjusts the observed time to what a normal worker could expect to accomplish. For example, a normal worker should be able to walk three miles per hour. He or she should also be able to deal a deck of fifty-two cards into four equal piles in thirty seconds. But even though there is a whole set of activity bench marks established by the Society for the Advancement of Management, performance rating is a very subjective task.

7. Compute the *standard time*. This adjustment to the normal time provides for other immeasurable allowances such as personal needs, unavoidable work delays, and worker fatigue.

$$\text{Standard time} = \frac{\text{normal time}}{1 - \text{allowance fraction}}$$

EXAMPLE 14.1

The time study of a work operation yielded a cycle time of 4.0 minutes. The analyst rated the worker observed at 85 percent. The firm uses a 13 percent allowance factor. We want to compute the standard time.

$$\text{Cycle time} = 4.0 \text{ min.}$$

$$\text{Normal time} = (\text{cycle time}) \times (\text{rating factor})$$

$$= (4.0)(0.85)$$

$$= 3.4 \text{ min.}$$

$$\text{Standard time} = \frac{\text{normal time}}{1 - \text{allowance fraction}} = \frac{3.4}{1 - 0.13} = \frac{3.4}{0.87}$$

$$= 3.9 \text{ min}$$

PROBLEM 14.1

An analyst clocked the cycle time for welding a part onto truck doors at 5.3 minutes. The performance rating of the worker timed was estimated at 105 percent. Find the normal time for this operation.

(continued)

According to a local union contract, each welder is allowed 3 minutes of personal time per hour and 2 minutes of fatigue time per hour. Further, it is estimated that there should be an average delay allowance of 1 minute per hour. Compute the allowance factor and then find the standard time for this welding activity.

Now that you can handle the basics, let us look at an example and problem in which all we are given is a series of actual stop-watch times for each element in an activity.

EXAMPLE 14.2

Management Science Associates promotes its management development seminars by mailing thousands of individually typed letters to various firms. A time study has been done on the job of preparing letters for mailing. Based on the readings below, Management Science Associates wants to develop a time standard for the whole job. The firm's allowance factor is 15 percent.

Job Element	Cycle Observed (in minutes)					Performance Rating
	1	2	3	4	5	
(A) Type letter	8	10	9	21*	11	120%
(B) Type envelope address	2	3	2	1	3	105%
(C) Stuff, stamp, seal, and sort envelopes	2	1	5*	2	1	110%

The procedure is as follows:

1. Delete all unusual or nonrecurring observations such as those marked with an asterisk (*). (They might be due to an unscheduled business interruption, a conference with the boss, or a mistake of an unusual nature.)

(continued)

2. Compute the *average cycle time* for each job element:

$$\text{Average time for A} = \frac{8 + 10 + 9 + 11}{4}$$

$$= 9.5 \text{ min.}$$

$$\text{Average time for B} = \frac{2 + 3 + 2 + 1 + 3}{5}$$

$$= 2.2 \text{ min.}$$

$$\text{Average time for C} = \frac{2 + 1 + 2 + 1}{4}$$

$$= 1.5 \text{ min.}$$

3. Compute the *normal time* for each job element:

$$\text{Normal time for A} = (\text{average time}) \times (\text{rating}) = (9.5)(1.2)$$
$$= 11.4 \text{ min.}$$

$$\text{Normal time for B} = (2.2)(1.05)$$
$$= 2.31 \text{ min.}$$

$$\text{Normal time for C} = (1.5)(1.10)$$
$$= 1.65 \text{ min.}$$

4. Add the element normal times to find the normal time for the whole job:

$$\text{Normal job time} = 11.40 + 2.31 + 1.65$$
$$= 15.36 \text{ min.}$$

5. Compute the *standard time* for the job:

$$\text{Standard time} = \frac{\text{normal time}}{1 - \text{allowance fraction}} = \frac{15.36}{1 - 0.15}$$

$$= 18.07 \text{ min.}$$

Thus, 18.07 minutes is the time standard for this job.

PROBLEM 14.2

A work operation consisting of three elements has been subjected to a stop-watch time study. The observations recorded are shown below. By union contract, the allowance time for the operation is 20 percent. Determine the standard time for the work operation.

Job Element	Cycle Observations (in minutes)						Performance Rating
	1	*2*	*3*	*4*	*5*	*6*	
A	0.1	0.3	0.2	0.9	0.2	0.1	90%
B	0.8	0.6	0.8	0.5	3.2	0.7	110%
C	0.5	0.5	0.4	0.5	0.6	0.5	80%

Time study is a sampling process, and the question of sampling error in the average cycle times naturally arises. Error, according to statistics, varies inversely with sample size. In order to determine just how many cycles should be timed it is necessary to consider the variability of each element in the study.

The easiest means of finding the necessary sample size is to use standard charts such as the one reproduced in Figure 14.1. Such charts help estimate sample sizes that offer the user 95 percent or 99 percent confidence that the sample average-cycle time will be within ±5 percent of the true average. To use the chart, we follow four steps:

1. Compute the average cycle time $\overline{X}$.
2. Find the standard deviation, s, based on the sample data:

$$s = \sqrt{\frac{\Sigma \,(\text{each sample observation} - \overline{X})^2}{\text{number in sample} - 1}}$$

3. Compute the *coefficient of variation*, which is just the standard deviation divided by the mean, that is

$$\text{Coefficient of variation} = \frac{s}{\overline{X}}$$

4. Find the appropriate coefficient of variation on the horizontal axis in Figure 14.1, proceed up to the curve that gives the confidence coefficient desired, and then read the sample size on the left-hand scale.

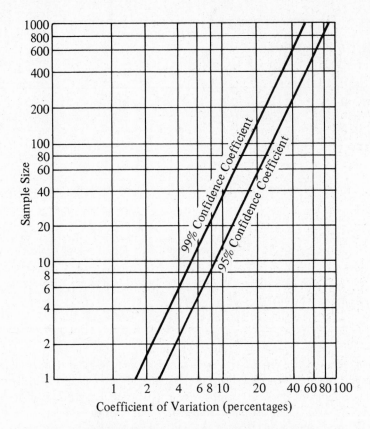

Figure 14.1. Chart for Estimating Sample Size with ± 5 Percent Accuracy for Given Coefficient of Variation Values

Source: From A. Abruzzi, *Work Measurement,* New York: Columbia University Press, 1952, p. 161, by permission of the publisher.

EXAMPLE 14.3

A sample of 12 cycles taken in a study resulted in an average cycle time of 2.80 minutes with a standard deviation of 0.56 minute. In order to be 95 percent confident that the resultant standard time is within ±5 percent of the true average, we need to know whether this sample size of 12 observations is large enough.

To find the answer we compute the coefficient of variation =

$$\frac{s}{\overline{X}} = \frac{0.56}{2.80}$$
$$= 0.20$$

Turning to Figure 14.1 for a coefficient of variation of 20 percent, we see that the required sample size is about 60 cycles. Thus, the sample of 12 cycles is not large enough and the observation process should continue.

PROBLEM 14.3

A time study of a factory worker revealed an average cycle time of 3.20 minutes, with a standard deviation of 1.28 minutes. These figures were based on a sample of 45 cycles observed.

Is this sample adequate in size for the firm to be 99 percent confident that the standard time is within 5 percent of the true value? If not, what should the proper number of observations be?

PREDETERMINED TIME STANDARDS

A second way to set production standards is to use *predetermined time standards*. This method assumes that all manual work is divisible into small basic elements that have predetermined times (based on very large samples of workers). To estimate the time for a particular task, it is necessary only to add the time factors for each element of that task.

The most common predetermined time standard is *methods time measurement* (MTM). MTM uses basic motions called *therbligs* (an anagram named after Frank and Lillian Gilbreth). Examples of therbligs include activities such as select, grasp, position, assemble, reach, hold, rest, and inspect. These activities are stated in terms of time-measurement units (TMUs), which are each equal to only 0.0006 minute. MTM values for various therbligs are set down in very detailed tables that are available in engineering stores. Table 14.1 provides, as an example, the set of time standards for the motion REACH. Note that reaching four inches for a part will have a very different TMU from reaching twelve inches.

Table 14.1 Methods Time Measurement Table for REACH Motion

REACH–R

Distance Moved Inches	Time TMU				Hand in Motion	
	A	B	C or D	E	A	B
3/4 or less	2.0	2.0	2.0	2.0	1.6	1.6
1	2.5	2.5	3.6	2.4	2.3	2.3
2	4.0	4.0	5.9	3.8	3.5	2.7
3	5.3	5.3	7.3	5.3	4.5	3.6
4	6.1	6.4	8.4	6.8	4.9	4.3
5	6.5	7.8	9.4	7.4	5.3	5.0
6	7.0	8.6	10.1	8.0	5.7	5.7
7	7.4	9.3	10.8	8.7	6.1	6.5
8	7.9	10.1	11.5	9.3	6.5	7.2
9	8.3	10.8	12.2	9.9	6.9	7.9
10	8.7	11.5	12.9	10.5	7.3	8.6
12	9.6	12.9	14.2	11.8	8.1	10.1
14	10.5	14.4	15.6	13.0	8.9	11.5
16	11.4	15.8	17.0	14.2	9.7	12.9
18	12.3	17.2	18.4	15.5	10.5	14.4
20	13.1	18.6	19.8	16.7	11.3	15.8
22	14.0	20.1	21.2	18.0	12.1	17.3
24	14.9	21.5	22.5	19.2	12.9	18.8
26	15.8	22.9	23.9	20.4	13.7	20.2
28	16.7	24.4	25.3	21.7	14.5	21.7
30	17.5	25.8	26.7	22.9	15.3	23.2

CASE AND DESCRIPTION

A Reach to object in fixed location, or to object in other hand or on which other hand rests.

B Reach to single object in location which may vary slightly from cycle to cycle.

C Reach to object jumbled with other objects in a group so that search and select occur.

D Reach to a very small object or where accurate grasp is required.

E Reach to indefinite location to get hand in position for body balance or next motion or out of way.

EXAMPLE 14.4

Riveting a hole to a casing in a transistor assembly process is assigned an MTM value of 70.0 TMU, based on industry data standards. Before riveting, a worker must reach 16 inches for a small part (17.0 TMU), grasp the part (9.1 TMU), move the part to the assembly (27.0 TMU), and position the transistor (32.3 TMU). This very small task, which consists of five elements, takes a total of 155.4 TMU (17.0 + 9.1 + 27.0 + 32.3 + 70.0). Translating TMU into minutes involves multiplying 155.4 TMU × 0.0006 minute = 0.0932 minute = 5.6 seconds.

PROBLEM 14.4

Sharpening your pencil is an operation that may be broken down into eight small elemental motions. In MTM terms, each element may be assigned a certain number of TMUs, as shown below.

1. Reach 4 inches for the pencil: 6 TMU
2. Grasp the pencil: 2 TMU
3. Move the pencil 6 inches: 10 TMU
4. Position the pencil: 20 TMU
5. Insert the pencil into the sharpener: 4 TMU
6. Sharpen the pencil: 120 TMU
7. Disengage the pencil: 10 TMU
8. Move the pencil 6 inches: 10 TMU

What is the total normal time for sharpening one pencil? Convert this time to minutes and seconds.

Predetermined time standards have several advantages relative to direct time studies. First, they may be established in a laboratory environment, which will not upset production activities (a consequence of time studies). Second, the standard can be set *before* a task is done and can be used for planning. In addition, no performance ratings are necessary—and the method is widely accepted by unions as a fair means of setting standards.

WORK SAMPLING

The last method of developing labor or production standards, *work sampling,* differs from the others discussed in one major way—it does not require a stop watch. Developed by an Englishman, L. Tippet, in the 1930s, work sampling estimates the percent of the time that a worker spends working and the percent of the time spent not working. The method involves random observations to record whether or not a worker is doing a productive activity.

The work-sampling procedure can be summarized in seven steps:

1. Take a preliminary sample to obtain an estimate of the parameter value (such as percent of time a worker is busy).
2. Compute the sample size required.
3. Prepare a schedule for observing the worker at appropriate times. The concept of random numbers (discussed in Unit 18) is used to provide for random observation.
4. Observe and record worker activities; rate the worker's performance.
5. Record the number of units produced during the study.
6. Compute the normal time per part.
7. Compute the standard time per part.

To determine the number of observations required, management must make a statement about the desired confidence level and accuracy. But first the work analyst must select a preliminary value of the parameter under study (step 1 above). The choice is usually based on a small sample of perhaps fifty observations. The following formula then gives the sample size for a desired confidence and accuracy.

$$n = \frac{Z_\alpha^2 \, p(1-p)}{h^2}$$

where

n = required sample size

Z_α = standard normal deviate for the desired confidence level

   ($Z_\alpha \cong 1$ for 68 percent confidence, $Z_\alpha \cong 2$ for 95 percent confidence, and $Z_\alpha \cong 3$ for 99 percent confidence—these values are obtained from the Normal table in Appendix A)

p = estimated value of sample proportion (of time worker is observed busy or idle)

h = accuracy level desired, in percent

EXAMPLE 14.5

The head of a large typing pool estimates that the typists are idle 25 percent of the time. The supervisor would like to take a work sample that would be accurate within ± 3 percent and wants to have 95 percent confidence in the results.

In order to determine how many observations should be taken, the head applies the equation

$$n = \frac{Z_\alpha^2 \, p(1-p)}{h^2}$$

(continued)

where

$$n = \text{sample size required}$$

$$Z_\alpha \cong 2 \text{ for 95 percent confidence level}$$

$$p = \text{estimate of idle proportion} = 25 \text{ percent} = 0.25$$

$$h = \text{accuracy desired of 3 percent} = 0.03$$

It is found that

$$n = \frac{(2)^2 (0.25)(0.75)}{(0.03)^2}$$

$$= 833 \text{ observations}$$

Thus, 833 observations should be taken. If the percent idle time noted is not close to 25 percent as the study progresses, then the number of observations may have to be recalculated and perhaps increased.

PROBLEM 14.5

A preliminary work sample of an operation indicates the following:

Number of times operator working:	60
Number of times operator idle:	40
Total number of preliminary observations:	100

What is the required sample size for a 99 percent confidence level with ± 4 percent precision?

PROBLEM 14.6

A bank wants to determine the percent of time its tellers are working and idle. They decide to use work sampling, and their initial estimate is that the tellers are idle 30 percent of the time. How many observations should be taken to be 95 percent confident that the results will not be more than 5 percent away from the true result?

Work sampling is used to set production standards in a fashion similar to that used in time studies. The analyst, however, simply records whether a worker is busy or idle during the period of time scheduled. After all the observations have been recorded, the worker rated, and the units produced counted (steps 4 and 5), we can determine the normal time by this formula:

$$\text{Normal time} = \frac{(\text{total study time}) \times \begin{pmatrix} \text{percent of time employee} \\ \text{observed working} \end{pmatrix} \times \begin{pmatrix} \text{performance} \\ \text{rating factor} \end{pmatrix}}{\text{number of pieces produced}}$$

The standard time is the normal time adjusted by the allowance fraction, computed as

$$\text{Standard time} = \frac{\text{normal time}}{1 - \text{allowance fraction}}$$

EXAMPLE 14.6

A work-sample study conducted over the 80 hours (or 4800 minutes of) a two-week period yielded the following data. The number of parts produced was 225 by an operator who was performance-rated at 100 percent. The operator's idle time was 20 percent and the allowance given by the company for this part is 25 percent.

To find the normal time and standard time per part, we proceed as follows:

$$\text{Normal time} = \frac{(\text{total time}) \times (\text{percent of time working}) \times (\text{rating factor})}{\text{number of units completed}}$$

$$= \frac{(4800 \text{ min.})(0.80)(1.00)}{225}$$

$$= 17.07 \text{ min./part}$$

(continued)

$$\text{Standard time} = \frac{\text{normal time}}{1 - \text{allowance fraction}}$$

$$= \frac{17.07}{1 - 0.25}$$

$$= 22.76 \text{ min./part}$$

PROBLEM 14.7

A work sample taken over a 160-hour work month produced the following results. What is the standard time for the job?

Units manufactured: 220
Idle time: 20 percent
Performance rating: 90 percent
Allowance time: 10 percent

PROBLEM 14.8

Sample observations of an assembly-line worker made over a 40-hour work week revealed that the worker produced a total of 320 completed parts. The performance rating was 125 percent. The sample also showed that the worker was busy assembling the parts 80 percent of the time. Allowances for work on the assembly line total 10 percent.

  Find the normal time and standard for this task.

LEARNING CURVES

It is accepted fact that the more you do a particular task, the easier it becomes. You normally can do it faster and better the second time than the first. Indeed, you have probably experienced this phenomenon as you have progressed through this book. The first time you use a new technique, it will take longer to solve a problem than after you have mastered the material and have solved a few similar problems. This is called the *learning-curve effect*. The basic assumptions underlying this effect are:

1. The more times you complete a given task, the less time it will take. For example, if it takes you 45 hours to complete the third unit, it may take you only 40 hours to complete the fourth unit.
2. The amount of time you save completing each unit normally decreases with each additional unit. Thus if you save 5 hours in producing unit 4 versus unit 3, you may only save 3 hours in producing unit 5 versus unit 4. In other words, it may take you 45 hours for the third unit, 40 hours for the fourth unit, 37 hours for the fifth unit, and so on.

Expressing the time it takes to produce a certain unit versus the number of units produced in the form of a mathematical relationship enables us to determine how long it will take to produce any unit as a function of how many units have been produced before it. Although this procedure helps in determining how long it takes to produce a given unit, the consequences of this type of analysis are more far-reaching. For example, if you don't take the learning-curve effect into account, it is possible to run out of inventory and raw materials because the units being produced are taking less and less time to finish. Severe problems in scheduling and labor planning can also occur if you don't take the learning-curve effect into account. Usually, managers will schedule more time for a project than is really necessary. As a result, the labor force and the productive facilities may be idle a significant portion of the time. Furthermore, you may have refused or turned down other projects or tasks because you didn't consider the effect of learning. Basically, you allowed too much time for the current project. These are only a few of the ramifications of not considering the effect of learning. We could apply similar arguments to problems and inefficiencies in marketing, production, and financial planning.

Many industries have experienced the learning-curve effect. The graph of the labor-hours per unit versus the number of units produced normally has the shape illustrated in Figure 14.2. This relationship can be

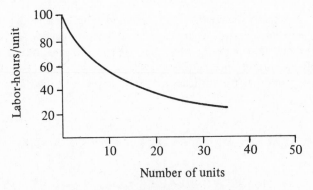

Figure 14.2. The Learning-curve Effect

expressed mathematically as follows:

$$Y_N = Y_1 N^x$$

where

Y_N = the number of labor-hours required to produce the Nth unit.

Y_1 = the number of labor-hours required to produce the first unit.

N = the unit number (N is 4 for the fourth unit, 5 for the fifth unit, and so on)

$X = \dfrac{\log L}{\log 2}$

L = the learning factor

If you know the learning factor and the time it takes to produce the first unit, you can determine how long it will take to produce any subsequent unit.

EXAMPLE 14.7

The learning factor for constructing the wings on the DC-13 jet is 0.8. If it took 56,000 hours to complete the first wing, how long will it take to complete the eighth one?

$$Y_N = Y_1 N^x$$

$$Y_8 = (56{,}000 \text{ hours})(8)^{\log 0.8/\log 2}$$

$$= (56{,}000 \text{ hours})(8^{-0.322})$$

$$= \frac{56{,}000 \text{ hours}}{8^{0.322}} = \frac{56{,}000 \text{ hours}}{1.95}$$

$$= 28{,}718 \text{ hours}$$

PROBLEM 14.9

How long does it take to complete the ninth wing in Example 14.7? How long does it take to complete the tenth wing?

Look at the results in Example 14.7 and Problem 14.9. First of all, it takes less time to complete each additional unit. It took 28,718 hours to complete the eighth unit; it took 27,586 hours to complete the ninth unit; and it took 26,666 hours to complete the tenth unit. Second, the time saving decreased for each additional unit. It takes $(28,718 - 27,586) = 1132$ hours less time to produce unit 9 versus unit 8. It takes $(27,586 - 26,666) = 920$ hours less time to produce unit 10 versus unit 9. Thus, the amount of time saved in completing each unit decreases with each additional unit. As you recall, these two points are the two underlying assumptions of the learning-curve effect. Thus the mathematical model for the learning-curve effect is consistent with the previously stated assumptions.

If you are a typical student, you probably did not solve Problem 14.9. This is not because you are lazy (we hope), but because you didn't have a sophisticated calculator or a computer at your command. Of course, many operations managers are in the same position. But there is a simpler method that makes the learning-curve technique usable and practical. This technique is embodied in Table 14.2 and the following equation:

$$Y_N = Y_B C$$

where

Y_N = the number of labor-hours required to produce the Nth unit

Y_B = the number of labor-hours required to produce the base (B) unit

C = a learning-curve coefficient

The learning-curve coefficient C is a function of the percent of the Nth unit divided by the base unit. You also need to know the learning factor L in order to use the technique.

The following example uses the preceding equation and Table 14.2 to calculate learning-curve effects.

EXAMPLE 14.8

It takes 125,000 hours to produce the first Ramex Super Computer. Using a learning factor of 86 percent, we can determine how long it takes to produce the fourth machine.

First, we compute the ratio of the desired unit to base percent:

$$\% \text{ base} = \frac{\text{unit } 4}{\text{unit } 1} = 400\%$$

Next, we search Table 14.2 for a percent base of 400 percent and a learning factor of 86 percent. We find that the learning-curve coefficient, C, is 0.7396. To produce the fourth unit, then, takes

$$Y_N = Y_B C$$
$$Y_4 = (125{,}000 \text{ hours})(0.7396)$$
$$= 92{,}450 \text{ hours}$$

PROBLEM 14.10

If it takes 80,000 hours to produce the first jet engine at T.R.'s aerospace division, and the learning factor is 90 percent, how long does it take to produce the eighth engine?

Table 14.2 Learning-curve Coefficients

% base	70%	74%	78%	80%	82%	84%	86%	88%	90%	94%	98%
2	7.486	5.469	4.065	3.523	3.065	2.675	2.343	2.058	1.812	1.418	1.121
5	4.672	3.674	2.927	2.623	2.358	2.125	1.919	1.738	1.577	1.307	1.091
10	3.270	2.718	2.283	2.098	1.933	1.785	1.651	1.529	1.419	1.228	1.069
20	2.290	2.012	1.781	1.674	1.585	1.499	1.420	1.346	1.277	1.155	1.048
30	1.858	1.687	1.540	1.473	1.412	1.354	1.300	1.249	1.201	1.113	1.036
40	1.602	1.489	1.389	1.343	1.300	1.259	1.221	1.184	1.149	1.085	1.027
50	1.429	1.351	1.282	1.250	1.220	1.190	1.163	1.136	1.111	1.064	1.020
60	1.300	1.248	1.201	1.178	1.158	1.137	1.118	1.099	1.081	1.047	1.015
70	1.201	1.167	1.137	1.121	1.108	1.094	1.081	1.088	1.056	1.032	1.010
80	1.122	1.101	1.083	1.074	1.066	1.058	1.050	1.042	1.034	1.020	1.007
90	1.056	1.047	1.039	1.034	1.031	1.027	1.023	1.020	1.016	1.010	1.003
100	1.000	1.000	1.000	1.000	1.000	1.000	1.000	1.000	1.000	1.000	1.000
110	0.9521	0.9593	0.9665	0.9696	0.9731	0.9764	0.9796	0.9827	0.9855	0.9916	0.9973
120	0.9105	0.9239	0.9369	0.9428	0.9492	0.9551	0.9610	0.9670	0.9726	0.9839	0.9947
125	0.8915	0.9076	0.9231	0.9307	0.9381	0.9454	0.9526	0.9552	0.9667	0.9803	0.9935
130	0.8737	0.8921	0.9104	0.9200	0.9279	0.9359	0.9447	0.9528	0.9609	0.9769	0.9923
140	0.8410	0.8640	0.8864	0.8974	0.9084	0.9188	0.9294	0.9399	0.9501	0.9704	0.9903
150	0.8117	0.8381	0.8645	0.8776	0.8905	0.9029	0.9156	0.9280	0.9402	0.9645	0.9882
160	0.7852	0.8152	0.8452	0.8595	0.8744	0.8885	0.9028	0.9170	0.9309	0.9590	0.9864
170	0.7611	0.7938	0.8270	0.8428	0.8591	0.8752	0.8910	0.9067	0.9225	0.9538	0.9847
175	0.7498	0.7842	0.8183	0.8352	0.8520	0.8687	0.8854	0.9020	0.9185	0.9513	0.9838
180	0.7390	0.7746	0.8103	0.8274	0.8452	0.8624	0.8798	0.8974	0.9144	0.9489	0.9830
190	0.7187	0.7568	0.7947	0.8133	0.8322	0.8510	0.8698	0.9885	0.9070	0.9443	0.9815
200	0.7000	0.7400	0.7800	0.8000	0.8200	0.8400	0.8600	0.8800	0.9000	0.9400	0.9800
220	0.6665	0.7098	0.7540	0.7759	0.7981	0.8201	0.8423	0.8646	0.8870	0.9321	0.9772
240	0.6373	0.6835	0.7306	0.7543	0.7783	0.8022	0.8265	0.8508	0.8754	0.9249	0.9748
260	0.6116	0.6602	0.7103	0.7349	0.7607	0.7863	0.8123	0.8384	0.8649	0.9182	0.9726
280	0.5887	0.6392	0.6915	0.7177	0.7447	0.7717	0.7992	0.8270	0.8550	0.9122	0.9704
300	0.5682	0.6203	0.6743	0.7019	0.7301	0.7586	0.7875	0.8161	0.8492	0.9066	0.9684
400	0.4900	0.5476	0.6084	0.6400	0.6724	0.7056	0.7396	0.7744	0.8100	0.8836	0.9604
500	0.4368	0.4970	0.5616	0.5956	0.6308	0.6671	0.7045	0.7432	0.7830	0.8662	0.9542
600	0.3977	0.4592	0.5261	0.5617	0.5987	0.6372	0.6771	0.7187	0.7616	0.8522	0.9491
700	0.3674	0.4294	0.4978	0.5345	0.5729	0.6129	0.6548	0.6985	0.7440	0.8406	0.9449
800	0.3430	0.4052	0.4746	0.5120	0.5514	0.5927	0.6361	0.6815	0.7290	0.8306	0.9412
900	0.3228	0.3850	0.4549	0.4929	0.5331	0.5754	0.6200	0.6668	0.7161	0.8219	0.9380
1000	0.3058	0.3678	0.4381	0.4765	0.5172	0.5604	0.6059	0.6540	0.7047	0.8142	0.9351

Source: R.W. Conway and Andrew Schultz, Jr., "The Manufacturing Progress Function," *Journal of Industrial Engineering,* vol. 10, no. 1, January–February 1959, pp. 39–54; and Thomas E. Vollman, *Operations Management*, Reading, Mass.: Addison-Wesley Publishing Company, 1973, pp. 381–4. Reproduced by permission of the AIIE and Addison-Wesley.

PROBLEM 14.11

It takes 28,718 hours to produce the eighth locomotive at a large French manufacturing firm. If the learning factor is 80 percent, how long does it take to produce the tenth locomotive?

ANSWERS

14.1

$$\text{Normal time} = (5.3 \text{ min.})(105\%)$$

$$= 5.565 \text{ min.}$$

$$\text{Allowance fraction} = \frac{\text{personal time} + \text{fatigue time} + \text{delay time}}{60 \text{ min.}}$$

$$= \frac{3 \text{ min.} + 2 \text{ min.} + 1 \text{ min.}}{60 \text{ min.}} = \frac{6}{60}$$

$$= 0.10$$

$$\text{Standard time} = \frac{5.565 \text{ min.}}{1 - 0.10} = \frac{5.565}{0.9}$$

$$= 6.183 \text{ min.}$$

14.2 First, delete the two observations that appear to be very unusual (0.9 min. for job element A and 3.2 min. for job element B). Then,

$$\text{A's ave. cycle time} = \frac{0.1 + 0.3 + 0.2 + 0.2 + 0.1}{5}$$

$$= 0.18 \text{ min.}$$

$$\text{B's ave. cycle time} = \frac{0.8 + 0.6 + 0.8 + 0.5 + 0.7}{5}$$

$$= 0.68 \text{ min.}$$

$$\text{C's ave. cycle time} = \frac{0.5 + 0.5 + 0.4 + 0.5 + 0.6 + 0.5}{6}$$

$$= 0.50 \text{ min.}$$

$$\text{A's normal time} = (0.18)(0.90)$$

$$= 0.16 \text{ min.}$$

$$\text{B's normal time} = (0.68)(1.10)$$

$$= 0.75 \text{ min.}$$

$$\text{C's normal time} = (0.50)(0.80)$$

$$= 0.40 \text{ min.}$$

(continued)

$$\text{Normal time for job} = 0.16 + 0.75 + 0.40$$

$$= 1.31 \text{ min.}$$

$$\text{Standard time} \quad = \frac{1.31}{1 - 0.20}$$

$$= 1.64 \text{ min.}$$

14.3

$$\text{Coefficient of variation} = \frac{s}{\overline{X}} = \frac{1.28}{3.20}$$

$$= 0.40$$

According to Figure 14.1, the correct sample size is 600 cycles.

14.4

$$\text{Normal time} = 6 + 2 + 10 + 20 + 4 + 120 + 10 + 10$$

$$= 182 \text{ TMU}$$

$$\text{Time in minutes} = (182 \text{ TMU}) (0.0006 \text{ min.})$$

$$= 0.1092 \text{ min.}$$

$$\text{Time in seconds} = (0.1092) (60 \text{ sec./min.})$$

$$= 6.55 \text{ sec.}$$

14.5

$$n = \frac{Z_\alpha^2 \, p(1-p)}{h^2} = \frac{(3)^2 (0.6)(0.4)}{(0.04)^2}$$

$$= 1{,}350 \text{ sample size}$$

14.6

$$p = 0.30, \; Z_\alpha \cong 2, \; h = 0.05$$

$$n = \frac{(2)^2 (0.3)(0.7)}{(0.05)^2}$$

$$= 336 \text{ observations}$$

14.7

$$\text{Normal time} = \frac{(9600 \text{ min.})(0.80)(0.90)}{220}$$

$$= 31.42 \text{ min./part}$$

$$\text{Standard time} = \frac{31.42 \text{ min.}}{1 - 0.10}$$

$$= 34.91 \text{ min./part}$$

14.8

$$\text{Normal time} = \frac{(2400 \text{ min.})(0.80)(1.25)}{320}$$

$$= 7.50 \text{ min./part}$$

$$\text{Standard time} = \frac{7.50}{1 - 0.10}$$

$$= 8.33 \text{ min./part}$$

14.9

$$Y_9 = (56,000 \text{ hours})(9)^{\log 0.8/\log 2}$$

$$= (56,000 \text{ hours})(9)^{-0.322}$$

$$= \frac{56,000 \text{ hours}}{9^{0.322}} = \frac{56,000 \text{ hours}}{2.03}$$

$$= 27,586 \text{ hours}$$

$$Y_{10} = (56,000 \text{ hours})(10)^{\log 0.8/\log 2}$$

$$= \frac{56,000 \text{ hours}}{10^{0.322}} = \frac{56,000 \text{ hours}}{2.10}$$

$$= 26,666 \text{ hours}$$

14.10

$$\% \text{ base} = \frac{\text{engine } 8}{\text{engine } 1}$$

$$= 800\%$$

$$C = 0.7290 \text{ from Table 14.2, where } \% \text{ base} = 800$$
$$\text{and the learning factor is } 90\%$$

$$Y_8 = (80,000 \text{ hours})(0.7290)$$

$$= 58,320 \text{ hours}$$

14.11

$$\% \text{ base} = \frac{\text{locomotive } 10}{\text{locomotive } 8}$$

$$= 125\%$$

$$C = 0.9307 \text{ from Table 14.2 where } \% \text{ base} = 125\%$$
$$\text{and the learning factor is } 80\%$$

$$Y_{10} = (28,718 \text{ hours})(0.9307)$$

$$= 26,728 \text{ hours}$$

Compare this result with Problem 14.9. The results are similar, but they are not exactly the same. Thus, it is up to the operations manager to decide whether to sacrifice accuracy for the convenience of using Table 14.2 (as opposed to the longhand method) to compute the learning-curve effect.

HOMEWORK PROBLEM

An analyst has timed an operator of a metal-working machine on a job that has four elements. The observed times and performance ratings for six cycles are shown below. The allowance for this type of work is 15 percent.

a. Find the average cycle time for each element.
b. Determine the normal time for each element.
c. Determine the standard time for this job.

Job Element	Performance Rating	Observations (minutes per cycle)					
		1	2	3	4	5	6
1. Set sheetmetal in place	90%	.44	.50	—	.46	.52	.40
2. Align drilling machinery	110%	1.05	.95	.85	.96	.80	1.00
3. Drill three holes	100%	1.55	1.50	1.70	1.60	1.45	1.65
4. Remove completed metal plate	130%	.25	.30	.28	.33	.25	—

Unit 15

Simulation

Simulation refers to the use of a numerical model, which represents various activities and relationships in a business system, in order to predict what will happen in the future. Using simulation, a production or operations manager can (1) define a problem, (2) introduce the variables associated with the problem, (3) construct a numerical model, and (4) set up possible courses of action for testing (see Figure 15.1). The advantage of simulation is that it determines the results of a particular decision (in a sort of laboratory fashion) before the firm tries to actually implement it. This way, a manager can ask a series of "what if" questions about the system, test several alternatives, and choose the one that provides the best results. *Computer simulation* allows the very rapid testing of many options and has advanced the popularity of this approach to problem solving. Just a few areas in which simulation is being used today are:

Table 15.1. Some Applications of Simulation

Ambulance and fire-fighting equipment location and dispatching
Assembly-line balancing
Design of parking lots, harbors, communication systems
Design of distribution systems
Scheduling aircraft
Job-shop scheduling
Manpower-hiring decisions
Personnel scheduling
Traffic-light timing

In this unit, we will examine the basic principles of simulation and then tackle some problems in the areas of inventory control, maintenance, and waiting-line analysis. Why use simulation in these areas when mathematical models discussed in other units can solve our problems? The answer is that simulation provides an alternative approach. For example, it can handle waiting-line problems in which arrivals at the facility and service times are not Poisson or exponentially distributed (two basic assumptions of Unit 16).

THE MONTE CARLO METHOD

The *Monte Carlo technique* for simulating events breaks down into four simple steps: (1) setting up a probability distribution for possible outcomes, (2) establishing an interval of random numbers for each outcome, (3) generating random numbers, and (4) actually simulating a series of trials. This section examines each of these in turn. In the following sections, we will use the Monte Carlo method to simulate a few production-operations management problems.

Establishing probability distributions. The basis of Monte Carlo simulation is the generation of values for the variables comprising the model under study. Examples of variables whose outcomes we may want to simulate include:

Inventory demand on a daily or weekly basis
Lead time for inventory orders to arrive
Times between machine breakdowns
Times between arrivals at a service facility
Service times
Project completion times

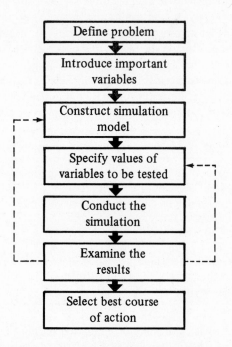

Figure 15.1. The Process of Simulation

One common way of establishing a *probability distribution* for a given variable is to examine historical outcomes. The probability, or relative frequency, for each possible outcome of a variable is found by **dividing the frequency of observation by the total number of observations. Example 15.1 illustrates this concept.**

EXAMPLE 15.1

Daily demand for radial tires over the past 100 days at Gibbs Auto Tire is shown below.

Demand	Number of Days
0	5
1	10
2	20
3	30
4	20
5	15
	100

We can convert this to a probability distribution (if we assume that past sales trends will hold in the future) by dividing each demand frequency by the total demand, 100.

Demand Variable	Probability of Occurrence
0	0.05
1	0.10
2	0.20
3	0.30
4	0.20
5	0.15
	1.00

PROBLEM 15.1

The number of autos arriving at Harry's Car Wash during the last 200 hours of operation is observed to be the following:

(continued)

Number of Cars Arriving	Frequency
4 or less	0
5	20
6	30
7	50
8	60
9	40
10 or more	0
	200

Set up a probability distribution for the variable of car arrivals.

Setting random number intervals. Once we have established a probability distribution for each variable to be included in the simulation, we must assign an interval of random numbers to represent each outcome. If there is a 5 percent chance that demand for a product will be zero units per day, then we will want 5 percent of the random numbers available to correspond to a demand of zero units. If a total of 100 two-digit random numbers is used in the simulation (think of them as being numbered chips in a bowl), we could assign a demand of zero units to the first five random numbers: 00, 01, 02, 03, and 04. Then a simulated demand for zero units would be created every time one of the numbers 00 to 04 was drawn. If there is also a 10 percent chance that demand for the same product will be one unit per day, we could let the next ten random numbers (05, 06, 07, 08, 09, 10, 11, 12, 13, and 14) represent that demand—and so on for other demand levels.

In general, if we set up a *cumulative probability distribution,* we can set the interval of random numbers for each level of demand in a very simple fashion, as Example 15.2 illustrates.

EXAMPLE 15.2

We can set an interval of random numbers for each outcome of tires demanded in Example 15.1 as follows:

(continued)

Daily Demand	Probability	Cumulative Probability	Interval of Random Numbers
0	0.05	0.05	00 to 04
1	0.10	0.15	05 to 14
2	0.20	0.35	15 to 34
3	0.30	0.65	35 to 64
4	0.20	0.85	65 to 84
5	0.15	1.00	85 to 99

Note that the interval of random numbers selected to represent each possible daily demand is closely related to the cumulative probability on its left. The top end of each interval is always one less than the cumulative probability percentage. The random number 04 is one less than .05, 14 is 1 less than .15, 34 is 1 less than .35 and so on.

PROBLEM 15.2

Establish an interval of random numbers for the random variable arrivals in Problem 15.1.

Generating random numbers. Random numbers, that is, numbers drawn in such a way that each digit (0 through 9) has an equal chance of being drawn, may be generated for simulation problems in two ways. If the problem is very large and the process being studied involves thousands of simulation trials, computer programs are available to generate the random numbers needed. If the simulation is being done by hand, as in this book, the numbers may be selected from a table of random digits such as Table 15.2.

Simulating the experiment. We may simulate outcomes of an experiment by simply selecting random numbers from Table 15.2 (beginning anywhere in the table) and noting the interval into which each falls. For example, if the random number chosen is 81 and the interval 65 to 84 represents a daily demand of 4 units, then we select a demand of 4 units.

Table 15.2. Table of Random Digits

97	95	12	11	90
02	92	75	91	24
80	67	14	99	16
66	24	72	57	32
96	76	20	28	72
55	64	82	61	73
50	02	74	70	16
29	53	08	33	81
58	16	01	91	70
51	16	69	67	16
04	55	36	97	30
86	54	35	61	59
24	23	52	11	59
39	36	99	50	74
47	44	41	86	83
60	71	41	25	90
65	88	48	06	68
44	74	11	60	14
93	10	95	80	32
20	46	36	19	47
86	54	24	88	94
12	88	12	25	19
42	00	50	24	60

Source: Excerpted from Harold Bierman, Jr., Charles P. Bonini, and Warren Hausman, *Quantitative Analysis for Business Decisions,* (Homewood, Ill.: Richard D. Irwin, 1977), p. 500.

EXAMPLE 15.3

Let us simulate ten days of demand for radial tires at Gibbs Auto Tire (see Example 15.2). We select the random numbers needed from Table 15.2, starting in the upper left-hand corner and continuing down the first column.

(continued)

Day Number	Random Number	Simulated Daily Demand
1	97	5
2	02	0
3	80	4
4	66	4
5	96	5
6	55	3
7	50	3
8	29	2
9	58	3
10	51	3
	Total ten-day demand:	32
	Average daily demand:	3.2 tires

It is interesting to note that the average demand of 3.2 tires in this ten-day simulation differs from the *expected* daily demand, which we may calculate from the data in Example 15.2:

$$\text{Expected demand} = \sum_{i=0}^{5} (\text{probability of } i \text{ units}) \times (\text{demand of } i \text{ units})$$

$$= (0.05)(0) + (0.10)(1) + (0.20)(2) + (0.30)(3) + (0.20)(4) + (0.15)(5)$$

$$= 0 + 0.1 + 0.4 + 0.9 + 0.8 + 0.75$$

$$= 2.95 \text{ tires}$$

If this simulation were repeated hundred or thousands of times, it is much more likely that the average *simulated* demand would be nearly the same as the *expected* demand.

Naturally, it would be risky to draw any hard and fast conclusions regarding the operation of a firm from only a short simulation such as we did above. Consequently the computer could be a very useful tool in carrying out the tedious work involved in such an undertaking. Nevertheless, simulating by hand demonstrates the important principles involved and may be useful in small-scale studies.

PROBLEM 15.3

Simulate eight hours of auto arrivals at Harry's Car Wash (Problem 15.2) and compute the average number of arrivals per hour. Select the random numbers needed from Table 15.2, beginning in the upper right-hand corner (the digit 90) and proceeding down that last column.

(continued)

Hour Number	Random Number	Simulated Hourly Arrivals

SIMULATION MODEL FOR A MAINTENANCE POLICY

Simulation is a valuable technique for analyzing various maintenance policies (see Unit 17) before actually implementing them. A firm can decide whether to add additional maintenance staff based on machine downtime costs and costs of additional labor. It can simulate replacing parts that have not yet failed in exploring ways to prevent future breakdowns. Many companies use computerized simulation models to decide if and when to shut down a whole plant for maintenance activities. This section provides a few relatively simple examples of the value of simulation in setting maintenance policy.

PROBLEM 15.4

The Mississippi Power Company is building a new generator for its Jackson plant. Management recognizes that even a well-maintained generator will have periodic failures or breakdowns. Historical figures for similar generators indicate that the relative frequency of failures during a year is as follows:

(continued)

Number of Failures	Probability (relative frequency)	Associated Interval of Random Numbers
0	0.75	
1	0.19	
2	0.03	
3	0.02	
4	0.01	

Complete the column headed "Associated Interval of Random Numbers," and assuming that the useful lifetime of the generator is twenty years, use simulation to estimate the number of breakdowns that will occur in twenty years of operation. Is it common to have three or more consecutive years of operation without a failure? (Note: So that we all reach the same conclusions, start selecting your random numbers at the top of the middle (third) column of Table 15.2, and proceed down that column.)

Year	Random Number	Number of Breakdowns

EXAMPLE 15.4

Cathy Innis, director of management analysis at the Cincinnati Manufacturing Company, is trying to decide whether to add a second full-time maintenance man to the staff. Innis has collected some historical data and has used the Monte Carlo method to simulate machine breakdown over a ten-hour period.

Time of Machine Breakdown	Total Hours of Repair Time Required
8:00 AM	1.0
9:30 AM	2.0
10:30 AM	1.0
1:00 PM	2.0
3:30 PM	1.5
	7.5

The firm's current maintenance man charges his time at a rate of $12.00 per hour (whether he is working or idle). The cost for a machine that is down is estimated by Ms. Innis to be $100 per hour.

Our objective in this example is to determine: (1) the service maintenance cost, (2) the simulated machine-breakdown cost, (3) the total simulated maintenance cost. Furthermore, we would like to know whether (based on this brief simulation) Innis should hire a second maintenance man. (This chore we will assign to *you* in Problem 15.5).

Breakdown Simulation with One Maintenance Man

Time of Breakdown	Repair Time Required (hours)	Time Repairs Begin	Time Repairs End	Number of Hours Machine Is Down
8:00 AM	1.0	8:00 AM	9:00 AM	1
9:30 AM	2.0	9:30 AM	11:30 AM	2
10:30 AM	1.0	11:30 PM	12:30 PM	2
1:00 PM	2.0	1:00 PM	3:00 PM	2
3:30 PM	1.5	3:30 PM	5:00 PM	1.5
				8.5

Note that repairs did not begin until 11:30 AM (when maintenance man completed earlier job)

(1) The service maintenance cost with one repairman on duty is ($12.00/hr.) × (10 hr.) = $120.
(2) The simulated machine-breakdown cost, from the rightmost column, is ($100/hr.) × (8.5 hr.) = $850.
(3) Simulated total maintenance cost = service + breakdown = $120 + $850 = $970.

PROBLEM 15.5

Assuming that adding a second maintenance man will result in twice the repair-time effectiveness of the one man in Example 15.4 (that is, they will work together and cut repair time by 50 percent), should Cincinnati Manufacturing Company hire another repairman? The additional person will cost $12.00 per hour.

Breakdown Simulation with Two Maintenance Men

Time of Breakdown	Repair Time	Time Repairs Begin	Time Repairs End	Number of Hours Machine Is Down

We would not, of course, want to make any major financial decisions based on either of these one-day simulations. We could run this basic model for hundreds of days, however, and it would prove a most worthwhile means of analysis.

SIMULATION AND INVENTORY ANALYSIS

Unit 7 introduced the subject of "deterministic" inventory models in which both demand per day and lead time were known, constant values. If we consider the case in which demand and lead time are variables, the analysis becomes extremely difficult to handle by any means other than simulation.

  In this section we will present an inventory problem with two decision variables and two probabilistic components. The owner of the hardware store described in the next example would like to establish *order quantity* and *reorder point decisions* for a particular product that has a probabilistic (uncertain) daily demand and reorder lead time. He wants to make a series of simulation runs, trying out various order quantities and reorder points, in order to minimize his total inventory cost for the item. Inventory costs in this case will include an ordering, holding, and stockout cost.

EXAMPLE 15.5

Simkin's Hardware sells the Ace model electric drill. Daily demand for the drill is relatively low but subject to some variability. Over the past 200 days, owner Simkin has observed the sales shown below. Our first step in this inventory problem is to form a probability distribution for the variable daily demand and to assign random number intervals.

Demand for Ace Drill	Frequency	Probability	Cumulative Probability	Interval of Random Numbers
0	10	0.05	0.05	00 to 04
1	20	0.10	0.15	05 to 14
2	40	0.20	0.35	15 to 34
3	80	0.40	0.75	35 to 74
4	30	0.15	0.90	75 to 89
5	20	0.10	1.00	90 to 99
	200 days	1.00		

We will use this information in Example 15.6.

PROBLEM 15.6

When Simkin places an order to replenish his inventory of Ace electric drills, there is a delivery lag, which we may also consider a "probabilistic" variable. The number of days it took to receive the past 50 orders is presented below. Establish a probability distribution for the variable lead time and assign random number intervals for each possible time.

(continued)

Lead Time in Days	Frequency
1	10
2	25
3	15
	——
	50

EXAMPLE 15.6

The first inventory policy that Simkin's Hardware wants to simulate is an order quantity of 10 with a reorder point of 5. That is, every time the on-hand inventory level at the end of the day is 5 or less drills, Simkin will call his supplier and place an order for 10 more drills. If the lead time is one day, by the way, the order will not arrive the next morning, but rather at the beginning of the following working day.

   The entire process is simulated below for a ten-day period. We assume that beginning inventory is 10 units on day 1. We took the random numbers from column 2 of Table 15.2.

   The following table was filled in by proceeding one day (or line) at a time, working from left to right. It was a four-step process:

1. Begin each simulated day by checking whether any ordered inventory has just arrived. If it has, increase the current inventory by the quantity ordered (10 units, in this case).
2. Generate a daily demand from the demand probability distribution by selecting a random number.
3. Compute ending inventory = beginning inventory minus demand. If on-hand inventory is insufficient to meet the day's demand, satisfy as much as possible and note the number of lost sales.
4. Determine whether the day's ending inventory has reached the reorder point (5 units). If it has, and if there are no outstanding orders, place an order. Lead time for a new order is simulated by choosing a random number and using the distribution in Problem 15.6.

(continued)

Inventory Simulation I

Order Quantity = 10 units   Reorder Point = 5 units

Day	Units Received	Begin Inventory	Random Number	Demand	End Inventory	Lost Sales	Order?	Random Number	Lead Time
1		10	95	5	5	0	Yes	92	3 days
2	0	5	67	3	2	0	No		
3	0	2	24	2	0	0	No		
4	0	0	76	4	0	4	No		
5	10	10	64	3	7	0	No		
6	0	7	02	0	7	0	No		
7	0	7	53	3	4	0	Yes	16	1 day
8	0	4	16	2	2	0	No		
9	10	12	55	3	9	0	No		
10	0	9	54	3	6	0	No		
Totals:					42	4			

$$\text{Average ending inventory} = \frac{42}{10} = 4.2 \text{ unit/day}$$

$$\text{Average lost sales} = \frac{4}{10} = 0.4 \text{ unit/day}$$

$$\text{Average number of orders placed} = \frac{2}{10} = 0.2 \text{ order/day}$$

EXAMPLE 15.7

Simkin estimates that the cost of placing each order for Ace drills is $10, the holding cost per drill held at the end of each day is $.50, and the cost of each lost sale is $8.

This information enables us to compute the total daily inventory cost for the simulated policy in Example 15.6.

Order cost = (cost of placing one order) × (number of orders placed per day)

= ($10)(0.2)

= $2.00

(continued)

Holding cost   = (cost of holding 1 unit for 1 day) × (average ending inventory)

   = ($.50)(4.2)

   = $2.10

Stockout cost = (cost per lost sale) × (average number of lost sales per day)

   = ($8)(0.4)

   = $3.20

Total daily inventory cost = $2.00 + $2.10 + $3.20

   = $7.30

Thus the total inventory cost to Simkin under this policy, as simulated above, is $7.30.

PROBLEM 15.7

Simkin's second inventory strategy for Ace drills is to consider ordering 12 drills, with a reorder point of 4 drills. Simulate this policy for a ten-day period, as we did in Example 15.6. Select the necessary random numbers by starting at the top of column 4 in Table 15.2. Assume that beginning inventory on day 1 is 12 units.

(continued)

Inventory Simulation II

Order Quantity = 12 units   Reorder Point = 4 units

Day	Units Received	Begin Inventory	Random Number	Demand	End Inventory	Lost Sales	Order?	Random Number	Lead Time

PROBLEM 15.8

Using the order, holding, and lost-sale costs given in Example 15.7, calculate the total daily inventory cost for the order policy just simulated. Compare your results to those found in the first simulation and comment.

We can repeat inventory simulations such as this one numerous times to test the effect of different order policies. After simulating all reasonable combinations or order quantities and reorder points, a firm would likely select the pair yielding the lowest total inventory cost.

SIMULATION OF A QUEUING PROBLEM

An important area of simulation application has been in the analysis of waiting-line problems. As mentioned earlier, the assumptions required for solving queuing problems analytically are quite restrictive. For most sophisticated queuing systems, simulation may actually be the only approach available.

This section illustrates the simulation at a barge unloading dock and the queue associated with it. Arrivals of barges at the dock are not Poisson distributed, as required for use of a mathematical waiting-line model, but follow a probability distribution given in Example 15.8.

EXAMPLE 15.8

Fully loaded barges arrive at night in New Orleans following their long trips down the Mississippi River from industrial midwestern cities. The number of barges docking on any given night ranges from zero to 5. We know the probability of 0, 1, 2, 3, 4, or 5 of them arriving and can establish a corresponding random number interval for each possible value.

(continued)

Barges are unloaded at a constant rate of three per day at the dock. Any more than three barges in the queue must wait till the following day for unloading. The unloading system operates on a "first-in, first-out" basis.

We can simulate the unloading process for a ten-day period by employing random numbers to generate arrivals each day. We drew the random numbers from rows 3 and 4 on Table 15.2.

Number of Arrivals	Probability	Random Number Interval
0	0.13	00 to 12
1	0.17	13 to 29
2	0.15	30 to 44
3	0.25	45 to 69
4	0.20	70 to 89
5	0.10	90 to 99
	1.00	

Queuing Simulation I

Day	Number Delayed from Previous Day	Random Number	Number of Nightly Arrivals	Total to Be Unloaded	Number Unloaded
1	–	80	4	4	3
2	1	67	3	4	3
3	1	14	1	2	2
4	0	99	5	5	3
5	2	16	1	3	3
6	0	66	3	3	3
7	0	24	1	1	1
8	0	72	4	4	3
9	1	57	3	4	3
10	1	32	2	3	3
	6		27		27

Average number of barges delayed to next day $= \dfrac{6}{10} = 0.6$

Average number unloaded each day $= \dfrac{27}{10} = 2.7$

Average number of nightly arrivals $= \dfrac{27}{10} = 2.7$

PROBLEM 15.9

A study by the dock superintendent reveals that the number of barges unloaded is not actually a constant three per day but tends to vary from day to day. The superintendent provides information from which we can create a probability distribution for the variable "daily unloading rate."

As the first step in resimulating the dock's waiting line, set up an interval of random numbers for the unloading rates below.

Daily Unloading Rate	Probability	Random Number Interval
1	0.05	
2	0.15	
3	0.50	
4	0.20	
5	0.10	
	1.00	

Now you may rerun the simulation shown in Example 15.8, but this time treat daily unloadings also as a variable. Use the third column of Table 15.2 (starting at the top for day 1) to provide random numbers to simulate ten days of unloading rates. The random numbers used to simulate arrivals in Example 15.8 may be used again for arrivals here.

Queuing Simulation II

Day	Number Delayed from Previous Day	Random Number	Number Nightly Arrivals	Total to Be Unloaded	Random Number	Number Unloaded
1						
2						
3						
4						
5						
6						
7						
8						
9						
10						
Totals:						

(continued)

Average number of barges delayed to next day =

Average number of barges unloaded each day =

Average number nightly arrivals =

It is interesting to compare the statistics computed in Example 15.8 and Problem 15.9. Introducing the number of barges unloaded daily as a variable in the problem above results in a different average delay rate (higher in this brief ten-day simulation). This is the kind of information that is both useful and important to the dock's management. Although simulation is a tool that cannot guarantee an optimal solution to problem situations, it can be very helpful in recreating a process and identifying good decision alternatives.

COMPUTER SIMULATION

As you may know, anything that a person can do with paper and pencil, a computer can do as well—and usually faster and more accurately. Computers make ideal aids in simulating complex tasks. They can generate random numbers, simulate thousands of time periods in a matter of seconds or minutes, and provide management with reports that make decision making easier. As a matter of fact, a computer approach is almost a necessity in order for us to draw valid conclusions from a simulation. Since we require a very large number of simulations—we surely would not want to make a major decision based only on a ten-day experiment—it would be a real burden to rely on pencil and paper alone.

In addition to general-purpose languages such as FORTRAN, BASIC, and COBOL, which have been used in simulation, there is a variety of special-purpose simulation languages. Such languages as GPSS, SIM-SCRIPT, and GASP are especially efficient in handling queuing, maintenance, and scheduling simulation problems.

ANSWERS

15.1 and 15.2

Random Variables Arrivals	Probability	Cumulative Probability	Interval of Random Numbers
5	0.10	0.10	00 to 09
6	0.15	0.25	10 to 24
7	0.25	0.50	25 to 49
8	0.30	0.80	50 to 79
9	0.20	1.00	80 to 99
	1.00		

15.3

Hour Number	Random Number	Simulated Hourly Arrivals
1	90	9
2	24	6
3	16	6
4	32	7
5	72	8
6	73	8
7	16	6
8	81	9
Total eight-hour arrivals:		59
Average hourly arrivals:		7.37

(continued)

15.4

Number of Failures	Random Number Interval
0	00 to 74
1	75 to 93
2	94 to 96
3	97 to 98
4	99

Year	Random Number	Breakdowns	Year	Random Number	Breakdowns
1	12	0	11	36	0
2	75	1	12	35	0
3	14	0	13	52	0
4	72	0	14	99	4
5	20	0	15	41	0
6	82	1	16	41	0
7	74	0	17	48	0
8	08	0	18	11	0
9	01	0	19	95	2
10	69	0	20	36	0

It is not uncommon for the generator to operate three or more consecutive years without a failure.

15.5 (1) The service maintenance cost with two men on duty is $(2)(\$12.00/hr.)(10)$
= \$240.

(2) Two repairmen will decrease by one-half the repair times in Example 15.4. As a result, there will be no delayed repairs and the total number of hours of machine downtime (the right-hand column) will be 3.75 hours. The simulated machine-breakdown cost is now $(\$100/hr.) \times (3.75\ hr.) = \$375$.

(3) Total maintenance cost is $\$240 + \$375 = \$615$. Thus, the company should hire a second man!

15.6

Lead Time in Days	Frequency	Probability	Cumulative Probability	Random Number Interval
1	10	0.20	0.20	00 to 19
2	25	0.50	0.70	20 to 69
3	15	0.30	1.00	70 to 99
	50			

15.7 and 15.8

Inventory Simulation II

Day	Units Received	Begin Inventory	Random Number	Demand	End Inventory	Lost Sales	Order?	Random Number	Lead Time
1		12	11	1	11	0	No		
2	0	11	91	5	6	0	No		
3	0	6	99	5	1	0	Yes	57	2 days
4	0	1	28	2	0	1	No		
5	0	0	61	3	0	3	No		
6	12	12	70	3	9	0	No		
7	0	9	33	2	7	0	No		
8	0	7	91	5	2	0	Yes	67	2 days
9	0	2	97	5	0	3	No		
10	0	0	61	3	0	3	No		
Totals:					36	10			

$$\text{Average ending inventory} = \frac{36}{10} = 3.6 \text{ units/day}$$

$$\text{Average lost sales} = \frac{10}{10} = 1.0 \text{ unit/day}$$

$$\text{Average number of orders placed} = \frac{2}{10} = 0.2 \text{ order/day}$$

$$\text{Order cost} = (\$10)(0.2) = \$2.00$$

$$\text{Holding cost} = (\$.50)(3.6) = 1.80$$

$$\text{Stockout cost} = (\$8)(1.0) = 8.00$$

$$\text{Total daily inventory costs} = 2 + \$1.80 + \$8 = \$11.80$$

Comments: The order policy simulated here appears to be significantly more expensive than the first one. Because the ten-day period is not a very long test, however, we would want to carry out further simulation trials before making any final decision.

15.9

Daily Unloading Rate	Probability	Random Number Interval
1	0.05	00 to 04
2	0.15	05 to 19
3	0.50	20 to 69
4	0.20	70 to 89
5	0.10	90 to 99
	1.00	

Queuing Simulation II

Day	Number Delayed	Random Number	Number of Nightly Arrivals	Total to Be Unloaded	Random Number	Number Unloaded
1	—	80	4	4	12	2
2	2	67	3	5	75	4
3	1	14	1	2	14	2
4	0	99	5	5	72	4
5	1	16	1	2	20	2 (but 3 could be)
6	0	66	3	3	82	3 (but 4 could be)
7	0	24	1	1	74	1 (but 4 could be)
8	0	72	4	4	08	2
9	2	57	3	5	01	1
10	4	32	2	6	69	3
Totals:	10		27			24

Average number of barges delayed $= \dfrac{10}{10} = 1$ barge/day

Average number of nightly arrivals $= \dfrac{27}{10} = 2.7$ (as in Example 15.8)

Average number unloaded $= \dfrac{24}{10} = 2.4$ barges /day

HOMEWORK PROBLEMS

15-1. Milwaukee's General Hospital has an emergency room that is divided into six departments: (1) the initial exam station to treat minor problems or make diagnoses, (2) an X-ray department, (3) an operating room, (4) a cast-fitting room, (5) an observation room (for recovery and general observation before final diagnoses or release), and (6) an out-processing department (where clerks check patients out and arrange for payment or insurance forms).

The probabilities that a patient will go from one department to another are presented in the accompanying table.

From	*To*	*Probability*
Initial exam at	X-ray Department	.45
emergency room	Operating Room	.15
entrance	Observation Room	.10
	Out-Processing Clerk	.30
X-ray Department	Operating Room	.10
	Cast-Fitting Room	.25
	Observation Room	.35
	Out-Processing Clerk	.30
Operating Room	Cast-Fitting Room	.25
	Observation Room	.70
	Out-Processing Clerk	.05
Cast-Fitting Room	Observation Room	.55
	X-ray Department	.05
	Out-Processing Clerk	.40
Observation Room	Operating Room	.15
	X-ray Department	.15
	Out-Processing Clerk	.70

a. Simulate the trail followed by ten emergency room patients. Proceed one patient at a time from each one's entry at the initial exam station until he or she leaves through out-processing. You should be aware that a patient can enter the same department more than once.
b. Using your simulation data, what are the chances that a patient returns to the X-ray department twice?

15-2. The Brennan Aircraft Division of TLN Enterprises operates a large number of computerized plotting machines. For the most part, the plotting devices are used to create line drawings of complex wing airfoils and fuselage part dimensions. The engineers operating the automated plotters are called loft lines engineers.

The computerized plotters consist of a minicomputer system connected to a 4-by-5-foot table with a series of ink pens suspended above it. When a sheet of clear plastic or paper is properly placed on the table, the computer directs a series of horizontal and vertical pen movements until the desired figure is drawn.

The plotting machines are highly reliable, with the exception of the four sophisticated ink pens that are built in. The pens constantly clog and jam in a raised or lowered position. When this occurs, the plotter is unusable.

Currently, Brennan Aircraft replaces each pen as it fails. The service manager has, however, proposed replacing all four pens every time one fails. This should cut down the frequency of plotter failures. At present, it takes one hour to replace one pen. All four pens could be replaced in two hours. The total cost of a plotter being unusable is $50 per hour. Each pen costs $8.

If only one pen is replaced each time a clog or jam occurs, the following breakdown data are thought to be valid:

Hours between Plotter Failures if One Pen Replaced during a Repair	Probability
10	.05
20	.15
30	.15
40	.20
50	.20
60	.15
70	.10

Based on the service manager's estimates, if all four pens are replaced each time one pen fails, the probability distribution between failures is:

Hours between Plotter Failures if All Four Pens Are Replaced during a Repair	Probability
100	.15
110	.25
120	.35
130	.20
140	.05

Simulate Brennan Aircraft's problem and determine the best policy. Should the firm replace one pen or all four pens on a plotter each time a failure occurs?

Waiting Lines and Service Systems

The subject of waiting lines, often called *queuing theory*, is a widely used means of evaluating the cost and effectiveness of service systems. An everyday occurrence, a waiting line may take the form of people or parts of machines waiting for service. The three basic components of queuing process are arrivals, service facilities, and the actual waiting line. Table 16.1 lists a few common production-operations management uses of queuing theory.

WAITING-LINE COSTS

Most waiting-line problems address the question of finding the ideal level of service that a firm should provide. Supermarkets must decide how many checkout counters should be open. Gasoline stations must decide how many pumps to open and how many attendants to have on duty. Manufacturing plants must determine the optimal number of mechanics to have on duty each shift to repair machines that break down.

One evaluation criterion is *total expected cost*, a concept illustrated in Figure 16.1. Total expected cost is the sum of *service costs* plus *waiting costs*. We can see that service costs increase as a firm attempts to raise its level of service. For example, employing three teams of stevedores, instead of two, to unload a cargo ship increases service costs by the additional price of wages. As service improves in speed, however, the cost of time spent waiting in lines decreases. This waiting cost may reflect lost worker productivity while tools or machines are awaiting repairs or may simply be an estimate of the cost of customers lost because of poor service and long queues.

Table 16.1 Common Queuing Situations

Situation	Arrivals in queue	Service process
Supermarket	Grocery shoppers	Checkout clerks at cash register
Highway toll	Automobiles	Collection of toll at booth
Doctor's office	Patients	Treatment by doctors and nurses
Airport	Airplanes	Takeoffs and landings
Bank	Customers	Transactions handled by teller
Restaurant	Diners	Waiters and cooks serve patrons
Machine maintenance	Broken machines	Repairmen fix machines
Port	Ships	Dockworkers load and unload

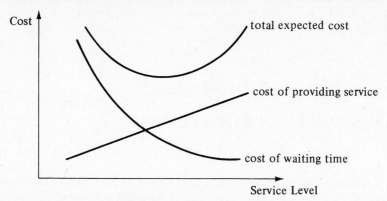

Figure 16.1. Queuing Costs

EXAMPLE 16.1

The Blank Brothers Shipping Company has a huge docking facility located on the Ohio River near Pittsburgh. Approximately five ships arrive to unload their cargoes of steel and ore during every 12-hour work shift. Each hour that a ship sits idle in line waiting to be unloaded costs the firm a great deal of money (about $1000 per hour). But each additional team of stevedores on duty to handle the unloading work is also an expensive proposition, due to union contracts. Blank's superintendent would like to determine the optimum number of teams of stevedores to have on duty each shift. The objective is to minimize total expected costs. The analysis is summarized below.

	Number of Teams of Stevedores			
	1	*2*	*3*	*4*
Average number of ships arriving per shift	5	5	5	5
Average time each ship waits to be unloaded	7 hr.	4 hr.	3 hr.	2 hr.
Total ship hours lost per shift	35 hr.	20 hr.	15 hr.	10 hr.
Estimated cost per hour of idle ship time	$1,000	$1,000	$1,000	$1,000
Value of ship's lost time	$35,000	$20,000	$15,000	$10,000
Stevedore team salary	$6,000	$12,000	$18,000	$24,000
Total expected cost	$41,000	$32,000	$33,000	$34,000

Note: Stevedore team salaries are computed as the number of stevedores in a typical team (assumed to be 50) times the number of hours each team member works per day (12 hours), times an hourly salary of $10 per hour. Employing two teams just doubles the rate.

In order to minimize the sum of service costs and waiting costs, the decision is made to employ two teams of stevedores each shift. The total cost of this is $32,000.

PROBLEM 16.1

The Super-shop Discount Department Store has approximately 300 customers shopping in its store between 9 AM and 5 PM on Saturdays. In deciding how many cash registers to keep open each Saturday, Super-shop's manager considers two factors: customer waiting time (and the associated waiting cost) and the service costs of employing additional checkout clerks. Checkout clerks are paid an average of $4 per hour. When only one clerk is on duty, the waiting time per customer is about 10 minutes (or 1/6 hour); when two clerks are on duty, the average checkout time is 6 minutes per person; when three clerks are working, it is 4 minutes; and when four clerks are on duty, it is 3 minutes.

Super-shop's management has conducted customer satisfaction surveys and has estimated that the store suffers approximately $5 in lost sales and goodwill for every *hour* of customer time spent waiting in checkout lines. Using the information provided, determine the optimal number of clerks to have on duty each Saturday in order to minimize the store's total expected cost.

Queuing theory helps in making decisions that balance desirable service costs with waiting-line costs. Some of the many measures of a waiting-line system's performance that are commonly obtained in a queuing theory analysis are as follows:

1. The average time each customer or object spends in the queue
2. The average queue length
3. The average time each customer spends in the system (waiting time plus service time)
4. The average number of customers in the system
5. The probability that the service facility will be idle
6. The probability of a specific number of customers in the system

A SINGLE-CHANNEL WAITING LINE

The most common case of queuing problems involves the *single-channel*, or single-server, waiting line. In this situation, arrivals form a single line to be serviced by a single station (Figure 16.2). We assume that the following conditions exist in this type of system:

1. Arrivals are served on a "first come, first served" (FIFO) basis and every arrival waits to be served, regardless of the length of the line or queue.
2. Arrivals are independent of preceding arrivals, but the average number of arrivals (arrival rate) does not change over time.
3. Arrivals are described by a Poisson probability distributon and come from an infinite (or very, very large) population.
4. Service times vary from one customer to the next and are independent of one another, but their average rate is known.
5. Service times occur according to the exponential probability distribution. (This is sometimes referred to as the negative exponential distribution.)
6. The service rate is faster than the arrival rate.

$$\lambda = \text{mean number of arrivals per time period}$$

$$\mu = \text{mean number of people or items served per time period}$$

Then the model is given by the following equations:

$$L = \text{average number of units (customers) in the system}$$

$$= \frac{\lambda}{\mu - \lambda}$$

SYSTEM

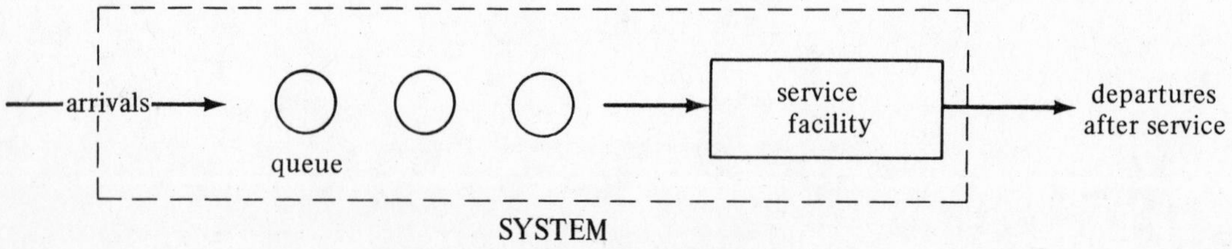

Figure 16.2. Single-channel Waiting Line

W = average time a unit spends in the system (waiting time + service time)

$$= \frac{1}{\mu - \lambda}$$

L_q = average number of units in the queue

$$= \frac{\lambda^2}{\mu(\mu - \lambda)}$$

W_q = average time a unit spends waiting in the queue

$$= \frac{\lambda}{\mu(\mu - \lambda)}$$

ρ = utilization factor for the system

$$= \frac{\lambda}{\mu}$$

P_0 = probability of 0 units in the system (that is, the service unit is idle)

$$= 1 - \frac{\lambda}{\mu}$$

$P_{n>k}$ = probability of more than k units in the system, where n is the number of units in the system

$$= (\frac{\lambda}{\mu})^{k+1}$$

EXAMPLE 16.2

Jones, the mechanic at Golden Muffler Shop, is able to install new mufflers at an average rate of three per hour (or about one every 20 minutes), according to an exponential distribution. Customers seeking this service arrive at the shop on the average of two per hour, following a Poisson distribution. The customers are served on a first in, first out basis and come from a very large (almost infinite) population of possible buyers.

From this description, we are able to obtain the operating characteristics of Golden Muffler's queuing system:

$$\lambda = 2 \text{ cars arriving per hour}$$

$$\mu = 3 \text{ cars serviced per hour}$$

$$L = \frac{\lambda}{\mu - \lambda} = \frac{2}{3 - 2} = \frac{2}{1}$$

$$= 2 \text{ cars in the system, on average}$$

$$W = \frac{1}{\mu - \lambda} = \frac{1}{3 - 2} = 1$$

$$= 1 \text{ hour average waiting time in the system}$$

(continued)

$$L_q = \frac{\lambda^2}{\mu(\mu - \lambda)} = \frac{2^2}{3(3 - 2)} = \frac{4}{3(1)} = \frac{4}{3}$$

$$= 1.33 \text{ cars waiting in line, on average}$$

$$W_q = \frac{\lambda}{\mu(\mu - \lambda)} = \frac{2}{3(3 - 2)} = \frac{2}{3} \text{ hr.}$$

$$= 40 \text{ min. average waiting time per car}$$

$$\rho = \frac{\lambda}{\mu} = \frac{2}{3}$$

$$= 67\% \text{ of time mechanic is busy}$$

$$P_0 = 1 - \frac{\lambda}{\mu} = 1 - \frac{2}{3}$$

$$= 0.33 \text{ probability there are 0 cars in the system}$$

Probability of More than *k* cars in the System

k	$P_{n>k} = (2/3)^{k+1}$
0	0.667 ⟵── Note that this is equal to $1 - P_0 = 1 - 0.33 = 0.667$
1	0.444
2	0.296
3	0.198 ⟵── Implies that there is a 19.8 percent chance that more than 3 cars are in the system
4	0.132
5	0.088
6	0.058
7	0.039

Once we have computed the operating characteristics of a queuing system, it is possible to do an economic analysis of their impact. The waiting-line model described above is valuable in predicting potential waiting times, queue lengths, idle times, and so on, but it does not identify optimal decisions or consider cost factors. As stated earlier, the solution to a queuing problem may require management to make a trade-off between the increased cost of providing better service and the decreased waiting costs derived from providing that service. Let us consider the costs involved in Example 16.2.

EXAMPLE 16.3

The owner of the Golden Muffler Shop estimates that the cost of customer waiting time, in terms of customer dissatisfaction and lost goodwill, is $10 per hour of time spent *waiting* in the line. Since the average car has a 2/3-hour wait (W_q) and there are approximately sixteen cars serviced per day (two per

(continued)

hour times 8 working hours per day), the total number of hours that customers spend waiting for mufflers to be installed each day is

$$\frac{2}{3}(16) = \frac{32}{3}$$

$$= 10 \ 2/3 \ hr.$$

Hence, in this case,

$$\text{Customer waiting-time cost} = \$10(10 \ 2/3)$$
$$= \$107 \text{ per day}$$

The only other major cost that Golden's owner can identify in the queuing situation is the salary of Jones, the mechanic, who earns $7 per hour, or $56 per day. Thus

$$\text{Total expected costs} = \$107 + \$56$$
$$= \$163 \text{ per day}$$

This information will be useful in the next problem.

PROBLEM 16.2

The owner of the Golden Muffler Shop finds out through the muffler business grapevine that The Rusty Muffler, a cross-town competitor, employs a mechanic named Smith who can efficiently install new mufflers at the rate of four per hour.Golden's owner contacts Smith and inquires as to his interest in switching employers. Smith says he would consider leaving The Rusty Muffler, but only for a $9 per hour wage. Golden Muffler's owner, being a crafty businessman, decides that it may be worthwhile to fire Jones and replace him with the speedier (although more expensive) Smith.

(continued)

Compute all of the operating characteristics shown in Example 16.2 using the new service rate of 4 mufflers per hour. Then determine the cost effectiveness of hiring Smith. Compare the costs to the ones computed for Jones in Example 16.3. What is your recommendation?

PROBLEM 16.3

G. White and Sons Wholesale Fruit Distributors employ one worker whose job is to load fruit on outgoing company trucks. An average of 24 trucks per day, or 3 per hour, arrive at the loading gate, according to a Poisson distribution. The worker loads them at a rate of 4 per hour, following approximately the exponential distribution in his service times.

Determine the operating characteristics of this loading-gate problem. What is the probability that there will be more than 3 trucks either being loaded or waiting? Discuss the results of your queuing model computation.

PROBLEM 16.4

G. White believes that adding a second fruit loader will substantially improve the firm's efficiency. He estimates that a two-person crew at the loading gate will double the loading rate from four trucks per hour to eight trucks per hour. Analyze the effect on the queue of such a change and compare the results to those found in Problem 16.3.

PROBLEM 16.5

Truck drivers working for G. White and Sons earn $10 per hour on the average. Fruit loaders receive about $6 per hour. Truck drivers waiting *in the queue or at the loading gate* are drawing a salary but are productively idle and unable to generate revenue during that time. What would be the *hourly* cost savings to the firm associated with employing two loaders instead of one?

MULTIPLE-CHANNEL WAITING LINES

In a *multiple-channel* queuing system, two or more servers or channels are available to handle customers who arrive for service. This system still assumes, however, that customers awaiting service form one single line and then proceed to the first available server. An example of a multiple-channel waiting line is found in many banks today, where a common line is formed and the customer at the head of the line proceeds to the first free teller. Figure 16.3 illustrates this system.

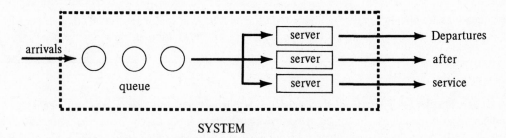

SYSTEM

Figure 16.3. Multiple-channel Queuing System

The multiple-channel system presented here also assumes that arrivals follow a Poisson probability distribution and that service times are exponentially distributed. Service is "first come, first served" and all servers are assumed to perform at the same rate.

If we let M equal the number of channels open, then we can use the following formulas in the waiting-line analysis:

$$\lambda = \text{average arrival rate}$$

$$\mu = \text{average service rate at each channel}$$

The probability that there are zero people or units in the system is

$$P_0 = \frac{1}{\left[\displaystyle\sum_{n=0}^{M-1} \frac{1}{n!} \left(\frac{\lambda}{\mu}\right)^n\right] + \frac{1}{M!}\left(\frac{\lambda}{\mu}\right)^M \frac{M\mu}{M\mu - \lambda}}$$

where $M\mu > \lambda$. The average number of people or units in the system is

$$L = \frac{\lambda\mu(\lambda/\mu)^M}{(M-1)!\,(M\mu - \lambda)^2}\, P_0 + \frac{\lambda}{\mu}$$

The average time a unit spends in the waiting line or being serviced (namely, in the system) is

$$W = \frac{\mu(\lambda/\mu)^M}{(M-1)!\,(M\mu - \lambda)^2}\, P_0 + \frac{1}{\mu} = \frac{L}{\lambda}$$

The average number of people or units in line waiting for service is

$$L_q = L - \frac{\lambda}{\mu}$$

The average time a person or unit spends in the queue waiting for service is

$$W_q = W - \frac{1}{\mu} = \frac{L_q}{\lambda}$$

These equations are obviously more complex than the ones used in the single-channel model, yet they are used in exactly the same fashion and provide the same type of information as the simpler model.

EXAMPLE 16.4

The Golden Muffler Shop has decided to open a second garage bay and to hire a second mechanic to handle muffler installations. Customers, who arrive at the rate of about $\lambda = 2$ per hour, will wait in a single line until one of the two mechanics is free. Each mechanic installs mufflers at the rate of about $\mu = 3$ per hour.

(continued)

To find out how this system compares to the old single-channel waiting-line system, we will compute several operating characteristics for the $M = 2$ channel system and compare the results with those found in Example 16.2.

$$P_0 = \cfrac{1}{\left[\displaystyle\sum_{n=0}^{1} \frac{1}{n!} \left(\frac{2}{3}\right)^n\right] + \frac{1}{2!} \left(\frac{2}{3}\right)^2 \frac{2(3)}{2(3) - 2}}$$

$$= \cfrac{1}{1 + \frac{2}{3} + \frac{1}{2}\left(\frac{4}{9}\right)\left(\frac{6}{6-2}\right)} = \cfrac{1}{1 + \frac{2}{3} + \frac{1}{3}} = \frac{1}{2}$$

$$= 0.5 \text{ probability of zero cars in the system}$$

$$L = \frac{(2)(3)(2/3)^2}{1! \, [2(3) - 2]^2} \left(\frac{1}{2}\right) + \frac{2}{3} = \frac{8/3}{16}\left(\frac{1}{2}\right) + \frac{2}{3} = \frac{3}{4}$$

$$= 0.75 \text{ average number of cars in the system}$$

$$W = \frac{L}{\lambda} = \frac{3/4}{2} = \frac{3}{8} \text{ hr.}$$

$$= 22.5 \text{ min. average time a car spends in the system}$$

$$L_q = L - \frac{\lambda}{\mu} = \frac{3}{4} - \frac{2}{3} = \frac{1}{12}$$

$$= 0.083 \text{ average number of cars in the queue}$$

$$W_q = \frac{L_q}{\lambda} = \frac{0.083}{2} = 0.0415 \text{ hr.}$$

$$= 2.5 \text{ min. average time a car spends in the queue}$$

We can summarize these characteristics and compare them to those of the single-channel model as follows:

(continued)

	Single Channel	Two Channels
P_0	0.33	0.5
L	2 cars	0.75 car
W	60 min.	22.5 min.
L_q	1.33 cars	0.083 car
W_q	40 min.	2.5 min.

The increased service has a dramatic effect on almost all characteristics. In particular, time spent waiting in line drops from 40 minutes to only 2.5 minutes.

PROBLEM 16.6.

G. White and Sons Wholesale Fruit Distributors are considering building a second platform or gate to speed the process of loading their fruit trucks. This system, they think, will be even more efficient than simply hiring another loader to help out on the first platform (as in Problem 16.4).

Assume that workers at each platform will be able to load 4 trucks per hour each and that trucks will continue to arrive at the rate of 3 per hour. Then apply the above equations to find the waiting line's new operating conditions. Is this new approach indeed more speedy than the other two considered?

THE USE OF NOMOGRAPHS

If you were patient enough to carefully follow the long, step-by-step calculations in Example 16.4 and correctly solved Problem 16.6, you deserve today's gold star! You can imagine the work involved in dealing with $M = 3, 4$, or 5 waiting-line models: the arithmetic becomes increasingly troublesome.

Fortunately, we can avoid much of the burden of examining multiple-channel queues by using a *nomograph*, such as the one reproduced in Figure 16.4. This nomograph is just a summary of large tables computed to represent the relationship between (1) service facility utilization ($\rho = \lambda/\mu$), (2) number of service channels open (M), and (3) the average number of people or things in the queue (L_q). For any ratio of λ/μ, you can quickly examine the effect of having $M = 1, 2, 3, 4, \ldots$ service channels open. This nomograph allows you to read off the appropriate values for L_q. Then it is a simple matter to compute the average waiting time in the queue, since $W_q = L_q/\lambda$.

EXAMPLE 16.5

A firm's customer arrival rate is $\lambda = 2$ per hour and the service rate is $\mu = 4$ per hour. What is the average number of customers in the queue if one service facility is open? If two service channels are open? If three channels are in use?

We note first that the firm's utilization rate is $\rho = \lambda/\mu = 2/4 = 0.50$. In Figure 16.4, we locate this value of ρ on the lower axis. Following the vertical line straight up (a ruler may help), we see that when we hit the $M = 1$ channel line, the corresponding value of L_q on the left scale is about 0.55 (customers in the queue).

Below this, we cross the $M = 2$ channel line at about $L_q = 0.038$ (customers waiting). Lower yet, we note that opening a third channel reduces the number of customers in the queue to an average of only $L_q = 0.003$. Obviously, opening even *more* service facilities will reduce the number of customers average in the queue to *none*.

PROBLEM 16.7

Take another look at Example 16.4 and Problem 16.6. Instead of using the complex formula approach to compute the average queue length L_q, try using the nomograph in Figure 16.4. How close are your answers? Which technique do you prefer?

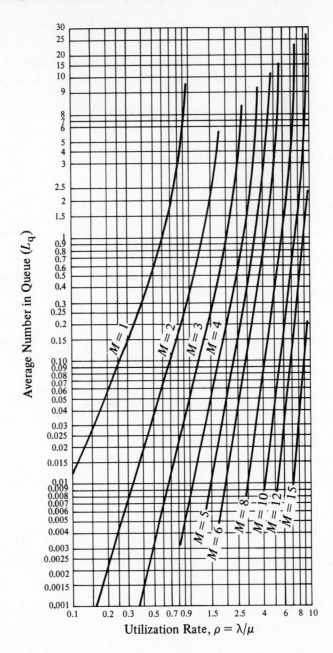

Figure 16.4. Nomograph for Simple Calculations of Average Queue Length (Lq)

Reprinted by permission of John Wiley and Sons, Inc. from Buffa, Elwood S., *Operations Management: The Management of Productive Systems*, New York, 1976, p. 319.

OTHER QUEUING MODELS

Numerous queuing models exist other than the single-channel and multiple-channel systems discussed in this unit. Many are more complex mathematically and require computer simulation (the topic of Unit 15). In particular, advanced production-operations management texts often discuss cases in which (1) the "first-in, first-out" discipline is not observed, (2) arrivals are not Poisson-distributed or service times are not exponentially distributed, (3) arrivals do not come from an infinite population, and (4) servicing involves a multiple-phase operation.

ANSWERS

16.1

	Number of Checkout Clerks			
	1	*2*	*3*	*4*
Number of customers	300	300	300	300
Average waiting time per customer	1/6 hr. (10 min.)	1/10 hr. (6 min.)	1/15 hr. (4 min.)	1/20 hr. (3 min.)
Total customer waiting time	50 hours	30 hours	20 hours	15 hours
Cost per waiting hour	$5	$5	$5	$5
Total waiting costs	$250	$150	$100	$75
Checkout clerk hourly wage	$4	$4	$4	$4
Total pay of clerks for eight-hour shift	$32	$64	$96	$128
Total expected cost	$282	$214	$196	$203

Optimal number of checkout clerks on duty = 3

16.2

$$\lambda = 2 \text{ cars arriving per hour}$$

$$\mu = 4 \text{ cars serviced per hour}$$

$$L = \frac{\lambda}{\mu - \lambda} = \frac{2}{4 - 2}$$

= 1 car in the system on the average

$$W = \frac{1}{\mu - \lambda} = \frac{1}{4 - 2}$$

= 0.5 hour in the system on the average

$$L_q = \frac{\lambda^2}{\mu(\mu - \lambda)} = \frac{2^2}{4(4 - 2)} = \frac{4}{8}$$

= 0.5 car waiting in line on the average

$$W_q = \frac{\lambda}{\mu(\mu - \lambda)} = \frac{2}{4(4 - 2)} = \frac{2}{8} = 0.25 \text{ hr.}$$

= 15 min. average waiting time per car in the queue

$$\rho = \frac{\lambda}{\mu} = \frac{2}{4}$$

= 50 percent of time mechanic is busy

(continued)

$$P_0 = 1 - \frac{\lambda}{\mu} = 1 - 0.5$$

= 0.5 probability there are zero cars in the system

Probability of More than k Cars in the System

k	$P_{n>k} = (2/4)^{k+1}$
0	0.5
1	0.25
2	0.125
3	0.062
4	0.031
5	0.016
6	0.008
7	0.004

To conduct an economic analysis of the costs incurred when Jones is the mechanic ($162 from Example 16.3) with the costs using Smith, we proceed as follows:

Total hours customers spend waiting = (16 cars/day) (1/4 hr/car)

= 4 hr

Customer waiting time cost = ($10/hr.) (4 hr.)

= $40

Salary of Smith, the new mechanic = (8 hr.) ($9/hr)

= $72

Total expected costs = $40 + $72

= $112

It appears that the owner of the Golden Muffler Shop should hire Smith at the higher salary. Doing so will reduce total expected costs by $163 − $112 = $51 per day.

(continued)

16.3 and 16.4

	Number of Fruit Loaders	
	1	*2*
Truck arrival rate (λ)	3/hr.	3/hr.
Loading rate (μ)	4/hr.	8/hr.
Average number in system (L)	3 trucks	0.6 trucks
Average time in system (W)	1 hr.	0.2 hr.
Average number in queue (L_q)	2.25 trucks	0.225 truck
Average time in queue (W_q)	3/4 hr.	0.075 hr.
Utilization rate (ρ)	0.75	0.375
Probability system empty (P_0)	0.25	0.625

Probability of More than k Trucks in System

	Probability $n > k$	
k	*One Loader*	*Two Loaders*
0	0.75	0.375
1	0.56	0.141
2	0.42	0.053
3	0.32	0.020

These results indicate that when only one loader is employed, the average truck must wait 3/4 hour before it is loaded. Furthermore, there are an average of 2.25 trucks waiting in line to be loaded. This situation may be unacceptable to management. Note the decline in queue size after the addition of a second loader.

16.5 Referring to the data in Problems 16.3 and 16.4, we note that the average number of trucks *in the system* is 3 when there is only one loader and 0.6 when there are two loaders.

	Number of Loaders	
	1	*2*
Truck driver idle time costs		
[(average number trucks) × (hourly rate)] = (3)($10) = $30		$6 = (0.6)($10)
Loading costs	$6	$12 = (2)($6)
Total expected cost per hour	$36	$18

The firm will save $18 per hour by adding the second loader.

16.6

$$P_0 = \cfrac{1}{\left[\displaystyle\sum_{n=0}^{1} \frac{1}{n!} \left(\frac{3}{4}\right)^n\right] + \frac{1}{2!}\left(\frac{3}{4}\right)^2 \frac{2(4)}{2(4)-3}}$$

$$= \cfrac{1}{1 + \frac{3}{4} + \frac{1}{2}\left(\frac{3}{4}\right)^2 \left(\frac{8}{8-3}\right)}$$

$$= 0.454$$

$$L = \frac{3(4)(3/4)^2}{(1)!\,(8-3)^2}\,(0.4545) + \frac{3}{4}$$

$$= 0.873$$

$$W = \frac{0.873}{3}$$

$$= 0.291 \text{ hr.}$$

$$L_q = 0.873 - 3/4$$

$$= 0.123$$

$$W_q = \frac{0.123}{3}$$

$$= 0.041 \text{ hr.}$$

(continued)

Looking back at Problems 16.3 and 16.4, we see that although length of the *queue* and average time in the queue are lowest when a second platform is open, the average number of trucks in the *system* and average time spent waiting in the system are smallest when two workers are employed loading at a *single* platform. Hence, we would probably recommend not building a second gate.

16.7   If you carefully interpolated values and drew a few straight lines, you found that the values of L_q that came from the nomograph are amazingly close to those computed in Example 16.4 and Problem 16.6. If you need a great deal of accuracy, use the formulas, otherwise use the nomograph.

HOMEWORK PROBLEMS

16-1. A university cafeteria line in the student center is a self-serve facility in which students select the food items they want, then form a single line to pay the cashier. Students arrive at a rate of about 4 per minute according to a Poisson distribution. The single cashier ringing up sales takes about 12 seconds per customer, following an exponential distribution.

a. What is the probability there are more than 2 students in the system? More than 3 students? More than 4?

b. What is the probability that the system is empty?

c. How long will the average student have to wait before reaching the cashier?

d. What is the expected number of students in the queue?

e. What is the average number in the system?

f. If a second cashier is added (who works at the same pace), how will the operating characteristics computed in (b), (c), (d), and (e) change? Assume customers wait in a single line and go to the first available cashier.

16-2. The wheat harvesting season in the Midwest is short, and most farmers deliver their truckloads of wheat to a giant central storage bin within a 2-week span. Because of this, wheat-filled trucks waiting to unload and return to the fields have been known to back up for a block at the receiving bin. The central bin is owned cooperatively, and it is to every farmer's benefit to make the unloading/storage process as efficient as possible. The cost of grain deterioration caused by unloading delays and the cost of truck rental and idle driver time are significant concerns to the cooperative members. Although farmers have difficulty quantifying crop damage, it is easy to assign a waiting and unloading cost for truck and driver of $18 per hour. The storage bin area is open and operated 16 hours per day and 7 days per week during the harvest season and is capable of unloading 35 trucks per hour according to an exponential distribution. Full trucks arrive all day long at a rate of about 30 per hour, following a Poisson pattern.

To help the cooperative get a handle on the problem of lost time while trucks are waiting in line or unloading at the bin, find the

a. Average number of trucks in the unloading system.

b. Average time per truck in the system.

c. Utilization rate for the bin area.

d. Probability that there are more than 3 trucks in the system at any given time.

e. Total daily cost to the farmers of having their trucks tied up in the unloading process.

f. The Cooperative, as mentioned, uses the storage bin heavily only about 2 weeks per year. Farmers estimate that enlarging the bin would cut unloading costs by 50 percent next year. It will cost $9,000 to do so during the off-season. Would it be worth the cooperative's while to enlarge the storage area?

Maintenance and Reliability

In recent years, production and operations managers have placed increased importance on keeping their facilities in working order. Machine and product failures can have far-reaching effects on a firm's operation and profitability. In highly mechanized and complex plants, the breakdown of one machine may result in hundreds of idle workers or even in the closing of the facility. Likewise, in an office, the failure of a generator, an air-conditioning system, or a computer may halt all normal operations.

Many costs are incurred when equipment breaks down. In this unit, we will look at how management might maintain the reliability of an operating system and keep a facility functioning, while keeping maintenance and breakdown costs under control. The two important topics we will discuss are *maintenance* and *reliability*. Generally speaking, *maintenance* includes all activities involved in keeping a system's equipment (and the entire production system) in working order. *Reliability* is the probability that a part or a product will function properly for a reasonable length of time after it is put into use. These two concepts are actually closely tied. If you were to inspect your automobile regularly—perhaps greasing it, changing spark plugs, replacing the battery, tires, and other major parts *every week*—the car would likely always start! Unfortunately, increasing the car's reliability with preventive maintenance is expensive. An alternative might be to increase the reliability of the auto and its parts during the manufacturing process. Let us begin by looking at the topic of reliability and its measurement.

RELIABILITY

When the U.S. submarine Thresher sank in the early 1960s, over one hundred crewmen perished. The cause was the failure of one pipe joint—out of 8000 on the ship. The equipment on the Thresher may have been designed and manufactured to the highest standards. Equipment for aircraft, rockets, computers, ovens, and typewriters is *all* generally designed to be of high quality. But failures *do* occur. This is an important fact in the concept of reliability.

We can view machines as comprising a series of individual components, each of which performs a certain job. If any one of these components fails to perform, for whatever reason, the overall system or machine can fail. Figure 17.1 illustrates that a system of 50 ($n = 50$) interacting parts, each of which has 99.5 percent reliability, has an overall reliability of about 78 percent. If the system or machine has 100 interacting parts, each with an individual reliability of 99.5 percent, the overall reliability will be only about 60 percent!

From Figure 17.1, we see that as the number of components in a series increases (as represented by the curved lines labeled $n = 50, n = 100, n = 200$, etc.), the reliability of the whole system declines very quickly (as evidenced by the scale on the vertical axis).

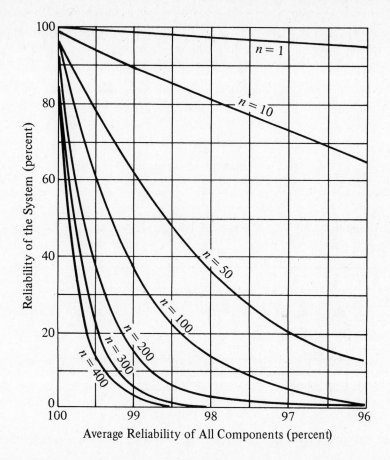

Source: R. Lusser, "The Notorious Unreliability of Complex Equipment," *Astronautics*, February, 1958. Reprinted with permission from the American Institute of Aeronautics and Astronautics, *Astronautics,* February, 1958.

**Figure 17.1. Overall System Reliability as a Function of Number of
Components and Component Reliability**

PROBLEM 17.1

The Beta II computer's electronic processing units contains 50 components in series. The average reliability of each component is 99.0 percent. Using Figure 17.1, determine the overall reliability of the processing unit.

To measure product reliability in which each individual part, or component, has its own rate of reliability, we cannot use the reliability curve. However, the method of computing system reliability R_s is simple. It consists of finding the product of individual reliabilities as follows:

$$R_s = R_1 \times R_2 \times R_3 \times \ldots \times R_n$$

where

$$R_1 = \text{reliability of component 1}$$

$$R_2 = \text{reliability of component 2}$$

and so on.

This equation assumes that the reliability of an individual component does not depend on the reliability of other components. We can use this method to measure the reliability of a product, such as the one we will examine in Example 17.1.

EXAMPLE 17.1

The typical electrical relay switch in an air compressor has three components that are set up in series:

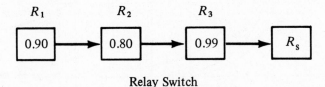

Relay Switch

If the individual component reliabilities are 0.90, 0.80, and 0.99, then the reliability of the entire relay switch is

$$R_s = R_1 R_2 R_3 = (0.90)(0.80)(0.99)$$

$$= 0.713, \text{ or } 71.3\%$$

PROBLEM 17.2

Transistors used in Monroe color televisions have five parts, each of which has its own reliability rate. Component 1 has a reliability of 0.90; component 2, 0.95; component 3, 0.80; component 4, 0.90; and component 5, 0.99. What is the reliability of one transistor system?

A *failure* is the change in a product or system from a working condition to a nonworking condition. The basic unit of measure for reliability is the product failure rate (FR). Firms producing high-technology equipment often provide failure rate data on their products. The failure rate measures the percentage of failures among the total number of products tested, FR (%), or a number of failures during a period of time, FR (N):

$$FR(\%) = \frac{\text{number of failures}}{\text{number of units tested}} \times 100\%$$

$$FR(N) = \frac{\text{number of failures}}{\text{number of unit-hours of operating time}}$$

One other common term in reliability analysis is the mean time between failures (MTBF), which is just the reciprocal of FR(N):

$$MTBF = \frac{1}{FR(N)}$$

EXAMPLE 17.2

Twenty air-conditioning systems to be used by astronauts in NASA space shuttles were operated for 1000 hours at NASA's Huntsville, Alabama, test facility. Two of the systems failed during the test— one after 200 hours and the other after 600 hours. To compute the percentage of failures,

$$FR(\%) = \frac{\text{number of failures}}{\text{number tested}} = \frac{2}{20} \ (100\%)$$

$$= 10\%$$

Next we compute the number of failures per operating hour:

$$FR(N) = \frac{\text{number of failures}}{\text{operating time}}$$

where

Total time	$= (1000 \text{ hr.}) \ (20 \text{ units})$
	$= 20,000 \text{ units-hrs.}$
Nonoperating time	$= 800 \text{ hrs. for 1st failure} + 400 \text{ hrs. for 2nd failure}$
	$= 1200 \text{ unit-hrs.}$
Operating time	$= \text{total time} - \text{nonoperating time}$

$$FR(N) = \frac{2}{20,000 - 1200} = \frac{2}{18,800}$$

$$= 0.000106 \text{ failure/unit-hr.}$$

(continued)

If the typical space shuttle lasts 60 days, NASA may be interested in the failure rate per trip:

$$\text{Failure rate} = (\text{failures/unit-hr.}) \, (24 \text{ hr./day}) \, (60 \text{ days/trip})$$

$$= (0.000106) \, (24) \, (60)$$

$$= 0.152 \text{ failure/trip}$$

Since this failure rate is likely too high, NASA will have to either increase the reliability of individual components and the whole system or else install several backup air-conditioning units on each space shuttle.

PROBLEM 17.3

A national medical equipment manufacturer subjected 100 heart pacemakers to 5000 hours of testing. Halfway through the testing, 5 of the pacemakers failed. What was the failure rate in terms of (a) percent of failures, (b) number of failures per unit-hour, and (c) number of failures per unit-year?

If 1100 people receive pacemaker implants, how many can we expect to fail during the following one year?

MAINTENANCE

Maintenance costs fall into two categories: preventive cost and breakdown cost. *Preventive maintenance* involves routine inspections and servicing and the general costs associated with keeping facilities in good repair. Preventive maintenance activities are intended to find potential failures and make changes or repairs that will prevent larger problems. *Breakdown maintenance* is usually more expensive: it occurs when equipment fails and then must be repaired on an emergency or priority basis.

Figure 17.2 shows the relationship between preventive maintenance and breakdown maintenance. As in many business situations, management needs to strike a balance between two costs. Allocating more money and crew to preventive maintenance will reduce the number of breakdowns. But, at some point, the decrease in breakdown maintenance costs will be less than the increase in preventive maintenance costs and the total cost curve will begin to rise. Beyond this optimal point, the firm will be better off waiting for breakdowns to occur and repairing them when they do.

We can easily compute this optimal level of maintenance activity on a theoretical basis. In real-world situations, we must have good historical data on maintenance costs, breakdown probabilities, and repair times. Example 17.3 and Problem 17.4 illustrate how to compare preventive and breakdown maintenance costs in order to select the least expensive maintenance policy.

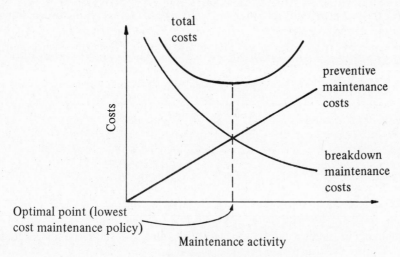

Figure 17.2. Maintenance Costs

EXAMPLE 17.3

Ashley, Gibbs, White and Associates is a CPA firm specializing in tax preparation. The accountants have been successful in automating much of their work by using a Digimatic 89 computer for processing and report preparation. The computerized approach is not without fault, however. Over the past twenty months, the computer system has broken down as indicated below.

(continued)

Number of Breakdowns	Number of Months that Breakdowns Occurred
0	4
1	8
2	6
3	2
Total:	20

Each time the computer breaks down, the partners estimate that the firm loses an average of $300 in time and service expenses. One alternative is for the firm to accept Digimatic's offer to contract for preventive maintenance. If they accept preventive maintenance, they expect an *average* of only one computer breakdown per month. The price that Digimatic charges for this service is $220 per month.

We will follow a four-step approach to answer the question of whether the CPA's should contract with Digimatic for preventive maintenance:

Step 1. Compute the *expected number* of breakdowns (based on past history) if the firm continues, as is, without the service contract.

Step 2. Compute the expected breakdown cost per month with no preventive maintenance contract.

Step 3. Compute the cost of preventive maintenance.

Step 4. Compare the two options and select the one that will cost less.

1.

Number of Breakdowns	Frequency
0	4/20 = 0.2
1	8/20 = 0.4
2	6/20 = 0.3
3	2/20 = 0.1

Expected number of breakdowns $= \Sigma$ (number of breakdowns) $\times$ (corresponding frequency)

$$= (0)(0.2) + (1)(0.4) + (2)(0.3) + (3)(0.1)$$

$$= 0 + 0.4 + 0.6 + 0.3$$

$$= 1.3 \text{ breakdowns per mo.}$$

2. Expected breakdown cost $=$ (expected number of breakdowns) $\times$ (cost per breakdown)

$$= (1.3)(\$300)$$

$$= \$390/\text{mo.}$$

(continued)

3.   Preventive maintenance cost   = cost of expected breakdowns if service contract signed + cost of service contract

$$= (1 \text{ breakdown/mo.})(\$300) + \$220/\text{mo.}$$

$$= \$520/\text{mo.}$$

4. Since it is less expensive to suffer the breakdowns *without* a maintenance service contract ($390) than with one ($520), the firm should continue its present policy.

PROBLEM 17.4

General Manufacturing Company operates its twenty-three large and expensive grinding and lathe machines on a 7 AM–11 PM basis, seven days a week. For the past year the firm has been under contract with Simkin and Sons for daily preventive maintenance (lubrication, cleaning, inspection, etc.). Simkin's crew works between 11 PM and 2 AM so as not to interfere with the daily manufacturing crew. Simkin charges $645 per week for this service. Since signing the maintenance contract, General Manufacturing has noted an average of only three breakdowns per week. When a grinding or lathe machine *does* break down during a working shift, it costs General about $250 in lost-production and repair costs.

After reviewing past breakdown records (for the period before signing a preventive maintenance contract with Simkin and Sons), General Manufacturing's production manager summarized the following patterns:

Number of Breakdowns per Week	Number of Weeks in Which Breakdowns Occurred
0	1
1	1
2	3
3	5
4	9
5	11
6	7
7	8
8	5
Total weeks of historical data:	50

The production manager is not certain that the contract for preventive maintenance with Simkin is in the best financial interest of General Manufacturing. He recognizes that much of his breakdown data is old, but is fairly certain that it is representative of the present picture.

(continued)

What is your analysis of this situation and what recommendation do you think the production manager should make?

Preventive maintenance is often a matter of overhauling an entire group of machines or a whole fleet of vehicles rather than operating them until they break down. The next example and set of problems deal with calculating which policy is best to use. Should we repair equipment only when it breaks down, or should we adopt a policy of regular weekly, monthly, bimonthly (or other periodic) overhauls?

EXAMPLE 17.4 and PROBLEM 17.5

New Orleans's famous French Quarter Hotel has five passenger elevators, which, like everything in life, tend to break down from time to time. A local service firm agrees to overhaul the five elevators on a preventive basis for a fee of $100 per overhaul visit. If an elevator *does* break down it costs an average of $250 to have it repaired. Records show that the probabilities of a breakdown after maintenance are as follows:

Months Until Breakdown After Overhaul	Probability of Breakdown
1	0.2
2	0.1
3	0.3
4	0.4

(continued)

You might have noted that the table shows a higher probability of a breakdown after only one month than after two. Experience shows that once in a while an overhaul is done improperly, and the equipment quickly breaks down. After this first "shakedown" month, the breakdown pattern is more as you would expect it to be.

The question faced by hotel management is whether to adopt a preventive maintenance policy. And if it does, how often should an elevator be overhauled?

The first step is to compute what a repair-on-breakdown policy would cost. The calculation is fairly simple and is based on the expected length of time the elevators can go without overhaul.

Expected time between breakdowns $= (0.2)(1 \text{ mo.}) + (0.1)(2 \text{ mo.}) + (0.3)(3 \text{ mo}) + (0.4)(4 \text{ mo.})$

$$= 2.9 \text{ mo.}$$

A repair-on-breakdown policy would cost an average of \$431 per month [Calculated as (5 elevators $\times$ \$250) $\div$ 2.9 mo. = \$431].

Calculating the cost of periodic overhauls (for example, preventive maintenance for each elevator every month, or every two months, every three months, or every four months) is more difficult. We know that it costs \$100 to overhaul all five elevators, but nevertheless there will be a few breakdowns. In addition, it is possible for a recently overhauled elevator to break down again soon. For longer intervals between preventive maintenance, more breakdowns and higher breakdown costs will occur; however, the preventive maintenance cost will drop.

The formula we need to compute the expected number of breakdowns (B_n) that will occur during the interval between overhauls is rather complex-looking. That equation is

$$B_n = N \sum_1^n p_n + B_{(n-1)} p_1 + B_{(n-2)} p_2 + B_{(n-3)} p_3 + \cdots + B_1 p_{(n-1)}$$

where

$n =$ the number of months (or time periods) between overhauls

$N =$ the number of machines or pieces of equipment in the group

$p_n =$ the probability of machine breakdown during the nth month after maintenance (for example, if maintenance was performed on a machine in period 3, then p_1 is the proability the same machine will break down in period 4, p_2 is the probability it will breakdown in period 5, and so on)

Policy of overhauling monthly. In this example, the expected number of breakdowns given monthly preventive maintenance is

$$B_1 = Np_1$$

$$= 5(0.2)$$

$$= 1$$

(continued)

Thus, the total cost of this policy is

$$\text{Total cost} = \text{preventive maintenance cost} + \text{breakdown cost}$$
$$= \$100 + (\text{expected number of breakdowns}) \times (\text{cost/breakdown})$$
$$= \$100 + (1)(\$250)$$
$$= \$350/\text{mo.}$$

Policy of overhauling every two months. Given a policy of overhauling equipment on a bimonthly basis, we find the expected number of breakdown in two months to be

$B_2 = N(p_1 + p_2) + B_1 p_1$ ◄———— What does this equation mean? It says that the expected
$\quad = 5(0.2 + 0.1) + 1(0.2)$ number of breakdowns (B_2) over two months is the number
$\quad = 1.5 + 0.2$ of elevators (N) times the probability an elevator will break
$\quad = 1.7$ down in month 1 or 2 ($p_1 + p_2$), plus the expected number of machines that will break down in the first month (B_1) times the probability that these machines will break down *again* in the second month (before the scheduled overhaul takes place).

The average number of breakdowns *per month* is $1.7/2 = 0.85$. Since the preventive maintenance cost of $100 is now spread over two months, the overhaul cost *per month* is $50.

$$\text{Total cost} = \$50 + (0.85 \text{ breakdowns}) (\$250/\text{breakdown})$$
$$= \$262.50/\text{mo.}$$

In tabular form, these two policies may be presented as follows:

French Quarter Hotel Elevator Maintenance

Overhaul Every n Months	Total Expected Breakdowns in n Months	Average Number of Breakdowns per Month	Expected Breakdown Cost per Month	Cost of Preventive Maintenance per Month	Expected Total Monthly Cost
1	1	1	$250	$100	$350
2	1.7	0.85	$212.50	$ 50	$262.50
3					
4					

This table and the hotel's policy analysis is not complete. Your job is to calculate the cost of overhauling the elevators *every three months* and *every four months*. Once you have determined

(continued)

these cost figures, then we can compare preventive maintenance costs to those costs established in the repair-on-breakdown policy and make a final decision.

PROBLEM 17.6

Judy Hess owns a fleet of twenty aging taxicabs operating in San Diego. The cabs have tended to break down frequently, mainly because of high mileage and rough driving by her cab drivers. Judy has heard a lot about preventive maintenance and, being cautious, has experimented with it on several cabs. She has found that weekly preventive maintenance checks and minor repairs cost an average of $12 *per cab* (or $240 for the whole fleet). Ms. Hess also knows that when a cab breaks down on the

(continued)

road, it costs an average of $40 (towing plus repairs) to get the car back in action. The record below is a summary of postpreventive maintenance breakdowns.

Weeks After Preventive Maintenance	Probability of Breakdown
1	0.15
2	0.10
3	0.20
4	0.25
5	0.30

What policy should Judy follow? Should she employ preventive maintenance, and if so, how often?

Preventive Maintenance Every n Weeks	Total Expected Breakdowns in n Weeks	Average Number of Breakdowns per Week	Expected Breakdown Cost per Week	Cost of Preventive Maintenance per Week	Expected Total Weekly Cost

(continued)

SIMULATION APPROACH

One other approach has become popular for studying maintenance problems and estimating breakdown costs. This technique, computer simulation, was the subject of Unit 15. Indeed, the advent of computers has been a real benefit to maintenance managers. Some computer programs, such as General Electric's FAME, are dedicated specifically to maintenance scheduling and to producing reports that help management monitor this important function.

ANSWERS

17.1   The overall reliability of the system is seen in Figure 17.1 to be approximately 62 percent.

17.2   Transistor system reliability $R_s = R_1 R_2 R_3 R_4 R_5$

$$= (0.90)(0.95)(0.8)(0.90)(0.99)$$

$$= 0.6094$$

Not very high, is it?

17.3   (a) $FR(\%) = \dfrac{5}{100}$

$$= 5.0\%$$

(b) $FR(N) = \dfrac{\text{number of failures}}{\text{total time} - \text{nonoperating time}}$

where

$$\text{Total time} = (5000 \text{ hr.}) (100 \text{ units})$$

$$= 500{,}000 \text{ unit-hr.}$$

$$\text{Nonoperating time of 5 failing pacemakers} = (2500 \text{ hr.}) (5 \text{ units})$$

$$= 12{,}500 \text{ unit-hr.}$$

Thus,

$$FR(N) = \frac{5}{500{,}000 - 12{,}500} = \frac{5}{487{,}500}$$

$$= 0.00001025 \text{ failure/unit-hr.}$$

(c) Failures per unit-yr. $= [FR(N) \, (24 \text{ hr./day}) \, (365 \text{ days/yr.})]$

$$= 0.08979$$

For 1100 pacemakers installed,

$$(0.08979 \text{ failure/unit-yr.}) (1100 \text{ units}) = 98.77 \text{ failures/yr.}$$

17.4   Step 1. Expected number of breakdowns/wk. *without* maintenance contract

$$= \sum_{n=0}^{8 \text{ breakdowns}} (\text{number of breakdowns}) \times (\text{probability})$$

$$= (0)\left(\frac{1}{50}\right) + (1)\left(\frac{1}{50}\right) + (2)\left(\frac{3}{50}\right) + (3)\left(\frac{5}{50}\right) + (4)\left(\frac{9}{50}\right)$$

$$+ (5)\left(\frac{11}{50}\right) + (6)\left(\frac{7}{50}\right) + (7)\left(\frac{8}{50}\right) + (8)\left(\frac{5}{50}\right)$$

$$= \frac{0}{50} + \frac{1}{50} + \frac{6}{50} + \frac{15}{50} + \frac{36}{50} + \frac{55}{50} + \frac{42}{50} + \frac{56}{50} + \frac{40}{50}$$

$$= \frac{251}{50} = 5.02 \text{ breakdowns/wk.}$$

Step 2. Expected cost of breakdowns without maintenance

$$= (\$250/\text{breakdown}) \, (5.02 \text{ breakdown/wk.})$$

$$= \$1,255$$

Step 3. Cost of breakdowns and service under maintenance contract

$$= (3 \text{ breakdowns/wk.}) \, (\$250/\text{breakdown}) + \text{Simkin's fee}$$

$$= \$750 + \$645$$

$$= \$1395$$

If we project the cost and service figures to stay the same and if the past breakdown data is valid, General Manufacturing Company should eliminate the preventive maintenance contract. The savings will be $1395 - $1255 = $140 per week.

17.5   *Overhauling every three months:*

$$B_3 = N(p_1 + p_2 + p_3) + B_2 p_1 + B_1 p_2$$
$$= 5(0.2 + 0.1 + 0.3) + (1.7)(0.2) + (1)(0.1)$$
$$= 3.00 + 0.34 + 0.10 = 3.44$$

Total cost = (cost of preventive maintenance/number of months) + (average number of breakdowns per month) $\times$ (cost per breakdown)

$$= (\$100/3) + (3.44/3)(\$250) = \$33.33 + \$285.00$$

$$= \$318.33$$

(continued)

Overhauling every four months:

$$B_4 = N(p_1 + p_2 + p_3 + p_4) + B_3 p_1 + B_2 p_2 + B_1 p_3$$

$$= 5(0.2 + 0.1 + 0.3 + 0.4) + (3.44)(0.2) + (1.7)(0.1) + (1)(0.3)$$

$$= 5 + 0.688 + 0.17 + 0.3$$

$$= 6.158$$

Total cost = average preventive maintenance cost + expected breakdown cost

$$= (\$100/4) + (6.158/4)(\$250) = \$25.00 + \$384.88$$

$$= \$409.88$$

Both of these policies are more expensive than the policy of overhauling every two months ($262.50). Since the policy of no preventive maintenance costs $431 per month, the best decision would be to overhaul the elevators bimonthly.

17.6   Cost *without* preventive maintenance:

Expected time between breakdowns $= (0.15)(2) + (0.10)(2) + (0.20)(3)$

$$+ (0.25)(4) + (0.30)(5)$$

$$= 3.6 \text{ wk.}$$

Average cost/wk. $= (20 \text{ cabs})(\$40)/(3.6 \text{ wk})$

$$= \$222.22$$

Costs *with* preventive maintenance:

$$B_1 = Np_1 = (20)(0.15)$$

$$= 3.0$$

$$B_2 = N(p_1 + p_2) + B_1 p_1 = 20(0.25) + 3(0.15)$$

$$= 5.45$$

$$B_3 = N(p_1 + p_2 + p_3) + B_2 p_1 + B_1 p_2$$

$$= 20(0.45) + (5.45)(0.15) + (3)(0.10)$$

$$= 10.12$$

(continued)

$$B_4 = N(p_1 + p_2 + p_3 + p_4) + B_3 p_1 + B_2 p_2 + B_1 p_3$$

$$= 20(0.70) + (10.12)(0.15) + (5.45)(0.10) + (3)(0.20)$$

$$= 16.66$$

$$B_5 = N(p_1 + p_2 + p_3 + p_4 + p_5) + B_4 p_1 + B_3 p_2 + B_2 p_3 + B_1 p_4$$

$$= 20(1.0) + 16.66(0.15) + (10.12)(0.10) + (5.45)(0.20) + (3)(0.25)$$

$$= 25.35$$

Preventive Maintenance Every n Weeks	Total Expected Breakdowns in n Weeks	Average Number of Breakdowns per Week	Expected Breakdown Cost per Week	Cost of Preventive Maintenance per Week	Expected Total Weekly Cost
1	3.0	3.0	$120.00	$240.00	$360.00
2	5.45	2.72	108.80	120.00	228.80
3	10.12	3.37	134.80	80.00	214.80
4	16.66	4.16	166.40	60.00	226.40
5	25.35	5.07	202.80	48.00	250.80

The least-cost policy is preventive maintenance every three weeks (total of $214.80). It is $7.42 (or $222.22 − $214.80) cheaper than *no* preventive maintenance policy.

HOMEWORK PROBLEM

A well-known North Carolina furniture manufacturer has maintained the following records on breakdowns of its power saws for a 250 day work year.

Number of Breakdowns	Frequency (in days)
0	25
1	30
2	50
3	100
4	35
5	10

The company's accounting department estimates that each breakdown costs $125. The production manager wishes to begin a preventive maintenance program that would cost $40 per day and limit the number of breakdowns to an average of 2 per day. What is the expected *annual* savings if the firm implements the preventive maintenance program?

Job Shop Scheduling

The *job shop* or *intermittent* processing system is one commonly found in business and government organizations. It is a production system in which products are not mass produced as on an assembly line, but made to order. Job shop orders usually differ considerably in terms of materials used, order of processing, processing requirements, time of processing, and setup requirements. Because of this uniqueness, the scheduling of tasks in job shops can be complex.

Scheduling in general deals with the timing of operations and must be considered at many stages. In the aggregate planning stage (discussed in Unit 12), the firm decides on the use of personnel, sub-contracting and facilities. In the project planning phase (the topic of Unit 19), techniques such as PERT and CPM are used in controlling and monitoring large activities. In job shop scheduling, two basic issues are addressed: how to assign the workload to various work centers and in what sequence to process waiting jobs.

Loading means the assignment of jobs to work or processing centers. When only one work center can perform a specific task, loading is not an issue. But in many cases, there are several jobs to be processed and more than one work center capable of handling the orders. Production managers need to commit work centers to jobs so that processing costs, idle time, or job completion times are kept to a minimum. In this unit, we present two approaches used for loading—*Gantt Charts* and the *assignment method* of linear programming.

Loading determines which jobs are to be processed at which work centers, but it does not tell us the order in which they should be done. Usually, a number of jobs will be waiting for processing. *Sequencing,* through priority rules, specifies their order of processing. *Johnson's Rule, priority rule heuristics* and the *critical ratio rule* will be discussed later in this unit.

GANTT CHARTS

Gantt charts are visual aids that are useful in loading and scheduling job shop operations. Their name is derived from Henry Gantt, who developed the concept in the early 1900s. The charts help describe the use of resources, such as work centers and overtime, which is usually in days.

When used in *loading,* Gantt charts show the loading and idle time of several departments, machines, or facilities. This displays the relative workloads in the system. For example, when one work center becomes overloaded, employees from a low load center can be transferred temporarily to increase the workforce. Or if waiting jobs can be processed at different work centers, some jobs at high load centers can be transferred to low load centers. Versatile equipment may also be transferred among centers. Example 18.1 illustrates a simple Gantt load chart.

EXAMPLE 18.1

A New York washing machine manufacturer accepts special orders for machines to be used in unique facilities such as submarines, hospitals, and large industrial laundries. The production of each machine requires varying tasks and durations. Figure 18.1 shows the load chart for the week of March 8.

There are four work centers and several jobs being processed during the week. This particular chart indicates that the Metal Works and Painting centers are completely loaded for the entire week. The Mechanical and Electronic centers have some idle time scattered during the week. We also note that the Metal Works center is unavailable on Tuesday, perhaps for preventive maintenance.

Figure 18.1

Work Center	Monday	Tuesday	Wednesday	Thursday	Friday
Metal Works	Job 349	✕		Job 350	
Mechanical			Job 349	Job 408	
Electronics	Job 408			Job 349	
Painting	Job 295		Job 408	✕	Job 349

  Processing

  Center not available
(e.g, maintenance time, repairs, shortages)

The Gantt load chart does have some major limitations. For one thing, it does not account for production variability such as unexpected breakdowns or human errors that require reworking a job. The chart must also be updated regularly to account for new jobs and revised time estimates.

A Gantt *schedule chart* is used to monitor jobs in progress. It indicates which jobs are on schedule and which are ahead or behind schedule. In practice, many versions of the chart are found. Example 18.2's schedule chart places "jobs in progress" on the vertical axis and "time" on the horizontal axis.

EXAMPLE 18.2

RMS Products Corporation uses the Gantt chart in Figure 18.2 to visualize the scheduling of three orders, Jobs A, B, and C. Each pair of brackets on the time axis denotes the estimated starting and finishing of a job enclosed within it. The solid bars reflect the actual status or progress of the job. Job A, for example, is about 1/2 day behind schedule at this point in time (the end of day 5). Job B has been completed, after a delay for equipment maintenance. Job C is ahead of schedule.

(continued)

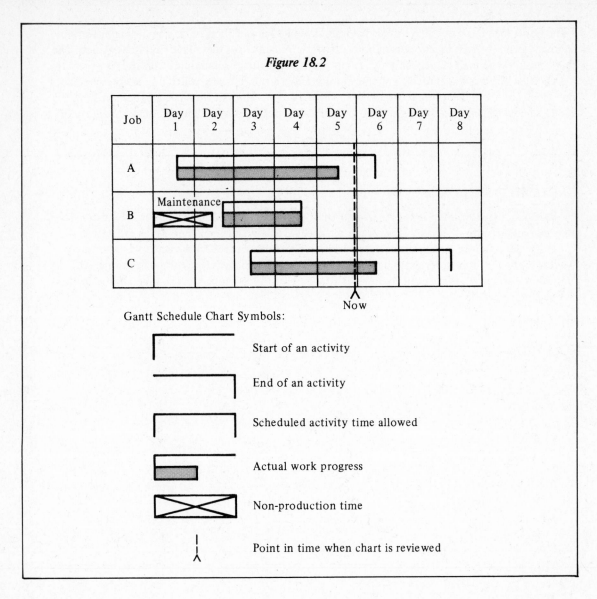

Figure 18.2

Gantt Schedule Chart Symbols:

	Start of an activity
	End of an activity
	Scheduled activity time allowed
	Actual work progress
	Non-production time
	Point in time when chart is reviewed

PROBLEM 18.1

RMS Products Corporation has four more jobs to be scheduled, in addition to those shown in Example 18.2. It is reviewing its chart at the end of day 4.

Job D was scheduled to begin early on day 2 and to end on the middle of day 10. As of now (the review point after day 4) it is 2 days ahead of schedule.

Job E should begin day 1 and end on day 3. It was on time.

Job F was to begin on day 3, but maintenance forced a delay of 1 1/2 days. The job should take now 5 full days. It is now on schedule.

Job G is a day behind schedule. It started at the beginning of day 2 and should require 6 days to complete.

Develop a Gantt schedule chart for RMS Corporation.

THE ASSIGNMENT METHOD

The assignment method is a special class of the linear programming model that involves assigning tasks or jobs to resources. Examples include assigning jobs to machines, contracts to bidders, people to projects, and salespeople to territories. The objective is most often to minimize total costs or time required to perform the tasks at hand. One important characteristic of assignment problems is that only one job (or worker) is assigned to one machine (or project).

Each assignment problem has a table associated with it. The numbers in the table will be the costs or times associated with each particular assignment. For example, if a job shop has three available machines (A, B, and C) and three new jobs to be completed, its table might appear as follows:

Job \ Machine	A	B	C
R-34	$11	$14	$6
S-66	$8	$10	$11
T-50	$9	$12	$7

The dollar entries represent the firm's estimate of what it will cost for each job to be completed on each machine.

The assignment method involves adding and subtracting appropriate numbers in the table in order to find the lowest *opportunity cost* for each assignment. There are four steps to follow:

1. Subtract the smallest number in each row from every number in that row and then subtract the smallest number in each column from every number in that column. This step has the effect of reducing the numbers in the table until a series of zeros, meaning *zero opportunity costs*, appear. Even though the numbers change, this reduced problem is equivalent to the original one and the same solution will be optimal.
2. Draw the minimum number of vertical and horizontal straight lines necessary to cover all zeros in the table. If the number of lines equals either the number of rows or the number of columns in the table,

then we can make an optimal assignment (see step 4). If the number of lines is less than the number of rows or columns, we proceed to step 3.

3. Subtract the smallest number not covered by a line from every other uncovered number. Add the same number to any number(s) lying at the intersection of any two lines. Return to step 2 and continue until an optimal assignment is possible.

4. Optimal assignments will always be at zero locations in the table. One systematic way of making a valid assignment is to first select a row or column that contains only one zero square. We can make an assignment to that square and then draw lines through its row and column. From the uncovered rows and columns, we choose another row or column in which there is only one zero square. We make that assignment and continue the above procedure until we have assigned each person or machine to one task.

EXAMPLE 18.3

The cost table shown earlier in this unit is repeated below. We find the minimum total cost assignment of jobs to machines by applying steps 1-4.

Job \ Machine	A	B	C
R-34	$11	$14	$6
S-66	$8	$10	$11
T-50	$9	$12	$7

Step 1.

Using the previous table, subtract the smallest number in each row from every number in the row. The result is shown below.

Using the previous table, subtract the smallest number in each column from every number in the column. The result is shown below.

Job \ Machine	A	B	C
R-34	5	8	0
S-66	0	2	3
T-50	2	5	0

Job \ Machine	A	B	C
R-34	5	6	0
S-66	0	0	3
T-50	2	3	0

(continued)

Step 2.

Draw the minimum number of straight lines needed to cover all zeros. Since two lines suffice, the solution is not optimal.

Job \ Machine	A	B	C
R-34	5	6	0̸
S-66	0̸	0̸	5̸
T-50	(2)	3	0̸

Smallest uncovered number

Return to step 2.

Cover all zeros with straight lines again.

Job \ Machine	A	B	C
R-34	3	4	0̸
S-66	0̸	0̸	5
T-50	0̸	1	0̸

Step 3.

Subtract the smallest uncovered number (2 in this table) from every other uncovered number and add it to numbers at the intersection of two lines.

Job \ Machine	A	B	C
R-34	3	4	0
S-66	0	0	5
T-50	0	1	0

Since three lines are necessary, an optimal assignment can be made (see step 4). Assign R-34 to machine C, S-66 to machine B, and T-50 to machine A

$$\text{Minimum cost} = \$6 + \$10 + \$9 = \$25$$

(Note: if we had S-66 assigned to machine A, we could not assign T-50 to a zero location.)

EXAMPLE 18.4

In a job-shop operation, four jobs may be performed on any of four machines. The following table lists the hours required for each job on each machine. The plant foreman would like to assign jobs in such a way as to minimize the total time.

(continued)

Worker \ Machine	W	X	Y	Z
A12	10	14	16	13
A15	12	13	15	12
B2	9	12	12	11
B9	14	16	18	16

Step 1.

Row subtraction

Job \ Machine	W	X	Y	Z
A12	0	4	6	3
A15	0	1	3	0
B2	0	3	3	2
B9	0	2	4	2

Column subtraction

Job \ Machine	W	X	Y	Z
A12	0	3	3	3
A15	0	0	0	0
B2	0	2	0	2
B9	0	1	1	2

Step 2.

Minimum straight lines to cover zeros

Job \ Machine	W	X	Y	Z
A12	0	3	0	3
A15	0	0	0	0
B2	0	2	0	2
B9	0	(1)	1	2

Smallest uncovered number

Step 3.

Smallest uncovered number subtracted from uncovered numbers, added to numbers at intersection of two lines

Job \ Machine	W	X	Y	Z
A12	0	2	3	2
A15	1	0	1	0
B2	0	1	0	1
B9	0	0	1	1

(continued)

Return to Step 2.
Cover all zeros

Job \ Machine	W	X	Y	Z
A12	0	2	3	2
A15	1	0	1	0
B2	0	1	0	1
B9	0	0	1	1

Assign:

job A12 to machine W
job A15 to machine Z
job B2 to machine Y
job B9 to machine X

Time = 10 + 12 + 12 + 16

= 50 hours

PROBLEM 18.2

The operations manager of Smith Manufacturing must assign three tasks to three machines. Cost data are presented below.

Job / Machine	#1	#2	#3
C-3	$800	$1100	$1200
C-5	$500	$1600	$1300
C-8	$500	$1000	$2300

Use the assignment algorithm to solve this problem.

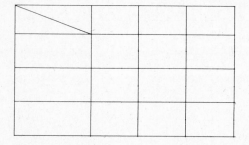

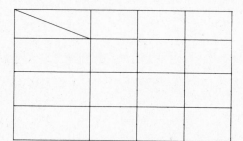

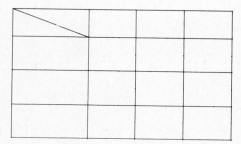

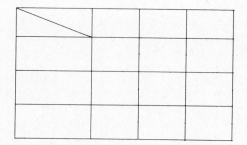

The solution procedure just discussed requires that the number of rows in the table equal the number of columns. Often, however, the number of people or objects to be assigned does not equal the number of tasks or clients or machines listed in the columns. When this is the case and we have more rows than columns, we simply add a *dummy column* or task. If the number of tasks that need doing exceeds the number of people available, we add a *dummy row*. Creating dummy rows and columns will give us a table of equal dimensions and allow us to solve the problem as before. Since the dummy task or person does not exist, it is reasonable to enter zeros in its row or column as the cost or time estimate.

PROBLEM 18.3

Dollar Finance Corporation, headquartered in New York, wants to assign three recently hired college graduates, Jones, Smith, and Wilson to regional offices. But the firm also has an opening in New York and would send one of the three there if it were more economical than a move to Omaha, Dallas, or Miami. It will cost $1000 to relocate Jones in New York, $800 to relocate Smith there, and $1500 to move Wilson. What is the optimal assignment of personnel to offices?

Hiree \ Office	Omaha	Miami	Dallas	
Jones	$800	$1100	$1200	
Smith	$500	$1600	$1300	
Wilson	$500	$1000	$2300	

(continued)

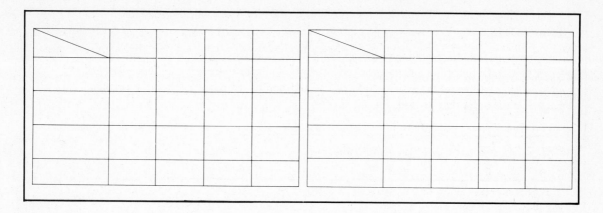

Some assignment problems entail *maximizing* the profit, effectiveness, or payoff of an assignment of people to tasks or of jobs to machines. It is easy to obtain an equivalent minimization problem by converting every number in the table to an *opportunity loss.* To perform this conversion, we subtract every number in each column from the largest number in that column. It turns out that minimizing opportunity loss produces the same assignment solution as the original maximization problem.

PRIORITY RULES FOR SEQUENCING

The loading decisions described above help the machines or work centers to be used to process specific jobs. *Priority decision rules* are simplified guidelines for determining the *sequence* in which orders will be processed. Priority rules are widely used and several of them are described below. The two other sequencing methods we shall later introduce are Johnson's rule and the critical ratio technique.

The most popular priority rules are:

FCFS   First come, first served. The first job to arrive at a work center is processed first.
EDD   Earliest due date. The job with the earliest due date is selected first.
SPT   Shortest processing time. The shortest jobs are handled first and gotten out of the way.
LPT   Longest processing time. The longer, bigger jobs are often very important and are selected first.

We can compare these rules by way of Example 18.5.

EXAMPLE 18.5

Five sheet metal jobs are waiting to be assigned at Ajax Company's Long Beach work center. Their processing times and due dates are given below. We want to determine the sequence of processing according to: (a) FCFS, (b) SPT, (c) EDD, and (d) LPT rules. Jobs were assigned a letter in the order they arrived.

Job	Job Processing Time in days	Job Due date (days)
A	6	8
B	2	6
C	8	18
D	3	15
E	9	23

(a) *FCFS* sequence is simply A–B–C–D–E. The "flow time" in the system for this sequence measures the time each job spends waiting plus being processed. Job B, for example, waits 6 days while Job A is being processed, then takes 2 more days of operation time itself. So it will be completed in 8 days—which is 2 days later than its due date.

Job Sequence	Processing time	Flow time	Job due date	Job lateness
A	6	6	8	0
B	2	8	6	2
C	8	16	18	0
D	3	19	15	4
E	9	28	23	5
	28	77		11

The first-come, first-served rule results in the following measures of effectiveness.

1. Average completion time =

$$\frac{\text{Sum of flow time totals}}{\text{no. of jobs}} = \frac{77 \text{ days}}{5} = 15.4 \text{ days}$$

2. Average number of jobs in the system =

$$\frac{\text{Sum of flow time totals}}{\text{total processing time}} = \frac{77 \text{ days}}{28 \text{ days}} = 2.75 \text{ jobs}$$

(continued)

3. Average job lateness =

$$\frac{\text{total late days}}{\text{no. of jobs}} = \frac{11}{5} = 2.2 \text{ days}$$

(b) *SPT* rule results in the sequence B–D–A–C–E (see below). Orders are sequenced according to processing time, with the highest priority given to the shortest job.

Job Sequence	Processing time	Flow time	Job due date	Job lateness
B	2	2	6	0
D	3	5	15	0
A	6	11	8	3
C	8	19	18	1
E	9	28	23	5
	28	65		9

Measures of effectiveness for SPT are:

1. Average completion time $= \dfrac{65}{5} = 13$ days

2. Average number of jobs in the system $= \dfrac{65}{28} = 2.32$

3. Average job lateness $= \dfrac{9}{5} = 1.8$ days

(c) EDD rule gives the sequence B–A–D–C–E. Note that jobs are ordered by earliest due date first.

Job Sequence	Processing time	Flow time	Job due date	Job lateness
B	2	2	6	0
A	6	8	8	0
D	3	11	15	0
C	8	19	18	1
E	9	28	23	5
	28	68		6

(continued)

Measures of effectiveness for EDD are:

1. Average completion time $= \dfrac{68}{5} = 13.6$ days

2. Average number of jobs in the system $\dfrac{68}{28} = 2.42$

3. Average job lateness $= \dfrac{6}{5} = 1.2$ days

(d) LPT results in the order E–C–A–D–B.

Job Sequence	Processing time	Flow time	Job due date	Job lateness
E	9	9	23	0
C	8	17	18	0
A	6	23	8	15
D	3	26	15	11
B	2	28	6	22
	28	103		48

Measures of effectiveness for the longest processing time approach are:

1. Average completion time $= \dfrac{103}{5} = 20.6$ days

2. Average number of jobs in the system $= \dfrac{103}{28} = 3.68$

3. Average job lateness $= \dfrac{48}{5} = 9.6$ days

The results of these four rules are summarized below,

Rule	Average Completion time (days)	Average no. job in system	Average lateness (days)
FIFS	15.4	2.75	2.2
SPT	13.0	2.32	1.8
EDD	13.6	2.42	1.2
LPT	20.6	3.68	9.6

As you can see, the LPT is least effective in each measure of effectiveness in this case. SPT is superior in two measures and EDD in the third (average lateness).   Tests show that SPT is generally the best technique for minimizing job flow and average number of jobs in the system.

PROBLEM 18.4

A well-known defense contractor in Dallas has six jobs awaiting processing. Processing time and due dates are given below. Assume jobs arrive in the order shown. Set the processing sequence according to FCFS and EDD. Which is preferable?

Job	Job Processing Time in days	Job Due date (days)
A	6	22
B	12	14
C	14	30
D	2	18
E	10	25
F	4	34

PROBLEM 18.5

The Dallas firm noted in Problem 18.4 wants to also consider job sequencing by the SPT and LPT priority rules. Apply them to the same data and provide a recommendation.

JOHNSON'S RULE

Johnson's rule can be used to minimize the processing time for sequencing a group of jobs through two machines or work centers. It also minimizes total idle time on the machines.

Johnson's rule involves four steps:

1. All jobs are to be listed and the time each requires on a machine shown.
2. We select the job with the shortest activity time. If the shortest times lies with the first machine, the job is scheduled first. If the shortest time lies with the second machine, schedule the job last. Ties can be broken, arbitrarily.
3. Once a job is scheduled, eliminate it.
4. Apply steps 2-3 to the remaining jobs, working toward the center of the sequence.

EXAMPLE 18.6

Five specialty jobs at a New York tool and die shop must be processed through two work centers (drill machine and lathe machine). The time for processing each job is shown below.

Processing time (in hours) for Jobs

Job	Work Center 1 (Drill)	Work Center 2 (Lathe)
A	5	2
B	3	6
C	8	4
D	10	7
E	7	12

We wish to set the sequence which will minimize the total processing time for the five jobs.

a) The job with the shortest processing time is A, in work center 2 (with a time of 2 hours). Since it is at the second center, schedule A last. Eliminate it from consideration.

				A

b) Job B has the next shortest time. Since it is at the first work center, we schedule it first and eliminate it from consideration.

B				A

---

c) The next shortest time is job C: it is placed as late as possible since it was on the second machine.

B			C	A

a) There is a tie for the shortest remaining job. We can place E, which was on the first work center, first. Then D is placed in the last sequencing position.

B	E	D	C	A

The sequential times are:

Work Center 1	3	7	10	8	5
Work Center 2	6	12	7	4	2

The time-phased flow of this job sequence is best illustrated graphically:

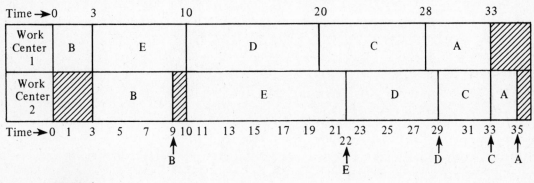

  Idle

↑ Job Completed

Thus, the five jobs are completed in 35 hours. The second work center will wait 3 hours for its first job and also wait one hour after completing job B.

PROBLEM 18.6

Use Johnson's rule to find the optimum sequence for processing the jobs below through two work work centers. Times at each center are in hours.

Job	Work Center 1	Work Center 2
A	6	12
B	3	7
C	18	9
D	15	14
E	16	8
F	10	15

PROBLEM 18.7

Illustrate the throughput time and idle time at the two work centers in Problem 18.6 by constructing a time phased chart.

CRITICAL RATIO

The third widely used sequencing rule is the *critical ratio*. The critical ratio (CR) is an index number computed by dividing the time remaining until due date by the work time remaining. As opposed to Johnson's rule and the priority rules, critical ratio is dynamic. It can be updated weekly and is useful in advance scheduling.

The critical ratio is set up to give priority to jobs that must be done to keep shipping on schedule. A job with a low critical ratio (less than 1.0) is one that is falling behind schedule. If CR is exactly 1.0, the job is on schedule. A CR greater than 1.0 means the job is ahead of schedule and has some slack.

The formula for critical ratio is:

$$CR = \frac{\text{Time remaining}}{\text{Work days remaining}} = \frac{\text{Due date} - \text{Today's date}}{\text{Work (lead) time remaining}}$$

EXAMPLE 18.7

Today is day 25 on B & R Food's production schedule. Three jobs are on order as indicated below

Job	Due date	Work days remaining
A	30	4
B	28	5
C	27	2

We compute the critical ratios using the formula for CR.

Job	Critical Ratio	Priority Order
A	(30 − 25)/4 = 1.25	3
B	(28 − 25)/5 = 0.60	1
C	(27 − 25)/2 = 1.00	2

Job B has a critical ratio less than one, meaning it will be late unless expedited, so it has the highest priority. Job C is on time, and job A has some slack.

PROBLEM 18.8

An Oregan lumber yard has four jobs on order, as shown below. Today is day 205 on the yard's schedule. Establish processing priorities.

Job	Due date	Remaining time in days
A	212	6
B	209	3
C	208	3
D	210	8

(continued)

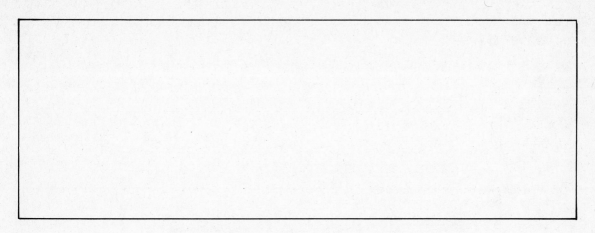

JOB SHOP SCHEDULING BY COMPUTER

Job shop scheduling is a difficult problem for operations managers. While the techniques described in this chapter are very useful, much scheduling is still done informally and intuitively.

Computer programs have been developed to provide another alternative. One popular program, developed by General Electric, is the General Job Shop Scheduler (GJSCH$). GJSCH$ can be used to assess capacity demands or to schedule jobs. The computer develops two reports. A job schedule report assigns jobs by machine, day, hours, operator, etc. The second report, a machine center load report, indicates idle time at each work center.

ANSWERS

18.1

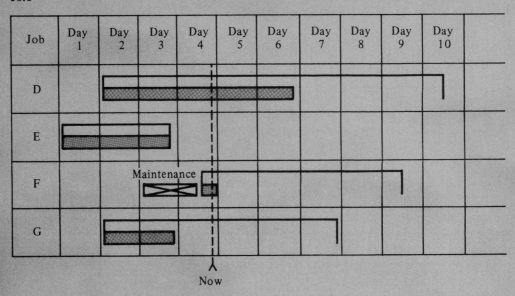

18.2

Row subtraction

Job \ Machine	#1	#2	#3
C-3	0	300	400
C-5	0	1100	800
C-8	0	500	1800

Column subtraction

Job \ Machine	#1	#2	#3
C-3	0	0	0
C-5	0	800	400
C-8	0	200	1400

(continued)

Cover zeros with lines

Job \ Machine	#1	#2	#3
C-3	0	0	0
C-5	0	800	400
C-8	0	(200)	1400

Subtract smallest number

Job \ Machine	#1	#2	#3
C-3	200	0	0
C-5	0	600	200
C-8	0	0	1200

Smallest uncovered number

Cover zeros with lines

Job \ Machine	#1	#2	#3
C-3	200	0	0
C-5	0	600	200
C-8	0	0	1200

Assign:

C-3 to #3
C-5 to #1
C-8 to #2

Cost = $1200 + $500 + $1000
    = $2700

18.3 The cost table has a fourth column to represent New York. To balance the problem, add a dummy row (person) with a zero relocation cost to each city.

Subtract smallest number in each row and cover zeros (column subtraction will give the same numbers and therefore is not necessary)

Hiree \ Office	Omaha	Miami	Dallas	New York
Jones	$800	$1100	$1200	$1000
Smith	$500	$1600	$1300	$800
Wilson	$500	$1000	$2300	$1500
Dummy	0	0	0	0

Hiree \ Office	Omaha	Miami	Dallas	New York
Jones	0	300	400	200
Smith	0	1100	800	300
Wilson	0	500	1800	1000
Dummy	0	0	0	0

(continued)

Subtract smallest uncovered number (200), add it to each square where two lines intersect, and cover all zeros.

Hiree \ Office	Omaha	Miami	Dallas	New York
Jones	0	100	200	0
Smith	0	900	200	100
Wilson	0	300	1600	800
Dummy	200	0	0	0

Subtract smallest uncovered number (100), add it to each square where two lines intersect, and cover all zeros.

Hiree \ Office	Omaha	Miami	Dallas	New York
Jones	0	0	100	0
Smith	0	800	500	100
Wilson	0	200	1500	800
Dummy	300	0	0	100

Subtract smallest uncovered number (100), add it to squares where two lines intersect, and cover all zeros.

Hiree \ Office	Omaha	Miami	Dallas	New York
Jones	100	0	100	0
Smith	0	700	400	0
Wilson	0	100	1400	700
Dummy	400	0	0	100

Assign:

Dummy (no one) to Dallas
Wilson to Omaha
Smith to New York
Jones to Miami

Cost = $0 + $500 + $800 + $1100
     = $2400

18.4 FCFS has the sequence A–B–C–D–E–F

Job sequence	Processing time	Flow time	Due Date	Job lateness
A	6	6	22	0
B	12	18	14	4
C	14	32	30	2
D	2	34	18	16
E	10	44	25	19
F	4	29	34	0
	48	163		41

1. Average completion time = 163/6 = 27.17
2. Average no. jobs in system = 163/48 = 3.4
3. Average job lateness = 41/6 = 6.83 days

EDD has the sequence B–D–A–E–C–F

Job sequence	Processing time	Flow time	Due Date	Job lateness
B	12	12	14	0
D	2	14	18	0
A	6	20	22	0
E	10	30	25	5
C	14	44	30	14
F	4	48	34	14
	48	168		33

1. Average completion time = 168/6 = 28.0 days (higher than FCFS)
2. Average no. jobs in system = 168/48 = 3.5 (higher than FCFS)
3. Average job lateness = 33/6 = 5.5 days (lower than FCFS)

18.5 SPT has the sequence D–F–A–E–B–C

Job sequence	Processing time	Flow time	Due Date	Job lateness
D	2	2	18	0
F	4	6	34	0
A	6	12	22	0
E	10	22	25	0
B	12	34	14	20
C	14	48	30	18
	48	124		38

1. Average completion time = 124/6 = 20.67 days
2. Average no. jobs in system = 124/48 = 2.58
3. Average job lateness = 38/6 = 6.33 days

LPT has the sequence C–B–E–A–F–D

Job sequence	Processing time	Flow time	Due Date	Job lateness
C	14	14	30	0
B	12	26	14	12
E	10	36	25	11
A	6	42	22	20
F	4	46	34	12
D	2	48	18	30
	48	212		85

1. Average completion time = 212/6 = 35.33 days
2. Average no. of jobs in system = 212/48 = 4.42
3. Average job lateness = 85/6 = 14.17 days

SPT provides the best average completion time (20.67 days) and average number of jobs in the system (2.58) of all four priority rules. EDD's average job lateness of 5.5 days is lowest. SPT is a good recommendation. SPT's major disadvantage is that it makes long jobs wait, sometimes for a long time.

18.6

B	A	F	D	C	E

The sequential times are:

Work Center 1	3	6	10	15	18	16
Work Center 2	7	12	15	14	9	8

18.7

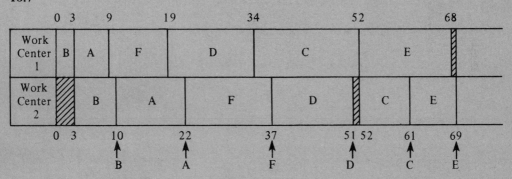

  Idle time

18.8

Job	Critical Ratio	Priority Order
A	(212 − 205)/6 = 1.17	3
B	(209 − 205)/3 = 1.33	4
C	(208 − 205)/3 = 1.00	2
D	(210 − 205)/8 = 0.62	1

HOMEWORK PROBLEM

The schedule at a small southwestern U.S. plant has six jobs that can be processed on any of six machines, with respective times as shown (in hours) below. Determine the allocation of jobs to machines that will result in minimum time.

	Machine					
Job	*#1*	*#2*	*#3*	*#4*	*#5*	*#6*
A-52	60	22	34	42	30	60
A-53	22	52	16	32	18	48
A-56	29	16	58	28	22	55
A-59	42	32	28	46	15	30
A-60	30	18	25	15	45	42
A-61	50	48	57	30	44	60

Project Planning with PERT

Large, complex projects are prevalent in all segments of government and industry. A building contractor might be constructing a hotel or an office complex. A shipbuilder may have just received a contract to build five large commercial oil tankers. A foundry might be in the process of installing a new pollution control device. NASA could be in the process of planning for the launching of a satellite. Perhaps at one time you spent some time planning what courses you had to take in order to meet all of the requirements and pre-requisites to graduate on a certain date.

The types of projects and programs just mentioned must be planned carefully if they are to completed by a certain date. Delays and cost overruns seem to be the rule these days instead of the exception. How can an organization organize and plan these types of projects to avoid delays and unnecessary costs? How can we find potential bottlenecks in a project? Are there any activities in a project that we can delay without jeop-ardizing the entire project? If so, how long can the delays be? If you want to complete a project in a relatively small amount of time, how can you do it at minimum cost? These are important questions. The answers could save thousands or even millions of dollars.

In the 1950s, the U. S. Navy developed a technique to answer these and related questions. Known as PERT (program evaluation and review technique), the Navy's method has since given rise to many related tech-niques. One such technique is CPM (critical path method). The techniques are popular because they work and have the potential to save thousands of dollars. We will begin this chapter by investigating some of the differences between PERT and CPM.

PERT and CPM are network techniques that provide operations managers with a graphical approach to project planning and scheduling. Both techniques have had widespread, successful application in large projects, including construction of buildings, ships, aircraft, and missiles. They are excellent for monitoring the progress of activities, for revealing potential bottlenecks, and for determining expected project-comple-tion dates.

Although PERT and CPM differ to some extent in terminology and in the construction of the network, their objectives are the same. Furthermore, the analysis used in both techniques is very similar. The major difference is that PERT employs three time estimates for each activity. Each estimate has an associated probability of occurrence, which, in turn, is used in computing expected values and standard deviations for the activity times. CPM makes the assumption that activity times are known with certainty and hence only one time factor is given for each activity. Although this chapter discusses PERT, most of the material ap-plies to CPM.

ACTIVITIES, EVENTS, AND NETWORKS

The first step in PERT is to break the entire project into events and activities. An event marks the start or completion of a particular task or activity. An activity, on the other hand, is a task or a subproject that occurs between two events. Table 19.1 restates these definitions and shows the symbols that analysts use to represent events and activities.

Table 19.1. Events and Activities

Name	Symbol	Description
Event	◯	A point in time, usually a completion date or a starting date
Activity	→	A flow over time, usually a task or subproject

Any project that can be described by activities and events may be analyzed by a **PERT** network.

EXAMPLE 19.1

Given the following information, develop a network.

Activity	Immediate Predecessors
A	—
B	—
C	A
D	B

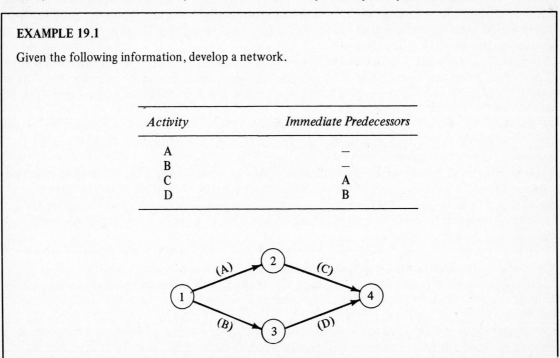

You will note that we have assigned each event a number. As you will see later, it is possible to identify each activity with a beginning and an ending node. For example, activity A in Example 19.1 is the activity that starts with node, or event, 1 and ends at node, or event, 2. In general, we number nodes from left to right. The beginning node, or event, of the entire project is number 1, while the last node, or event, in the entire project bears the largest number. In Example 19.1 the last node shows the number 4.

PROBLEM 19.1

Given the following information; develop a network.

Activity	Immediate Predecessors
A	—
B	—
C	A
D	A
E	C,B

PROBLEM 19.2

Given the information below, construct a network.

Activity	Immediate Predecessors
A	—
B	—
C	A
D	B
E	C
F	D

We can also specify networks by events and the activities that occur between events. The following example shows how to develop a network based on this type of specification scheme.

EXAMPLE 19.2

Given the following table, develop a network.

Beginning Event	Ending Event	Activity
1	2	1-2
1	3	1-3
2	4	2-4
3	4	3-4
3	5	3-5
4	6	4-6
5	6	5-6

Instead of using a letter to signify activities and their predecessor activities, we can specify activities by their starting event and their ending event. Beginning with the activity that starts at event 1 and ends at event 2, we can construct the following network.

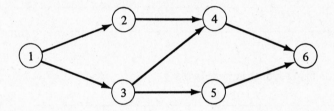

PROBLEM 19.3

Given the following table, construct a network.

Beginning Event	Ending Event	Activity
1	2	1-2
1	3	1-3
2	4	2-4
3	4	3-4
4	5	4-5
5	6	5-6

All that is required to construct a network is the starting and ending event for each activity.

EXAMPLE 19.3

Construct a network based on the following table.

Activity
1-2
1-3
1-4
2-5
3-5
4-6
5-7
6-7

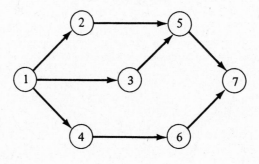

PERT AND ACTIVITY TIME ESTIMATES

As mentioned earlier, one distinguishing difference between PERT and CPM is the use of three time estimates for each activity in the PERT technique. Only one time factor is given for each activity in CPM.

For each activity in PERT, we must specify an optimistic, a most probable (or most likely) and a pessimistic time estimate. We then use these three time estimates to calculate an expected completion time and variance for each activity. If we assume that activity times follow a beta probability distribution, we can use the following formulas:

$$t = \frac{a + 4m + b}{6}$$

$$v = \left(\frac{b - a}{6}\right)^2$$

where

$$a = \text{optimistic time for activity completion}$$

$$b = \text{pessimistic time for activity completion}$$

$$m = \text{most likely time for activity completion}$$

$$t = \text{expected time of activity completion}$$

$$v = \text{variance of activity completion time}$$

In PERT, after we have developed the network, we compute expected times and variances for each activity.

EXAMPLE 19.4

Compute expected times and variances of completion for each activity based on the following time estimates:

Activity	a	m	b
1-2	3	4	5
1-3	1	3	5
2-4	5	6	7
3-4	6	7	8

Activity	$a + 4m + b$	t	$\dfrac{b-a}{6}$	v
1-2	24	4	$\dfrac{2}{6}$	$\dfrac{4}{36}$
1-3	18	3	$\dfrac{4}{6}$	$\dfrac{16}{36}$
2-4	36	6	$\dfrac{2}{6}$	$\dfrac{4}{36}$
3-4	42	7	$\dfrac{2}{6}$	$\dfrac{4}{36}$

PROBLEM 19.4

Determine expected times and variances for each activity based on the following data:

Activity	a	m	b
1-2	1	2	3
1-3	5	6	7
2-3	2	4	6
2-4	2	5	8
3-4	2	5	6

Activity	$a + 4m + b$	t	$\dfrac{b - a}{6}$	v
1-2				
1-3				
2-3				
2-4				
3-4				

PROBLEM 19.5

Calculate expected times and variances for every activity.

Activity	a	m	b
1-2	2	3	5
1-3	2	3	4
2-4	1	4	8
3-5	6	7	8
4-6	1	2	4
5-6	4	6	8

Activity	$a + 4m + b$	t	$\dfrac{b-a}{6}$	v
1-2				
1-3				
2-4				
3-5				
4-6				
5-6				

CRITICAL PATH ANALYSIS

The objective of critical path analysis is to determine the following quantities for each activity:

ES = earliest activity start time. *All predecessor* activities must be completed before an activity can be started. This is the earliest time an activity can be started.

LS = latest activity start time. *All following* activities must be completed without delaying the entire project. This is the latest time an activity can be started without delaying the entire project.

EF = earliest activity finish time.

LF = latest activity finish time.

S = activity slack time, which is equal to (LS – ES) or (LF – EF).

For any activity, if we can calculate ES and LS, we can find the other three quantities as follows:

$$EF = ES + t$$

$$LF = LS + t$$

$$S = LS - ES$$

$$= LF - EF$$

Once we know these quantities for every activity we can analyze the overall project. Typically this analysis includes:

1. The critical path—the group of activities in the project that have a slack of zero. This path is "critical" because a delay in any activity along this path would delay the entire project.
2. T—the total project completion time, which is calculated by adding the expected time (*t*) values of those activities on the critical path.
3. V—variance of the critical path, which is computed by adding the variance (*v*) of those individual activities on the critical path.

Critical path analysis normally starts with the determination of ES and EF.

The following example illustrates the procedure.

EXAMPLE 19.5

Given the following information, determine ES and EF for each activity.

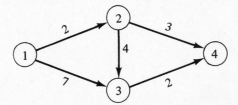

(continued)

Activity	t
1-2	2
1-3	7
2-3	4
2-4	3
3-4	2

We find ES by moving from the starting activities of the project to the ending activities of the project. For the starting activities, ES is either zero or the actual starting date, say, August 1. For activities 1-2 and 1-3, ES is zero.

There is one basic rule. Before an activity can be started, *all* of its predecessor activities must be completed. In other words, we search for the *longest* path leading to an activity in determining ES. For activity 2-3, ES is 2. Its only predecessor activity is 1-2, for which $t = 2$. By the same reasoning, ES for activity 2-4 also is 2. For activity 3-4, however, ES is 7. It has two predecessor paths: activity 1-3 with $t = 7$ and activities 1-2 and 2-3 with a total expected time of 6 (or 2 + 4). Thus, ES for activity 3-4 is 7 because activity 1-3 must be completed before activity 3-4 can be started. We compute EF next by adding t to ES for each activity. See the following table.

Activity	ES	EF
1-2	0	2
1-3	0	7
2-3	2	6
2-4	2	5
3-4	7	9

PROBLEM 19.6

Given the following data, determine ES and EF for each activity.

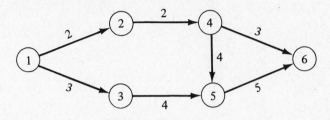

Activity	t
1–2	2
1–3	3
2–4	2
3–5	4
4–5	4
4–6	3
5–6	5

Activity	ES	EF
1–2		
1–3		
2–4		
3–5		
4–5		
4–6		
5–6		

The most difficult part of the Problem 19.6 is determining ES for activity 5-6. The main point to remember is that *all* predecessor activities must be completed. The "bottleneck" is formed by activities 1-2, 2-4, and 4-5, for which the total expected completion time is 8 (or 2 + 2 + 4).

PROBLEM 19.7

Determine ES and EF for each activity in the network given below.

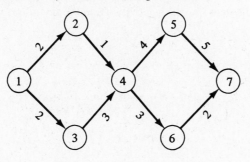

Activity	t
1-2	2
1-3	2
2-4	1
3-4	3
4-5	4
4-6	3
5-7	5
6-7	2

Activity	ES	EF
1-2		
1-3		
2-4		
3-4		
4-5		
4-6		
5-7		
6-7		

The next step is to calculate LS, the latest activity starting time for each activity. We start with the last activities and work backward to the first activities. The procedure is to work backward from the last activities to determine the latest possible starting time (LS) without increasing the earliest finishing time (EF). This task sounds more difficult than it really is.

EXAMPLE 19.6

Determine LS, LF, and S (the slack) for each activity based on the following data:

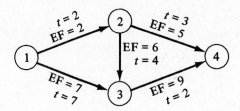

Activity	t	ES	EF
1–2	2	0	2
1–3	7	0	7
2–3	4	2	6
2–4	3	2	5
3–4	2	7	9

The earliest time by which the entire project can be finished is 9 because activities 2-4 (EF = 5) and 3-4 (EF = 9) *both* must be completed. Using 9 as a basis, we now will work backwards by subtracting the appropriate *t* values from 9.

The latest time we can start activity 3-4 is at time 7 (or 9 − 2) in order to still complete the project by time period 9. Thus LS for activity 3-4 is 7. Using the same reasoning, LS for activity 2-4 is 6 (or 9 − 3). If we start activity 2-4 at 6 and it takes 3 time units to complete the activity, we can still finish in 9 time units. The latest we can start activity 2-3 is 3 (or 9 − 2 − 4). If we start activity 2-3 at 3 and it takes 2 and 4 time units for activities 2-3 and 3-4, respectively, we can still finish on time. Thus LS for activity 2-3 is 3. Using the same reasoning, LS for activity 1-3 is zero (or 9 − 2 − 7). Analyzing activity 1-2 is more difficult because there are two paths. Both must be completed in 9 time units.

(continued)

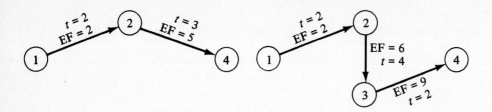

Since both of the above paths must be completed, LS for activity 1-2 is computed from the most binding, or slowest path. Thus, LS for activity 1-2 *is 1* (or $9 - 2 - 4 - 2$) and *not 4* (or $9 - 3 - 2$). Noting the following relationships, we can construct a table summarizing the results.

$$LF = LS + t$$
$$S = LF - EF$$
$$= LS - ES$$

Activity	ES	EF	LS	LF	S
1-2	0	2	1	3	1
1-3	0	7	0	7	0
2-3	2	6	3	7	1
2-4	2	5	6	9	4
3-4	7	9	7	9	0

PROBLEM 19.8

From the following information, determine LS, LF, and S for each activity.

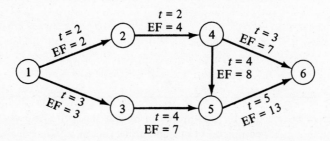

(continued)

Activity	t	ES	EF
1-2	2	0	2
1-3	3	0	3
2-4	2	2	4
3-5	4	3	7
4-5	4	4	8
4-6	3	4	7
5-6	5	8	13

Activity	LS	LF	S
1-2			
1-3			
2-4			
3-5			
4-5			
4-6			
5-6			

Once we have computed ES, EF, LS, LF, and S, we can analyze the entire project. Analysis includes determining the critical path, project completion time, and project variance. Consider the following example.

EXAMPLE 19.7

What is the critical path, total completion time T, and project variance V, of the following network?

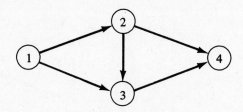

Activity	t	v	ES	EF	LS	LF	S
1-2	2	$\frac{2}{6}$	0	2	1	3	1
1-3	7	$\frac{3}{6}$	0	7	0	7	0
2-3	4	$\frac{1}{6}$	2	6	3	7	1
2-4	3	$\frac{2}{6}$	2	5	6	9	4
3-4	2	$\frac{4}{6}$	7	9	7	9	0

The critical path consists of those activities with zero slack. These are activities 1-3 and 3-4.

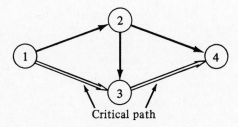

Critical path

The total project completion time is 9 (or 7 + 2).

The project variance is the sum of the *activity variances* along the *critical path* which is 7/6 (or 3/6 + 4/6).

PROBLEM 19.9

Calculate the critical path, completion time T, and variance V, based on the following information.

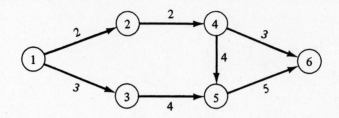

Activity	t	v	ES	EF	LS	LF	S
1-2	2	$\frac{2}{6}$	0	2	0	2	0
1-3	3	$\frac{2}{6}$	0	3	1	4	1
2-4	2	$\frac{4}{6}$	2	4	2	4	0
3-5	4	$\frac{4}{6}$	3	7	4	8	1
4-5	4	$\frac{2}{6}$	4	8	4	8	0
4-6	3	$\frac{1}{6}$	4	7	10	13	6
5-6	5	$\frac{1}{6}$	8	13	8	13	0

Critical path is

$$T =$$

$$V =$$

Knowing a network and values for activity times and variances (t and v), makes it possible to perform a complete critical-path analysis, including the determination of ES, EF, LS, LF, and S for each activity as well as the critical path, T, and V for the entire project.

PROBLEM 19.10

Given the following information, perform a critical path analysis.

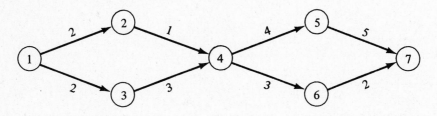

Activity	t	v
1–2	2	$\dfrac{1}{6}$
1–3	2	$\dfrac{1}{6}$
2–4	1	$\dfrac{2}{6}$
3–4	3	$\dfrac{2}{6}$
4–5	4	$\dfrac{4}{6}$
4–6	3	$\dfrac{2}{6}$
5–7	5	$\dfrac{1}{6}$
6–7	2	$\dfrac{2}{6}$

The solution begins with the determination of ES, EF, LS, LF, and S. We can determine these values from the above information and then enter them into the following table:

(continued)

Activity	t	v	ES	EF	LS	LF	S
1–2	2	$\frac{1}{6}$					
1–3	2	$\frac{1}{6}$					
2–4	1	$\frac{2}{6}$					
3–4	3	$\frac{2}{6}$					
4–5	4	$\frac{4}{6}$					
4–6	3	$\frac{2}{6}$					
5–7	5	$\frac{1}{6}$					
6–7	2	$\frac{2}{6}$					

Then we can find the critical path, T and V:

$$\text{Critical path} =$$

$$T =$$

$$V =$$

THE PROBABILITY OF PROJECT COMPLETION

Having computed the expected completion time T and completion variance V, we can determine the probability that the project will be completed at a specified date. If we make the assumption that the distribution of completion dates follows a normal curve, we can calculate the probability of completion as in the following example.

EXAMPLE 19.8

If the expected project completion time T is 20 weeks and the project variance V is 100, what is the probability that the project will be finished on or before week 25?

$$T = 20$$

$$V = 100$$

$$\sigma = \text{standard deviation} = \sqrt{\text{project variance}} = \sqrt{V} = \sqrt{100}$$

$$= 10$$

$$C = \text{desired completion date}$$

$$= 25 \text{ weeks}$$

The normal curve would appear as follows:

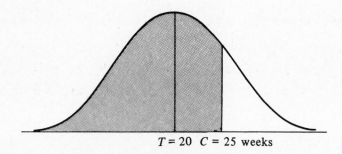

$$T = 20 \quad C = 25 \text{ weeks}$$

$$Z = \frac{C - T}{\sigma} = \frac{25 - 20}{10}$$

$$= 0.5$$

where Z equal the number of standard deviations from the mean. The area under the curve, for $Z = 0.5$, is 0.6915. (See the normal curve table in Appendix A.) Thus the probability of completing the project in 25 weeks is approximately 0.69, or 69 percent.

PROBLEM 19.11

A network has a total expected completion time of nine months and a variance of completion of four. What is the probability that the project will be completed in twelve months or less?

PROBLEM 19.12

The following information has been computed from a project:

$$T = 62 \text{ weeks}$$

$$V = 81$$

(continued)

What is the probability that the project will be completed eighteen weeks *before* its expected completion date?

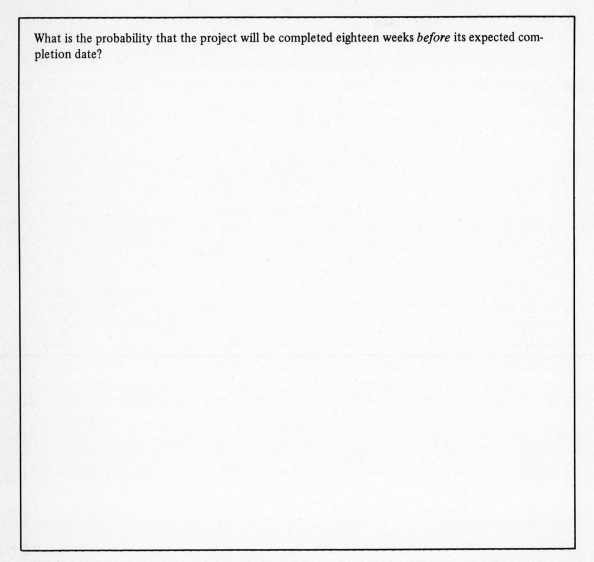

We must point out that the foregoing analysis should be used with caution. If a noncritical path activity has a large variance, it is possible for it to become a critical path activity. This occurrence would cause the analysis to be in error. Consider the network pictured in Figure 19.1. The critical path is 1-3 and 3-4 with $T = 12$ and $V = 4$. If the desired completion date is 14, the Z value is 1 [or $(14 - 12)/\sqrt{4}$]. The chance of completion is 84 percent from the normal distribution in the appendix. What would happen if activities 1-2 and 2-4 became the critical path? Because of the high variance, this event is not unlikely. With the same values for C and T, Z becomes 0.4 [or $(14 - 12)/\sqrt{25}$]. Looking at the normal distribution, we see that the chance of project completion is 66 percent. If activities 1-2 and 2-4 became the critical path, the chance of project completion would drop significantly due to the large total variance ($25 = 16 + 9$) of these activities. A computer simulation of the project could prevent this problem.

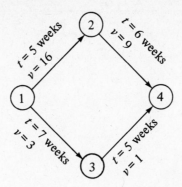

Figure 19.1. Critical Path Analysis

DUMMY ACTIVITIES AND EVENTS

You may encounter a network that has two activities with identical starting and ending events. "Dummy" activities and events can be inserted into the network to prevent this problem.

EXAMPLE 19.9

Insert dummy activities and events to correct the following network:

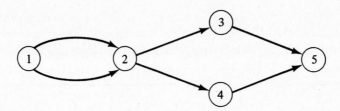

We can add the following dummy activity and dummy event to obtain the correct network:

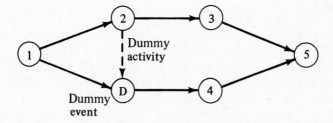

This network can be analyzed as usual. A dummy activity should have completion time, t of zero.

PROBLEM 19.13

Insert dummy activities and events to correct the following network:

The use of dummy activities and events is especially important when computer programs are to be employed in determining the critical path, project completion time, project variance, and so on. Dummy activities and events can also ensure that the network properly reflects the project under consideration. The following example reveals the procedure.

EXAMPLE 19.10

Develop a network based on the following information:

Activity	Immediate Predecessors
A	—
B	—
C	A
D	B
E	C, D
F	D
G	E
H	F

(continued)

Given those data, you might develop the following network

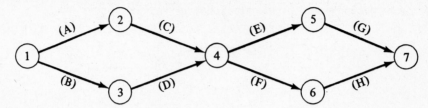

Look at activity F. According to the network, both activities C and D must be completed before we can start F, but in reality, only activity D must be completed (see the table). Thus the network is not correct. The addition of a dummy activity and a dummy event can overcome this problem as shown below.

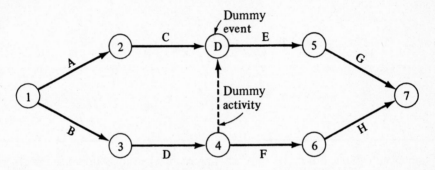

Now, the network embodies all of the proper relationships.

PROBLEM 19.14

Consider the following *part* of a large network:

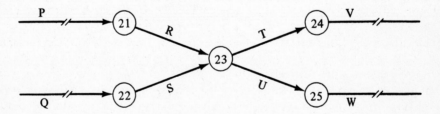

Given the following information, determine if this partial network reveals the correct relationships. If it doesn't, make the appropriate alterations.

(continued)

Activity	Immediate Predessor
R	P
S	Q
T	R
U	R, S

PERT/COST

Until now, we have assumed that it is not possible to reduce activity times. This is usually not the case, however. Perhaps additional resources can reduce activity times for certain activities within the project. These resources might be additional labor, more equipment, and so on. Although it can be expensive to shorten activity times, doing so might be worthwhile. If a company faces costly penalties for being late with a project, it might be economical to use additional resources to complete the project on time. There may be fixed costs every day the project is in process. Thus, it might be profitable to use additional resources to shorten the project time and save some of the daily fixed costs. But which activities should be shortened? How much will this action cost? Will a reduction in the activity time in turn reduce the time needed to complete the entire project? Ideally, we would like to find the least expensive method of shortening the entire project. This is the purpose of PERT/cost.

In addition to time, the operations manager is normally concerned with the cost of the project. Usually it is possible to shorten activity times by committing additional resources to the project. Figure 19.2 shows cost-time curves for two activities. For activity 5–6, it costs $300 to complete the activity in eight weeks,

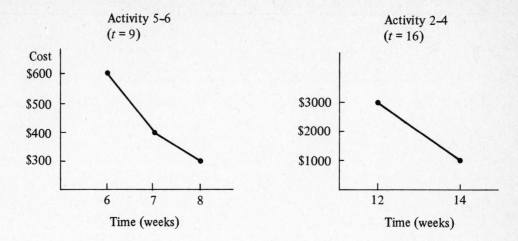

Figure 19.2. Cost-time Curves Used in PERT/Cost Analysis

$400 for seven weeks, and $600 for six weeks. Activity 2–4 requires $3000 of additional resources for completion in twelve weeks and $1000 for fourteen weeks. Similar cost-time curves or relationships can usually be developed for all activities in the network.

The objective of PERT/Cost is to reduce the entire project completion time by a certain amount at the least cost. Although there are several good computer programs that perform PERT/Cost, it is useful to understand how to complete this process by hand. To accomplish this objective, we must introduce a few more variables. For each activity, there will exist a reduction in activity time and the cost incurred for that time reduction. Let

$$M_i = \text{maximum reduction of time for activity } i$$

$$C_i = \text{additional cost associated with reducing activity time for activity } i$$

$$K_i = \text{cost of reducing activity time by one time unit for activity } i$$

$$K_i = \frac{C_i}{M_i}$$

With this information it is possible to determine the least cost of reducing the project completion date.

EXAMPLE 19.11

Given the following information, determine the least cost of reducing the project completion time by one week.

(continued)

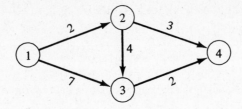

Activity	t (weeks)	M (weeks)	C
1–2	2	1	$300
1–3	7	4	$2000
2–3	4	2	$2000
2–4	3	2	$4000
3–4	2	1	$2000

Activity	ES	EF	LS	LF	S
1–2	0	2	1	3	1
1–3	0	7	0	7	0
2–3	2	6	3	7	1
2–4	2	5	6	9	4
3–4	7	9	7	9	0

The first step is to compute K for each activity:

Activity	M	C	K	Critical Path
1–2	1	$300	$300	No
1–3	4	$2000	$500	Yes
2–3	2	$2000	$1000	No
2–4	2	$4000	$2000	No
3–4	1	$2000	$2000	Yes

The second step is to locate that activity on the critical path with the smallest K_i value. The critical path consists of activities 1–3 and 3–4. Since activity 1–3 has a lower K_i value, we can reduce the project completion time by one week to eight weeks by incurring an additional cost of $500.

We must be very careful in using this procedure. Any further reduction in activity time along the critical path would cause the critical path to also include activities 1–2, 2–3, and 3–4. In other words, there would be two critical paths.

PROBLEM 19.15

Determine the least cost of reducing the project completion date by three months based on the following information:

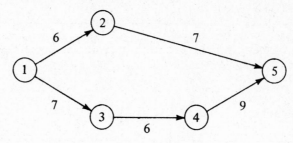

Activity	t (months)	M (months)	C
1–2	6	2	$400
1–3	7	2	$500
2–5	7	1	$300
3–4	6	2	$600
4–5	9	1	$200

Activity	ES	EF	LS	LF	S
1–2					
1–3					
2–5					
3–4					
4–5					

(continued)

Activity	M	C	K
1–2	2	$400	
1–3	2	$500	
2–5	1	$300	
3–4	2	$600	
4–5	1	$200	

ANSWERS

19.1

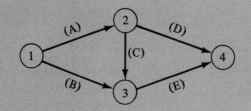

19.2

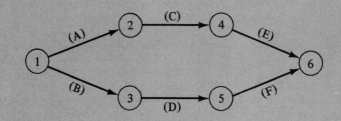

19.3

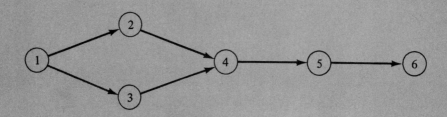

19.4

Activity	$a + 4m + b$	t	$\dfrac{b-a}{6}$	v
1–2	12	2	$\dfrac{2}{6}$	$\dfrac{4}{36}$
1–3	36	6	$\dfrac{2}{6}$	$\dfrac{4}{36}$
2–3	24	4	$\dfrac{4}{6}$	$\dfrac{16}{36}$
2–4	30	5	$\dfrac{6}{6}$	1
3–4	28	4.67	$\dfrac{4}{6}$	$\dfrac{16}{36}$

19.5

Activity	$a + 4m + b$	t	$\dfrac{b - a}{6}$	v
1–2	19	3 1/6	3/6	9/36
1–3	18	3	2/6	4/36
2–4	25	4 1/6	7/6	49/36
3–5	42	7	2/6	4/36
4–6	13	2 1/6	3/6	9/36
5–6	36	6	4/6	16/36

19.6

Activity	ES	EF
1–2	0	2
1–3	0	3
2–4	2	4
3–5	3	7
4–5	4	8
4–6	4	7
5–6	8	13

19.7

Activity	ES	EF
1–2	0	2
1–3	0	2
2–4	2	3
3–4	2	5
4–5	5	9
4–6	5	8
5–7	9	14
6–7	8	10

19.8

Activity	LS	LF	S
1–2	(13 − 5 − 4 − 2 − 2) = 0	2	0
1–3	(13 − 5 − 4 − 3) = 1	4	1
2–4	(13 − 5 − 4 − 2) = 2	4	0
3–5	(13 − 5 − 4) = 4	8	1
4–5	(13 − 5 − 4) = 4	8	0
4–6	(13 − 3) = 10	13	6
5–6	(13 − 5) = 8	13	0

Note: In calculating LS for activities 1–2 and 2–4, we must take the *longest* path. This path is 1–2–4–5–6.

19.9   The critical path consists of activities 1–2, 2–4, 4–5, and 5–6.

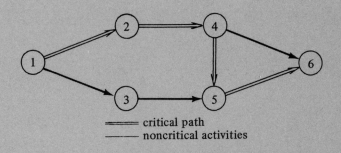

======= critical path
———— noncritical activities

$$T = 2 + 2 + 4 + 5$$

$$= 13$$

$$V = \frac{2}{6} + \frac{4}{6} + \frac{2}{6} + \frac{1}{6} = \frac{9}{6}$$

$$= \frac{3}{2}$$

19.10

Activity	t	v	ES	EF	LS	LF	S
1–2	2	$\frac{1}{6}$	0	2	2	4	2
1–3	2	$\frac{1}{6}$	0	2	0	2	0
2–4	1	$\frac{2}{6}$	2	3	4	5	2
3–4	3	$\frac{2}{6}$	2	5	2	5	0
4–5	4	$\frac{4}{6}$	5	9	5	9	0
4–6	3	$\frac{2}{6}$	5	8	9	12	4
5–7	5	$\frac{1}{6}$	9	14	9	14	0
6–7	2	$\frac{2}{6}$	8	10	12	14	4

The critical path comprises activities 1-3, 3-4, 4-5, and 5-7. These activities all have zero slack.

$$T = 2 + 3 + 4 + 5$$

$$= 14$$

$$V = \frac{1}{6} + \frac{2}{6} + \frac{4}{6} + \frac{1}{6}$$

$$= \frac{8}{6}$$

19.11

$$T = 9$$

$$V = 4$$

$$\sigma = \sqrt{V}$$

$$= 2$$

$$C = \text{desired completion date}$$

$$= 12$$

The normal curve for the problem is:

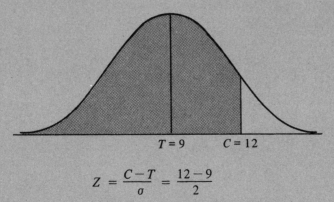

$$Z = \frac{C-T}{\sigma} = \frac{12-9}{2}$$

$$= 1.5$$

From a normal curve table, the area under the normal curve is 0.93319. Thus, the probability that the project will be completed in twelve months is approximately 0.93, or 93 percent.

19.12   The desired completion date is 18 weeks before the expected completion date, 62 weeks. The desired completion date is 44 (or 62 − 18) weeks.

$$Z = \frac{C - T}{\sigma} = \frac{44 - 62}{9} = \frac{-18}{9}$$

$$= -2.0$$

The normal curve appears as follows:

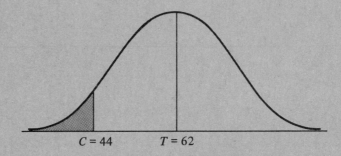

$$C = 44 \qquad T = 62$$

Since the normal curve is symmetrical and table values are calculated for positive values of Z, the area desired is equal to 1 − (table value). For $Z = +2.0$, the area from the table is 0.97725. Thus the area, corresponding to a Z values of −2.0, is 0.02275 (or 1 − 0.97725). Hence the probability of completing the project 18 weeks before the expected completion date is approximately 0.02, or 2 percent.

19.13

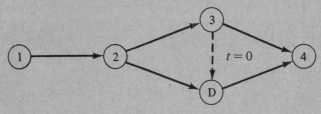

19.14   The network is not correct. It should include a dummy event and a dummy activity, as shown below:

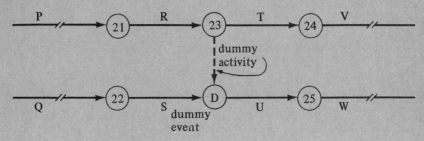

19.15 The first step in this problem is to compute ES, EF, LS, LF, and S for each activity.

Activity	ES	EF	LS	LF	S
1–2	0	6	9	15	9
1–3	0	7	0	7	0
2–5	6	13	15	22	9
3–4	7	13	7	13	0
4–5	13	22	13	22	0

The critical path consists of activities 1–3, 3–4, and 4–5.

Next, K must be computed for each activity by dividing C by M for each activity.

Activity	M	C	K	Critical Path?
1–2	2	$400	$200/mo.	No
1–3	2	$500	$250/mo.	Yes
2–5	1	$300	$300/mo.	No
3–4	2	$600	$300/mo.	Yes
4–5	1	$200	$200/mo.	Yes

Finally, we will select that activity on the critical path with the smallest K_i value. This is activity 4–5. Thus we can reduce the total project completion date by one month (because $M = 1$ month) for an additional cost of $200. We still need to reduce the project completion date by two more months. This reduction can be achieved at least cost along the critical path by reducing activity 1–3 by two months for an additional cost of $500. This solution is summarized in the following table:

Activity	Months Reduced	Cost
4–5	1	$200
1–3	2	$500
	Total:	$700

HOMEWORK PROBLEMS

19-1. Tom Schriber, director of personnel of Management Resources, Inc., is in the process of designing a program that their customers can use in the job-finding process. Some of the activities include preparing resumes, writing letters, making appointments to see prospective employers, researching into companies and industries, etc. Some of the information on the activities appears in the accompanying table.

Activity	a	(days) m	b	Immediate Predecessors
A	8	10	12	
B	6	7	9	
C	3	3	4	
D	10	20	30	A
E	6	7	8	C
F	9	10	11	B, D, E
G	6	7	10	B, D, E
H	14	15	16	F
I	10	11	13	F
J	6	7	8	G, H
K	4	7	8	I, J
L	1	2	4	G, H

a. Construct a network for this problem.
b. Determine the expected times and variances for each activity.
c. Determine ES, EF, LS, LF and slack for each activity.
d. Determine the critical path and project completion time.
e. Determine the probability that the project will be finished in 70 days.
f. Determine the probability that the project will be finished in 80 days.
g. Determine the probability that the project will be finished in 90 days.

19-2. Zuckerman Wiring and Electric is a company that installs wiring and electrical fixtures in residential construction. John Zuckerman has been very concerned with the amount of time that it takes to complete wiring jobs. Some of his workers are very unreliable. A list of activities and their optimistic completion time, pessimistic completion time, and most likely completion time is given in the accompanying table.

(continued)

Activity	a	m	b	Immediate Predecessors
A	3	6	8	
B	2	4	4	
C	1	2	3	
D	6	7	8	C
E	2	4	6	B, D
F	6	10	14	A, E
G	1	2	4	A, E
H	3	6	9	F
I	10	11	12	G
J	14	16	20	C
K	2	8	10	H, I

Determine the expected completion time and variance for each activity. John Zuckerman would like to determine the total project completion time and the critical path for installing electrical wiring and equipment in residential houses. In addition, determine ES, EF, LS, LF, and slack for each activity.

What is the probability that Zuckerman will finish the project in forty days or less?

Appendix

The Standardized Normal Distribution Function, F(Z)

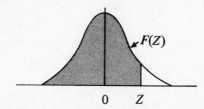

Z	0.00	0.01	0.02	0.03	0.04	0.05	0.06	0.07	0.08	0.09
0.0	0.5000	0.5040	0.5080	0.5120	0.5160	0.5199	0.5239	0.5279	0.5319	0.5359
0.1	0.5398	0.5438	0.5478	0.5517	0.5557	0.5596	0.5636	0.5675	0.5714	0.5753
0.2	0.5793	0.5832	0.5871	0.5910	0.5948	0.5987	0.6026	0.6064	0.6103	0.6141
0.3	0.6179	0.6217	0.6255	0.6293	0.6331	0.6368	0.6406	0.6443	0.6480	0.6517
0.4	0.6554	0.6591	0.6628	0.6664	0.6700	0.6736	0.6722	0.6808	0.6844	0.6879
0.5	0.6915	0.6950	0.6985	0.7019	0.7054	0.7088	0.7123	0.7157	0.7190	0.7224
0.6	0.7257	0.7291	0.7324	0.7357	0.7389	0.7422	0.7454	0.7486	0.7517	0.7549
0.7	0.7580	0.7611	0.7642	0.7673	0.7703	0.7734	0.7764	0.7794	0.7823	0.7852
0.8	0.7881	0.7910	0.7939	0.7967	0.7995	0.8023	0.8051	0.8078	0.8106	0.8133
0.9	0.8159	0.8186	0.8212	0.8238	0.8264	0.8289	0.8315	0.8340	0.8365	0.8389
1.0	0.8413	0.8438	0.8461	0.8485	0.8508	0.8531	0.8554	0.8577	0.8599	0.8621
1.1	0.8643	0.8665	0.8686	0.8708	0.8729	0.8749	0.8770	0.8790	0.8810	0.8830
1.2	0.8849	0.8869	0.8888	0.8907	0.8925	0.8944	0.8962	0.8980	0.8997	0.90147
1.3	0.90320	0.90490	0.90658	0.90824	0.90988	0.91149	0.91309	0.91466	0.91621	0.91774
1.4	0.91924	0.92073	0.92220	0.92364	0.92507	0.92647	0.92785	0.92922	0.93056	0.93189
1.5	0.93319	0.93448	0.93574	0.93699	0.93822	0.93943	0.94062	0.94179	0.94295	0.94408
1.6	0.94520	0.94630	0.94738	0.94845	0.94950	0.95053	0.95154	0.95254	0.95352	0.95449
1.7	0.95543	0.95637	0.95728	0.95818	0.95907	0.95994	0.96080	0.96164	0.96246	0.96327
1.8	0.96407	0.96485	0.96562	0.96638	0.96712	0.96784	0.96856	0.96926	0.96995	0.97062
1.9	0.97128	0.97193	0.97257	0.97320	0.97381	0.97441	0.97500	0.97558	0.97615	0.97670
2.0	0.97725	0.97778	0.97831	0.97882	0.97932	0.97982	0.98030	0.98077	0.98124	0.98169
2.1	0.98214	0.98257	0.98300	0.98341	0.98382	0.98422	0.98461	0.98500	0.98537	0.98574
2.2	0.98610	0.98645	0.98679	0.98713	0.98745	0.98778	0.98809	0.98840	0.98870	0.98899
2.3	0.98928	0.98956	0.98983	$0.9^2 0097$	$0.9^2 0358$	$0.9^2 0613$	$0.9^2 0863$	$0.9^2 1106$	$0.9^2 1344$	$0.9^2 1576$
2.4	$0.9^2 1802$	$0.9^2 2024$	$0.9^2 2240$	$0.9^2 2451$	$0.9^2 2656$	$0.9^2 2857$	$0.9^2 3053$	$0.9^2 3244$	$0.9^2 3431$	$0.9^2 3613$
2.5	$0.9^2 3790$	$0.9^2 3963$	$0.9^2 4132$	$0.9^2 4297$	$0.9^2 4457$	$0.9^2 4614$	$0.9^2 4766$	$0.9^2 4915$	$0.9^2 5060$	$0.9^2 5201$
3.0	$0.9^2 8650$	$0.9^2 8694$	$0.9^2 8736$	$0.9^2 8777$	$0.9^2 8817$	$0.9^2 8856$	$0.9^2 8893$	$0.9^2 8930$	$0.9^2 8965$	$0.9^2 8999$
3.5	$0.9^3 7674$	$0.9^3 7759$	$0.9^3 7842$	$0.9^3 7922$	$0.9^3 7999$	$0.9^3 8074$	$0.9^3 8146$	$0.9^3 8215$	$0.9^3 8282$	$0.9^3 8347$
4.0	$0.9^4 6833$	$0.9^4 6964$	$0.9^4 7090$	$0.9^4 7211$	$0.9^4 7327$	$0.9^4 7439$	$0.9^4 7546$	$0.9^4 7649$	$0.9^4 7748$	$0.9^4 7843$

For example: $F(2.41) = .9^2 2024 = .992024$.

*From A. Hald, *Statistical Tables and Formulas* (New York: John Wiley & Sons, Inc., 1952): reproduced by permission of Professor A. Hald and the publishers.

Index